Religion and the Sciences of Origins

DATE DUE

HIGHSMITH #45115

RELIGION AND THE SCIENCES OF ORIGINS

Historical and Contemporary Discussions

Kelly James Clark

First published in 2014 by
PALGRAVE MACMILLAN®
in the United States—a division of St. Martin's Press LLC,
175 Fifth Avenue, New York, NY 10010.

Where this book is distributed in the UK, Europe and the rest of the world,
this is by Palgrave Macmillan, a division of Macmillan Publishers Limited,
registered in England, company number 785998, of Houndmills,
Basingstoke, Hampshire RG21 6XS.

Palgrave Macmillan is the global academic imprint of the above companies
and has companies and representatives throughout the world.

Palgrave® and Macmillan® are registered trademarks in the United States,
the United Kingdom, Europe and other countries.

ISBN: 978–1–137–41483–0 (hardcover)
ISBN: 978–1–137–41480–9 (paperback)

Library of Congress Cataloging-in-Publication Data is available from the
Library of Congress.

A catalogue record of the book is available from the British Library.

Design by Newgen Knowledge Works (P) Ltd., Chennai, India.

First edition: May 2014

10 9 8 7 6 5 4 3 2 1

To Sid and Cate Jansma
In gratitude

Contents

Acknowledgments   ix

1   Science and/or Religion   1

2   Conflict, Separation, Integration   9

3   The Fabric of the Universe   31

4   "The Galileo Affair"   45

5   Darwin, God, and Creation   61

6   Evidence and Evolution   79

7   Chance and Creation   97

8   The Evolution of God?   115

9   Evolution and Ethics   137

10 God and the Good Life   153

11 In Search of the Soul   165

12 This Most Beautiful System   185

13 Judaism and Evolution   207

14 Islam and Evolution   223

Notes   245

Bibliography   259

Index   271

Acknowledgments

I am indebted to four research assistants, Emmalon Davis, Sean Cristy, Sarah C. Dahlstrom, and David Leestma, for their invaluable help. I am also grateful to my colleagues at various institutions who read some of the chapters and offered helpful comments and criticism: Sheldon Kopperl and Gamal Gasim of Grand Valley State University, Nuh Aydin of Kenyon College, Ted Davis of Messiah College, Alvin Plantinga of the University of Notre Dame, Kevin Timpe of Eastern Nazarene College, Steve Horst of Wesleyan University, Michael Murray of the John Templeton Foundation, and Justin Barrett of Fuller Theological Seminary.

This work was supported by the generous funding of the John Templeton Foundation.

CHAPTER 1

Science and/or Religion

THE PRIMEVAL ATOM

Consider two diametrically opposed creation stories, the first from ancient China and the second from twentieth-century Belgium:

> Long, long ago, when heaven and earth were still one, the entire universe was contained in an egg-shaped cloud. All the matter of the universe swirled chaotically in that egg. Deep within the swirling matter was Pan Gu, a huge giant who grew in the chaos. For 18,000 years he developed and slept in the egg. Finally one day he awoke and stretched, and the egg broke to release the matter of the universe. The lighter purer elements drifted upwards to make the sky and heavens, and the heavier impure elements settled downwards to make the earth. (Hamilton, 1988: 21)

> The radius of space began at zero; the first stages of the expansion consisted of a rapid expansion determined by the mass of the initial atom, almost equal to the present mass of the universe. The expansion took place in three phases: a first period of rapid expansion in which the atom-universe was broken into atomic stars, a period of slowing-down, followed by a third period of accelerated expansion. It is doubtless in this third period that we find ourselves today, and the acceleration of space which followed the period of slow expansion could well be responsible for the separation of stars into extra-galactic nebulae. (Lemaître, 1931: 422)

In these two quotations, we have stumbled onto a collision between religious and scientific accounts of the origin of the universe. While few contemporary Chinese and even fewer non-Chinese lend credence to the Pan Gu story, religious creation stories have nonetheless been enthusiastically embraced around the world and throughout history. Australia's aborigines believed that Baiame, the Maker of Many Things, brought up water, plants, animals, and even humans from underground to inhabit a previously barren, lifeless plain; the sun, moon, and stars came into existence when Emu and Eagle ancestors threw each other's eggs into the sky, and they burst into flames where they are continually fueled by Baiame (Parker, 1905). Mayans believed that Tepeu and Gugumatz *thought* mountains, trees, the sky, and animals into existence (Sproul, 1979: 285). Scandinavian tradition holds that Odin, the All-Father and most powerful of the gods, made the earth from the flesh of the brutal frost giant Ymir, while the rivers and seas flowed from Ymir's blood (Sturluson, 1987). The Egyptian god, Khepri, spat out the gods She and Tefnut from his stomach and then united himself with them; when Khepri was united with She and Tefnut, he wept for joy, and from those tears humans arose (Sproul, 1979: 99). Perhaps the most influential, based on the number of people who believe it, is the creation story in Genesis: God *speaks* the world into existence out of nothing. God speaks and it is done (Genesis 1).

The account of "the creation" offered by Lemaître, a twentieth-century physicist, never mentions God. His account appeals only to an initial state (where time = zero), expansion, mass, and the tiniest of particles (such as protons, neutrons, and electrons). It assumes laws of physics, such as gravity and quantum forces. Imagine, according to Dr Lemaître, a universe contained within the casing of an exploding, cosmic firework, with its embers (galaxies) bursting forth in brilliant splendor. His view, which would be called "the Big Bang theory," requires only material particles and natural forces. Lemaître was the first physicist to demonstrate that all of the matter of the universe was, at the beginning, contained within an initial point, which he called "the Primeval Atom." Imagine, again with Lemaître, all of the matter of the universe squished uncomfortably together into a tiny point—smaller than the period at the end of this sentence. All of those tiny particles, like Aladdin crammed into his tiny lamp, were itching to get out. Lemaître called this point, likely without reference to the Chinese creation story, "the Cosmic Egg exploding at the moment of the creation." The Egg, which he also called "the Primeval Atom," was the birthplace of everything (Lemaître, 1950). When the Egg erupted, the particles of the universe rapidly expelled, but then, over billions of years, came together to form stars, planets, and galaxies. Like many scientists endeavoring into a new scientific field that yet lacks adequate language and concepts, Lemaître used metaphors. But his intent was to offer a completely scientific, completely natural, completely physical description of the beginning of the universe. Lemaître learned of the observational confirmation of his theory shortly before his death in 1966.

Prior to Lemaître, most scientists believed that the universe was infinite and eternal with matter relatively evenly distributed throughout, with the same unchanging shape and form forever. Lemaître argued that the universe was finite and temporal yet rapidly expanding and that, by mathematically tracing the expansion backwards, one could discover the very beginnings of the universe. The Big Bang occurred on "a day without yesterday," as he elegantly stated it.

On the one hand, we've got Pan Gu's Cosmic Egg and gods thinking or speaking things into existence and human beings created from divine tears while, on the other hand, we have science. Put this way, it is hard not to cast one's lot with science.

Religion and science are at war, no mere rumors here, and religion is losing all of the key battles. Or so it is claimed.

THE LIMITLESS POWER OF SCIENCE

Peter Atkins, professor of chemistry at Oxford University, assumes science and religion are in a conflict in which God has been decisively defeated. In so doing, he ironically treats science as a religion substitute. In his 1995 essay, "The Limitless Power of Science," Atkins assesses the status of religion in an age of test tubes and telescopes: "Science and religion cannot be reconciled, and humanity should begin to appreciate the power of [science] and to beat off all attempts at compromise. Religion has failed, and its failures should be exposed. Science, with its currently successful pursuit of universal competence...should be acknowledged the king" (1995: 132).

Any attempt to reconcile science and religion is, according to Atkins, "muddle-headed sentiment and intellectually dishonest emotion." Surprisingly, Atkins describes science in religious, even godlike, terms. Science is "limitless" (the Alpha and the Omega, the beginning and the end), and science "liberates" (the Truth shall make you free). Science will "blow back the fog that shrouds the mind of those who have not yet seen" (the Light of the world). Finally, sounding like a medieval theologian's omni-god (omnipotent, omniscient, omnipresent), Atkins commends "the omnicompetence of science." In a nutshell, says Atkins, "Science respects more deeply the potential of humanity than religion ever can." Science is the new sacred. God is out, Science is in. After apologizing for his exuberance, Atkins declares that it is not possible to be intellectually honest and believe in gods; likewise, he claims that it is not possible to believe in gods and be a true scientist. Religious belief, he concludes, is "outmoded and ridiculous" (1996).

Are we forced then to choose between outmoded, ridiculous religion on the one hand and omnicompetent science on the other? Does, for example, Lemaître's now widely accepted scientific theory stand in stark opposition to religion?

FATHER LEMAÎTRE

In 1927, Albert Einstein met Lemaître at a physics conference where the two discussed Lemaître's theory of an expanding universe. Einstein expressed his disagreement rather sharply. He was dubious partly because Lemaître's theory seemed too close to the Christian doctrine of creation. Lemaître, in addition to being a fine physicist, was also a Catholic priest. Since the opening sentence of the Bible suggests a beginning of the universe: "In the beginning God created the heavens and the earth," Einstein suspected the priest of smuggling God into his equations. Concomitantly, Lemaître's mentor, Sir Arthur Eddington, publicly declared Lemaître's claims about a beginning of the world "repugnant" (perhaps for antireligious reasons) (Farrell, 2005: 107). Sir Fred Hoyle, an award-winning British astronomer and physicist, long rejected Lemaître's Big Bang theory in part because it entailed a beginning to the universe (and if a beginning, then a creator). He disparaged belief in an exploding universe, declaring it, in a BBC interview in the 1950s, as unseemly and undignified "as a party girl jumping out of a cake."

But in January 1933, Einstein, now a good friend of Lemaître, listened carefully at a seminar where Lemaître painstakingly presented the evidence for a beginning of the universe. At the conclusion, Einstein offered Lemaître a standing ovation, declaring, "This is the most beautiful and satisfactory explanation of creation to which I have ever listened" (Farrell, 2005: 115). Shortly thereafter, Einstein nominated Lemaître for the Franqui Prize, Belgium's highest award for scientific accomplishment. Einstein came to regard his rejection of an expanding universe as one of the biggest blunders of his life. Eddington, one of the twentieth century's greatest astrophysicists, would become Lemaître's biggest fan, commending his theories to other prominent physicists. Hoyle's later work on the generation of new elements through the evolution of stars (a central concept of the Big Bang theory) would move him from atheism to belief in a "supercalculating Intellect" (Hoyle, 1981).

Of course, Father Lemaître was keenly aware of the religious implications of his theory. In an unpublished paper written in 1922, five years before he published his first scientific paper on the theory, he claimed that that the universe had begun in light "as Genesis suggested it."[1]

Science and/or Religion

We started with primitive religious myths that were apparently refuted by science. But upon further inspection, some science, say the Big Bang, may confirm or coincide with religious myths. The relationship between science and religion may be more complicated than the claim to warfare makes readily apparent. While those like Atkins proclaim religion's demise at the hands of science, religion is still alive and kicking. To paraphrase Mark Twain, reports of religion's death have been greatly exaggerated. While science and religion may hit an occasional bump in the road, their differences may not be irreconcilable. The relationship between science and religion is, to be sure, complicated. And their courtship has been fraught with both peril and promise. But it is not all peril, as Atkins assumes.

Science and religion have mutually shaped our beliefs about the world. The way we dress and the food we eat, the methods by which we educate our children, and how we manage our health have all been influenced by both scientific discovery and religious commitment. Science may have proven that smoking is dangerous, but religions that prohibit smoking (such as Mormonism) are decidedly more effective in preventing smoking. Alcohol and drugs may likewise have negative health consequences, but Alcoholics Anonymous, with its reliance on a Higher Power, has proven to be one of the most successful cures for alcoholism and drug abuse. We have flown to the moon and split the atom; we can clone potatoes and, maybe one day, people. But we are soiling and maybe even destroying our planet at an astonishingly rapid rate with the very technology that has driven those remarkable discoveries. Science, of course, may save us from ecological disaster and mutually assured destruction. But it may not. Science is not ("omnicompetence" aside) our Lord and Savior. And religion is here to stay (for better and, admittedly, sometimes for worse).

Better, then, to understand both science and religion, and their fascinating relationship, than remain in ignorance.

The claim that theism and evolution are incompatible assumes that *religion is a scientific hypothesis.* Richard Dawkins writes: "A universe with a God would look quite different from a universe without one. A physics, a biology where there is a God is bound to look different. So the most basic claims of religion are scientific. Religion is a scientific theory." Religion and science, then, compete on the same field. So Dawkins claims: "The existence of God is a scientific hypothesis like any other.... God's existence or non-existence is a scientific fact about the universe, discoverable in principle if not in practice" (2006: 50). The great twentieth-century philosopher Willard Van Orman Quine concurs with Dawkins: "If I saw indirect explanatory benefit in positing sensibilia, possibilia, spirits, a Creator, I would joyfully accord them scientific status too, on a par with such avowedly scientific posits as quarks and black holes" (1995: 252). The God Hypothesis, Quine claims, is on a par with the periodic table of the elements, the kinetic theory of gases, Newton's inverse law of gravitation, the germ-theory of diseases, and quarks and black holes. We can lay them all alongside reality to see which measures up.

Many of our primitive (and not so primitive) ancestors did suppose God to be a scientific explanation of this or that. If theism were a scientific hypothesis, it would stand or fall by how well it explains the relevant scientific data. Such primitive peoples, requiring an explanation for thunder, postulated Zeus or Hadad; Aeolus or Vayu were thought to control the winds, while Tialoc or Chiuta brought on the rain; those in need of a little love could call on Cupid. There was no end of alleged deities in charge of reproductive success: Famian, Ison, Njambi, Ruhanga, Unkulunkulu, and Xesiovo, to name just a few. Even Aristotle called upon the Unmoved Mover to do some heavy planetary lifting. With the development of meteorology, the reproductive sciences, the principle of inertia, and the law of gravity, these gods have fallen by the intellectual wayside.

If God's existence is, as Dawkins claims, "unequivocally a scientific question," one must tot up the evidence for and against, and see how God fares. If God fares badly as a scientific explanation, then belief in God is rationally undermined. With respect to explaining the origin of species, Dawkins plumps for gradual evolution over divine design. The evidence, he claims, is "terminally fatal to the God Hypothesis" (2006: 61).

Is theism, the so-called God Hypothesis, a scientific hypothesis? I will occasionally revert to the colloquial usage of "God" for ease of communication and to remind ourselves that, unlike most scientific theories, the God Hypothesis involves propositions about a person, and to acknowledge that many believers treat belief in God more like belief in a person than a theory.[2]

Theism, at least for many modern believers, is not a scientific hypothesis, one in competition with the sciences of origins.[3] Many think that belief in God is more like belief in other minds (persons) than belief in a scientific theory such as the kinetic theory of gases or the structure of the atom. We don't believe in other minds (persons) as an explanatory hypothesis or scientific theory. We simply find ourselves believing in other persons, a belief that is an immediate product of our cognitive equipment, not the conclusion of an inference. We don't withhold belief in other persons until we observe a great deal of person-like behavior (thoughts, pains, feelings) and then, finally, affirm the belief as an induction from that set of data. Rather, we just believe in other persons. We can't do otherwise.

If God is a person, theism is not a scientific theory awaiting proof from physics or biology. If God is a person, one might simply find oneself believing in God through, say, religious experience or the testimony of those one loves and respects.

Belief in God is not, on this view, a scientific theory held tentatively or not at all until the available evidence piles up to confirm God's existence. Theism is not a scientific theory in competition with other scientific theories such as evolutionary theory. Even if evolutionary theory were well supported by the evidence, rational belief in God would not be precluded by it. Of course, various religious believers such as young earth creationists and Intelligent Design theorists do conceive of God as a scientific hypothesis in competition with evolutionary theory; such believers do, indeed, have a problem.

Dawkins and Quine (and others) may object and sternly assert that theism *is* a scientific hypothesis.[4] But it's religious believers' beliefs that are in question, not Dawkins and Quine's construal of their beliefs. And if the religious believer's belief is not a scientific hypothesis, then it need not await the decision of the scientific community or the accumulation of empirical evidence before she's permitted to hold it, and she need not fear that the accumulation of scientific knowledge will drive God into obsolescence. God is not competing with scientific theories because, at least for them, God is not a scientific theory.

Science cannot rule out the existence of the nonnatural, nor do (most) scientists try to do such a thing; but scientists cannot as scientists enter into discourse regarding the nonnatural. They are limited in their methods to the natural world and the natural processes found therein. God, if there is one, lies outside the naturalistic methodologies and measurements of science.

While God is the metaphysical explanation of why there is a world at all, God is not a scientific competitor with theories about how particular things work in the world. God is not a scientific explanation of some particular aspect of reality (like the motions of the planets or the origin of the species), God is a metaphysical explanation of everything. God, properly speaking, falls under the domain of the philosopher not the scientist. God is not on the scientific radar.

It's not the God Hypothesis that's defective. It's the assumption that God is a scientific hypothesis.[5]

Religion and the Sciences of Origins

We started with creation myths and the Big Bang because the religious rubber meets the science road in discussions of origins. In the development and reception of the Big Bang theory, we see the worry that the scientist-priest might be reading his religion into his data. We see the dismay on the part of some scientists that science might provide some sort of confirmation of an important religious doctrine, the doctrine of creation. Religious believers, on the other hand, are apprehensive because the sciences of origins keep offering naturalistic explanations that were once the special preserve of a supernatural God; when it comes to origins, science seems to keep trumping religion. And so there is the fear: the sciences of origins will crush God once and for all.

Rather than consider every issue in science and religion, I will focus, then, on the rubber meeting the road: on the sciences of origins.

Two topics will be obvious and have received the most attention in the past century: the origin of the universe and the origins of species (Big Bang cosmology and Darwinism). The former seems to corroborate belief in a creator, whereas the latter is often taken, by believer and unbeliever alike, to be clean contrary to belief in a creator.

Before we can discuss such issues in science and religion, we have to come to some sort of understanding of just what science and religion are. So we begin at the beginning with a quest for understanding both the nature of science and the nature of religion. We will learn that gaining such an understanding is not so easy.

Our first look at origins is a discussion of the origins of modern science. There we find deeply religious thinkers—Galileo, Newton, and Kepler, for example—grappling simultaneously with science and theology without the distinctions and fears of twentieth-century thinkers. At the very origins of modern science, we find science and religion deeply intertwined both in the minds of the scientists and in the theories they are considering. Moreover, we can find in the theological reflection of these thinkers, resources for negotiating the relationship between science and religion.

While Darwin may have made the world safe for atheism, he, for most of his life, was not an atheist, and did not view his theory as a competitor to belief in God. After considering Darwin's religious beliefs (in relation to Darwinism), we move from the nineteenth- to the fourth century where we find St Augustine already puzzling over the proper interpretation of the biblical story of creation. Augustine suggests a profound way of reconciling the biblical creation stories in the Book of Scripture with scientific discoveries.

What precisely are the scientific discoveries that support evolution? What, in short, is the evidence for evolution? In "Evidence and Evolution" we examine two things: how the case for evolution is shaped and how precisely the case is made. From the perspective of religion, we are looking for clues as to how to read the Book of Nature, the companion book to the Book of Scripture. Of course, one might wonder how God could create a world if the world is at bottom random (apparently out of God's control). That is the following chapter.

What does science say about the origins of religious belief itself? Is religious belief immune from scientific inquiry? Recent work in the cognitive and evolutionary psychology of religion affords insights into the operations of the human mind that incline us towards religious beliefs. But if belief in God involves a natural process, doesn't that somehow undermine rational religious belief?

In the next two chapters, we consider what science says about the origin of morality, and whether or not it leaves any room for God in one's understanding of goodness and the good life.

In "In Search of the Soul," we consider the source or origin of our humanity. While religious conceptions of the human person typically include an immaterial soul or spirit, recent work in the science of the brain has called the soul into question. We will look into the science of the mind and see what consequences it has for an understanding of ourselves as persons. We conclude with a discussion of the science of free will.

Finally, we return to the discussion that begins the book—the origin of the universe. The Big Bang suggests a consilience between the science of origins and the doctrine of creation. And the universe seems apparently exquisitely fine-tuned for the existence of life. Some have argued that this fine-tuning offers evidence of a Fine-Tuner.

The book concludes with two chapters, one each on Jewish and Muslim approaches to the science of origins. Owing to the cultural dominance of Western science and Christianity, discussions of science and religion are typically discussions of Western science and Christianity. It is time for consideration of these issues from the perspective of non-Christian religions. So while the main chapters primarily discuss Christian thinkers, and thinkers who played major roles in the development of modern Western science, we will conclude with a consideration of Judaism's and Islam's understandings of evolution.

CHAPTER 2

Conflict, Separation, Integration

CSI

One of the most popular television shows of the past decade is *CSI: Crime Scene Investigation*. Its wily supersleuths examine grisly crimes for the slightest of clues. Slowly, carefully, patiently, the clues emerge and then converge on the perpetrator. Grissom, the sagely veteran, repeatedly reminds his younger, impetuous investigators not to rush to a conclusion based on preconception, hasty judgment, or circumstantial evidence. He insistently and constantly reminds them: Don't focus on a single suspect, be open to surprising possibilities, and accumulate the evidence. Only when they heed his wise counsel are they able to discern the true pattern in their increasing and remarkably varied array of evidence.

"Conflict, Separation, and Integration" was a deliberately selected title for this chapter to remind us not to rush to hasty conclusions about the relationship between science and religion based on preconceptions, rushed judgments, or circumstantial evidence. We must proceed like Grissom on *CSI: Crime Scene Investigation*.

Most of us come to discussions of science and religion with preconceptions, typically armed with *conflict* metaphors such as "combat," "warfare," and "battle." This militaristic tone was set in the nineteenth century by influential books titled *History of the Conflict between Religion and Science* and *A History of the Warfare of Science with Theology in Christendom* (Draper, 1898; White, 1908). The casualty of this war: God. In less militaristic terms, belief in God is no longer an intellectually viable option. One need not look too hard to find a skirmish or two. In the United States, for example, the battle over beginnings (biblical creationism vs evolution) has been carried on in both the public square and the courts. Stephen Hawking has recently proclaimed that the law of gravity, not God, spontaneously created the world from nothing (Hawking, 2010). In the battle between gravity and God, gravity wins by a knockout. Hear biologist Richard Dawkins's assessment of Hawking's claim: "Darwin kicked [God] out of biology, but physics remained more uncertain. Hawking is now administering the coup de grace" (Dawkins, 2010). Conflict, it must be conceded, is the dominant metaphor.

What about *separation*? Religion and science also seem, sometimes or at least to some, quite separate or distinct from each other. For example, physicist Freeman Dyson writes: "Science and religion are two windows that people look through, trying to understand the big universe outside, trying to understand why we are here. The two windows give different views, but both look out at the same universe. Both views are one-sided, neither is complete. Both leave out essential features of the real world. And both are worthy of respect."[1] Religion, according to this view, is more the home of ethics and the meaning of life; science, on the other hand, is concerned with how things go in the natural world. Religion is the world of value (how things ought to be); science is the world of facts (the way things are). Religion speaks of repentance, restoration, and reconciliation, whereas science speaks of atoms, absolute zero, and albatrosses. Science is concerned with things in the world, but God transcends the world. Pop-rock band Lone Justice's wistful lyrics "Soap, soup and salvation, tired hearts sing in jubilation, restoration at the rescue mission, soap, soup and salvation" tell of radically different persons, places, and things from the sober scientist in her laboratory carefully pouring from her beaker, poring over her notes, and deducing a natural law. No possibility for science–religion conflict there. Never the twain shall meet.[2]

Science and religion have also had, meaningfully and powerfully, *integration*. The science–religion twain have met and embraced. For Isaac Newton, as good a scientist as has ever lived, science and religion were the two threads of an intricately interwoven tapestry. Newton wrote: "This most beautiful system of the sun, planets and comets, could only proceed from the counsel and dominion of an intelligent and powerful being. This Being governs all things...as Lord over all."[3] Nineteenth-century physicist James Clerk Maxwell viewed his work as worship. He regularly prayed to God for increased wisdom so that he could better understand the work of God's hands (nature). The modern theory of genetics was discovered by Gregor Mendel, a Catholic monk who humbly and patiently observed successive generations of pea plants. Believing the universe to be the creation of a God of order, he did not believe hereditary characteristics were simply due to chance and sought to discover God's laws of inheritance.

So a little bit of conflict here, some separation there, and a dash of integration over there. Perhaps the relationship between science and religion is just plain messy: sometimes conflict, sometimes separation, and sometimes integration. It's not C, S, or I; it's C, S, *and* I. Before deciding how science and religion are related, one would do well to follow Grissom's advice: Don't focus on a single suspect, be open to surprising possibilities, and accumulate the evidence. Don't rush to judgment based on preconceptions or scanty evidence. You may very likely find yourself, as you do with the television show, surprised by a careful consideration of all of the evidence.

The purpose of this chapter is to canvass the various options—conflict, separation, and integration—for understanding the relationship between science and religion. But if we are going to address the relationship between science and religion, we must have some understanding of our subject matter: just what is science and what is religion?

DEFINING SCIENCE AND RELIGION

Q: How many physicists does it take to change a light bulb?
A: Two. One to hold the bulb, and the other to rotate the universe.

Was that a good joke? For that matter, what is a joke? It is difficult to come up with a definition of "joke." Likewise it is difficult to define "science" and "religion." Whatever definition one comes up with for "joke," someone will quickly think of a joke that doesn't fit that definition. If we define "joke" as "a funny remark," we ignore the fact that some jokes are not funny. If we define it as a "remark intended to provoke laughter," we omit jokes that are actions without words (e.g., practical jokes or pantomime). If actions and intentions are included in the definition, applications to people or careers are left out, as in, "Richard Nixon's presidency was a joke." But if a person's life, such as Nixon's, can be a joke, the concept of a joke has been completely transformed: a life that is a joke is marked more by tragedy than humor. Moreover, Nixon never intended the tragedy. Our definition went from humorous remark, through intended humorous remark, to humorous act, and ended at unintended tragedy (and there are many more sorts of jokes than the ones I've just canvassed). By the time we got to Nixon, our definition of "joke" had none of the characteristics that we started with. There is no single definition of "joke" that contains all and only attributes of jokes. We know roughly what a joke is. We use the term. But we can't really come up with an adequate definition.

Science and religion are similarly afflicted.[4]

There are caricatures of science and religion at the outset: science is an objective, fact-oriented practice; religion is subjective and emotional. Where science is heralded as universal and based on objective observations in the world, religion is characterized by specific traditions based on subjective experience. The difficulty is coming up with a meaningful definition that includes all and only what we want it to include (and excluding everything we want to exclude). Should science include, for example, both Aristotle's biology and Einstein's $E = mc^2$? Should it exclude magic, astrology, alchemy (changing base elements like lead into precious metals like gold), and religion? And that's just science.

We start by taking a long look at scientists and their practices before taking a much briefer look at the definition of "religion." We will find, I think, that those whom we count as scientists and that which we call "science" can't be squeezed into any simple definition.

SCIENCE AND SOME SCIENTISTS

Defining "science" so that it includes exactly what it should throughout all of human history is complicated because science has included a great many beliefs, many of which are no longer held today, and scientific practices can differ wildly.

Throughout history "scientific" theories have held that the earth is at the center of the universe, that lead can be changed into gold, that the earth is only a few thousand years old, that the body contains four humors: blood, yellow bile, black bile, and phlegm (and that medicine, properly practiced, regulates the humors), that the earth is flat, and that various life-forms can be spontaneously generated out of nothing.

We can find a diversity of scientific practices as well, even in our own day and age. Imagine a white-coated scientist hunched over test tubes or peering through a microscope in a pristine, germ-free laboratory. He (our typical image of a scientist is, sadly, a male) makes very careful measurements, keen observations, and keeps meticulous records. After running hundreds of experiments, he ponders his numerical data and then applies very complicated mathematics. Soon a universal law of nature emerges. He adds this law of nature to the ever-increasing stockpile of confirmed laws of nature.

Is the work of the lab-coated experimenter—carefully deducing laws from observations, then adding his theory to the stockpile of science—the paradigm of science?

My father-in-law is a theoretical physicist. He seldom visits a laboratory and, when he does, he is there only briefly. In a lab, he is more tourist than technician. His tools of trade are a fountain pen and yellow legal pad. His "laboratory" is his imagination. He doesn't look out at the world; he sits at his desk and thinks. He "sees" the world in numbers and then jots down numerical patterns on paper. He derives theorems from fundamental axioms and assumptions. He believes the world, underneath all of its complexity, is simple and beautiful. Simplicity, beauty, and mathematical precision drive his scientific theorizing as much as, perhaps even more than, observations and experiments.

The greatest theoretical physicist of all, Albert Einstein, claimed that one of his best ideas came from thinking about what it would be like to ride on a beam of light. His general theory of relativity rejected the traditional view that light travels in a straight line, and he boldly predicted that light would bend around very heavy objects (like the sun). The solar eclipse of 1919 permitted the first testing of Einstein's prediction. So certain was he of the truth of his theory, Einstein couldn't be bothered to travel to Brazil or the island of Principe in Guinea where the observations would be made. When the results were announced, Einstein instantly became world famous. Einstein conducted his research in his mind, through thought-experiments, not in laboratories. He was guided by intuitions about the nature of reality not reflection on piles of observations. Of his method he said, "When I assess a theory, I ask myself, if I was God, would I have arranged the universe that way?" (Isaacson, 2007: 335). He was so convinced of the beauty and truth of his special theory of relativity that when he was informed that some new experiments refuted the theory, he questioned the experimental results rather than giving up his theory (and he was right—further experiments refuted those alleged to refute his theory).

While scientific theories came to Einstein in thought experiments, they came to others in dreams.[5] Otto Loewi (1873–1961), the Nobel-prize winning "Father of Neuroscience," first had the idea that nerve impulses were transmitted chemically in a dream. In the early 1920s, Loewi dreamed about an experiment that would show how nerve impulses were transmitted. Waking up in the middle of the night, he excitedly jotted the experiment down on paper and fell back asleep. However, the following morning, he couldn't read his own notes. But wait, wait; all is not lost. He had the same dream the next night. This time he attended carefully to his drowsy handwriting and quickly and correctly transcribed his Nobel-prize winning experiment.

Consider the caricature of Isaac Newton (1642–1727)—young Isaac got plunked on the head with an apple, thereby discovering gravity and going on to a great career in science. There is a grain of truth here: he likely did see apples fall on the family farm. Maybe he even saw falling apples as he was thinking about what kept the moon in its place and the relationship of the moon to tides. It took him years to calculate the law of gravity. Moreover, he didn't discover gravity—it's not as though people were floating around helplessly in space awaiting Newton's discovery! He did, however, discover the *law* of gravity, as well as the laws of motion, the light spectrum, and the calculus.

Newton also spent a great deal of his "scientific time" studying the Bible. Like many scientists of his day, Newton was involved in the illegal practice of alchemy—attempting to turn base elements, like lead, into gold. He wrote over a million words on alchemy, but they weren't made widely available until the twentieth century. Of Newton's alchemical research, physicist Arthur Eddington writes: "The science in which Newton seems to have been chiefly interested, and on which he spent most of his time was alchemy. He read widely and made innumerable experiments, entirely without fruit so far as we know" (Eddington, 2007: 69). In fact, Newton's discoveries of the theory of gravity and the nature of light may have arisen out of his alchemical research (not from the mythical apple). Newton fervently studied Scripture because he believed that the secrets of alchemy were hidden in and then transmitted through various sacred writings. He believed that various supernatural agents had long ago passed on this alchemical wisdom to earthly emissaries like Moses who then passed them on to successors including Pythagoras and Plato. Newton cautioned his contemporaries who had likewise embarked on alchemical research to remain silent on the topic because it was feared that whoever held the secret of the transmutation of lead into gold would be strangled in his bed to extract the secret.

In the seventeenth century, alchemy was called "chymistry" from which we get our term "chemistry." Since chemistry arose from chymistry, and since the first chemists were also chymists, it is difficult to define "science" so that it includes chemistry but excludes chymistry (i.e., alchemy).

Aristotle (384 BC–322 BC), often referred to as "the father of today's scientific method," wore no lab coat, didn't darken the door of a laboratory, used no microscopes or telescopes, and came up with exactly zero laws of nature. Yet he was the greatest scientist of his day and his theories dominated science until the sixteenth century.[6] Ancient and medieval physics was Aristotelian physics. Ancient and medieval biology was Aristotelian biology. Medieval scientific method was Aristotelian. Yet virtually every aspect of Aristotle's physics was rejected during the scientific revolution, and most of his biology was rejected by Darwin. While he did endorse some sort of empirical method (which relies on sense experience), his naïve but understandable reliance on the senses and common sense were shown to limit scientific inquiry.

Aristotle was the teacher of Alexander the Great (356–323 BC), King of Macedonia, one of history's great military geniuses. Through a series of remarkable military conquests, Alexander extended the Macedonian empire from north Africa through Europe and into India—the largest in the world. Legend has it that Alexander wept because he had no more worlds left to conquer. Yet upon Alexander's death, Macedonia was plunged into civil war, was besieged by outside forces and, in 146 BC, was reduced to a Roman province. Aristotle's science and scientific method, like Alexander's empire, have disappeared from the world. Yet it would be folly to exclude Aristotle's work and beliefs from science by definition.

Of course, not all scientific discoveries are made through dreams, through alchemical secrets, or by reading the mind of God. Many scientists, at least in the late twentieth century and later, work in laboratories and assiduously collect data. Some test predictions made by a theory. Some are more exploratory. But these quirky examples, and the study of history, show that if we define science too narrowly so as to exclude alchemy, religion, hunches, and educated guesses, we may end up excluding, for example, Newton, Aristotle, and early physics and chemistry.[7]

SCIENCE, NATURAL PHILOSOPHY, AND *SCIENTIA*

If our definition of science must include all of the above, we shall have no easy task.[8] From Archimedes and Aristotle, on the one hand, to Newton and Einstein, on the other, there is no single method or even common field of inquiry. The term "scientist" itself was not invented until the nineteenth century (Ross, 1962: 71–72) and even then it was introduced as a joke (since we don't know exactly what a joke is, we don't know if "scientist" could have been meant as a joke!). The term didn't catch on until the beginning of the twentieth century. Until the word "scientist" stuck, those who sought an understanding of nature referred to themselves as natural philosophers. While *we* might call Newton a scientist or physicist and his writings "science" or "physics," he did not. He didn't entitle his most famous work *Principles of Science* or even *Principles of Physics*. Newton's greatest work was *The Mathematical Principles of Natural Philosophy* (*Philosophiae naturalis principia mathematica*—usually referred to simply as "Principia"). Newton was, by his own account, a natural philosopher and considered his results natural philosophy. We impose, anachronistically, the term "science" and "scientist" when we apply them to pre-twentieth-century thinkers. In so doing, we impose what we now think is proper science and what we now think are proper scientific methods into domains where they simply don't apply.

The Latin *scientia*, from which we get the term "science," simply means "knowledge" or "certainty" and in the Middles Ages included anything about which humans have attained the highest level of confidence; *scientia* is a true and certain knowledge of reality. Historically, *scientia* was not restricted to the natural world but included ethics (moral philosophy), metaphysics, and theology. Various medieval thinkers thought that one could acquire, after very extensive and careful study, *scientia*—certain knowledge—about such statements as "Keep your promises," "The interior angles of a triangle total 180 degrees," "God loves you and has a wonderful plan for your life,"[9] and "Nothing can be completely red and completely green." Natural philosophy, what we might rather call "science," was organically related to (not distinct from) all of those other disciplines in the unified domain of *scientia*; it was just one more item of knowledge in the big pile of human knowledge. For the medievals, there is nothing special that distinguishes natural philosophy, what we might now call science, from other fields of knowledge, including theological knowledge, in that pile.

Yet, in our day and age, it is impossible to deny that there is something special and even distinctive about science. What is it, then, that defines science and makes it so special?

DEFINING SCIENCE

We sometimes think of scientists as special, almost priestly, people who study a very special, almost sacred, topic. I think we can agree that science is special and that it is not just any old piece in the pile of knowledge. The universal law of gravitation and the germ theory of disease are somehow better than more ordinary knowledge claims such as "I had oatmeal for breakfast" and "Wow, that sunset sure is pretty." Some go further: they consider it the highest form of human knowledge; some even considered it the *sole* form of human knowledge. But we don't need to go that far to concede that science is a uniquely special and important sort of human knowledge and inquiry.

The image of the contemporary scientist in the laboratory conveys the following ideas about the nature of science:

1. Science is *empirical*—it is both beholden to and restricted to information gained from our five senses.
2. Science is *objective*—there are no subjective factors involved in scientific judgment.
3. Science is *cumulative*—the history of science is the progressive accumulation of knowledge with each success simply an addition to previous successes.

Let us briefly consider these.

Science Is Empirical?

Science, you might think, is just the simple accumulation of empirical, objective facts. But while empirical facts are surely the touchstone of science, most scientific theories are not limited to what can be observed; they often involve explicit reference to various unobservable entities or powers. A scientist may start with trees, planets, and radium, all of which can be clearly observed. But they quickly move to the unseen realm of genes, gravity, and atoms. Scientific theories often invoke these extraordinary and unseen things and forces to explain the things that we can see. Even when scientific laws are restricted to things that can be seen, such laws apply to the vast regions of space and the distant past and future, so their content involves things that no human being could possibly see. For example, the law of universal gravitation states that every body in the universe is attracted to every other body in the universe (in direct proportion to their masses and indirect proportion to their distance from each other). This is true for *every* body in the universe at *every* time (past, present, and future). We—even if we include every human who has ever existed—could never see into the vast reaches of space, or into the past or into the future. Every body in every place at every time—such is the subject matter of the universal law of gravitation. So scientific theories and laws go vastly beyond what any human or any group of humans could possibly observe. Science may start with the observable, and it may be answerable to the observable, but it certainly does not end with the observable.

Thinking of infinite realms beyond what humans could possibly experience is science's charm and curse. Not curse in a bad sense—curse in the sense that it is very, very difficult to comprehend the reality that exceeds our five senses.

Imagine that you, for the first time in your life, are sailing across the surface of a vast and deep and beautiful ocean. As the sun glints off its silver surface, you can't visually penetrate its dark underside. You reach out and touch the limpid surface; it feels cool, silky, and liquid. Then, breaking through its skin, you delve below. Your grasp is limited to the length of your arm—a couple of feet at most. You feel around—only water strikes your fingertips. You bring the water to your nose and smell vague, some identifiable and some unidentifiable, scents. What lies below is mystery. You look all around and, as far as you can see, there is water everywhere. Beyond the horizon lies what? Beneath the surface contains what?

Science is like that. We seek to peer beneath or behind or beyond what we can see, hear, touch, taste, or smell to the secret springs and powers that cause our perceptions. We gaze beyond the present toward the horizons of the past and future, seeking principles that apply at all times. And we look at the universe from our little point within a point within a point, seeking laws that hold true throughout entire cosmos. We constantly return to what we can experience—experience *is* our touchstone to reality—but it is just our starting point. Science beckons us beyond the bounds of finite human experience.[10]

Science Is Objective?

As every scientist well knows (but few publicly concede) subjective evaluations are essentially involved in scientific theorizing. While scientists aim at the truth, the target is not easy to hit. And it can't be hit with a quiver of observable data alone. Even running observable data through the filter of "the scientific method" won't hit the target. Some of the most brilliant thinkers in human history have attempted to grasp the nature of reality and been woefully mistaken. Science is just plain hard—it requires a grasp of a huge amount of data, the ability to think very abstractly and often in defiance of common sense, and very high-level mathematics. If science were easy—if there were some easy, rule-based, foolproof system of moving from the seen to the unseen—humans would have discovered quantum mechanics and the structure of the DNA molecule long ago (and with a lot less effort).

Even conceding our limitations, there's another problem for developing the true scientific theory on the basis of observation. Many competing theories are consistent with any set of observations. The data don't point unequivocally in the direction of a single theory. And so other factors, *value judgments*, are called upon to decide which theory is the "best explanation" of the relevant data (Kuhn, 1977; McMullin, 2012).

Consider an example. Suppose that you are a physicist trying to explain quantum phenomena—the stuff that atomic bombs and lasers are made of. According to contemporary physics, this quantum stuff is notoriously unpredictable. So scientists postulate unseen and unseeable electrons that hop, skip, and jump around inside atoms in a random manner; no scientific law could capture this carefree motion. But while electrons are widely accepted, various entities could fully account for all of the data. Scientists initially postulated that quantum phenomena are produced by the smallest pieces of material reality: invisible and indivisible pieces of matter called atoms ("atom" in Greek means "indivisible"). These entities, in turn, constitute the ultimate building blocks of reality. Some believe protons, neutrons, and electrons themselves are actually further divisible into even tinier pieces of matter called quarks. Others believe that the most basic units of reality are not pieces of matter at all but are packets of energy. And, given certain wave-like, particle-like behavior of the apparent cause of quantum phenomena, others believe that ultimate reality is a wave-particle. So far we've got, as the ultimate building blocks of reality: protons, neutrons, and electrons, or quarks, packets of energy, or wave-particles. Theories involving each of these entities could be made fully, mathematically consistent with the data (of course, they may require some tinkering). And we're just getting started. A vast number of other theories could account for quantum phenomena. Contemporary scientists limit their imaginations because they are committed to theories in terms of matter and energy (or matter/energy) and their various manifestations. So contemporary theories exclude nonmatter/energy explanations of quantum phenomena at the outset.

However, ultimate, unseen reality may not be matter and energy at all; it could be really, really small person-like things that, like most persons, behave capriciously (I don't offer this as a serious option; it's just a logical possibility).[11] Teeny, tiny elves dart about in this unseen world in a manner captured by the mathematics of quantum theory. Except for prejudice (prejudgment, which is not always bad, certainly not in ruling out tiny elf theory) against persons as the causes of material reality, we might have seen twentieth-century scientists develop elvic theory instead of atomic theory. I'm not commending elvic theory over atomic theory, but a theory involving elves *could* account for the observable data as effectively as atomic theory. A value commitment to *material causes*, not simply reflection on the observable data, has guided us toward favoring atomic theories. But even commitment to material causes is not sufficient to settle whether wave-particles, packets of energy, or indivisible matter are the ultimate stuff of reality.[12]

We've already seen one value commitment that guides scientific theorizing—a commitment to explanations in terms of matter and energy (in their various manifestations). But there is a host of other values that scientists rely on to sort through the huge number of competing theories that could fully account for the empirical data.

For example, scientists bring to the evaluation of the data a commitment to *simple* theories; they embrace the adage that *the simple is the sign of the true*. But perhaps reality is extraordinarily complex and the assumption of simplicity is systematically misleading. Scientists also prefer theories that are *fertile*—theories that suggest or unite other domains of research. But, again, reality may be dappled and disjoint with lots of unrelated things and our quest for unifying explanations, again, may be systematically misleading.[13]

Scientists also prefer theories that are *beautiful*—the true is the beautiful, according to this view. Paul Dirac, Nobel-prize winning physicist, once advised his students to be concerned only with the beauty of their theories (Weinberg, 1994). When Watson and Crick discovered the structure of the DNA molecule, Watson wrote that some found the DNA's double-helical structure "too pretty not to be true" (Watson, 1968: 124). In his *Dreams of a Final Theory*, Steven Weinberg, again a Nobel laureate in physics, contends that beauty will be a defining characteristic of the final, absolutely true, scientific theory of the world: "When it turns out that mathematically beautiful ideas are actually relevant to the real world, we get the feeling that there is something behind the blackboard, some deeper truth foreshadowing a final theory that makes our ideas turn out so well...The beauty in our present theories may be 'but a dream' of the kind of beauty that awaits us in the final theory." Beauty, to follow the theme of this chapter, compounds the problem of the definition of science: "professionals have stopped using this word [beauty] because they realize how impossible it is to define...you do not define these things; you know them when you feel them" (Weinberg, 1994: 6, 17, 134).

Commitments to matter/energy, simplicity, fertility, and beauty are not forced upon us by the objective data. We don't observe them in or infer them from the world, *we bring them to the world* and use them to assess the data. Such values guide scientists in their assessments of various theories. They are necessary precisely because the empirical phenomena can be accounted for perfectly adequately by a wide variety of complex, disjointed, and ugly theories that invoke any number of entities as the ultimate sources of reality. But the fundamental conviction that the world must be a certain way—simple and beautiful, for example—guides our understanding of the observable data. Because science involves values as well as observations, it is not a purely objective discipline. Yet let us remind ourselves that the use of subjective values has not prevented scientific discoveries of the first order. In fact, it is only through the judicious use of such values that scientific discoveries are possible at all.

Science Is Cumulative?

Many people assume that science is cumulative, and that each new piece of scientific knowledge is added to the top of the ever-growing pile of scientific knowledge. But science is not the simple accumulation of fact-based hypotheses. Newton's physics overthrew much of Aristotle's, and Einstein's physics overthrew Newton's. Darwin's biology was a rejection of much of Aristotle's. There are serious inconsistencies in contemporary physics, and these inconsistencies suggest the possibility of a radically new theory. So there may be a greater-than-Einstein who offers a new theory that leads to the rejection of the theories of both Einstein and Darwin.

Scientific theories are subject to radical change as scientists discard old hypotheses, methods, and assumptions.[14] In attempting to define "science," we often ignore the fact that today's science is the result of a long chain of wrong but brilliant guesses. Items that were once considered absolutely central to the best scientific theories of their day have been consigned to the trash heap of knowledge, from things like phlogiston, crystalline spheres, and the caloric to forces like *vis viva*, impetus, and astrology.[15] Don't worry if you aren't familiar with these (I'm just making a point): they were once the stuff of well-established theories. In their day, every well-educated person, including persons we now call "scientists," firmly believed in them. They are now just quaint (and mostly unknown). They weren't preserved in the sciences that succeeded them; they were simply discarded.[16]

Science is not strictly speaking empirical, objective, or cumulative. Moreover, values like simplicity and elegance play a role in the acceptance of theories.[17] Yet none of this has precluded scientific knowledge (though it has muddied our understanding of what precisely science is and how it is practiced). Let us illustrate the success of science, and its use of values like simplicity and elegance, with an actual example, the sixteenth-century discussion of the nature of the cosmos.

SIMPLICITY AND THE CENTER OF THE UNIVERSE

The historical debate about the center of the universe illustrates how science is not strictly empirical, objective, and cumulative. Since this debate also figures in the science–religion discussion of the next chapter, it will be useful to consider here. Prior to, say, 1600 AD virtually every Western astronomer believed that the earth was at the center of the universe (which, sadly, 20% of Americans still believe [Crabtree, 1999]): all of the stars, planets, and the sun, like the moon, revolve around the earth. The evidence for this view is, well, evident. Sit outside one evening, focus your gaze on the heavens, and *see* the cosmos revolve around you. Moreover, you don't *feel* the earth move. It was widely believed, following Aristotle, that material things (all made of the element Earth), seeking their "natural place," fell toward the center. Since all earthy things fell toward the earth, the earth was the center. Finally, it was widely believed that heavenly motions, being heavenly, were perfect. Since astronomers believed that the most perfect motion was circular, they also believed that everything revolved around the center point (the earth) in perfect, circular motion. Again, when you are gazing at the heavens at night, you will see the stars and planets arc around the earth in perfection—circular motion. Aristotle's view of the cosmos was systematically and mathematically developed by Ptolemy in the second-century AD. The Ptolemaic system was widely accepted, with an amendment here and there, until around 1600 AD. At the center of the Ptolemaic system—both literally and figuratively—was the earth.

But as observations accumulated, the earth-centered system grew vastly more complicated, even unwieldy.

The earth-centered system would find its final expression in the work of Tycho (pronounced "Teeko") Brahe (1546–1601). So great was Tycho's reputation that the King of Denmark gave him an island and funds to build an observatory. He was determined to improve on the observational foundation of astronomy—no more amateurs relaxing in their backyards gazing at stars. He dramatically improved instruments, in this pretelescope era, for observing and measuring the stars and planets. The observations of Tycho and his many assistants were 10–30 times more accurate than previous astronomical observations. His improved observations made it increasingly difficult, mathematically, to model the solar system with the earth at its center. Copernicanism—the view that the sun is at the center of the universe—was a controversial but live option for astronomers of his day. But Tycho couldn't bring himself to believe that the earth was not at the center of the universe or that the earth was in motion.

Nonetheless, Tycho's new and improved observations led him to reject Ptolemy's simple, earth-centered, circular system. In Tycho's system, while the important things—the sun, moon, and stars—rotated around the earth, Mars and the other planets orbited around the sun. Tycho's system was mathematically no better than Ptolemy's system. Both could equally well account for all of the observable data.

In 1600 AD, in order to complete the new calculations of the orbits of the planets, Tycho hired a more mathematically adept astronomer named Johannes Kepler (1571–1630). The two had had a stormy relationship. The younger scholar repeatedly insulted his elder and Tycho was concerned that Kepler would use his data to discredit the earth-centered system that he had defended. Upon Tycho's death a year later, his fears were realized: Kepler coopted Tycho's massive set of observational data that he had carefully collected for over 40 years.

Kepler then used Tycho's observational data in defense of the Copernican system. Kepler improved on Copernicus's system when he realized that the planetary orbits were not perfect circles as Copernicus (following Aristotle) supposed, but were instead "flattened circles" (ellipses). The chief virtue of Kepler's system: it is mathematically simpler than the earth-centered systems of Ptolemy and Tycho.[18]

Aside from simplicity and elegance, though, the Ptolemaic, Tychonic, and Copernican systems could account equally well for the observational data.[19] There is no mathematical advantage, other than simpler calculations, of the sun-centered view of the cosmos over any earth-centered view. The three systems are mathematically equivalent, and identical predictions can be made within any system. As far as the observations go, there is nothing to recommend one system over the other—you have to bring in nonobservational values like simplicity and beauty. On those grounds, the Copernican system, as modified by Kepler, wins hands down over the Ptolemaic system.

Science, though not a rule-governed process, is remarkably successful in discovering the truth. However science works and whatever its precise definition is, we know that the earth rotates around the sun, that the heart is a pump that circulates blood throughout our bodies, that diseases are sometimes caused by germs, that gases expand when heated in accordance with Boyle's law, that light is made up of many colors, that the basic elements arrange themselves very neatly into the periodic table, that the universe is billions of years old, that $E = mc^2$, and that all biological species evolved from a single ancestor. Science is, without a doubt, one of the most astounding of all human intellectual achievements.

So What is Science?

When a contemporary scientist makes a creative guess, he or she formulates that guess into a hypothesis and then the hypothesis is put to some sort of test. The sorts of tests that hypotheses are subjected to can be very rigorous, involving incredibly complex equipment; these tests are often repeated. The sorts of tests involved vary depending on the science and the hypothesis. A test of a hypothesis for the destruction of dinosaurs will be completely different from a test for the existence of black holes, the special theory of relativity, or the structure of the DNA molecule, each of which in turn requires its own specific means of evaluation.

Scientists today invent hypotheses and put them to various tests. That's about all we need at this point in our understanding of the scientific process. This is sometimes called *the hypothetico-deductive method*: scientists come up with various testable hypotheses (by whatever creative and mysterious processes are involved in the imagining of new theories). Testable predictions or consequences are then deduced from the hypotheses. At that point, an experimental scientist takes over: he or she seeks to confirm or deny the hypothesis based on its testable predictions. While many accept the hypothetico-deductive method as the "true" scientific method, others reject it.[20] Moreover, it does not apply to all of the instances of what we might call science throughout human history. Yet it is as good as any definition of the current practice of science.

As we proceed in our discussion, though, we can look more at the *results* of the practice of science than at the *process* or *definition* of science itself. We will consider, for example, where some particular claims of well-established science is alleged to be in conflict with or to support some claims of religion.

DEFINING RELIGION

We have seen the difficulty of defining "science." Are we any better off in defining "religion?" I was once at a conference with a group of theologians discussing the nature of religion. After several academic and abstract definitions, the earthy theologian Stanley Hauerwas exclaimed, "That's a pile of horseshit. I'll tell you what religion is. Religion is a farmer sittin' on his stool readin' his Bible." Taken literally, that definition is likewise a pile—it restricts religion to so-called "religions of the Book" and, very likely, to Christianity. Taken metaphorically, it may mean that religion involves deeply human ritual practices in response to the divine. But like science, religion cannot be bundled into a neat word or phrase that concisely describes its many facets. In 1990, the Barnes and Noble Cambridge Encyclopedia stated that "no single definition will suffice to encompass the varied sets of traditions, practices, and ideas which constitute different religions." The difficulty in defining "religion" parallels the difficulty in defining "science"—there is no single definition that can capture everything we mean when we use the word "religion."

In the West, religions are widely associated with belief in or beliefs about gods or even God (Yahweh, the Father Almighty, or Allah, most notably). But if the definition of religion were to require god beliefs, then the Buddha and some Buddhists (those who, following the Buddha, are atheists) would not be religious.[21] Some religions, such as Buddhism, essentially involve proper behaviors. Others, such as various forms of Gnosticism, involve esoteric knowledge and show little concern for human behavior; these religions are more concerned with having proper beliefs rather than proper practices. Some religions, such as Roman Catholicism, have a highly hierarchical priesthood, while others, say Quakers, are more egalitarian. Some forms of religious Confucianism are completely private (the rituals take place within one's own home). Some, such as Protestant Christianity, involve a set of authoritative texts and doctrinal beliefs, while others, Sufi mystics, for example, reject such linguistic barriers between the individual and transcendent, ineffable reality. Some involve highly articulated liturgical practices such as the burning of incense, singing of choirs, and hoisting of holy books at the precisely right moments. Quakers, on the other hand, sit together in silence during worship. Others, such as shamanistic ecstatic religions, involve more chaotic, feeling-driven, body-shaking practices. From such widely varying beliefs to such vastly diverging practices, it is hard to fit all of religion under a single umbrella.

Philosopher William Alston, after analyzing various definitions of religion, finds them all wanting because no single definition can fit every case of what we might consider religion (Alston, 1967). Instead of thinking of religion in terms of a single, unifying definition, he suggests a web of "religion-making characteristics." These sorts of characteristics, some of which are partly overlapping with others, tend to make something count as a religion. These characteristics include the following:

1. Belief in supernatural beings.
2. A distinction between sacred and profane objects.
3. Ritual acts focused on sacred objects.
4. A moral code believed to be sanctioned by the gods.
5. Characteristic religious feelings (awe, sense of mystery, and adoration).
6. Prayer and other forms of communication with gods.
7. A worldview, or general, picture of the world as a whole, and the place of the individual therein.
8. A more or less total organization of one's life based on the worldview.
9. A social group bound together by the above.

This list is not exhaustive. Moreover, a religion could have as few as one and as many as nine of these characteristics.

No need to belabor the point: it's impossible to define "religion" in a handy, single, useful, and comprehensive way. But if we can't adequately define "science" and "religion," how can we hope to understand the relationship between science and religion?

The Relationship between Science and Religion

We've been so far unsuccessful in precisely defining "science" and "religion" so that they fit all times and all places. Yet this book is about science and religion. What gives? Surely some claims of some actual religions are relevant to science (by some definition). Instead of talking about religion and science in very general terms, let's restrict ourselves to something more manageable—the specific claims of a single religion, Christianity, and the specific claims of modern, Western science.[22] So instead of talking about science in general (which can't be precisely defined) and religion in general (which can't be precisely defined), we will talk about specific scientific claims, such as the law of universal gravitation or the age of the earth, and their relationship to specific Christian beliefs or doctrines, such as divine creation or divine providence. Let's put this together into more useful questions: How have science and Christianity been related? How are, can, or should they be?

There are various options, as mentioned earlier in this chapter, for conceiving of the relationship between science and religion. Some hold that science and religion are fundamentally in conflict. Others hold that science and religion occupy distinctively separate, nonoverlapping realms (and so couldn't possibly conflict). And still others, like Kepler and Newton, believed that science and religion can be integrated together in mutually beneficial ways. These general positions—conflict, separation, and integration—are three main ways to interpret the complex relationship between science and religion.[23]

> *Conflict*: Science and religion are in continual conflict, both historically and fundamentally.
> *Separation*: Science and religion are entirely independent, and operate within separate realms.
> *Integration*: Science and religion are fundamentally related, and can correct and enhance each other.

Let us briefly consider these three models of the relationship between science and religion.

Conflict

Reflecting on the travails of Galileo and the reception of Darwin, it is fashionable to assert that science and religion are locked in mortal combat. Such high-profile examples are seized upon in historically influential but deeply flawed and misleading books such as John William Draper, *History of the Conflict between Religion and Science* (1874) and Andrew Dickson White, *A History of the Warfare of Science with Theology in Christendom* (1896). Of Galileo, Draper wrote:

> Galileo was accused of heresy, blasphemy, atheism. He was summoned before the Holy Inquisition, under an accusation of having taught that the earth moves round the sun, a doctrine "utterly contrary to the Scriptures." He was ordered to renounce that heresy, on pain of being imprisoned. He was directed to desist from teaching and advocating the Copernican theory, and pledge himself that he would neither publish nor defend it for the future. Knowing well that Truth has no need of martyrs, he assented to the required recantation, and gave the promise demanded.
>
> For sixteen years the Church had rest. But in 1632 Galileo ventured on the publication of his work entitled "The System of the World," its object being

the vindication of the Copernican doctrine. He was again summoned before the Inquisition at Rome, accused of having asserted that the earth moves round the sun. He was declared to have brought upon himself the penalties of heresy. On his knees, with his hand on the Bible, he was compelled to abjure and curse the doctrine of the movement of the earth. What a spectacle! This venerable man, the most illustrious of his age, forced by the threat of death to deny facts which his judges as well as himself knew to be true! He was then committed to prison, treated with remorseless severity during the remaining ten years of his life, and was denied burial in consecrated ground. (Draper, 1898: 171–72)

This sounds bad for any hope of reconciliation between science and religion.[24]

Of Darwin, White wrote:

DARWIN'S *Origin of Species* had come into the theological world like a plough into an ant-hill. Everywhere those thus rudely awakened from their old comfort and repose had swarmed forth angry and confused. Reviews, sermons, books light and heavy, came flying at the new thinker from all sides.

The keynote was struck at once in the *Quarterly Review* by Wilberforce, Bishop of Oxford. He declared that "the principle of natural selection is absolutely incompatible with the word of God"; that it "contradicts the revealed relations of creation to its Creator." Nor did the bishop's efforts end here; at the meeting of the British Association for the Advancement of Science he again disported himself in the tide of popular applause. Referring to the ideas of Darwin, who was absent on account of illness, he congratulated himself in a public speech that he was not descended from a monkey. The reply came from Huxley, who said in substance: "If I had to choose, I would prefer to be a descendant of a humble monkey rather than of a man who employs his knowledge and eloquence in misrepresenting those who are wearing out their lives in the search for truth." (White, 1908: 70).

Such combative and pugnacious language is widely accepted as the god-honest truth.[25]

Suppose we take these exaggerations and half-truths as the whole truth and nothing but the truth. Two examples scarcely amount to a fundamental or continual conflict between science and religion. Cases of actual conflict between science and Christianity are few and far between. The conflict thesis gains momentum by dramatizing and emphasizing relatively few and typically exaggerated historical events.

Yet there surely is conflict sometime between some science and some religion. For example, young earth creationism blatantly contradicts the science of a very old earth. The scientific consensus that humans descended from preexisting species conflicts with the widely held belief that humans were created by a direct act of God breathing life into dust.

But the myth of continual and irreconcilable differences needs to be put to its well-deserved final rest.

Separation

Imagine Muhammad Ali versus Smokin' Joe Frazier in the Boxing Match of the Century. Ali, dancin' like a butterfly and stingin' like a bee, throwing and landing countless clever jabs, amazingly, is seldom hit. Smokin' Joe lumbers around the ring delivering punch after powerful punch but, again, is the recipient of scarcely a blow. At the end of the final round, the bell rings and both Ali and Smokin' Joe are declared the winner. How could that happen? Turns out, they were boxing side by side but in entirely different rings.

Maybe science versus religion is like this imaginary boxing match. Perhaps science and religion are not in conflict because they aren't in the same ring. Perhaps science and religion are wholly independent of one another. They don't actually conflict with each other because they *can't* conflict. According to the separation model, science and religion cannot step on each other's toes because they walk within totally isolated realms. Science and religion address different issues and answer different questions using different methods and different languages.

One version of the separation model holds that science and religion have different foundations: science rests on human observation and reason, religion rests on divine revelation. In a *National Geographic* issue that included an article on the evolution of life, the editor offered his view on science and religion:

> Faith and science have at least one thing in common: Both are lifelong searches for truth. But while religion is an unshakable belief in the unseen, science is the study of testable, observable phenomena. The two coexist, and may at times complement each other. But neither should be asked to validate or invalidate the other. Scientists have no more business questioning the existence of God than theologians had telling Galileo the Earth was at the center of the universe.
>
> Bill Allen, *National Geographic*, March 1998

The editor holds that since science and religion have different methods and start from different foundations, their beliefs *can't* conflict (they might even complement one another).

The recently deceased Harvard biologist Stephen Jay Gould proposed that science and religion belong to separate domains, which he calls "nonoverlapping magisteria" (NOMA, for short). Nonoverlapping magisteria is "a principle of respectful noninterference." Gould writes: "The lack of conflict between science and religion arises from a lack of overlap between their respective domains of professional expertise—science in the empirical constitution of the universe, and religion in the search for proper ethical values and the spiritual meaning of our lives. The attainment of wisdom in a full life requires extensive attention to both domains" (1997). Because science and religion inhabit such different arenas of thought, each serves a different purpose in human life and inquiry. Science operates within the domain of the *how*; that is, science aims to discover the ways in which things operate—science explores *what is*. On the other hand, religion operates within the domain of the *why*, answering questions about meaning and purpose—religion explores *what ought to be*. The separation model avoids conflict and preserves the unique aims of both science and religion.

Religion, the domain of value and meaning, can help us to change ourselves for the better and to become other-regarding. The magisterium of religion governs self-understanding, our hopes and fears, choices, decisions, personal crisis, meaning, relationships, morality, miracles, and virtue.

Science, the ream of natural facts, can say little of the existence of miracles, morality, and deities. It can neither affirm nor deny the existence of a supernatural creator. While science may influence the way that some people live and understand their lives, it does not require those who study it to adopt a naturalistic worldview. Science helps us to understand objective truth both in the cosmos and at the molecular level. Scientific answers are observable and repeatable. Ultimately, science is limited to the observable, the measurable, the tangible.

By restricting science and religion to their own magisterium, conflict is avoided. Gould states that, "If religion can no longer dictate the nature of factual conclusions properly under the magisterium of science, then scientists cannot claim higher insight into moral truth from a superior knowledge of the world's empirical constitution. This mutual humility has important practical consequences in a world of such diverse passions" (Gould, 1997). For example, the separation model states that cosmology is outside the domain of religion, and as such, the Bible has no grounds to teach us anything about the science of the cosmos. Adopting a separation approach, Ian Barbour states we should "read the opening chapters of Genesis as a symbolic portrayal of the basic relation of humanity and the world to God, a message about human creatureliness and the goodness of the natural order. These religious meanings can be separated from the ancient cosmology in which they were expressed" (Barbour, 1997: 85). Just as we wouldn't look to the weather channel for clues about how to work through a stormy relationship, we shouldn't read the book of Genesis for scientific facts about the planet.

But a simple fact remains—some scientists and some Christians make assertions that seem for all intents and purposes to conflict. As seen in the opening chapter, Richard Dawkins claims that religion is a science: "[Y]ou can't escape the scientific implications of religion. A universe with a God would look quite different from a universe without one. A physics, a biology where there is a God is bound to look different. So the most basic claims of religion *are* scientific. Religion *is* a scientific theory" (Dawkins, 1994). While Dawkins' claim is exaggerated, it is difficult to maintain that religious beliefs could never, in principle, conflict with scientific beliefs. Perhaps religion is mostly about sin and salvation, but it has also made claims that constitute an incursion into territory claimed by science. We may need to look further for a completely adequate account of the relationship between religion and science.

Integration

On the integration model, science and religion both contribute to the formation of a consistent set of beliefs. Unlike the separation model, the integration model encourages mutual interaction between science and religion. And unlike the conflict model, the integration model encourages a healthy give and take between science and religion. Why consider the integration model?

It's easy to see that religion, on various points, could and should seek and find guidance from science. For example, ancient religious accounts of creation are likely to be long on myth and short on math. Religious conceptions of the human person might stand some insights from psychology and neuroscience. While we all know that the earth revolves around the sun, the authors of most sacred texts did not. Science provokes religious thinkers to do some much-needed rethinking. For example, how should science aid the interpretation of a sacred text (almost certainly written in a prescientific, preliterate, age)?

But what about the other direction? Does religion have anything to offer science? The most common answer is that theology provides a worldview in which the assumptions of science, the subjective values discussed in the preceding sections, find their home. Scientists make crucial assumptions, assumptions that science itself is incapable of justifying. For example, scientists assume that our senses and reasoning processes are reliable and that they can assist in our quest to understand the world. Since science *starts* with the reliability of our senses and intellect, it cannot prove or justify their reliability. But if God created us in his image, as knowers, we have good reason to trust the reliability of our cognitive faculties. Scientists also assume the uniformity of nature—that the universe is the same everywhere and at all times. The uniformity of nature, like the reliability of our cognitive faculties, is quite at home within a religious worldview.

Religion may legitimately advise and caution science as well. Scientists have made claims that dramatically exceed their evidential base, often moving from physics or psychology into metaphysics or ethics. Behavioral psychologist B. F. Skinner, for example, articulated a quasi-scientific view of human psychology that left no room for moral responsibility or human dignity (Skinner, 1971). Religious believers, with a strong commitment to human responsibility and dignity, rightly objected to Skinner's excessive claims.

Some scientists clothe antitheistic diatribe in scientific garb. For example, Stephen Hawking, perhaps the most famous living physicist, has recently argued that the Big Bang, properly understood, leaves no room for God as creator of the universe: "Spontaneous creation is the reason there is something rather than nothing, why the universe exists, why we exist." Hawking claims: "Because there is a law such as gravity, the universe can and will create itself from nothing" (2010: 180). Hawking offers a theological conclusion based on scientific jargon. Thus adorned, it is hard for nonscientists to know what to think. Religious believers should not be overawed when a scientist, however lauded, proclaims the irrelevance of the creator. While the quantum theory of gravity may allow for the *possibility* of an infinite universe, it looks, for all intents and purposes, to be *actually* finite, to have a beginning in time. While it takes a certain courage to chastise Stephen Hawking, religious thinkers may need to respond to poorly established scientific theories that are contrary to deeply entrenched religious beliefs.

Finally, science may require the kind of moral guidance that religious believers can offer. Einstein's claim that science needs religion was partly based on his fear of nuclear warfare. Although his theories provided the theoretical basis for nuclear bombs, he fervently opposed their development and deployment. We can make bombs that kill hundreds of thousands of people and devastate a country, but should we? We might be able to clone humans, but should we? Science itself, in our contemporary understanding, is about *what is*; morality is about what *ought to be*. So science, properly speaking, has nothing to say about ethics. But, to twist Einstein's words a bit, science without ethics is blind.

Conclusion

The integration model suggests various ways that religion might incorporate well-established science into religion. It is also open to ways in which religion might be incorporated into a complete scientific worldview—by justifying the foundations or methodology of science, by courageously questioning brash and poorly established science, by warning science when it has exceeded its bounds, or by providing science with a moral conscience. Religion, of course, sometimes intrudes improperly into well-established science. We are all aware of the ignorant theist demanding his day (sometimes in court) in the face of well-established science. Various debates in evolution and creation are cases in point. Let's reserve judgment about these matters until we've studied them in detail in the chapters that follow.

CHAPTER 3

The Fabric of the Universe

THE MYTH OF WARFARE

Recent headlines scream the conflict thesis: "God vs. Science" and "Religion and Science Will Always Clash" (Atkins, 1998; Van Biema, 2006). Sam Harris, in "Science Must Destroy Religion," writes, "The conflict between science and religion is inherent" (2006). One reviewer of Richard Dawkins's *The God Delusion* sketched out the cultural import of his book: "It was refreshing to see the publication of Richard Dawkins's book *The God Delusion*. It is not every day that one of the premier evolutionary biologists in the world publishes a text dedicated to the defense of atheism. Dawkins has done us a service, if only in making more acceptable the general proposition that religion and science are at odds with each other, and that it is science that should win out" (Kay, 2007). According to the conflict thesis, as science fills the cup of reason, irrational religion spills out. When the cup of reason is finally full, religion will have evaporated.

In spite of being widely held, the Conflict Thesis has been rejected by historians, philosophers, and scientists—theists and atheists alike. For example, when we look at the scientific revolution (the scientific developments that began in the sixteenth century and progressed through the seventeenth century), the place where science as most of us know it began, we discover that the scientists involved, people like Copernicus, Galileo, Robert Boyle, and Isaac Newton, were deeply and sincerely religious. Modern science sprang from religious believers and religious belief. Not only were these early scientists religious, their religious beliefs motivated and even informed their pursuit of science.

What was it about their religious beliefs that proved such fertile ground for the development of modern science? Why Christian belief and not the belief systems that preceded it? Why did modern science develop in the Christian West and not, for example, in the advanced culture of China?

While we can't answer all of these fascinating questions, we will examine three key thinkers—Francis Bacon (1561–1626), Robert Boyle (1627–91), and Isaac Newton (1642–1727)—who exerted a profound influence on the "new science." Bacon, considered the father of the modern scientific method, was not himself a scientist, yet he provided the philosophical foundation of the scientific revolution. Boyle, the father of chemistry, put into practice the experimental philosophy advocated by Bacon. Newton, the father of physics, was one of the greatest scientific thinkers of all time.[1] Each of these thinkers was motivated in their scientific pursuits by their deeply held religious beliefs.

BACON'S BUSY BEE

Francis Bacon (1561–1626) is widely praised for his influence on Britain's Royal Society for Improving Natural Knowledge (i.e., science), founded in 1660 for the advancement of "Physico-Mathematicall Experimentall Learning." The Royal Society was the first society of scholars devoted to the development of natural philosophy (we will use the term that was not used at that time—"science"). Its exclusive membership was astounding. Robert Boyle was one of the Society's founders and Isaac Newton one of its early members. Membership in the Society would subsequently include a who's who list of all-time great scientists: Charles Darwin, Ernest Rutherford (the father of nuclear physics), Albert Einstein, Francis Crick and James Watson (who cracked the DNA code), and Stephen Hawking. Among its current members are more than 70 Nobel Prize winners.

Bacon's impact on the particulars of science was slight; his general ideas, insights, and outlook inspired generations of followers to collect empirical (observational) data and to postpone theorizing until adequate evidence had been gathered. Consider Bacon's maxim: "What nature is or does must not be thought up or reasoned out but discovered." Bacon believed that the rational speculation and neglect of observation by his predecessors had proven a hindrance to the progress of science. His recommendation of proceeding on the basis of observation and experiment and not on, say, traditional authorities or metaphysical speculation, was captured in the motto of the Royal Society, "*Nullius in Verba*" ("On the words of no one"). Although not much of a scientist himself, his philosophy exerted an extraordinary and timely influence on the development of science in this significant period.

Bacon was born into a family with connections to the royal family of England (Bacon's father was the Lord Keeper of the Seal for Queen Elizabeth; Bacon himself was Lord Chancellor of England under King James). Bacon, who entered Cambridge at the age of 12, left his mark on a host of disciplines: he was a philosopher, lawyer, statesman, and writer. But he is most famous for his "invention" of the new, observational, and experimental method in science. This method would provide the light that "would eventually disclose and bring into sight all that is most hidden and secret in the universe." The new science would require a new method—Bacon's method.

Bacon felt that previous natural philosophers constructed theories prematurely and with little grounding in observable reality; he called their approach "Anticipations of the Mind." They proceeded top-down: they erected theories based on reason alone and then found illustrations (rationalizations) of the veracity of these theories in nature. Their method was to spin a theoretical web, like a spider, entirely from within; Bacon writes: "For the wit and mind of man, if it work upon matter, which is the contemplation of the creatures of God, worketh according to the stuff, and is limited thereby; but if it work upon itself, as the spider worketh his web, then it is endless, and brings forth indeed cobwebs of learning, admirable for the fineness of thread and work, but of no substance or profit" (Bacon, 1605: Bk. I.5). Bacon contends that without observations of the world—that is, when the mind doesn't work on matter—the mind works upon itself producing empty but elegant constructions, spinning out ephemeral theories with no correspondence to reality.

Bacon emphasized a bottom-up approach: collect data (through careful and extensive observation), begin to theorize, do experiments (i.e., make more and highly specialized observations based on the theory), and then reassess the theory. Scientific theorizing must be based on observations: "Man, being the servant and interpreter of Nature, can do and understand so much and so much only as he has observed in fact or in thought of the course of nature. Beyond this he neither knows anything nor can do anything" (Bacon, 1620: Bk. I.1). Theorizing in science should be based on careful observations and experiments that are then judiciously interpreted to reveal the regularities in the world. Bacon's "bottom-up" approach to scientific theorizing begins on empirical *and* rational grounds rather than on rational grounds alone. From observed particulars, scientific knowledge would slowly rise up to the realm of general principles. Bacon argued, "Neither the naked hand nor the understanding left to itself can affect much. It is by instruments and helps that the work is done, which are as much wanted for the understanding as for the hand. And as the instruments of the hand either give motion or guide it, so the instruments of the mind supply either suggestions for the understanding or cautions" (Bacon, 1620: Bk I.2). Both observation and understanding, Bacon argued, are essential ingredients to human knowledge.

Proper science is not the simple, blind accumulation of observed facts. The mind must reflect on the facts to extract their significance or meaning. Consider, for example, these observations: ball fell to the ground, dead bird fell to the ground, I tripped and fell to the ground, a tree crashes to the ground, a feather gracefully glides to the ground, and so on. We can develop a long list of observations concerning falling down things, but we don't have a science of falling down things. Lists of observations, however complete, aren't good science.

In the passage below, Bacon discusses the deficiencies of those who rely on sense experience alone (men of experiment) as well as those who rely on reason alone (the reasoners). He writes:

> The men of experiment are like the ant, they only collect and use; the reasoners resemble spiders, who make cobwebs out of their own substance. But the bee takes a middle course: it gathers its material from the flowers of the garden and of the field, but transforms and digests it by a power of its own. Not unlike this is the true business of philosophy; for it neither relies solely or

chiefly on the powers of the mind, nor does it take the matter which it gathers from natural history and mechanical experiments and lay it up in the memory whole, as it finds it, but lays it up in the understanding altered and digested. Therefore from a closer and purer league between these two faculties, the experimental and the rational (such as has never yet been made), much may be hoped (Bacon, 1620: Bk. I.95).

The Baconian method is the rational-empirical busy bee—while it begins with observations, it takes these accumulated observations into the mind for transformation into a significant scientific theory (which could then be tested through experimentation).

With respect to falling down things, we can see Newton's transformation of observations into a significant theory—the universal law of gravitation. On the basis of careful observations (and analysis of the countless observations of others), Newton determined that there was a constant relation between bodies (masses) in the universe: any two bodies are attracted to each other. Moreover, the closer they are to each other, the more they are attracted to one another; the bigger they are, the more they attract another. He calculated the universal law of gravity to be

$$F = G \frac{m_1 m_2}{r^2}$$

where

m_1 is the mass of one of the objects.
m_2 is the mass of the other object.
r is the radius of separation between the center of masses of each object.
F_G is the force of attraction between the two objects.

Now *that* is good Baconian science. This transformational and rational process begins with the incremental accumulation of observed facts, which are then taken up by the mind and developed into a rational principle.

Bacon's work was motivated by his belief in the *Doctrine of the Two Books*— the belief that God revealed himself in two ways, the *Book of Scripture* and the *Book of Nature*. A full and complete understanding of reality requires careful readings of both books. He writes:

> For our Saviour saith, You err, not knowing the Scriptures nor the power of God; laying before us two books or volumes to study, if we will be secured from error; first the Scriptures, revealing the will of God, and then the creatures expressing his power; whereof the latter is a key unto the former; not only opening our understanding to conceive the true sense of the Scriptures, by the general notions of reason and rules of speech; but chiefly opening our belief, in drawing us into a due meditation of the omnipotency of God, which is chiefly signed and engraven upon his works. (Bacon, 1605: Bk. I.VI.16)

Through the *Book of Scripture* we can learn of God's will for our lives and God's character. Through the *Book of Nature* we can learn of God's power and intellect as manifested in his well-ordered universes. A diet restricted to one book or the other is intellectually and spiritually impoverished. Bacon's friend, Thomas Browne, expressed the Doctrine of the Two Books in a way that Bacon would agree with: "The world was made to be inhabited by Beasts but studied and contemplated by man; 'tis the Debt of our Reason we owe unto God, and the homage we pay for not being Beasts...The Wisdom of God receives small honor from those vulgar Heads that rudely stare about, and with a gross rusticity admire His works: those highly magnify Him, whose judicious inquiry into His Acts, and deliberate research into His Creatures, return the duty of a devout and learned admiration" (Browne, 1974: 33).

Bacon was so persuaded of the Doctrine of the Two Books that he came to see natural philosophy (science) as a sort of theology and natural philosophers (scientists) as priests.

The task of scientific priests, according to Bacon, is to restore God's creation to its pristine pre-fall state. According to the dominant Christian (Augustinian) view, God created an unblemished world, a paradise, that was ruined by the sin of Adam (the fall). According to Bacon and to Christian tradition, Adam's fall from grace wreaked havoc on God's orderly creation. The fall also plunged humanity into a moral, spiritual, and intellectual darkness from which it had not yet recovered by Bacon's day. The fall disrupted God's perfect creation and put blinders on humans that prevented them from seeing God's natural order. In order to restore humanity to its pre-fall state, God had to forgive and redeem humans through the life, atoning death and resurrection of his son, Jesus; God could thereby transform us body, mind, and soul. We can then and only then get into the right relationship with God and God's world. In order to understand the natural world, Bacon is clear: it all begins with God. Thus restored by God, we can, following Bacon's methods, cooperate with God in the restoration of the world to its perfect, pre-fall state. God's restoration of our pre-fall intellectual capacities is crucial to our ability to truly understand the world. Only by understanding the world can we begin to recreate paradise.

When divine grace and Bacon's methods restore the powers of human understanding, we can comprehend the world. We can comprehend the world because God has created both an orderly world and human minds capable of grasping that order—the so-called *correspondence of mind and world*. It is astounding that our mental capacities are capable of grasping the world. There might have been problems on both ends—the world may have been disorderly and chaotic, and we might have been cognitively incapable of grasping order. A failure on either end, and science is impossible.[2] Our world is precisely mathematically ordered, according to Bacon, because it is a reflection of the mind of God. God's mind got melded into the order of this world.[3]

Successful science requires more than an orderly world—humans must also have the ability to grasp and communicate that order. Monkeys, slugs, and bananas, to name just a few, lack the capacities for a scientific understanding of the world. Humans could have been really good at understanding whatever is necessary for human survival—gathering food, say, or seeking a mate—but lousy at understanding the ultimate structure of reality—for example, adducing the law of gravity or the structure of DNA. We are all familiar with the Peter Principle—every employee tends to rise to his level of incompetence. Natural science may have been one or two levels above humanity's competence. But it is not: we can understand the natural world. Like our orderly world, Bacon believed that human minds capable of grasping that order is a sign of divine handiwork. God put his mind into the world and then into humanity. Human minds and the natural world were, according to Bacon, made for one another. Mind and world match.[4]

For Bacon, knowledge is also power. Because of the fall, humanity had fallen from its proper place in nature. Humans had lost their dominion—their place of prominence, authority, and control—over nature. Through great effort (the sweat of their brows) and faith, humanity can be restored to its pre-fall place, and the world will then supply us with all human necessities. Bacon unites the themes of fall, restoration, dominion, and power into a single concluding paragraph:

> For man by the fall fell at the same time from his state of innocence and from his dominion over creation. Both of these losses however can even in this life be in some part repaired; the former by religion and faith, the latter by arts and sciences. For creation was not by the curse made altogether and forever a rebel, but in virtue of that charter, "In the sweat of thy face shalt thou eat bread," it is now by various labors at length and in some measures subdued to the supplying of man with bread; that is, to the uses of human life. (Bacon, 1620: Bk. II.52)

Bacon viewed nature as God's creation, which could be understood and even tamed through technological advancement. Bacon, like other modern scientists, believed that science has a practical function—of making life better for everyone by giving us some measure of control over nature. Consider all the practical ways in which knowledge of the world gained through experimentation and keen observation has led to an improvement in the quality of human life: home heating, indoor plumbing, electricity, pharmaceutical development, and advances in medical technology.[5] According to Bacon, such technologies constitute our partial recreation of paradise. Bacon believed that human beings working hand-in-hand with God would restore humankind's dominion over the earth and return us to Eden.

INSTRUMENTS OF HAND AND MIND

Bacon imagined, rightly or wrongly, his predecessors sitting alone in their studies, thinking. The modern scientist, according to Bacon, walks outside and observes the motions of the planets and stars, or goes into the laboratory to carefully perform an experiment; only then does he sit back and reflect. The differences in approach, and hence results, couldn't be more obvious.

Very smart people started looking long and hard, carefully and closely at things and, lo and behold, a revolution in human knowledge—the monumental discoveries of Copernicus, Galileo, Boyle, and Newton.

One of the great innovations of this scientific revolution was the regular use of experiments to discover the world around us. Scientific knowledge comes from an engagement with the world: knowledge of natural objects is discovered, not deduced. Bacon complained about those who "hunt more after words than matter." He believed that the world would give up its secrets only if we put mind and hand together: "the instruments of the hand either give motion or guide it [understanding of the world], so the instruments of the mind supply either suggestions for the understanding or cautions" (Bacon, 1620: Bk. I.2). The mind alone spins meaningless webs, but the world alone is vast and incomprehensible. The world needs to be broken down into bite-size bits so that we can begin to understand it. Experiments break the world down into graspable bits.

We read the *Book of Nature* through experimentation. Bacon believed that experiments can break down the language of the world into the letters of its alphabet, and only then, through reflection, can those letters be put back together into scientific sentences (a theory) that we can understand. Boyle similarly claimed that through experimentation the philosopher is able "to read the stenography of God's omniscient hand" (Boyle, 166: 62–63).

Science uses mind *and* hands, theorizing *and* experimentation, speculation *and* observation. Science utilizes reason as it conducts experiments, gathers data, organizes the data coherently, and then theorizes by attempting to establish universal principles, which it tests and retests, repeating the entire process. Thomas Sprat, a seventeenth-century historian, bishop and member of the Royal Society said: "Philosophy will then attain to perfection, when either the Mechanic Labourers shall have philosophical heads, or the Philosophers shall have Mechanical Hands" (Sprat, 1722: 397).

Bacon believed that, God helping us, we can use the experimental method to understand the world. But without the agreement between our mind and the world, we should despair of grasping the world at all. Yet there is hope: God has equipped us with the capacities to read the *Book of Nature* and restore humanity to paradise.

Ironically, one of Bacon's experiments led to his premature demise. While stuffing a chicken with snow to determine the preservative effects of low temperatures, Bacon contracted pneumonia. He died a few days later. Bacon might just be the first martyr to the experimental method.

BOYLE'S LAW AND THE LAWS OF GOD

Robert Boyle (1627–91), the founder of the field of chemistry, is immortalized for "Boyle's Law," which says that for a given amount of gas the product of its volume and pressure is constant. Boyle himself and his influence are often overlooked in discussions of the history of science and religion. This is unfortunate. Boyle, one of the greatest of modern scientists, was a clear thinker on issues of science and religion and is representative of the mindset of an early modern scientist—committed to both experimental science and the Christian faith. He wrote that his chemical investigations of our wonderful creation were "a means of discovering the nature and purpose of God." Boyle's scientific achievements and natural philosophical insights shed light on the extent to which modern science was propelled by religious considerations. Boyle took Bacon's maxim to heart: "What nature is or does must not be thought up or reasoned out but discovered." So Boyle became perhaps the first genuine experimentalist in science.

Robert Boyle was the fourteenth child of the Earl of Cork, at that time one of the wealthiest men in Britain. The Earl had come to wealth through his own gumption and hard work, purchasing estates at cheap prices at just the right time. He impressed the Queen enough that he was appointed Clerk to the Council in Ireland. As is often the case for self-made men, the Earl of Cork decided that his children should be brought up without excessive material comforts, luxuries, and privileges. For the Earl's sons, this meant being sent away to live with a family in the country as a baby and returning around age 5. All of the Earl's children were expected to take their studies seriously, and Robert especially excelled.

While traveling through Italy with his brother and their tutor, Boyle heard the news of the great astronomer Galileo's death. His curiosity piqued, Boyle decided to read Galileo's writings and began to develop an interest in science. An Irish rebellion in the early 1640s and civil war thereafter altered the family's financial position. Boyle's father passed away before Robert turned 18, and, although he died a far less wealthy man than he had been only a few years earlier, the Earl of Cork was able to leave a small manor in the country for Robert.

In the early 1650s, the political climate in Britain stabilized, and Boyle reestablished his father's estate and fortunes. After a few years, Boyle earned sufficient rental income from these estates to afford to live a comfortable life. Boyle moved to Oxford to be part of its exciting intellectual and scientific climate. There he hired a number of assistants to help him perform experiments in chemistry and physics.

Boyle's scientific experiments, especially in the fledgling field of chemistry, contributed greatly to the development of science in this period. It is Boyle's interest in science and religion, however, that is of interest to us here. His groundbreaking book, *The Skeptical Chymist*, was followed by three books defending the Christian faith, concluding with his book, *The Christian Virtuoso*. His Baconian experimental outlook was closely allied with his Christian beliefs. Consider, for example, the following: "It more sets off the wisdom of God in the fabric of the universe that he can make so vast a machine perform all those many things which he designed it should by the mere contrivance of brute matter, managed by certain laws of local motion and upheld by his ordinary and general concourse, than if he employed from time to time an intelligent overseer—such as nature is fancied to be—to regulate, assist, and control the motions of the parts" (Boyle, 1996: 11).

Boyle's mission "was to formulate a view of nature that allowed us to understand and marvel at the wonder of the created order, so that we might better appreciate the glory of the Creator" (Ashworth, 2003: 80). This goal could be achieved, he believed, through the mechanical philosophy. His mechanical philosophy was not a form of deism (a view that holds that God creates the cosmos and then leaves it alone to run on its own), but one in which God is intimately involved in the ongoing operation of his creation. Boyle writes, "And it is intelligible to me that God should at the beginning impress determinate motions upon the parts of matter, and guide them as he thought requisite for the primordial construction of things; and that since, he should by his ordinary and general concourse maintain those powers which he gave the parts of matter to transmit their motion thus and thus to one another" (Boyle, 1996: 24–25). God, according to Boyle, is continually active in sustaining the world.

Rather than conflict or tension, we find in Boyle's writing the peaceful coexistence of science and religion.[6] Boyle's life shows that religious beliefs can encourage the development of science. The integration of science and religion is not only possible, it actually happened. Boyle argued that science likewise can and should encourage the development of religious belief. The new "Experimental Philosopher" was "dispos'd to make use of the knowledge of the Creatures to confirm his Belief, and encrease his Veneration, of the Creator" (Boyle, 1690: 7).

Standing on the Shoulders of Giants

Isaac Newton (1642–1727) discerned the law of universal gravitation not because of that pesky apple but "By thinking on it continually." Along with Galileo, Newton had perhaps the most indelible impact on the development of modern science. It seems fitting then that Newton was born in 1642, the same year Galileo died. Although he was no orthodox Christian believer, Newton was a devout theist and a firm believer that the study of nature was at the same time the study of God.

When Isaac's mother was pregnant with him, Isaac's father passed away. His mother remarried when Isaac was 3 years old, and young Isaac was sent to live with strict yet caring grandparents until he was 10, at which time Isaac returned to his mother who was again widowed. Isaac was an excellent student, demonstrating an aptitude for designing and constructing elaborate models, such as a working model of a windmill. Although he excelled at school, it was not until he failed at managing the family farm that Isaac enrolled at university. At Cambridge University, Newton often ignored the prescribed curriculum in favor of pursuing his own scientific interests. Spending little time studying the curriculum sponsored by the university, however, did not prevent Newton from winning a competitive fellowship to stay on at Cambridge.

Newton's best-known scientific and mathematical achievements were the development of the calculus and his discernment of the law of universal gravitation. It is our interest in this chapter, however, to explore Newton's views on science and religion, especially how Newton's religious views influenced his approach to science. Few people know that Newton spent more time in serious study of the Bible than he did in his scientific ventures. Newton scholar James Force writes, "Newton's universe is *not*, and for Newton can *never* be, stripped of 'metaphysical considerations' because its creator, owner, and operator is the Lord God" (Force, 2000: 268). These metaphysical-religious considerations were the roots of Newton's scientific views.

In his preface to Newton's *Principia*, Roger Cotes writes:

> Without all doubt this world...could arise from nothing but the perfectly free will of God...From this fountain...[what] we call the laws of nature have flowed, in which there appear many traces indeed of the most wise contrivance, but not the least shadow of necessity. These therefore we must not seek from uncertain conjectures, but learn them from observations and experiments. He who is presumptuous enough to think that he can find the true principles of physics and the laws of natural things by the force alone of his own mind, and the internal light of reason, must either suppose that the world exists by necessity, and by the same necessity follows the laws proposed: or, if the order of Nature was established by the will of God, that himself, a miserable reptile, can tell what was fittest to be done. (Newton, 1687)

This passage reveals the foundational principles of science that were held not just by Newton but by his contemporaries as well. Among these principles are

1. God voluntarily created the world.
2. God freely established laws of nature.
3. We can learn about these laws through observations and experiments.

From this modest theological foundation, Newton would erect his remarkable scientific edifice. He had learned the lessons of Bacon and Boyle (and others) well. Bacon cleared the ground upon which Boyle, Copernicus, and Galileo walked. Newton gave them due credit, confessing, "If I have seen further it is only by standing on the shoulders of giants."[7]

A perfect and simple god, Newton thought, would make a simple world. A passage from one of Newton's manuscripts states: "Truth is ever to be found in simplicity, and not in the multiplicity and confusion of things. As the world, which to the naked eye exhibits the greatest variety of objects, appears very simple in its internal constitution when surveyed by a philosophic understanding, and so much the simpler, the better, it is understood, so it is in these visions. It is the perfection of all God's works that they are done with the greatest simplicity" (Newton, 1974). Newton viewed mathematical formulas as examples of simplicity in which "truth is ever to be found."

The view that mathematics could be applied with such precision to the natural world is one of the lasting insights of the scientific revolution. Modern-day developments in physics—relativity theory, quantum mechanics, and string theory, to name a few—are the fruits of this idea. Newton believed that precise mathematical formulas could be used to describe nature because God created the world, organized it by his laws, and established building blocks of perfect simplicity. According to Newton, God speaks to us in the *Book of Nature* through the language of mathematics.

Newton viewed his work in *Principia* as a long and complex argument for design, which, in turn, leads irresistibly to the Designer. This conclusion, he claims, follows as surely from his natural philosophical principles as his physical laws. He concludes his discussion of the theological implications of his physics with the following: "And thus much concerning God; to discourse of whom from the appearances of things, does certainly belong to Natural Philosophy" (Newton, 1729: 546). God, so he argues, is the ultimate conclusion of physics. For Newton the thought that science could be opposed to religion would seem most odd: theology and physics, for Newton, jointly constitute natural philosophy.

Even more, Newton believed that his natural philosophy would and should move us to obedience to God and love of one another. By leading us to God, natural philosophy leads us to the source and authority over our lives: "If natural Philosophy in all its Parts, by pursuing this Method [i.e., experiment], shall at length be perfected, the Bounds of Moral Philosophy will be also enlarged. For so far as we can know by natural Philosophy what is the first Cause, what Power he has over us, and what Benefits we receive from him, so far our Duty towards him, as well as that towards one another, will appear to us by the Light of Nature" (Newton, 1704: 405). The study of the *Book of Nature* is devotionally and morally uplifting: it leads us to love of God and humans alike.

CHRISTIANITY AND THE RISE OF MODERN SCIENCE

Francis Bacon, Robert Boyle, and Isaac Newton—three of the greatest thinkers of the scientific revolution—were keenly attuned to the role their theological beliefs played in their investigations of nature. Through their hard work and brilliant insights, modern science was born. Far from being antagonistic toward science, their faith motivated and even informed the development of science. In his *Principia*, Newton would write: "This most beautiful system of the sun, planets, and comets could only proceed from the counsel and dominion of an intelligent and powerful Being. And if the fixed stars are the centers of other like systems, these, being formed by the like wise counsel, must be all subject to the dominion of One" (Newton, 1713). The religious beliefs of these early scientists provided a foundation— a God-created cosmos and a God-created mind—for investigating nature. This investigation was carried out with the confidence that a world created by God is orderly and regular. By experimentation and observation we can attain to an understanding of the created world.

Science found fertile ground in the Christian West.[8] As contemporary physicist Paul Davies reminds us: "Science began as an outgrowth of theology, and all scientists, whether atheists or theists accept an essentially theological worldview" (Davies, 1995: 138). Science arose among natural philosophers who believed the world to be the design of God. In their quest for *scientia*, a complete and full understanding of reality, they perused God's two books—Scripture and Nature—to learn the mind of God. Kepler, for example, conceived of astronomers as "priests of the most high God, with respect to the book of nature." Robert Boyle regarded the activities of natural philosophers as intellectual worship of God. This is the theological worldview within which modern science blossomed.

Exclude God from the definition of science and, in one fell definitional swoop, you exclude the greatest natural philosophers of the so-called scientific revolution—Kepler, Copernicus, Galileo, Boyle, and Newton (to name just a few).

METHODOLOGICAL VERSUS METAPHYSICAL NATURALISM

While religion was there nurturing modern science, contemporary science can and should proceed without consideration of supernatural entities or forces. Most contemporary scientists believe, and I concur, that *science should proceed as if there were no God*. Science, at least nowadays, should restrict itself to the natural world and the natural laws that operate within the natural world. The claim that science should not appeal to the divine, sometimes called "methodological naturalism," is the dominant assumption of scientific practice in our day and age. *Methodological naturalism* holds that, in the practice of science, supernatural entities or forces (like God, ghosts, or qi^9) are not allowed; scientists should restrict their explanatory theories to those that invoke or involve only natural entities or forces (like atoms and planets, or gravity and electromagnetism). Physicist Steven Weinberg puts it as follows: "Science should be taught not in order to support religion and not in order to destroy religion. Science should be taught simply ignoring religion" (2000). The days of scientific appeals to God are over.

Like simplicity and beauty, values that inform scientific decision making, methodological naturalism is an assumption; one I think warranted, but it is an assumption nonetheless. Why accept this assumption?

The biggest reason to think methodological naturalism appropriate for contemporary science is the remarkable success of science when scientists grew increasingly dissatisfied with "God did it!" explanations and sought natural explanations. Invocations of the divine—to explain thunder, say, or valleys—were usually little more than theologically veiled ignorance (if we didn't know how something was done, then we presumed that God did it). Our understanding of the weather advanced when people stopped appealing to the gods of thunder and started appreciating the dynamic and interactive forces of, for example, heat conduction and convection. Astronomy yielded its secrets when people stopped believing that God was the prime mover of the planets and began understanding planetary motion in terms of inertia and gravity. Modern geology developed when slow, gradual, natural forces replaced Noah's flood as the movers and shakers of the earth's surfaces. Science, human knowing, dramatically progressed when it was no longer satisfied with "God did it" explanations and sought the underlying natural causes of the phenomena in question. The remarkable progress of science, when theologically veiled ignorance is conceded and natural causes are sought, is the biggest reason in favor of methodological naturalism. The continued success and progress of science demand methodological naturalism.

Does methodological naturalism entail metaphysical naturalism—the view that there are no supernatural entities or powers?

James Watson, the co-discoverer of the structure of the DNA molecule, contends that the increasing success of science counts decisively against the existence of God; he writes: "Every time you understand something, religion becomes less likely" (Highfield, 2003). The more successful science is at explaining, Watson argues, the less intellectual space there is for God. The very success that motivates the assumption of methodological naturalism supports, Watson claims, metaphysical naturalism.

While this narrative is all too common, it is flawed. Scientific explanations are restricted by their method to the material world. So it shouldn't come as a surprise that scientific theories say nothing about the immaterial world (should it exist). If God should exist, God is beyond the physical and, therefore, lies outside the domain and methods of science. In 1960 Soviet cosmonaut Yuri Gagarin, the first human to venture into space, confidently declared that his atheism was confirmed because when he peered into space, he didn't see God. But Gagarin's confidence was misplaced. God isn't out there, in space. God isn't in the world at all. Gagarin couldn't find God because he was looking in the wrong place.

Believing that supernatural explanations have no place in science does not require an affirmation of metaphysical naturalism. Methodological naturalism—understanding the natural world without appeal to the supernatural—is neutral with respect to the existence of God. Even if the weather is best understood in terms of heat conduction and convection, and even if dinosaurs died out because a meteor crashed into the earth, God might still exist. Imagine how odd it would be if someone based their atheism on science's ability to explain the switching on of a light in terms of electricity. Understanding the natural world in natural terms implies nothing about the existence or nonexistence of a supernatural God.

Bacon, Boyle, and Newton commended methodological naturalism *and* believed in God. They were inspired to methodological naturalism by their belief that God acts in natural, law-like ways. According to this view, God's dominant mode of action is through natural law, not through sporadic and miraculous divine interventions. If you want to understand how God works, you have to understand the natural laws that undergird God's world. That is how God did it.

When doing science—explaining how things work in the natural world—one should not go beyond the natural world; one should seek to understand the physical laws that operate within the natural world. Contemporary scientists, theists or not, should not bring God into their labs or theories. Scientists should follow methodological naturalistic principles: "Leave God and god-like entities out of science." God's existence is an independent, non-scientific question (one scientists are not any better equipped to answer).

CONCLUSION

We have discovered the profound influence of religion on the origin of modern science. Without exception, the first great modern scientists were devoutly religious. Yet they also affirmed some sort of separation between science and religion. Kepler, for example, repeatedly asserted that it is not the purpose of the Scriptures to instruct men in natural things. Like Kepler, most of these scientists affirmed something like the Doctrine of the Two Books, but believed that the two books should be kept entirely separate.[10] Bacon seemed likewise concerned that theology should not intrude on science; he wrote that "natural philosophy [science] has, in every age, met with a troublesome and difficult opponent: I mean superstition, and a blind and immoderate zeal for religion" (1620: Bk. I.89). We must be careful readers here. He is not claiming that religion has a negative effect on science—he denounces superstition and blind and excessive zeal. He leaves open the possibility that true religion might have a positive effect on science. While it is not clear that true religion will have much to add to the mathematical formulae for plate tectonics or the kinetic theory of gases, it may have a great deal to say about the reliability of our cognitive faculties, or the match between mind and world, or, perhaps, many other things that are essential assumptions for the practice of science. True religion may serve, as it did for Bacon, Boyle, and Newton, to justify the presuppositions of science (the scientific values discussed in the preceding chapter).

Of course, *claiming* no conflict between science and religion, and there *being* no conflict between science and religion are two entirely different stories. Christian slaveholders might have blithely maintained their convictions about Christian beliefs and the rightness of slavery, but Christian belief is in deep conflict with slavery. So people can hold beliefs that are in conflict. Perhaps Bacon, Boyle, and Newton were simply self-deceived. They held religious beliefs and they held scientific beliefs, but those beliefs are fundamentally in conflict (and perhaps they should have known better). We need to examine particular religious beliefs and particular scientific beliefs and then determine if they invariably conflict.

CHAPTER 4

"The Galileo Affair"

MISDIRECTIONS

There is a familiar and oft-told story about the fate of the famous astronomer, Galileo (1564–1642). Galileo, meek and mild, patiently gazed into starry, starry nights through his self-made telescopes and saw that the earth, like all of the other planets, revolves around the sun. The new, sun-centered (heliocentric) view of science was thus established and the old, earth-centered (geocentric) view of the Bible and the Church was thus refuted. The earth-centered cosmos, better known as the Ptolemaic view (named after the astronomer, Ptolemy), held to a stationary earth at the center of the universe around which the sun, stars, and planets revolve. The Ptolemaic view was first challenged by the astronomer Copernicus who contended that the sun is the center of our galaxy with the earth and the other planets revolving around it (heliocentrism would be also called "Copernicanism"). With Galileo's decisive falsification of Ptolemy and the Bible, Copernicanism was once and for all vindicated; thus was the earth displaced from the center of the cosmos and the Bible from science.

Fearing for its very life, the Church struck back branding Galileo a heretic and using the Roman Inquisition to force him to recant his heretical views; when the inquisitor pounded on your door, you were sorely tempted to concede to his wishes. Given their tactics—for example, getting one's body stretched and bones broken on the rack—you'd recant, too. Although Galileo promised to recant, he wrote one last, defiant defense of the sun-centered cosmos and, after a hasty and unfair trial, the elderly, decrepit Galileo was banished by the Pope to a cold, clammy jail for the remainder of his life.

On this telling of the tale, Galileo was the first martyr in the warfare between science and religion. Perched at the end of the Dark Ages, a time of Church-directed ignorance and superstition, Galileo peered into humanity's bright future, shining on it the light of reason. With his telescope, Galileo could see more clearly both into the nighttime skies and into the nature of reality than the Church could see with its Bible and its ignorant interpreters. In Galileo's epic battle of religion versus science, reason versus revelation, and scientific observation versus religious authority, religion won. Religion's triumph was due to power and coercion, not the unfettered commitment to the truth and careful assessment of evidence. Galileo's army of one was no match for the Holy Roman Empire, his light snuffed out by a fearful and power-hungry Pope.

Religion won this battle but lost the war: truth would eventually win out over superstition and scientific inquiry over religious authority. Galileo's light was not extinguished completely; its tiny flicker was nurtured into the flame of modern science through the mighty winds of, among many others, Isaac Newton (and the scientific method). The Bible and religious authority would finally bow at the altar of science.

This story, in both essence and detail, is nearly completely false—influential and widely held, yes, but nonetheless nearly wholly fabricated. Let us take a careful look at "the Galileo Affair," the popular name for Galileo's trial and the events that led up to it, and see what lessons might really be gleaned about the relationship between science and religion.

Redirections

To understand the Galileo Affair, we must first take a look at the cultural, political, and religious milieu of sixteenth- and seventeenth-century Italy. Galileo engaged in his scientific endeavors during a period of history in which the predominant scientific and natural philosophical view for nearly two millennia, namely Aristotelianism, was being questioned and reexamined. Galileo also lived and worked within a religious context in which the sole power for centuries, the Roman church, was seeing its authority profoundly challenged. As the medieval (Ptolemaic) conception of the cosmos began to lose its hold within the scientific community due to the insights of Copernicus, Bacon, Descartes, and Galileo, questions of the relation between religion and science were being raised with increasing intensity. Because the Ptolemaic system was believed contained within the Bible itself, there was extraordinary pressure to understand Copernicanism within the context of Scripture. Both Aristotle's and the Roman church's supremacy were beginning to be defied by Renaissance and Reformation thinkers and would continue to be tested in political, religious, and scientific matters. Let us now consider how Aristotelians understood scientific matters and how the Roman church interpreted what the Bible had to say regarding matters of the physical world.

Aristotelianism assumed geocentrism, which holds that the earth's position in the universe is fixed and stable and that the sun, planets, and stars revolve around the earth. The earth is at the center of the universe. Hence, we are singularly placed to contemplate the cosmos, our unique place in it, and the god who creates it.

Geocentrism was not a view unique to Aristotelians; nearly everyone for millennia believed that geocentrism was true. It's easy to see why. Both our sensory experience and common sense support geocentrism. For example, we don't see or feel the rotation of the earth. Imagine putting small models of people on a large ball and spinning it rapidly. The "people" would fly off instantly. Likewise, if we were on a rapidly spinning ball, say the earth (the earth rotates at more than a thousand miles per hour at the equator), we should fly off into space. But we don't. So our senses and our common sense tell us that we are on a fixed and stable object. Score one for geocentrism. We all know the feeling of driving 65 miles per hour in a car with the windows down—the wind blows back our hair and tears fall from our eyes. Imagine what it would feel like if we were driving 65,000 miles per hour. Our hair and eyes would likely get blown out of our skulls. But on planet Earth we don't feel like we are hurtling through space at a vast speed (even though the earth travels more than 65,000 miles per hour around the sun). Score two for geocentrism. Finally, if one evening you were to lie on the ground and watch the stars and planets (and the sun—if you could avoid going blind), you would see them all move around the earth, and you would not see or feel the earth moving around the sun. And you would see them move in circles around you. Since we see celestial objects revolve around us and not vice versa, score three for geocentrism (or, strike three for heliocentrism).[1] Our senses and common sense, then, unanimously support geocentrism.

Because Aristotelian physics emphasized the role of common sense and the senses, it is natural that those using Aristotelian physics came to believe that the earth was fixed and that the sun revolved around it. Nothing in our sense experience gives us cause to believe that the sun is fixed or that the earth is moving. Our senses give us every reason to believe otherwise.

Natural philosophers (what we might today call "scientists"), relying on their senses, were not the only ones who argued for geocentrism. Geocentrism was also assumed in passages throughout the Bible. For example, in Joshua 10: 12–13 we read:

> On the day the LORD gave the Amorites over to Israel, Joshua said to the LORD in the presence of Israel:
>
> "O sun, stand still over Gibeon,
> O moon, over the Valley of Aijalon."
> So the sun stood still,
> and the moon stopped,
> till the nation avenged itself on its enemies,
> as it is written in the Book of Jashar.
>
> The sun stopped in the middle of the sky and delayed going down about a full day.

Joshua's prayer is for more time in the day. The way to increase the length of the day? Stop the sun in its orbit around the earth: "O sun, stand still." And, according to the text, the sun stopped, giving Joshua an extra day to avenge his enemies. If, in response to Joshua's prayer, God caused the sun to stand still, then the sun must be moving (only a moving thing can be stopped). Joshua clearly did not believe that the earth should or could stop rotating to lengthen the day. Other biblical passages are also apparently geocentric:

> The world is firmly established; it cannot be moved (Psalm 93:1).
> He set the earth on its foundations; it can never be moved (Psalm 104:5).

Prior to the scientific revolution, the vast majority of biblical interpreters—lay and clergy alike—accepted a very literal interpretation of the Joshua passage and the other passages like it. Thus geocentrism became the official view of the Christian church.

In opposing geocentrism—a belief supported by common sense and our physical senses, the philosophical heft of Aristotelianism, the religious authority of the Bible, and the Holy Roman Empire—Galileo was a brave man indeed.

NICHOLAS COPERNICUS

Geocentrism was first challenged in the fifteenth century by the mathematician, natural philosopher, and cleric, Nicholas Copernicus (1473–1543). A devout Catholic his entire life, Copernicus was esteemed within the church for his impressive intellect. Although some deemed Copernicus' discoveries to be contrary to the Bible and thus the Church, Copernicus himself viewed his discoveries as service to the Church. Furthermore, Copernicus did not distinguish markedly between his religious vocation and his scientific experiments, hypotheses, and discoveries. All were done to the glory of God. If science and religion were at war, someone forgot to inform Brother Copernicus.

Having been commissioned by Pope Leo X to reexamine the church calendar, Copernicus attended to matters of astronomy. During these investigations, squeezed in between his religious duties, Copernicus became convinced that the sun was motionless and that the earth rotated around the sun. By shifting the center of the universe to the sun, and relegating the earth to planet status (in orbit around the sun), Copernicus could resolve some difficulties inherent in the Ptolemaic system.

On the Celestial Revolutions (*De revolutionibus orbium coelestium*) was published while Copernicus was on his deathbed. In it Copernicus argued that heliocentrism is the correct model of our universe, and that Aristotelian geocentrism is incorrect. This revolutionary work (the movement he started would come to be called "the Copernican Revolution") met with little acceptance; fewer than a dozen sixteenth-century thinkers endorsed his views. While it is not fair to say the work was ignored, it is safe to say that Copernicus' work was greeted with neither enthusiasm nor disagreement. It would take nearly half a century before the debate over heliocentrism exploded. The revolution was getting off to a slow start.

GALILEO GALILEI

Galileo Galilei was born in 1564 in Pisa to a noble family. A precocious child, fond of music as well as mathematics, Galileo considered becoming a monk, but his pious intentions were redirected by his father, and Galileo was enrolled in university to study medicine. Medicine, however, could scarcely contain Galileo's interests, and he was enticed into studying mathematics and physics. Soon Galileo began to dispute Aristotelianism, which downplayed the role of mathematics in understanding the natural world. Galileo considered mathematics indispensable to a greater knowledge of the natural world.

Galileo's first academic position was teaching mathematics at the University of Pisa. His intellect, however, when coupled with an acerbic wit and a confident demeanor, endeared Galileo to some and aroused animosity in others. There's a thin line between wit and confidence, on the one hand, and sarcasm and arrogance, on the other; one that Galileo seemed determined to cross. Galileo's ability to attract enemies and raise the ire of his colleagues led him not to seek reappointment at the University of Pisa, for he knew that he had overstayed his welcome. Galileo moved to Padua as professor of mathematics where his work in mathematics, physics, and astronomy continued full force.

Leaving university life in 1610, Galileo became the "Philosopher and Mathematician to the Grand Duke." In addition to a very a generous stipend, this position afforded Galileo more time to carry out experiments. Galileo continued to see the importance of mathematics and precise measurements in understanding the natural world and further distanced himself from the Aristotelianism prevalent in the universities.

Unlike Copernicus's work, Galileo's work was considered controversial. Through his work on supernovas (which contradicted Aristotle's assertion that no change could take place in the perfect heavens) and making his writings accessible to nonscientists, Galileo angered the Aristotelians and professional scientists within the universities. Most controversial of all was Galileo's Copernicanism.

Copernicanism, as we have already noted, conflicted with Aristotelianism, the best science of more than a millennium, one that was in accord with both good sense and the Bible. Thus, those within the scientific community and those within the Church found ample reasons to disagree with Galileo. Questions arose regarding Galileo's commitment to Scripture and how he could reconcile this new science with the Bible.

The Grand Duchess (mother of Galileo's employer, the Grand Duke) expressed worries that Copernicanism and the Bible were at odds. These worries prompted Galileo to write her a letter, his *Letter to the Grand Duchess Christina* in 1615, which was circulated widely throughout Italy. The main argument of this letter is that God has written two books—the *Book of Nature* and the *Book of Scripture*—and that these two books do not, because they cannot, contradict one another. If these books do not contradict one another, it means that if one can infer a proper explanation of the physical world that seems to contradict a passage of Scripture, then one has good reason to reconsider the proper interpretation of Scripture. The surface meaning of the Bible, then, may not be its true meaning. We will return to these issues in greater detail later.

Two important events occurred shortly after the *Letter* was written. First, the Church convened a panel to investigate the relation of Copernicanism to the Holy Bible. The panel decided that the Copernican claim that the sun was immobile was "stupid and absurd in philosophy." Furthermore, the panel decided that a heliocentric position was heretical, for it contradicted the literal interpretation of certain biblical passages. On the issue of geokinetics (the movement of the earth), the panel declared that Copernicus was merely mistaken (not heretical). The second important event was Galileo's meeting with Cardinal Bellarmine, an influential figure within the Church, who warned Galileo that he must avoid making public proclamations of Copernicanism. Bellarmine, however, was willing to cut Galileo a deal. Bellarmine told Galileo that he must not advocate Copernicanism as a reality. Nonetheless, Galileo would be permitted to argue from within a *hypothetical* Copernican position regarding the motion of the earth. That is, Galileo could affirm the Copernican system as a mathematically useful fiction (it was simpler, mathematically, than the Ptolemaic system), useful for making predictions, but he could not endorse it as reality. The terms of this deal were acceptable to Galileo, who was more interested in continuing scientific experiments than in learning to knit in jail. By acquiesing in this ruse, he avoided ecclesiastical censure and civil punishment (Pederson, 1983).

Cardinal Bellarmine took a cautious approach to the issue of Copernicanism. He was concerned that the reinterpretation of the Bible in a Copernican manner would start a trend: with each new scientific theory, the Bible would need to be reinterpreted. Bellarmine was concerned about where this would all end and, like other theologians, was worried about who—scientists or theologians—would carry out the task of reinterpreting scripture. Given that there was as yet precious little evidence in favor of Copernicanism, and a mountain of common sense evidence against it, there seemed little reason to jump on board Copernicanism. Slow and steady seemed the wiser plan.

Bellarmine's caution stemmed from two important but as yet unanswered questions. First, does the evidence support Copernicanism? Second, does Copernicanism conflict with the Bible? In Galileo's time, the answer to the scientific question, despite Galileo's insistence, was a resounding "NO!" While it is easy to condemn Bellarmine and the Roman Church's treatment of Galileo from our twenty-first-century vantage point, we must remember that from the seventeenth-century perspective, there was little scientific evidence in favor of Copernicanism. Most scientists were opposed to Copernicanism.[2] The second question should be answered, Bellarmine thought, by theologians working within the Church. Scientists must accept whatever answer the theologians and the Church proposed to the second question. Cardinal Bellarmine's caution was prompted by both the lack of evidence in favor of Copernicanism and his desire to maintain fidelity to the Church and biblical authority.

With the publication of Galileo's *Dialogue on the Two Principal World Systems—Ptolemaic and Copernican* in 1632, the hostility exhibited by clergy and other scientists toward Galileo boiled over. Galileo's *Dialogue* contained three characters: an Aristotelian (Ptolemaic), a Copernican, and a neutral interlocutor, who weighed the evidence and arguments of the other two. The Copernican character, Salviati, offered the best evidence and arguments, to which the Aristotelian, Simplicio, offered weak and unconvincing objections.

Salviati was the mouthpiece of Galileo; Simplicio may have represented the Pope or at least the views forced on Galileo by the Roman Catholic Church. Even if Simplicio did not mean "simpleton" (simpleton is *sempliciotto* in Italian), it sure sounded like it, and Simplicio's simple arguments were much like similar arguments previously advanced by the Pope. Whatever the truth, the Pope felt mocked. Since the Pope had formerly supported Galileo and considered him a friend—having once written a poem in Galileo's honor—Galileo's caricature was taken as a personal insult. Galileo's caustic wit would cost him dearly.

Galileo's timing was poor: the Roman Catholic Church was stinging from the effects of the century-old Protestant Reformation. Protestants had won the hearts of half of Europe, and the Roman Catholic Church felt compelled to shore up its bulwark by establishing orthodox Catholic belief against its Protestant critics once and for all. In the mid-1500s, the Roman Catholic Church issued an anti-Protestant decree which stated that "in matters of faith and morals no one, relying on his own judgment and distorting the Sacred Scriptures according to his own conceptions, shall dare to interpret them contrary to that sense which the Holy Mother Church has held or does hold."[3] Galileo, though a loyal son of the Roman Church, was indeed endorsing an interpretation of the Scriptures contrary to the meaning endorsed by the Holy Mother Church. In spite of his argument to the contrary, Copernicanism was considered, for better or worse (worse for Galileo), a matter of faith and morals.[4]

While it is easy to judge historical issues by contemporary standards, we must keep in mind that Galileo lived in a time when popes and politicians alike thought that the sun's revolving around the earth *really* mattered, even to one's eternal destiny; to go against the Bible on this matter was viewed as spiritually dangerous. And consider their concern with authority: who has the rightful authority to speak on such matters—the Church (on behalf of God) or maverick natural philosophers (with less than compelling evidence)? Rebel priests and theologians, Calvin and Luther, had decimated the Roman Catholic Church; Rome wasn't about to let that happen again. Galileo found himself caught up in the anti-Protestant juggernaut unleashed by a Church that had lost patience with dissenters.

A kinder and gentler Galileo might have succeeded where the actual Galileo failed. Some theologians were upset with an outsider encroaching on their territory, sharing Cardinal Bellarmine's concerns about the authority of the Church. The Church, and it alone, was considered God's instrument on Earth for interpreting the Bible and determining theological doctrine. Just as the earth was fixed and stable (and made so by God), so too Church doctrine was fixed and stable (and made so by God's earthly administrators—the Pope and his councils). Galileo was a scientist, after all, who was trespassing on theological grounds, unabashedly sharing his views on biblical interpretation and theology. What business did a mathematician have doing theology?

Galileo, charged with violating an official injunction against proclaiming Copernican views, was summoned to Rome for a trial in 1633. After five days, with Galileo having lost the Pope's good will, the judges declared that Galileo had most assuredly defended the truth of Copernicanism, thus violating the terms of his deal with Bellarmine. Galileo was condemned as a heretic and the *Dialogue* was prohibited. Entering into a plea bargain, Galileo signed a deposition renouncing Copernicanism, and then affirmed his commitment to a fixed earth around which the sun revolves.

Although Galileo's trial was ostensibly a heresy trial—and so apparently a conflict between science and religion—Galileo's chief problem was not conflict with religion; it was, rather, *lack of scientific evidence*. The conflict, and there surely was one, was more science versus science than science versus religion. That religion factored into this very complex case is undeniable. But Galileo's chief problem was lack of evidence for a view that would require systematic and radical scientific rethinking. For example, using his telescope, Galileo noticed for the first time in history that Venus went through phases like the moon. While this was difficult to account for on the Ptolemaic system, it could be accounted for on the Tychonic system. So the phases of Venus do not favor Copernicanism over the Tychonic system. Moreover, Galileo's theory of tides, which would favor a sun-centered system, was just plain wrong. Little wonder that the majority of scientists opposed his views.

Galileo spent the remainder of his days under house arrest, obliged to recite penitential Psalms for the remainder of his life (which task was carried out by one of his illegitimate daughters [a nun]). He lived the remainder of his days in relative ease in a rented house in the Florentine countryside—not tortured, not imprisoned, and not killed. He was allowed to leave the premises to receive medical treatment, and he continued his scientific writing and experiments until his death in 1642.

LETTER TO THE GRAND DUCHESS CHRISTINA

Galileo's *Letter to the Grand Duchess Christina*, written nearly four hundred years ago, is still a wonderful fount for understanding the relationship between science and religion. Galileo's letter offers valuable insights into learning how to proceed when we meet an apparent contradiction between science and religion. We shall quote extensively from Galileo, using his own words as much as possible, to highlight those aspects of the letter that are most germane to the contemporary discussion of possible conflicts between science and religion. In the *Letter*, we find four major themes: the Naturalistic Stance, the Accommodation Principle, the Doctrine of the Two Books, and Interpretive Humility. We shall see that these themes were not only useful for Galileo in discussing his own situation but also that they are useful today for understanding the relationship between science and religion.

First, let us define our terms.

The Naturalistic Stance: When we examine the physical world we ought to bracket out religious considerations.

The Naturalistic Stance denies explanations of natural phenomena like the weather or the growth of crops in terms of supernatural agents like the gods bowling or germinating goblins; proper scientific explanations invoke strictly natural processes. The Naturalistic Stance does *not* claim or entail that there are no supernatural agents. Rather, the Naturalistic Stance says that science should proceed, methodologically, independent of any particular religious considerations. Today we call the Naturalistic Stance "methodological naturalism."[5]

Methodological naturalism, as seen in the previous chapter, is the working assumption that scientists should not include or invoke any supernatural entities or powers in their scientific theorizing. They should appeal completely to material entities and their powers. Those who take the Naturalistic Stance can, like Galileo, still be deeply committed religious believers. However, when they are gazing into the heavens or thinking about the atomic structure of reality, they should simply leave those religious beliefs to one side. In their practice as scientists, they should restrict themselves to the natural world.[6]

If the Bible is the infallible, how can it contain untruths concerning nature? Galileo argued that God permitted such language because he had deeper, more important truths to communicate. And so he suggested the following principle for understanding Scripture:

The Accommodation Principle: When speaking of the natural world, the Bible accommodates the opinions and views of the common people.

Galileo was constantly asked why he claimed (against the Bible) that the earth moved. Galileo argued that the Bible puts its message into the language of the common people "lest the shallow minds of the common people should become confused, obstinate, and contumacious [stubbornly disobedient] in yielding assent to the principal articles that are absolutely matters of faith" (Drake, 1957: 200). The Accommodation Principle recognizes what might now seem obvious (but was not so obvious in the seventeenth century): the Bible was written in a prescientific, preliterate culture and so we should not expect its writers to be cognizant of modern science. If God wished to communicate divine truths to human beings, he would have to *accommodate* himself to their ways of understanding. He would have to use their language, their concepts, and their understanding as vehicles for communicating divine information. The Almighty would have to stoop down, so to speak, to the finite, human, historically conditioned level. The Accommodation Principle is better known, in our day and age, as accommodationism. We should expect God to accommodate himself, in various ways, to the common understandings of human beings in order to effectively communicate divine truths crucial to human harmony and salvation. According to this view, the "science" of the Hebrews is incidental to God's message of love, justice, and forgiveness. They are false but irrelevant items that were permitted in the Bible for the sake of the effective communication of vastly more important truths.

God might be inclined to accommodative language if God has provided us with different sources of information about himself (and our relationship to him) and nature. Galileo believes that God has indeed written two books that communicate different but complementary truths.

The Doctrine of the Two Books: God has revealed truth both in Scripture and in nature. On matters of faith, the Book of Scripture has the authority; on matters relating to the natural world, the Book of Nature has the authority.

According to this doctrine, God has revealed himself truly in two books—scripture and nature—and, in their proper domains, neither has primacy over the other. Since "all truth is God's truth," these two books, when properly understood, cannot contradict each other. There cannot be a conflict between science, rightly understood, and scripture, rightly understood. The Doctrine of the Two Books maintains that the Holy Scriptures have primacy in matters of faith, but in areas on which the Scriptures do not speak or speak only as a concession to human limitations (see the Accommodation Principle), it is best to read and understand God's other book, the *Book of Nature*.

Galileo did not invent the Doctrine of the Two Books. It can be found (as mentioned in the previous chapter) in the works of Bacon among others. By the end of the sixteenth century, we find a clear and typical statement of this doctrine by Hieronymus Zanchius:

> There are two divine books through which God thought it proper to express his eternal essence and perfect nature, and to communicate his best will and highest love toward us. First is the Book of the Creatures or Works; the other is the book Sacred Scripture or the word of God. If you compare these a little, you will see that although they are different, they have this common character: to show forth and work together for this end, the knowledge of God and our happiness. (found in Harrison, 2006b)

The chief error then of ignoring the Doctrine of the Two Books is to let one book intrude into the other's proper domain.

Finally, Galileo commends humility in relation to our understandings of the Bible, especially when it speaks of relative incidentals, like nature.

Interpretive Humility: We ought not think our interpretation of the Bible is final, especially when dealing with matters extrinsic to the central message of the Scriptures.

Interpretive Humility does not mean that there is no right interpretation, nor does it state that no interpretation is better than another. Rather, Interpretive Humility is a guiding principle that stresses human fallibility, that is, the human tendency to misread and take things out of context, to obscure the main message and intent of a passage, and to become overconfident with one's own interpretation of a passage. Interpretive Humility stresses the need for interpreters to remain open to new evidence and to judge such evidence fairly. It would be especially imprudent, Galileo thought, to commit oneself, on the basis of Biblical texts alone, to a view of nature that might one day be refuted "by the senses or demonstration."

With these themes in mind, we can now turn to Galileo's *Letter*, which begins with an explanation of why he is writing:

> Some years ago, as Your Serene Highness well knows, I discovered in the heavens many things that had not been seen before our own age. The novelty of these things, as well as some consequences which followed from them in contradiction to the physical notions commonly held among academic philosophers, stirred up against me no small number of professors—as if I had placed these things in the sky with my own hands in order to upset nature and overturn the sciences. They seemed to forget that the increase of known truths stimulates the investigation, establishment, and the growths of the arts, not their diminution or destruction. Showing a greater fondness for their own opinions than for truth, they sought to deny and disprove the new things, which, if they had cared to look for themselves, their own senses would have demonstrated to them. To this end they hurled various charges and published numerous writings filled with vain arguments, and they made the grave mistake of sprinkling these with passages taken from places in the Bible which they had failed to understand properly, and which were ill-suited to their purposes. (Drake, 1957: 175)

In the last sentence Galileo claims that his accusers lack Interpretive Humility. Furthermore, this passage alleges other shortcomings of his opponents: his opponents care less about truth than their own opinions, less about settling scientific disputes than settling personal vendettas, and less about understanding the proper domains of the *Book of Scripture* and the *Book of Nature* than in twisting the message of the *Book of Scripture* to fit their own ends. If their objections had been limited merely to science or philosophy, or had concerned themselves mainly with the questions of what counts as evidence and how to understand this evidence, then Galileo claims that he could easily have responded to these scientific objections. His opponents, however, didn't want an academic debate. They were pushing for heresy charges against Galileo. Galileo, then, was forced to defend himself both on scientific and on theological and interpretive grounds.

According to Galileo, the theological issues should be set aside as theologically insignificant or even irrelevant. He considered the main point to be Copernicanism (heliocentrism) and the evidence for and against it. About this Galileo writes:

> I hold the sun to be situated motionless in the center of the revolution of the celestial orbs while the earth rotates on its axis and revolves about the sun. They know also that I support this position not only by refuting the arguments of Ptolemy and Aristotle, but by producing many counter-arguments; in particular, some which relate to physical effects whose causes can perhaps be assigned in no other way. In addition there are astronomical arguments

derived from many things in my new celestial discoveries that plainly confute the Ptolemaic system while admirably agreeing with and confirming the contrary hypothesis. Possibly because they are disturbed by the known truth of other propositions of mine which differ from those commonly held, and therefore mistrusting their defense so long as they confine themselves to the field of philosophy, these men have resolved to fabricate a shield for their fallacies out of the mantle of pretended religion and the authority of the Bible. These they apply, with little judgment, to the refutation of arguments that they do not understand and have not even listened to. (Drake, 1957: 177)

Along with a shared commitment to heliocentrism, Galileo and Copernicus share methodological views, namely, the Naturalistic Stance.

Finding both a support and a strategic guide, Galileo turns to Copernicus's work to discover how Copernicus preempted charges of heresy by invoking the Naturalistic Stance and the Doctrine of the Two Books. Galileo writes:

For Copernicus never discusses matters of religion or faith, nor does he use arguments that depend in any way upon the authority of sacred writings which he might have interpreted erroneously. He stands always upon physical conclusions pertaining to the celestial motions, and deals with them by astronomical and geometrical demonstrations, founded primarily upon sense experiences and very exact observations. He did not ignore the Bible, but he knew very well that if his doctrine were proved, then it could not contradict the Scriptures when they were rightly understood. (Drake, 1957: 179–80)

Galileo's opponents, on the other hand, exhibited Interpretive Pride and a disregard for the Doctrine of the Two Books. Galileo presents the strategy of his opponents as follows:

They go about invoking the Bible, which they would have minister to their deceitful purposes. Contrary to the sense of the Bible and the intention of the holy Fathers, if I am not mistaken, they would extend such authorities until even in purely physical matters—where faith is not involved—they would have us altogether abandon reason and the evidence of our senses in favor of some biblical passage, though under the surface meaning of its words this passage may contain a different sense. (Drake, 1957: 179)

By arguing that Galileo's conclusions are contrary to the message of the Bible, his opponents were able to muster the troops against him. Galileo endeavors to demonstrate why his conclusions and hypotheses are not contrary to the Bible and how the Bible may in fact even support them. In so doing, Galileo holds tightly to the four themes defined above.

This following lengthy passage ties together all four doctrines:

Hence I think that I may reasonably conclude that whenever the Bible has occasion to speak of any physical conclusion (especially those which are very abstruse and hard to understand), the rule has been observed of avoiding confusion in the minds of the common people which would render them contumacious [disobedient] toward the higher mysteries. Now the Bible, merely to condescend to popular capacity, has not hesitated to obscure some very important pronouncements, attributing to God himself some qualities extremely remote from (and even contrary to) His essence. Who, then, would positively declare that this principle has been set aside, and the Bible has confined itself rigorously to the bare and restricted sense of its words, when speaking but casually of the earth, of water, of the sun, or of any other created thing? Especially in view of the fact that these things in no way concern the primary purpose of the sacred writings, which is the service of God and the salvation of souls—matters infinitely beyond the comprehension of the common people.

This being granted, I think that in discussions of physical problems we ought to begin not from the authority of scriptural passages, but from sense-experiences and necessary demonstrations; for the Holy Bible and the phenomena of nature proceed alike from the divine Word, the former of the dictate of the Holy Ghost and the latter as the observant executrix [follower] of God's commands. It is necessary for the Bible, in order to be accommodated to the understanding of every man, to speak many things which appear to differ from the absolute truth so far as the bare meaning of the words is concerned. But Nature, on the other hand, is inexorable and immutable; she never transgresses the laws imposed upon her, or cares a whit whether her abstruse reasons and methods of operation are understandable to men. For that reason it appears that nothing physical which sense-experience sets before our eyes, or which necessary demonstrations prove to us, ought to be called in question (much less condemned) upon the testimony of biblical passages which may have some different meaning beneath their words. For the Bible is not chained in every expression to conditions as strict as those which govern all physical effects; nor is God any less excellently revealed in Nature's actions than in the sacred statements of the Bible. (Drake, 1957: 182–3)

Galileo states that by carefully and humbly reading the Two Books, and following the methods peculiar to each book, one may come to a fuller and richer understanding of divine truth.

Because the Bible can be difficult to understand, Galileo emphasizes the need for Interpretive Humility. If we take seriously the Doctrine of the Two Books, it can prevent us from falling into Interpretive Pride and will also help us discern when the surface meaning of a passage is not its true meaning. Galileo writes:

The reason produced for condemning the opinion that the earth moves and the sun stands still is that in many places in the Bible one may read that the sun moves and the earth stands still. Since the Bible cannot err, it follows as a necessary consequence that anyone takes an erroneous and heretical position who maintains that the sun is inherently motionless and the earth movable. With regard to this argument, I think in the first place that it is very pious to say and prudent to affirm that the holy Bible can never speak untruth—whenever its true meaning is understood. But I believe nobody will deny that it is often very abstruse, and may say things which are quite different from what its bare words signify. Hence in expounding the Bible if one were always to confine oneself to the unadorned grammatical meaning, one might fall into error. (Drake, 1957: 181)

One can use the knowledge gained in science to understand the message of Scripture. In other words, the *Book of Nature* informs the *Book of Scripture*. Galileo writes, "[H]aving arrived at any certainties in physics, we ought to utilize these as the most appropriate aids in the true exposition of the Bible and in the investigation of those meanings which are necessarily contained therein, for these must be concordant with demonstrated truths" (Drake, 1957: 183). Humanity can fully grasp the Truth only when it humbly learns all that both books have to teach us.

Recall that each book has authority and primacy within its own domain. In matters of science and religion, Galileo is of the same opinion as Cardinal Baronius:

> The intention of the Holy Ghost is to teach us how one goes to heaven, not how heaven goes. (Drake, 1957: 186)

The import of this famous quotation is that the Bible primarily concerns matters of faith and practice and should not intrude into knowledge of the natural world. There can be no conflict when each book is restricted to its proper domain.

In general, Galileo advises against using the Bible as a source of information about the natural world. Given the necessity of divine accommodation to the common understanding of the prescientific Hebrews, we should not expect the Bible to be a scientific textbook. While previous generations had been given little reason to reject the science of the Bible, Galileo's generation must face that issue squarely. The lesson is simple: "Hence I should think it would be the part of prudence not to permit anyone to usurp scriptural texts and force them in some way to maintain any physical conclusion to be true, when at some future time the senses and demonstrative or necessary reasons show the contrary" (Drake, 1957: 187). Not clinging too tightly to one's cherished opinions when Scripture intrudes on the natural world is a good practice (for such claims may be shown to by reason to be false). Of course, one should keep in mind that by showing the *scientific* beliefs of the early Hebrews to be false, one has not thereby shown the *theological* beliefs of the early Hebrews to be false.

Galileo commends a general principle, namely, that "in questions of nature which are not matters of faith it is first to be considered whether anything is demonstrated beyond doubt or known by sense-experience, or whether such knowledge or proof is possible; if it is, then, being the gift of God, it ought to be applied to find out the true senses of Holy Scripture in those passages which superficially might seem to declare differently" (Drake, 1957: 199). This general principle or strategy is what informs the Doctrine of the Two Books. We can use the *Book of Nature*, he contends, to better understand the *Book of Scripture*, and we can use the *Book of Scripture* to better understand the *Book of Nature*.

Galileo's Contradiction

Galileo's brilliant letter to the Grand Duchess is one of the finest discussions of the relation between science and religion in all of human history; its rich and deep reflection have seldom been equaled. The principles that he commended are now held by the Church that condemned him. Yet this very text would betray him. Let us outline Galileo's self-contradiction very briefly.

Galileo's Doctrine of the Two Books, each with its own proper domain and methodologies, seems eminently sensible. While the domain restriction seems clear, the standard he set for understanding the *Book of Nature* was very high. In one passage, he writes: "In discussions of physical problems we ought to begin not from the authority of scriptural passages, but from sense-experiences and necessary demonstrations" (Drake, 1957: 182). As we have already seen, sense experience nearly uniformly counts against heliocentrism. We don't see the earth revolving around the sun, and we don't feel the earth rotating rapidly. In fact, if anything, we see the sun and planets revolve around the earth. While Galileo did see some unexpected and significant things with his telescope—for example, the moons of Jupiter (and so proved that not everything celestial revolved around the earth)—they were not sufficient to overcome the nearly universal experiences of a fixed earth and a revolving sun.

Galileo offered more advice on methodology in understanding the natural world. He writes: "In questions of nature which are not matters of faith it is first to be considered whether anything is demonstrated beyond doubt or known by sense-experience, or whether such knowledge or proof is possible" (Drake, 1957: 199).[7]

While Galileo asserted Copernicanism as a fact, he had not *demonstrated* it. Copernicanism may have been mathematically simpler than Ptolemy's vastly more cumbersome model, but mathematical simplicity is not proof of truth. The case for Copernicanism had scarcely any demonstration, let alone demonstration beyond doubt. Galileo's letter sowed his own seeds of a scientific rejection of the hypothesis of heliocentrism.

Conclusion

I don't endorse the Roman Church's condemnation of Galileo. But in 1633 his view had not been established—on scientific grounds alone—as a matter of indisputable fact. While Galileo's standard of proof was surely too high, it would take another 50 years and another genius, Isaac Newton, to scientifically confirm heliocentrism. The Church itself would later concede that Galileo was right. It removed Galileo's *Dialogue* from the Index of Banned Books and, in 1822, affirmed Copernicanism as a physical fact and no longer hypothetical. In 1992, Pope John Paul II set up a special committee to reexamine Galileo's trial, and the Church offered a formal apology for Galileo's sentence.

We have seen that the conflict thesis is a poor description of the Galileo affair. The affair was a mixture of competing and conflicting forces: political, personal, theological, interpretive, and, most importantly, scientific.

Galileo's *Letter to the Grand Duchess Christina* can help us understand deep issues in science and religion. Providing us with a host of arguments and useful concepts, Galileo shows us that science and religion are not at an eternal impasse, but may be two ways of knowing the world. The Naturalistic Stance, the Accommodation Principle, the Doctrine of the Two Books, and Interpretive Humility are themes that are still useful today in understanding the perhaps complementary relationship between science and religion.

The Christian holds that there is a unity to truth, and it is manifest in God's Two Books—the *Book of Nature* and the *Book of Scripture*. If there is only one truth that God reveals both through nature and through scripture, there cannot be a conflict or contradiction. The conflict thesis, failing to concede the possible unity of truth, presents a historically inaccurate and conceptually inadequate view of the relationship between science and religion.

CHAPTER 5

Darwin, God, and Creation

THE DAY BELIEF IN GOD DIED

Charles Darwin drove a stake into the heart of religious belief in 1859 when he published *On the Origin of Species by Means of Natural Selection*. Darwin proved that the biblical account of creation is a fairy tale of epic proportions. The biblical narrative tells the story of the miraculous creation in six days of the heavens and the earth and all that they contain. God speaks the world into existence one day, then shapes and populates it over the next few days. Finally, God breathes into the dust of the earth and creates the first man, Adam, and from Adam he extracts a rib and fashions the first woman, Eve. Prior to the fall of Adam, there was no suffering and no death. Finally, the Bible offered a means by which the days of the earth could be numbered: by tracing back the chronology of events recorded therein, the seventeenth-century Irish Bishop James Ussher calculated that the earth's birthday was October 23, 4004 BC.[1]

Darwin argued that all that the earth contains resulted from very natural processes over a very long period of time. Natural selection, not supernatural intervention, produced amoebae, camels, sharks, and trees. Suffering, death, and destruction did not enter into creation *after* the fall of Adam. All three were always and integrally part and parcel of the struggle for existence and the production of species.

This is the story of how Darwin confounded belief in God.

Once again, this story is influential and widely believed, but not true. While geological and biological processes supplant certain conceptions of God and certain beliefs about how and when God created the world, they don't refute belief in a supernatural deity. Darwin himself, as we shall see, did not view his work as opposed to belief in God. As he once wrote to a friend: "It seems to me absurd to doubt that a man may be an ardent Theist & an evolutionist" (Darwin, Personal Communication, 1879).

In this chapter, I will argue that geology and evolution are not in conflict with the Genesis story of creation properly understood. Of course, a creation spanning six 24-hour days is in conflict with science. But Genesis, properly understood, does not offer a scientific account of creation.

THE GENESIS STORY OF CREATION

One can't reasonably assess Darwin's alleged undermining of belief in God without a better understanding of the Biblical creation narrative. Let us begin at the beginning with the book of Genesis (in Hebrew "genesis" means beginnings)—the opening salvo of the Bible:

> In the beginning God created the heavens and the earth. Now the earth was formless and empty, darkness was over the surface of the deep, and the Spirit of God was hovering over the waters.
>
> And God said, "Let there be light," and there was light. God saw that the light was good, and He separated the light from the darkness. God called the light "day," and the darkness he called "night." And there was evening, and there was morning—the first day.
>
> And God said, "Let there be an expanse between the waters to separate water from water." So God made the expanse and separated the water under the expanse from the water above it. And it was so. God called the expanse "sky." And there was evening, and there was morning—the second day.
>
> And God said, "Let the water under the sky be gathered to one place, and let dry ground appear." And it was so. God called the dry ground "land," and the gathered waters he called "seas." And God saw that it was good. Then God said, "Let the land produce vegetation: seed-bearing plants and trees on the land that bear fruit with seed in it, according to their various kinds." And it was so. The land produced vegetation: plants bearing seed according to their kinds and trees bearing fruit with seed in it according to their kinds. And God saw that it was good. And there was evening, and there was morning—the third day.
>
> And God said, "Let there be lights in the expanse of the sky to separate the day from the night, and let them serve as signs to mark seasons and days and years, and let them be lights in the expanse of the sky to give light on the earth." And it was so. God made two great lights—the greater light to govern the day and the lesser light to govern the night. He also made the stars. God set them in the expanse of the sky to give light on the earth, to govern the day and the night, and to separate light from darkness. And God saw that it was good. And there was evening, and there was morning—the fourth day.
>
> And God said, "Let the water teem with living creatures, and let birds fly above the earth across the expanse of the sky." So God created the great creatures of the sea and every living and moving thing with which the water teems, according to their kinds, and every winged bird according to its kind. And God saw that it was good. God blessed them and said, "Be fruitful and increase in number and fill the water in the seas, and let the birds increase on the earth." And there was evening, and there was morning—the fifth day.
>
> And God said, "Let the land produce living creatures according to their kinds: livestock, creatures that move along the ground, and wild animals, each according to its kind." And it was so. God made the wild animals according to their kinds, the livestock according to their kinds, and all the creatures that move along the ground according to their kinds. And God saw that it was good.
>
> Then God said, "Let us make man in our image, in our likeness, and let them rule over the fish of the sea and the birds of the air, over the livestock,

over all the earth, and over all the creatures that move along the ground." So God created man in his own image, in the image of God he created him; male and female he created them. God blessed them and said to them, "Be fruitful and increase in number; fill the earth and subdue it. Rule over the fish of the sea and the birds of the air and over every living creature that moves on the ground."

Then God said, "I give you every seed-bearing plant on the face of the whole earth and every tree that has fruit with seed in it. They will be yours for food. And to all the beasts of the earth and all the birds of the air and all the creatures that move on the ground—everything that has the breath of life in it—I give every green plant for food." And it was so. God saw all that he had made, and it was very good. And there was evening, and there was morning—the sixth day.

Thus the heavens and the earth were completed in all their vast array. By the seventh day God had finished the work he had been doing; so on the seventh day he rested from all his work. (Genesis 1.1–2.2 NIV)

This is how God did it. Omnipotence spoke and it was so; six quick but very productive days, and then time off for some well-deserved rest (I get tired just thinking about it). The first three days are spent creating the heavens and the earth; the next three days, God created all the birds, fish, land animals, and even human beings that inhabit the earth. Work, work, work, work, work, work. Sleep.

Young Earth Creationism

Young earth creationists, claiming compatibility between their "scientific" account of creation and an allegedly literal and faithful reading of Genesis, believe that the earth is, well, young; they believe it is six to ten thousand years old and has attained its present state through an initial series of miraculous creative activities and a subsequent series of catastrophes—like floods and earthquakes. God threw down the earth and populated it with every kind of living creature in six days, then earthquakes threw up mountains and floods drew down valleys. While the earth has the appearance of age, that is simply to deceive the unbeliever. The true believer can see, through faith and the God-given information in the Bible, that the earth is in its infancy.

The processes that shaped the earth—miracles and catastrophes—are sudden and extreme; God initially created everything out of nothing, and then catastrophes dramatically reshaped that something into the world that we see today. Young-earth creationists reject both *uniformitarianism* (the view that the slow and gradual processes we see today, like erosion, have predominantly shaped the earth) and evolution. They affirm *catastrophism* (the view that the earth was shaped and formed by sudden catastrophes such as Noah's flood). God has revealed both the earth's age and the flood of Noah that reshaped the earth very rapidly.

Using radiometrics and isochronal dating (to use some scientific jargon), the earth's age has been calculated to be about 4.5 billion years old and life on the earth dates back some 3.8 billion years. The estimates of young-earthers are off by a factor of millions! The universe itself is 13.7 billion years old. It is hard to cram all that into the six-day package of the Bible.

In the beginning was the cosmic big bang—one grand explosive force disgorging all of the tiny little particles that would come together to form atoms, stars, and planets. The earth, like all the other planets, was spit out of a star.

Animals and plants weren't created in a day or two. They evolved by natural, evolutionary processes from preexisting species. Love doesn't make the world go round, survival of the fittest does. Humans were not created out of dust in the image of the omnipotent God but out of animals in the image of the not-so-great apes from which they descended.

How can anyone any longer believe, as the ancient Apostles' Creed states, "I believe in God the Father, Almighty, maker of heaven and earth?"

Faced with this apparent conflict between Genesis and evolution, many Christians–Muslims–Jews have dismissed evolution outright (Newport, 2012). They have drawn their faith line in the sand, and science is not permitted to cross it.

PALEY AND NATURAL THEOLOGY

William Paley was an eighteenth-century theologian who had a big influence on nineteenth-century science and upon the early thinking of Charles Darwin. Born in 1743, Paley was educated at Cambridge University where he displayed an interest in mathematics, law, and theology. After graduation, Paley was ordained as a priest in the Anglican Church and taught moral and political philosophy at Cambridge. Paley's natural theology sought to provide a rational foundation for Christianity in order to enhance its credibility. *Natural theology* is a philosophical and theological discipline that attempts to infer the existence of God from the natural world (without recourse to special revelation such as the Bible).

During the eighteenth century, philosophy of nature was dominated by a kind of *mechanical philosophy*, one which viewed the world as something like a collection of gears and pulleys. Those inspired by mechanical philosophy were constantly searching for the causes (the hidden gears and pulleys) behind the visible phenomena. The view of the world as a kind of machine (usually a clock) implied the existence of a divine craftsman. If you could peek just behind the face of the clock of the universe, you could see the face of God. Paley writes:

> In crossing a heath, suppose I pitched my foot against a *stone*, and were asked how the stone came to be there, I might possibly answer, that, for anything I knew to the contrary, it had lain there forever: nor would it perhaps be very easy to show the absurdity of this answer. But suppose I had found a *watch* upon the ground, and it should be enquired how the watch happened to be in that place, I should hardly think of the answer which I had before given, that, for any thing I knew, the watch might have always been there. Yet why should

not this answer serve for the watch, as well as for the stone? Why is it not admissible in the second case, as in the first? For this reason, and for no other, namely that, when we come to inspect the watch, we perceive that its several parts are framed and put together for a purpose,...the inference, we think, is inevitable; that the watch must have had a maker...who comprehended its construction, and designed its use. [E]very indication of contrivance, every manifestation of design, which existed in the watch, exists in the works of nature. (2012: 7–8, 16)

Paley's famous Watchmaker Argument functions as an analogy. Instead of a watch, consider the human eye—nature's telescope. The eye is truly an amazing and extremely complex mechanism. All of the eye's parts—retinas, corneas, lenses, and nerves—come together in a way that enables us to see. Just as a watch points back to a watchmaker, the eye points back to an eye-maker (God). God, like a human watchmaker, designs his mechanisms for a purpose. Paley would argue that "every indication of contrivance, every manifestation of design, which existed in the watch" is present in the eye. Now instead of the eye, think of, Paley writes, "all large terrestrial animals" in which one can see "the uniformity of plan observable in the universe." Where there's a plan, there is likewise a Planner.

Paley argued, rather convincingly for the time, that the hump of the camel, the web of the duck, and the eye of the human are so remarkably and manifestly designed that there must have been a designer. Indeed, "every organized natural body," plant and animal alike, likewise leads one to the conclusion that they too must have a maker. He wrote: "The hinges in the wings of an earwig, and the joints of its antennae, are as highly wrought, as if the Creator had nothing else to finish." From this remarkable design found everywhere, he concluded: "The marks of design are too strong to be got over. Design must have had a designer. That designer must have been a person. That person is GOD."

Natural theology sought to place religion on a rational foundation and to provide a solid and rigorous framework for understanding how to balance theological knowledge with scientific inquiry. For a time these goals were met, but scientists started noticing a lack of design: arbitrariness, waste, death, suffering, and caprice in nature.[2] Was the world, with its violent fits and starts, really the handiwork of a benevolent and omnipotent creator? Would a benevolent creator have produced new species through mass death (extinctions) or have designed parasites that devour their hosts from the inside? Darwin noticed the "clumsy, wasteful, blundering low & horridly cruel works of nature" and found himself moving away from seeing the world through the lens of design (Personal Communication, 1856).

Darwin, Paley, and God

Darwin was born into a wealthy family in 1809. From an early age, he was interested in the natural world, collecting bugs and plants, and performing chemistry experiments when not in class at the classical school he attended. Charles' father decided that his son should follow a career path similar to Charles' grandfather's, Erasmus Darwin, a medical doctor who had shared Charles' interest in the natural world. Erasmus, interestingly, defended an early but widely rejected theory of evolution. Charles was enrolled in the University of Edinburgh to study medicine but quickly discovered that he lacked the stomach for such a career. In those days, patients were operated on without anesthesia, causing them considerable pain and discomfort. Darwin's father enrolled him in Cambridge to study theology and prepare for a career as a clergyman (which, at the time, meant something like a gentlemanly life of leisure to explore one's other interests).

While at Cambridge, Darwin became interested in natural theology, falling under the spell of William Paley. Darwin not only read Paley, he also lived in Paley's former college room. Darwin was deeply impressed with Paley's arguments. Paley's ideas were widely accepted, even by Darwin, and his *Evidence of Christianity* was required reading at Cambridge up to the twentieth century. In his *Autobiography*, Darwin would write:

> In order to pass the B.A. examination, it was, also, necessary to get up Paley's *Evidences of Christianity*, and his *Moral Philosophy*...The logic of this book and as I may add of his *Natural Theology* gave me as much delight as did Euclid. The careful study of these works, without attempting to learn any part by rote, was the only part of the Academical Course which, as I then felt and as I still believe, was of the least use to me in the education of my mind. I did not at that time trouble myself about Paley's premises; and taking these on trust I was charmed and convinced of the long line of argumentation. (Darwin, 1958: 59)

Although he would come to reject Paley's conclusions—his *Origin of Species* is a systematic critique of Paley's arguments—Darwin always admired Paley's arguments and keen observations.

Mentors at Cambridge encouraged Darwin's pursuit of science. One of them, John Stevens Henslow, suggested to Darwin upon his graduation that he take up an offer to join the crew of the ship the *Beagle* as a naturalist. The *Beagle* was commissioned to explore the coast around South America. Darwin soon departed on a voyage that would last nearly five years, from December 1831 to October 1836. Darwin's time on the *Beagle* marked a turning point in his life. What Darwin saw on this journey convinced him that Paley's natural theology, the theological and scientific worldview that had so profoundly shaped and influenced him, left too many unanswered questions.

In the Galapagos Islands, Darwin observed a different species of tortoise on each island. This seemed rather extravagant on the part of God, but more importantly, it showed the precise adaptation of each species to its unique environment. On some islands that were perfect for mammalian life, he found only one mammalian species: bats. Omnipotence seemed to have run out of creative steam by the time it got to those islands. The appearance of flightless birds on some islands further deepened Darwin's skepticism concerning the argument from design. Why would a bird have wings if it did not fly? More disturbing were observations like that of a scorpion wasp that lays an egg inside a caterpillar with the emerging larva devouring its host. How could such destruction be designed by God?

Around South America, Darwin collected fossils that he then sent home along with letters explaining his geological conclusions. He made notes and sketches outlining his fledgling ideas concerning *natural selection* (the idea that certain traits make an individual more fit for its environment and lead to its reproductive success) and *common descent* (the idea that all species on earth have a common ancestor and are, therefore, related). These ideas would form the basis of Darwin's scientific work for the remainder of his life.

Upon completion of the *Beagle*'s journey, Darwin continued to develop his theory. Although he was excited about his observations and the revolutionary ideas they suggested, he was reluctant to publish his findings. He was concerned that his theory would lead others to doubt theological truths they took to be rock solid, and he was reticent to be at the center of a controversy. He was also concerned about the effects of his beliefs on his relationship with his devoutly Christian wife, Emma. The threat of being scooped by Alfred Russell Wallace, who had independently developed a theory of evolution by natural selection, forced his hand. Darwin's *On the Origin of the Species by Means of Natural Selection* was rushed into publication in 1859.

While Darwin learned from Paley the idea of species being well adapted to their environments, he came to believe that such adaptations were due to *natural* selection, not *supernatural* creation. The suffering and waste in the natural world led Darwin to conclude that natural selection was a better explanation of the natural world than a benevolent designer. The charms of Paley's argument had been lost. Darwin would write: "The old argument of design in nature, as given by Paley, which formerly seemed to me so conclusive, fails, now that the law of natural selection has been discovered. We can no longer argue that, for instance, the beautiful hinge of a bivalve shell must have been made by an intelligent being, like the hinge of a door by man" (1958: 87). Believing that nature evinces perhaps more cruelty than compassion, the foundations of Darwin's Christian beliefs (allied as they were to Paley's arguments) began to crumble.[3]

In 1851, Darwin experienced an "insufferable grief" upon the death of his beloved daughter Annie at the age of 10. In his memorial he wrote: "We have lost the joy of the Household, and the solace of our old age:— she must have known how we loved her; oh that she could now know how deeply, how tenderly we do still & shall ever love her dear joyous face. Blessings on her."[4] In spite of widespread claims that Annie's death decisively assured Darwin's atheism, there is no evidence to support this view. Darwin had already given up on his Christian faith, which was a great source of personal distress because he now believed he would never see Annie again (in heaven).

Darwin had long thought that it was difficult to reconcile God's action in the natural world with so much suffering, waste, and destruction. He slowly became convinced that an omnipotent and benevolent being was not acting in the physical world. Yet Darwin himself was never an atheist; his beliefs ranged between some sort of *deism* (belief in a deity who is not actively involved in the world) and *agnosticism* (withholding belief or disbelief in God). In 1879, just three years prior to his death, in a private letter to a friend, he wrote:

> It seems to me absurd to doubt that a man may be an ardent Theist & an evo-lutionist. What my own views may be is a question of no consequence to any one except myself. But as you ask, I may state that my judgment often fluctu-ates. In my most extreme fluctuations I have never been an atheist in the sense of denying the existence of a God.—I think that generally (& more and more so as I grow older) but not always, that an agnostic would be the most correct description of my state of mind. (Personal Communication, 1879)

Although Darwin likely died an agnostic, he thought one could be both a theist and an evolutionist. That is, one might believe that God created the world through natural, evolutionary processes. While Darwin abandoned his Christian beliefs, in the second and subsequent editions of the *Origin*, he concluded with the following:

> There is grandeur in this view of life, with its several powers, having been originally breathed *by the Creator* into a few forms or into one; and that, whilst this planet has gone cycling on according to the fixed law of gravity, from so simple a beginning endless forms most beautiful and most wonderful have been, and are being, evolved. (emphasis mine)[5]

If God and evolution are incompatible, Darwin himself was unaware of it.

Is evolution, Darwin's personal opinion to the contrary, the destroyer of faith?

Interpreting Genesis

Some claim that Darwinian evolutionary theory contradicts the book of Genesis taken straight up. But does it wreak havoc on all defensible interpre-tations of the biblical account of the beginning of the world?

Already in the third century, church father Origen contended that the opening chapter of Genesis could not be understood literally. He wrote: "What man of intelligence will believe that the first and second and the third day, and the evening and the morning existed without sun and moon and stars, while the first day was even without a heaven?...I do not think anyone will doubt that these are figurative expressions which indicate certain mysteries through a semblance of history and not through actual events" (Origen, 1966: Bk. 4, ch. 3). The arrangement of days in the text demands a figurative interpretation of the opening chapter of Genesis.

St. Augustine (354–430 AD) likewise argued that the interpretation of Genesis involving six literal 24-hour days could not be the correct interpreta-tion. Augustine is worth attending to because he wrote and lived more than a millennium prior to Darwin. As such, he could scarcely be accused of capitulating to science or being held captive by the spirit of our secular age. He argued, relying on the biblical text alone, for a very different understanding of Genesis 1.

In *The Literal Meaning of Genesis*, Augustine offers interpretive principles and guidelines for properly understanding not only Genesis but also the rest of the Bible. He argues that the position he defends, one that rejects 24-hour days, *is* the literal meaning. Taken in its literary context, *the text itself* precludes an interpretation of 24-hour days. Let us consider some of Augustine's interpretive principles that lead to this conclusion.

Because Scripture is sometimes ambiguous, proceed with caution. Since Scripture may have multiple plausible meanings, one must remain humble and open when reading it. Here Augustine understands "ambiguity" quite literally: biblical texts often admit of two equally likely and defensible meanings. Since it is difficult to interpret an ambiguous text, it is better to hold lightly to one's own interpretation. He writes:

> In matters that are obscure and far beyond our vision, even in such as we may find treated in Holy Scripture, different interpretations are sometimes possible without prejudice to the faith we have received. In such a case, we should not rush in headlong and so firmly take our stand on one side that, if further progress in the search of truth justly undermines this position, we too fall with it. That would be to battle not for the teaching of Holy Scripture but for our own, wishing its teaching to conform to ours, whereas we ought to wish ours to conform to that of Sacred Scripture. (Augustine, 1982: 41)

When we encounter a difficult passage, the best thing to do is adopt a tentative interpretation of the text, remaining eager and open to reexamine it in light of any new evidence that comes along. We should not be so wedded to our own, cherished interpretation of the text that we mistake our own voice for the voice of God.

Because all truth is God's truth, science and Scripture cannot conflict. Augustine did not limit truth to the bible; instead he held that a Christian "should understand that wherever he may find truth, it is his Lord's." So the Christian need not fear, as many do, that science is nothing but a continual assault on their beliefs. Science may assault false beliefs, but eliminating false beliefs and false interpretations of Scripture is a good thing. Science cannot conflict with the Christian's true beliefs. Augustine writes, "When [scholars] are able, from reliable evidence, to prove some fact of physical science, we shall show that it is not contrary to our Scripture" (1982: 45). There can be no real contradictions between true science and the proper interpretation of Scripture. This principle would provide the foundation for the Doctrine of the Two Books—that God speaks to us in the *Book of Nature* and in the *Book of Scripture* (and the two cannot conflict). One need not, of course, adjust one's interpretation of Scripture according to just any scientific claims. But science well supported by evidence cannot contradict Scripture properly understood.

Because the Genesis creation story cannot be completely factual, it must contain figurative elements. Augustine cautions readers to interpret carefully what is meant by the word "day" in the Genesis account. It cannot mean literal 24-hour day. He writes, "It is a laborious and difficult task for the powers of our human understanding to see clearly the meaning of the sacred writer in the matter of these six days" (1982: 103). If night and day are not created until the fourth day, how could there possibly be a day in the first three days of creation? And if "day" doesn't mean "a 24-hour period" in verses 1–3, it doesn't mean "a 24-hour period" in the remaining verses. Augustine carries on this line of reasoning, arguing:

> Thus, in all the days of creation there is one day, and it is not to be taken in the sense of our day, which we reckon by the course of the sun; but it must have another meaning, applicable to the three days mentioned before the creation of the heavenly bodies. This special meaning of "day" must not be maintained just for the first three days, with the understanding that after the third day we take the word "day" in its ordinary sense. But we must keep the same meaning even to the sixth and seventh days. Hence, "day" and "night," which God divided, must be interpreted quite differently from the familiar "day" and "night," which God decreed the lights that He created in the firmament should divide when He said, *And let them divide day and night.* For it was by this latter act that He created our day, creating the sun whose presence makes the day. But that other day which was originally made had already repeated itself three times when, at its fourth recurrence, these lights of the firmament were created. That day in the account of creation, or those days that are numbered according to its recurrence, are beyond the experience and knowledge of us mortal earthbound men. And if we are able to make any effort towards an understanding of the meaning of those days, we ought not to rush forward with an ill-considered opinion, as if no other reasonable and plausible interpretation could be offered. Seven days by our reckoning, after the model of the days of creation, make up a week. By the passage of such weeks time rolls on, and in these weeks one day is constituted by the course of the sun from its rising to its setting; but we must bear in mind that these days indeed recall the days of creation, but without in any way being really similar to them. (1982: 134–35)

Augustine says that the term "day" serves a purpose, but, given that days are not even possible until the fourth day, its purpose must be figurative—it is not equivalent to our ordinary, everyday use of the term.

To communicate to this audience, the author of Genesis followed a practice that Augustine calls *accommodation*. The doctrine of accommodation, which we likewise saw in Galileo's *Letter to the Grand Duchess Christina*, states that the truths of a text should be communicated using concepts and terms that the audience is familiar with, even if such concepts and terms are not entirely accurate. When the author of Genesis discussed the beginnings of the world, he spoke in terms familiar to his ancient Near Eastern audience. A basic understanding of the context in which Genesis was written and for whom it was written is essential for understanding its intended message. Genesis was written about 2,500 years ago to an audience of ancient

Hebrews, a small and distinct people group located among the diverse peoples of the ancient Near East.

Suppose some early Hebrews had heard a dim but distinct reverberation and asked God, "What was that?" God replied, "Oh, that was the echo of the big bang from when I created the world." They replied, "Ooh, God, that's impressive. How'd you do that, anyway?" God responded as follows:

$$\frac{S_0 + \int |\aleph(t)| \, \partial t + \delta \vartheta - \delta \Im + \left[\Re^3 - \downarrow \Pi \right] + \sqrt{\beta \varphi^2 \gamma^4 \phi^3}}{\delta \Lambda} = \text{the heavens and earth}$$

"What the heck does that mean?" the ancient Hebrews retorted and stared blankly. Reminding himself that the average Hebrew was a shepherd and not a theoretical physicist, God replied, "Sorry. What I meant to say was, "I said, 'Let there be light...'"

The Genesis account states that God "spoke" the land and sea, fish, birds, mammals, and humans into existence. But, as Augustine reminds us, this is deeply poetic language that tells us nothing about God's method. How could God have revealed the precise mode of creation to a group of people who had only recently discovered the wheel? How exactly did he speak the land into mountains, for example? What did he say to call skunks, camels, and dinosaurs into existence? What sacred incantation did God breathe into the dust to create the first human? Just as six days is a metaphor without reference to the passage of time, so too God's speech is a metaphor without reference to the creative process.

Ancient Near Eastern cosmology held that the earth was a round disc with waters above the heavens and below the earth and that the sky was a glasslike solid. The idea that an original body of water gets separated by land was also a common feature of ancient Near Eastern cosmology. The author of Genesis presented the account of God's creation by accommodating to these widely held cosmological concepts. "Seven days" is also an accommodative literary device. For ancient Near Eastern cultures, the numeral 7 indicated such ideas as completion and perfection. Furthermore, the idea of a seven-day cycle was an established convention for conveying information. Within this shared cosmological and numerological context, Genesis presents a theological message but has precious little to say of scientific interest.

Scripture speaks primarily of salvation. Here is perhaps Augustine's key point. God's chief concern is not to advance science, but to transform people. If God's chief concern is salvation, then it would be imprudent for God to try to rectify every false scientific belief first. Since the Bible is a guide to moral and spiritual transformation, readers of the Bible should not expect to find scientific claims, hypotheses, and experiments in the Bible. Augustine warns of the potential dangers associated with mistaking biblical claims for scientific assertions. Genesis was written to shape the identity of the Israelites, showing them who they are, where they came from, what they should believe, and how they should live (not to teach the forming and shaping of the heavens):

> It is also frequently asked what our belief must be about the form and shape of heaven according to Sacred Scripture. Many scholars engage in lengthy discussions on these matters, but the sacred writers with their deeper wisdom have omitted them. Such subjects are of no profit for those who seek beatitude, and what is worse, they take up very precious time that ought to be given to what is spiritually beneficial. (Augustine, 1982: 58–59)

The theological message of Genesis is radically different from the message of all other ancient Near Eastern creation accounts. Other creation accounts, such as the *Enuma Elish*, present multiple gods, nature gods, and humanlike gods. Genesis presents a God who is one and is wholly other from nature and human beings. Genesis is a theological polemic against nature deities and highly anthropomorphic gods. The point of the book of Genesis is to show that the God of Israel is the one true God, and that he is a God of order and is in complete control of the universe, including all the creatures inhabiting the universe. The sun is not a god, the earth is not a god, the moon is not a god, and, finally, we are not gods. By using terms and concepts familiar to the ancient Israelites, the author of Genesis was able to make these important theological points; namely, that the world is created and governed by the one true, living God who is distinct from nature and humanity and who created heaven and Earth.

Interpreting Genesis as an accommodative text with a distinct theological message allows present-day believers to grasp the salvific message without being forced to accept an antiquated cosmology as science. Because the Bible is not a scientific text, it does not make scientific claims. We are not required to believe, for example, that the earth is flat because the early Hebrews did. The best interpretive strategy, then, is to understand that biblical passages that seem contrary to well-established knowledge likely contain accommodating features. Any interpretation of a biblical text that involves a scientific claim should only be accepted tentatively, while we remain open to new evidence from science that may change the interpretation.

God, Genesis, and Evolution

Reading Genesis as a scientific account of creation violates Augustinian (and Galilean) interpretive principles. While Genesis unequivocally asserts that God is the creator, it is not intended to teach how God did it or when God did it (or how long it took). Imagine what an odd book it would be if, in addition to revealing God's creative power and love for God's creatures, God had to explain how he did all of his marvelous works. Suppose that before he could explain his love for his creations, God had to describe, in detail, the nature and structure of the cosmos. *That* version of Genesis, let us call it *The Precise Account of Creation*, would have contained thousands of pages, most of which would be completely incomprehensible to the prescientific Hebrews to whom he was writing. It would contain mathematical formulas and scientific concepts that vastly exceeded their knowledge.

Albert Einstein once lamented that only one or two people understood his theories. If God had written *The Precise Account of Creation* instead of the succint poem we find, he could have lamented that no one, even Einstein, understood his theories. And, while people might have purchased *The Precise Account*, they would have only looked at the pictures, promptly placing it on their coffee tables to show off to their neighbors. No one would have made it to the part where God tells us that he loves and cares for us and explains how we should live as his creatures. Not a great way for God to get his point across.

Given the primitive state of Hebrew science, God would need to communicate his salvific message in terms that they could understand. God is not commending the primitive cosmology of the Hebrews; he is condescending to use it to communicate something vastly more important.

Augustine offers wise counsel to Christians who speak out of ignorance on scientific matters:

> Even a non-Christian knows something about the earth, the heavens, and the other elements of this world, about the motion and orbit of the stars and even their size and relative positions, about the predictable eclipses of the sun and moon, the cycles of the years and the seasons, about the kinds of animals, shrubs, stones, and so forth, and this knowledge he holds to as being certain from reason and experience. Now, it is a disgraceful and dangerous thing for a [nonbeliever] to hear a Christian, presumably giving the meaning of Holy Scripture, talking nonsense on these topics; and we should take all means to prevent such an embarrassing situation, in which people show up vast ignorance in a Christian and laugh it to scorn. (1982: 42–43)

Many contemporary religious believers, in the name of piety, criticize evolution as though they were speaking the very voice of God. By demonstrating their ignorance on scientific matters, they have made it easy for detractors to laugh and scorn (and to assume they are ignorant on religious matters as well). Augustine writes, "If [nonbelievers] find a Christian mistaken in a field which they themselves know well and hear him maintaining his foolish opinions about [the Bible], how are they going to believe [the Bible] in matters concerning the resurrection of the dead, the hope of eternal life, and the kingdom of heaven, when they think [the Bible's] pages are full of falsehoods on facts which they themselves have learnt from experience and the light of reason" (Augustine, 1982: 43)? Such behavior, Augustine warns, is disgraceful and dangerous.

EVOLUTION AND EVIL

Augustine has offered us a way to read Genesis so that it is not in conflict with evolution. Yet evolution raises a problem for divine goodness, one not countenanced if the world were very young and if suffering entered the world only after the fall of Adam. William Paley argued that life was unfailingly harmonious and happy. Of God's nature, he writes: "It is a happy world after all. The air, the earth, the water, teem with delighted existence. In a spring noon, or a summer evening, on whichever side I turn my eyes, myriads of happy beings crowd upon my view." The kind creator that Paley envisioned ordered the universe, and humans recognize and appreciate that order. Nature, like the Bible, is a moral treatise. Charles Darwin, who initially agreed with Paley, would come to demur:

> We behold the face of nature bright with gladness, we often see superabundance of food; we do not see, or we forget, that the birds which are idly singing round us mostly live on insects or seeds, and are thus constantly destroying life; or we forget how largely these songsters, or their eggs, or their nestlings, are destroyed by birds or beasts of prey; we do not always bear in mind, that though food may be now superabundant, it is not so at all seasons of each recurring year. (Darwin, 1859: 49)

Darwin came to believe, quoting Tennyson, that "nature red in tooth and claw" was considerably less reassuring than the evidence appealed to so selectively by Paley. He grew increasingly aware that far more offspring are produced than can possibly survive and that competition for scarce resources, resulting in suffering and death, shapes living organisms.

The God of Abrahamic theism is difficult to square with a world with so much waste, suffering, and death. As Darwin wrote: "A being so powerful and so full of knowledge as a God who could create the universe, is to our finite minds omnipotent and omniscient, and it revolts our understanding to suppose that his benevolence is not unbounded, for what advantage can there be in the sufferings of millions of the lower animals throughout almost endless time?" (1958: 13). It's difficult to be unmoved by Darwin's concerns. Omnipotence, omniscience and perfect goodness do not lead us to expect a world with mass extinctions and mosquitoes, predation and parasites, and starvation and snakes. Surely Omnipotence would have done things neat and clean. Death and destruction seem poor ingredients when Perfect Goodness cooks up worlds. How can one remain a theist given the natural evil that the history of the world presents to us?

A variety of *theodicies*, explanations of why God allows evil, have been offered but, frankly, I find them all wanting especially when applied to natural evil. How can one justify belief in God given the facts of evil? God—omnipotent, omniscient, and wholly good may he be—may yet have a perfectly good reason (or two) for allowing evil.

The *free will theodicy* claims that God permits evil so that humans can meaningfully exercise their free will. Without the ability to choose, human choices would be morally insignificant and humans reduced to puppets. If the free will theodicy were true, the bulk of human suffering would be explained. But the free will theodicy is a sorry explanation for natural evils, none of them to be sure, the result of free human choices. Natural evils result from the laws of nature; natural evils seem built into the very cosmos itself.

The most promising theodicy of natural evil is *the soul-making theodicy*, which unites the free-will explanation of moral evil with a view of human nature as less than perfect. On the traditional, Augustinian view of human nature, humans were created perfect (but with free will) and placed in paradise. How such humans in such circumstances could have fallen is a mystery. However, if human beings were less than perfect, and were not placed in paradise, then human failure seems almost inevitable. What could justify God's placing people in harm's way? According to the soul-making theodicy, facing real dangers and challenges is the only way that God could accomplish the goal that he set for human beings—to freely become children of God. Natural evils provide the training ground for the development of such virtues as courage, patience, and generosity. Natural evil is justified because it provides the necessary struggles, dangers, and opportunities for immature, incomplete people to become heirs of eternal life.

This would be a great theodicy of natural evil if humans played a more central role in the history of the planet. The vast amount of natural evil—at least the sufferings of sentient animals—occurred prior to the entrance of *Homo sapiens* onto the scene. Their suffering couldn't possibly have contributed to human soul-making.

Maybe animals don't really suffer, or maybe the cosmos demands a maximal contrast of good to evil, or maybe the suffering of animals is the unavoidable side effect of the otherwise really top-notch physical laws that God selected for the universe. Or maybe God's bringing order out of chaos required doing battle with cosmic chaos-monsters or principalities and powers (which wreaked their havoc on Earth), or maybe all natural evil can be attributed to Satan and his minions. Maybe, maybe, and more maybes. But the fact is, I think we simply don't know why God, if there is one, created the world in this manner.

Suppose the theist doesn't know why God permits natural evil. Does unexplained natural evil undermine rational belief in God?

Let us proceed by way of example with an outstanding and troubling problem in fundamental physics. It is well known that quantum theory and the general theory of relativity are incompatible. The two greatest achievements of twentieth-century physics can't be made to fit together. I won't develop the problem, I'll just note it. You can read about it yourself in any good physics textbook or in any number of websites.

Given their incompatibility, are physicists required by reason to give up one or the other theory? Or do they live in the tension of not knowing for sure which theory is false (or if both are)? Or do they hope for a deeper, underlying theory, one which preserves the truth of both?

Most physicists live very slightly in the tension but much more in the hope that someone, a greater than Einstein or Newton, will discover a more fundamental theory that incorporates both without remainder. Some think that we've reached the limit of human cognition and will never know if these competing theories can be reconciled. If so, the best one can do is to accept both theories but trust that reality is ultimately rational and that there is an unknowable solution. We'll reach the limits of human understanding some time; perhaps we are at the limit. Finally, some physicists reject both theories; after all, they can't both be true. Some of those who hold this view believe that quantum mechanics plumbs a "reality" that so vastly exceeds what we can see, hear, touch, taste, or smell we're liable to be wrong about it. Better to be cautious than wrong. So this sort of physicist takes the theories as predicting devices without any commitment to their reality.

I doubt there's a principle of reason that dictates what the ideally rational physicist should do in these circumstances. Moreover, I suspect that all three responses are rational; each person might reasonably believe as they do. None of the three positions is optimal but we aren't in an optimal situation: information is limited, intuitions differ, background commitments don't coincide, and we have different policies when it comes to belief-assessment (e.g., some physicists take more risks than others when it comes to belief, some are more conservative). Physicists do the best they can to make their best judgments in these areas, knowing that they might be wrong.

With respect to theistic beliefs and natural evil, the theist is in a similar position. Some will live in the tension all the while hoping that someone will discover a theodicy that explains how a good God could create a world like ours. Some will, like Job, believe that we've reached the limits of human understanding and simply find themselves believing that there is an unknowable solution that reconciles God and natural evil; such believers will no doubt believe that access to God's purposes is limited by our cognitive capacities. And, finally, some may reject the plain teaching of science (remain a young earth creationist) or the reality of evil (as a practitioner of Christian Science does). Others will find their religious beliefs wilting away.

Again, I doubt there's a principle of reason that dictates what should be done in these circumstances. None of these positions is optimal but, again, we aren't in an optimal believing situation: we have to do the best we can to make our best judgment about God and natural evil knowing that we might be wrong. I don't think that there's a one-size-fits-all belief or belief policy in this area either.

A deeply committed believer may continue trusting, without ignoring or diminishing natural evil, that God is good and has a plan that incorporates suffering and death. If however, one's religious belief is shaky, one may find one's religious beliefs overwhelmed by the suffering of animals and the tears of humanity.[6] Both options are, as best I can tell, reasonable.

CONCLUSION

The apparent tensions between natural, scientific explanations and specific religious beliefs may be remedied by coming to see that the Bible is not a scientific textbook. The early Hebrews were a prescientific, largely uneducated, agrarian people who lived within a particular Middle-Eastern culture and who, like everyone else in that day and age, had a primitive view of the world. If God wished to communicate to such a group of people, God would have to accommodate himself to their finite, even incorrect natural (and perhaps even theological) beliefs. God's challenge was to communicate, in language prescientific people could understand, what was necessary for their greatest good. Suppose in order to grasp, "Choose justice, love mercy, and walk humbly before your God," God would have had to explain big bang cosmology, $E = mc^2$, the periodic table of elements, plate tectonic geology, and the transmutation of species. The stiff-necked Hebrews had a difficult enough time being kind to the poor, widow, and orphan; they didn't need to worry about grasping the special theory of relativity.

God, according to this Augustinian way of thinking, communicated redemptive truths within a context of uncorrected scientific errors. Religious believers who cling to the primitive scientific worldview within which these normative truths were communicated are mistaking the medium for the message. One great blessing of science is to separate the redemptive wheat from the cultural chaff.

While Darwin himself would come to reject his Christian heritage, he did not think that descent with modification required one to give up belief in God. Many of his contemporaries, including geologist Charles Lyell, believed his theory consistent with their religious beliefs. Charles Kingsley, a prominent clergyman and historian, wrote one of the earliest reviews of the *Origin of Species*, praising its ideas in an Augustinian manner: "Of old it was said by Him without whom nothing is made: 'My Father worketh hitherto, and I work.' Shall we quarrel with Science if she should show how those words are true?" (Kingsley, 1871) Theologian James Orr suggested that Genesis should not be taken as literal fact: "I do not enter into the question of how we are to interpret the third chapter of Genesis—whether as history or allegory or myth, or most probably of all, as old tradition clothed in oriental allegorical dress." (1897: 185)

Yet Darwin would be demonized by religious believers and increasingly so in the twentieth century. As the scientific evidence has accumulated in favor of Darwinism, many Christians have defensively retreated into unscientific, untenable biblical literalism. Conflict is an apt metaphor for the ongoing battle between Darwinian evolution and biblical literalism.

If one surrenders the view that their Holy Writ is a scientific textbook, the cost to genuine religious belief may be minimal. Religious believers who claim God as a scientific hypothesis may find their beliefs squeezed by increases in scientific knowledge. But if God is not a scientific hypothesis in competition with other scientific hypotheses, belief in God will be untouched by increases in scientific knowledge, including evolutionary theory. If one rejects God-as-Scientific-Hypothesis, one need not fear that future scientific developments will find increasingly natural explanations for everything under the sun.

CHAPTER 6

Evidence and Evolution

God and/or Evolution?

"I believe in God, the Father Almighty, Maker of Heaven and Earth" is oft-repeated in Christian churches. Combine a belief in the Almighty with the biblical creation narrative in which the heavens and the earth and all they contain are created in seven days and you have all the ingredients necessary for a showdown with science. God Almighty, according to this view, is the omnipotent creator of the universe; he speaks the world into instantaneous existence; on one day he says that the land should produce vegetation and, voilà, all of the plants and trees inhabit the earth; on another day he fills the waters with sea creatures and the sky with birds; on the sixth day, he populates the land with wild animals. And then, in the blink of an eye, he spoke humankind into existence. Humans, like all of the other animals, were created directly by Omnipotence. God spoke, it was done, and it was good.

In the previous chapter we offered ample Augustinian resources for rejecting this "literal" 24-hour-day interpretation of Genesis. In short, we discussed the *Book of Scripture*. What does God's other book, the *Book of Nature*, say about species and their origins? A proper reading of the *Book of Nature* requires a deeper understanding of evolution than we've offered so far.

The Theory of Evolution

"Evolution" covers several different (sometimes overlapping) concepts or theories. "Evolution" can refer to change over time in systems of any kind, like the evolution of the computer from mechanical calculators, the evolution of President Barack Obama from mixed-raced poor child to President, or the evolution of rock 'n' roll music from the Delta blues. Or evolution may refer to the widely accepted fact of change in biological organisms over time (within the same species). For example, the descendants of grey moths in England became mostly black in response to the increasingly sooty trees of the Industrial Revolution,[1] and sparrows in the northern United States became larger than those in the south as a result of adaptations to survive colder temperatures. Such changes within a species, more precisely called *microevolution*, are widely accepted even by the most conservative young earth creationists.

Macroevolution refers to the fundamental changes in organisms that generate entirely new forms or species. When we look at the changes in dinosaurs (say the Archaeopteryx or the newly discovered feathered dinosaurs in China) as they shifted into the first birds, the changes in small mammals that led to horses, or the changes in primitive plants that led to the explosive diversity in modern-day plants, we are looking at macroevolutionary changes. From this point on, we will take *evolution* to be synonymous with macroevolution, the change from one species into another.

There are two central aspects of Darwinian evolutionary theory.[2] The first is *common descent*, also known as common ancestry. The second is *natural selection*.

Darwin seldom used the word *evolution* in *The Origin of Species*. He more often used the phrase "descent with modification" to describe his theory. Universal common descent holds that all organisms alive today descended from a common ancestor that lived in the distant past. All living creatures—from amoebae to mammoths, from lobsters to crab grass, from hippos to humans—are cousins; distant cousins, admittedly, but we all share ancestral relatives.

The resulting picture of biological development, a "family tree," is *the tree of life*: a gigantic pedigree encompassing all organisms throughout all of earth's history. Each currently living organism or species is represented by a twig at the end of a branch of the tree. From any particular twig on the periphery there is a backwards path representing ancestral lineage that traces back to the trunk of the tree: all paths end in (i.e., begin with) a common ancestor. The primary lesson of the tree of life is that all organisms are *related by ancestry*.[3]

Common descent affirms biological *relationships* among organisms: we—all living things—are family. As Darwin put it, "All true classification is genealogical." And the genealogy traces back, ultimately, to original and primitive forms of life from which all other species have descended. The scope is universal—from bacteria to *Homo sapiens*, we all share a common ancestor. Descendants of our common ancestor diversified spectacularly, yielding millions of species exhibiting innumerable forms and sizes—"endless forms most beautiful and most wonderful," in Darwin's words. How did this come about?

The second central aspect of evolutionary theory is *natural selection*. Darwin focused famously on the role of natural selection acting on diverse populations of organisms, with individuals exhibiting higher fitness being selected for survival and reproduction. Adaptation is the process by which a population changes over time in ways that enhance its success in a particular environment or set of circumstances. Individuals with traits that allow them to live longer or to better attract mates than other members of their group will be able to pass on these favorable traits to succeeding generations. Resistance to antibiotics in species of bacteria, the scales on the flat feet of the Round Island Day Gecko (which help them climb smooth surfaces), and the hair that lines the ears of Bactrian camels (which prevent the entrance of sand) are adaptations that were brought about by selection.

The basic structure of Darwin's theory consists of three observations and a conclusion that follows from them:

1. *Variation*: Traits in individuals of a species may be different.
2. *Inheritance*: Traits in individuals may be passed on to offspring.
3. *Competition*: Individuals in a species compete for survival and reproduction.

From these three observations, we can conclude natural selection: those individuals with traits that help them survive and reproduce will generally leave offspring that possess those useful traits. These traits will, in turn, provide those offspring with a competitive advantage (in terms of either survival or reproduction) over those that lack such traits.

Let us develop this in a bit more detail. There is a keen and sometimes desperate competition among individuals within a species often for very scarce resources, such as food or mates; in addition, various predators and even nature itself (e.g., lack of rain or a hurricane) conspire against the existence of these individuals. Life in nature is nasty, brutish, bloody, and, often, short. Some individuals have traits or characteristics (variations) that enable them to better compete with other individuals (maybe they are faster or can grasp food better or see better) and so are able to survive a bit longer, perhaps long enough to reproduce. Likewise, some individuals demonstrate greater abilities (variations) to meet the challenges of their environment (they are harder for a predator to spot or can withstand the cold better or can live longer without water) and, again, are able to survive a bit longer, perhaps to reproduce. The traits that enable such individuals to survive and reproduce better than other individuals are passed on to the next generation, which subsequently passes them on to the next generation, and so on. These traits come to predominate in a species and so, gradually, the species as a whole comes to exhibit greater "fitness"—that is, better adaptation to its environment.

The mechanism that ties all this together is natural selection. In Darwin's words, "I have called this principle, by which each slight variation, if useful, is preserved, by the term Natural Selection." Useful variations, under the pressure of competition, are preserved. Hear Darwin's eloquent, godlike statement of natural selection: "It may be said that natural selection is daily and hourly scrutinizing, throughout the world, every variation, even the slightest; rejecting that which is bad, preserving and adding up all that is good; silently and insensibly working, whenever and wherever opportunity offers, at the improvement of each organic being" (1859: 168).

Consider a simple example. Suppose individuals in a school of fish are both brown and green. Now suppose that the brownish-green river in which these fish live slowly changes to a decidedly brownish hue due to the increasing erosion of its banks. Since the green fish are now more visible, predators gobble up most of them. The brown fish, which blend in better with the muddy river, are not gobbled up as readily and so more survive to pass on their brown genes to their offspring. Shortly thereafter, all of the fish in that stream are brown. Nature (in the form of the changed environment and the predators) has selected out the unfavorable variations (the green fish gene), and successful reproduction has selected the favorable variations (the brown fish gene).

Natural selection can be thought of as a process of elimination. Those that are not adapted to their circumstances and environment and who cannot compete effectively for scarce resources will die out and thus not pass on their genes. In other words, unfavorable traits are not selected. Only those individuals that can compete effectively and adapt to their circumstances hang around long enough to pass along their genes.

Everything that has been said so far—"adapt or die"—is undeniable; new traits in species have indeed come to predominate in response to changing environmental pressures.[4]

Here is the fascinating but religiously difficult part: given millions of years, natural selection has formed each new species, starting with microscopic bacteria and ending with every currently existing species. Natural selection, acting on the small variations presented to it, has in the right circumstances slowly and gradually produced big results: every species that has ever existed. A single common ancestor, a single-celled organism, gave rise to protists (like amoebas), which gave rise to plants and to animals like sponges and worms, which gave rise to animals like crustaceans and fish; those fish gave rise to birds, amphibians, and mammals; those mammals gave rise to dogs and elephants and primates, out of which humans arose.[5]

CHARLES LYELL AND THE AGE OF THE EARTH

If species evolved the way Darwin described, a vast amount of time, millions of years, was needed. The earth had to be much more than 6,000 years old. Up until around 1820, most believed that the earth was very young and that it had rapidly acquired its present shape and form through various natural disasters (such as the Bible's universal flood). Let us briefly look at the study of Earth history at the time of Darwin. This will show us how Darwin first realized that there was enough time for species to evolve.

The first great science–religion controversy of the nineteenth century was not over Darwin's theory; it was over the age of the earth. Since Genesis seems to suggest a very young earth, it is helpful to understand the outlines of this great debate.

In the nineteenth-century debate over the age of the earth, there were two major views: catastrophism and uniformitarianism. *Catastrophism* maintains that the earth was shaped and formed by sudden "catastrophes" or natural disasters, perhaps of supernatural origin, like earthquakes and floods. These intense processes, of relatively short duration, very rapidly raised up mountains, carved canyons, and destroyed dinosaurs (and so laid down the fossil record). Catastrophism holds that slow and steady did not win the race to shape the earth.

Catastrophists believed that the biblical, Noahic flood explains the earth's essential features. While catastrophism is now viewed as more a biblical than a scientific geology, there was ample empirical evidence to support it. There are many well-known catastrophes, like earthquakes and volcanic explosions, ones that both create and destroy landmasses in very short periods of time. While it is impossible to reconcile geological history with a universal flood, the geologic record is nonetheless rife with catastrophes.

The structure of the fossil record is relatively straightforward. Stratified rock contains fossils that are in a sequential order. Think of stratified rock like the layering of a cake. At the base of the cake is the oldest part—the cake mix that has been baked; the top layer of the cake, the frosting, is the most recent. In fossil rock, the bottom layers are full of the fossils of older, simpler species, whereas the more recent layers contain the fossils of more complex species. The structure of the fossil record generally shows a trajectory of simple to complex, just as evolutionary theory would have us imagine. The oldest rocks contain fossilized bacteria, simple single-celled organisms. More recent rocks contain the fossilized remains of more complex species, like dinosaurs. But, in support of catastrophism, the geologic record is sometimes mixed up with "modern" layers beneath "ancient" layers (suggestive of a catastrophe).

Uniformitarianism states that the very slow and gradual natural processes we see on earth today—rainfall, earthquakes, wind, and so on—have always been in effect. According to this view, the history of the earth can be adequately explained in terms of the natural processes that are presently observed. Uniformitarianism holds that the natural processes of the universe were always in effect (with roughly the same intensity); that is, the past was like the present. Moreover, these natural processes are all that are needed to explain the changes that have taken place throughout natural history. Essential to uniformitarianism are the concepts of gradualism and continuity (indeed, it is sometimes called "gradualism").

Charles Lyell, Darwin's close friend, defended uniformitarianism in his influential *Principles of Geology*. His lengthy subtitle, *An Attempt to Explain the Former Changes of the Earth's Surface by Reference to Causes Now in Operation*, reveals his geological philosophy—"Present is key to the past." Given the rates at which we now see wind and rain carving rocks, sedimentation forming, and volcanoes coughing up new landmasses, and so on, Lyell showed how slow, gradual processes could produce great changes. Moreover, on the basis of these rates of geologic change, Lyell could very roughly extrapolate backward to the age of the earth. His calculation: really, really old. He believed the earth to be vastly more than 6,000 years (he calculated the Cenozoic era alone to be about 80 million years). Lyell, it might be thought, gave Darwin the gift of time that he needed for species to evolve.

Lyell's influence on Darwin is clear. His uniformitarianism made sense of earth's history, furnished the vast amount of time that Darwin's theory required, and provided a well-established model of gradual, step-like natural processes that could produce—given sufficient time—remarkable changes. If slow, gradual changes produced mountains and valleys, perhaps slow, gradual changes could produce new species. Finally, the detailed fossil record provided a key piece of evidence for Darwin's theory. So great was Lyell's influence on Darwin that he would write: "I feel as if my books came half out of Sir Charles Lyell's brain." (1844)

The influence was reciprocated: although initially a staunch opponent of human evolution, Lyell would become persuaded by Darwin of its truth.

STONES AND BONES

Geology also provided Darwin with a fossil snapshot of evolution. The unearthing of the fossil record began in the late eighteenth century. As people began to dig, a host of fossils—traces in rock of dead organisms—were found. The fossils began to change how people thought about the age of the earth. The fossil evidence shows a long natural history before the appearance of humans. Darwin's theory offered a framework for understanding the fossil record. Let us look into the fossil record and the support it affords evolution in more detail.

A fossil is a trace left behind by a long-dead organism. We're all accustomed to rock casts of the hard parts—the bones—of dead animals, but footprints, burrows, eggs, and even subtle but distinctive chemical remnants are all considered fossils. Our world contains a vast array of such tracings, and their assemblage—the fossil record—is a record of Earth's biological past. The fossil record is not a random collection of artifacts; it is a chronologically ordered sequence in which the individual entries (the fossils) represent organisms from particular times and places. Several aspects of the fossil record find elegant and comprehensive explanation by common ancestry.

Patterns of Succession

While the fossils that document the existence of gigantic reptiles and other seemingly alien creatures are remarkable, even more remarkable is the fact that the fossil record tells the story of life's past. It tells of an ancient and ongoing parade of organisms that exhibits a clear pattern of successive relatedness. For example, the fossil record reveals the time at which flowering plants first appeared on Earth and then their subsequent variations throughout succeeding eras, and all this in orderly succession. Mammals appear at a particular time in the past and have remained since, changing through time; horses appear, primates appear and, very late in the game, humans appear. The fossil record is an enduring image of this orderly succession.

The fossil record presents a chronologically ordered assemblage of organisms laid down in layers, with each layer containing forms that morphed into subsequent forms (which we find in later layers). The fossil record is a mirror of the tree of life: the set of fossil traces matches the branching system of the tree of life.

Extinction is a notable feature of the succession of life forms, and the fossil record indicates that some chapters of Earth's history have seen spectacular levels of extinction in which nearly every animal species disappeared. Since extinction, like a diamond, is forever, species that disappear from the record don't reappear later. Episodes of mass extinction are often followed by explosions in diversity; it's almost as though extinct species stepped aside to make room for new life forms. This extinction-explosion process has been preserved in the fossil record. The tree of life does not branch endlessly, growing out of control: it has been pruned, repeatedly and sometimes severely.

The match between the ordered pattern of the fossil record and the tree of life cries out for an explanation. Common descent offers a simple explanation: the shared pattern records a succession of life forms that are related through biological ancestry. Ancient organisms are the ancestors of less ancient ones, and those in turn are the ancestors of all species today.

Transitional Organisms

It is commonly asserted by anti-evolutionists that gaps in the fossil record indicate a decided lack of transitional forms between one species and the next. Microevolution is certainly true and present in the fossil record, but the lack of transitional fossils is, so it is claimed, decisive evidence against macro-evolution. The fossil record shows, or so the anti-evolution story goes, that while organisms have undergone relatively minor changes, it does not show species morphing into new species. This assertion, however, has been refuted by an increasingly developed fossil record, which offers dramatic examples of fossils with characteristics intermediate between similar but quite different species in earlier and later eras. Consider two fascinating discoveries of transitional organisms: walking whales and "fishapods."

Researchers working in Pakistan and Egypt have assembled nearly complete fossil skeletons of whales and similar animals with peculiar combinations of land and water-based characteristics. The different species have limbs of varying sizes, showing a remarkable progression from four-legged mammals that look as if they could swim to large swimming mammals with comically tiny hind limbs. The biggest find, called the "smoking gun" by the late Stephen Jay Gould, was named *Ambulocetus natans* ("walking whale"). These animals are intermediate in form and in time. Before *Ambulocetus'* time, there were no whales of any kind, and since that time modern whales are represented in the fossil record. *Ambulocetus natans* is a transitional species preserved in hardened mud as a transitional fossil precisely between whale-like mammals and whales.

Paleontologists have also found fossil fish in Greenland that display a striking combination of fish-like and land animal-like characteristics. The most famous of these new fossil fish, *Tiktaalikrosae*, nicknamed the "fishapod," is a fish that possesses several distinctive features of tetrapods (four-limbed land animals such as pandas and people). Like the walking whale, the fishapod is not merely intermediate structurally; it lived in the era before tetrapods appear in the fossil record and after which the planet was filled with four-legged animals. *Tiktaalikrosae* is a transitional species preserved in hardened mud as a transitional fossil precisely where it should have been found, between animal-like fish and animals (tetrapods).

The fossil record presents us with compelling evidence of transitional species from land mammals to sea mammals, and from sea fish to land fish, two of the most remarkable morphs in the history of the world. Common descent explains these features of the fossil record. Transitional organisms such as *ambulocetus* and *tiktaalik*, and their specific position within the succession documented in the fossil record, are elegantly and simply explained by common ancestry.

But it's not just walking whales and fishapods. Dinosaurs may have given rise to birds, and several transitional organisms attest to this, most strikingly, feathered dinosaurs. Horses arose from small, dog-sized ancestors through an extensively documented series of transitional forms. Transitional plant forms have also been discovered documenting key branch points, such as the appearance of seeds. There are at least two serious candidates for the transition between lizards and snakes. And there's a detailed assemblage of fossil primates pointing to key transitions in the evolution of primates. The fossil record documents evolutionary transitions, and the fossil record, replete with transitional fossils, is most reasonably explained by common descent.

The fossil record paints a fairly consistent picture. A layering of fossils from simple organisms to more complex creatures is what one should expect to find in the fossil record if evolution were true. Again and again, these expectations are confirmed. There are, to be sure, gaps in the fossil record, areas where the record seems to be incomplete or lacking expected forms. Many former gaps, however, have been closed by subsequent discoveries, and the expectation is that at least some current gaps in the fossil record will be closed by future discoveries. There has been some mixing up of the layers due, no doubt, to the odd catastrophe. Yet the overall trajectory is clear, and neither the few gaps in the fossil record nor the occasional muddy mix-up overturns the abundance of evidence that the fossil record provides in support of evolution.

A CONSILIENCE OF INDUCTIONS

Darwin's theory doesn't stand (or fall) on the single leg of the fossil record. The case for Darwin's theory is its ability to explain, better than any competing explanation, a wide variety of data. The case for evolution has been called *a consilience of inductions.* Consilience means "a jumping together," "unity," or "putting together." The concept was invented in 1840 by Cambridge philosopher and scientist, William Whewell, who wrote: "Accordingly the cases in which inductions from classes of facts altogether different have thus *jumped together*, belong only to the best established theories which the history of science contains. And as I shall have occasion to refer to this peculiar feature in their evidence, I will take the liberty of describing it by a particular phrase; and will term it the *Consilience of Inductions*." (Whewell, 1847, vol. 2: 65) A consilience of inductions involves linking together various kinds of evidence in order to make a mutually supportive case for a particular claim. In a successful consilience, bodies of data, otherwise unrelated, are explained by a single, unifying theory. The unifying theory sheds light on the disparate sets of data by revealing their underlying similarities and causes. Taken together, the various forms of evidence mutually support and illuminate the theory (which, in turn, illuminates the evidence).

During a criminal trial, a judge or a jury typically relies on a consilience of inductions. While a single piece of evidence is seldom adequate to convict a criminal, carefully bringing together various lines of inquiry—fingerprints, DNA, eyewitness testimony, rejection of alibis, gunshot residue—is often decisive in demonstrating guilt. The various lines of inquiry are mutually supportive of the claim that the defendant is guilty.

In the case of evolution, a consilience of inductions involves various previously unrelated lines of evidence. These lines of evidence include *the fossil record, biogeography, comparative anatomy, embryology*, and *genetics*. Shared ancestry brings the data from these disparate areas of inquiry together under a single explanatory tent. Common descent unites the distant past with the present, and unites continent-sized ecological observations with molecular-sized DNA sequences. The case for evolution involves complementary, coinciding, and reciprocally supportive evidence. For example, biogeography and the fossil record are mutually reinforcing. These in turn mutually reinforce genetics, and so on. The light (of reason) switches on as these various disciplines are unified under and illuminated by the theory of evolution.

Believers in the two books, the *Book of Scripture* and the *Book of Nature*, can turn to either book for information about the nature of reality. Let us, reading the *Book of Nature*, consider the evidence for evolution, much of which has been discovered since Darwin's death in 1882. Advances in genetics and molecular biology, which Darwin could never have imagined, confirm his theory. It has been said that all biological evidence points back to evolution, so much so that the geneticist Theodosius Dobzhansky once wrote that "nothing in biology makes sense except in the light of evolution" (1973).

BIOGEOGRAPHY

Biogeography is the study of the geographical distribution of species. Recall Darwin's observation that on each of the islands in the Galapagos, there was a different species of tortoise; such an observation is a biogeographical observation. The geographical distribution of species gives us the idea of branching evolution and, ultimately, points back to a common ancestor. For example, Darwin noticed that there were three different species of mockingbird on three different Galapagos Islands. This struck him as curious because in

South America there was only one species of mockingbird. Darwin reasoned that these different species of mockingbird branched off from "the parent species" on the coast of South America.

Different parts of the world are home to wildly diverse and even peculiar types of organisms. Australia, for example, is famous for its rich collection of marsupials. These mammals, known for their pouches and unique mode of development (outside of the mother's body in the pouch), came to be so dominant in Australia that there are few native representatives of the other major group of mammals (the placentals). Placentals develop inside of the mother's body in a womb. The near-total absence of native placentals in Australia led to a curious ecological phenomenon: marsupials play ecological roles in Australia that are filled by placentals in the rest of the world. Until the mid-twentieth century, Australia was home to a now-extinct marsupial "wolf" (*thylacine*), and is still home to the marsupial mouse, anteater (the numbat), flying squirrel (*phalanger*), groundhog (wombat), and rabbit (bandicoot). These animals are distinct from their placental namesakes. For example, the bandicoot is not a rabbit at all—it just looks and acts like one—and fills the ecological niche that rabbits fill in the rest of the world.

In the mid-nineteenth century, naturalists (including Darwin) recognized that the reigning paradigm based on the repopulation of the earth following a global Noahic flood could not explain such striking patterns of distribution. The best explanation is common descent. At least 125 million years ago, mammals split into marsupials and placentals. As the Australian island broke off from the ancient landmass Gondwanaland, its mammals followed a unique evolutionary trajectory: modern wolf-like, mouse-like, anteater-like, and rabbit-like marsupial mammals developed as successful descendants of earlier successful marsupials.

What about the biogeography of the past? Paleontologists have discovered that ancient land animals arose in particular parts of the world and that similar organisms often succeed them in the fossil record of that same part of the world. This geographical pattern holds right into the present day, resulting in a geographically specific succession of species that links the past and the present. In other words, the fossil record of regions of Earth inhabited by distinctive land animals—the Australian marsupials again a dramatic example—includes those distinctive organisms and the distinctive extinct species that resemble them. The remarkable overlap of the fossil record and the geographical distribution of unique life forms proved compelling to Darwin. He wrote:

> Mr. Clift many years ago showed that the fossil mammals from the Australian caves were closely allied to the living marsupials of that continent. In South America, a similar relationship is manifest, even to an uneducated eye, in the gigantic pieces of armor like those of the armadillo, found in several parts of La Plata; and Professor Owen has shown in the most striking manner that most of the fossil mammals, buried there in such numbers, are related to South American types. This relationship is even more clearly seen in the

wonderful collection of fossil bones made by M. M. Lund and Clausen in the caves of Brazil. I was so much impressed with these facts that I strongly insisted, in 1839 and 1845, on this "law of the succession of types,"—on "this wonderful relationship in the same continent between the dead and the living" (Darwin, 1859: 339).

Both biogeography and the fossil record *and* their remarkable correspondence are elegantly and simply explained by a single theory: descent with modification. Without descent with modification, biogeography and the fossil record are poorly explained and their remarkable correspondence is a shocking coincidence.

COMPARATIVE ANATOMY

Comparative anatomy is the study and comparison of different species' anatomical or bodily structures. Comparative anatomy supports evolutionary theory through its support of common descent. When we see similarities among the anatomical structures of differing species, especially when similar structures serve different purposes (in different species), common descent helps put the pieces together. Natural history offers many examples of anatomical structures performing one function that are slowly and gradually modified to perform an entirely different function.

Consider the human hand, which has five fingers that can perform rather complex tasks, such as typing on a keyboard, playing stringed instruments, and grasping a hammer. Primates, no surprise here, have hands that look and function like human hands. We also see similarities to the human hand in the structures of bats, cats, and whales. Bats have an extended digit-like structure that makes up their wings. Cats have a similar structure in which the digits are smaller and adapted to walking. And the whale's digit-like fins are used for swimming. Hands–wings–paws–fins: all share similar structures suggesting a common plan. The common plan suggests that bats, cats, whales, and humans had a common ancestor, one with a digit-like structure that was passed on to subsequent generations, but modified given various environmental differences. As Darwin put it, descent with modification.

Richard Owen (1804–92) was one of the greatest anatomists and paleontologists of all time. His work undergirded many of Darwin's claims, and he espoused evolutionary ideas throughout the mid-nineteenth century. Best known now for coining the term "dinosaur," Owen devoted his professional life to the study of animal form, especially *homologies*: "the same organ in different animals under every variety of form and function." In his 1849 classic *On the Nature of Limbs*, Owen described the uncanny similarities of structural design among the vertebrate limbs of every species: a similar pattern is repeated in the arm of a human, the wing of a bat, the wing of a bird, the flipper of a whale, and even the fins of some fish. Anatomist Neil Shubin summarizes the pattern very simply as "one bone, followed by two bones, then little blobs, then fingers or toes" (Shubin, 2009: 31). There are no exceptions. The limbs of all four-limbed animals are built according to that basic design. Remarkably similar homologies also exist among jaws, teeth, eyes, and hair.

To explain these similarities, Owen developed the concept of the Archetype, a kind of ideal, Platonic vertebrate plan upon which all vertebrate forms are based. While Owen toyed with evolutionary ideas, Darwin supplied the unifying explanation. Owen was partly right—animal limbs are variations on a theme—but the "Archetype" was not a Platonic ideal but the very real common ancestor from which the plan has been inherited. There's a shared plan because all animals share a common ancestor; all successive animal arms, skulls, hair, teeth, and jaws are variations on that ancestral theme.

Comparative anatomy reveals homologies, and common descent explains why. The basic limb plan appears first at a particular time in the fossil record, specifically in the species that document the fish-to-animal transition, and that limb plan has characterized animals for at least a quarter of a billion years. The first successful limb plan was passed on with modifications from a common descendent through all subsequent species.

EMBRYOLOGY

Early in the nineteenth century, scientists noticed striking similarities between human embryos and other mammalian embryos. Scientists also noticed that in the early stages of development, mammalian embryos exhibit similarities with embryos of reptiles and fish, possessing tails and webbed hands and feet. Why would the embryos of lizards and fish resemble 2-month-old human embryos?

The marriage of evolutionary biology and developmental biology has spawned a new field called "evo-devo." Evo-devo seeks to understand the evolution of form by examining the developmental processes that create form. Biologists have uncovered a striking unity in the embryological processes that underlie the construction of animal bodies. Animal limbs, as different as they look at birth in different animals, arise through similar forms and structures in the embryo. The initial structure in the embryo, called a limb bud, is the same in all animals, and the genes that control the formation of that structure are the same in all animals. You could transfer these genes from one species to another with scarcely a difference.

This profound conservation of limb-making genetic machinery led to the coining of the term *deep homology*. According to this deep homology, animal limbs display unity in every detail of their construction as well as in their design. Common descent provides the ready explanation of why every limb undergoes the same embryological development under the control of the same genes: shared plan, shared genes, and similar limbs are due to shared ancestry. An ancient but successful limb plan has been genetically transferred (with modifications) to successive generations.

The discovery of DNA revealed that these conserved and constant patterns of development are controlled by similar genes. The same genes in completely different animals (or bacteria or plants, for that matter) provide independent evidence of common descent. Consider two examples: genes that control basic body plans and genes that control the formation of eyes.

First, body plans. All animals are constructed during embryonic development through the formation of different regions, or segments. Whether you're a tiny worm or a humpback whale, you have a head and a tail, a top and a bottom, and various segments in between. These patterns are set up in the early embryo through the orchestration of gene activity by proteins that specialize in turning genes on and off. In other words, bossy *regulatory genes* are responsible for the activity of submissive genes. These bossy genes are in control of developmental pattern formation. In the 1980s, biologists studying the development of the fruit fly discovered that many of the regulatory genes that control development are similar to each other, forming a gene family. In addition, each member of this bossy family controls a specific region of the embryo. Remarkably, the genes are housed in a complex in the genome and are ordered according to their pattern in the embryo: genes that control the front of the embryo are at one end of the complex and genes that control the back of the embryo are at the other end. Biologists also found the same gene complexes in mammalian genomes. The same genes, controlling the same parts of an embryo, are housed in a complex in the genome, in the same order, in fruit flies, felines, and humans. This stunning discovery revealed that homology in animals was deeper than imagined, extending all the way down to the most basic genetic controls of development. Common ancestry, again, provides a simple explanation: fly, feline, and human genomes similarly control fly, feline, and human embryological development because flies, felines, and humans share a common ancestor.

Molecular biology also discovered a master race of genes that are such powerful regulators they can activate an entire developmental program, leading to the construction of, say, a limb or a muscle. Consider the development of eyes. Curiously, "Eyeless" is the name of the master regulator gene in the development of the eyes of fruit flies: flies in which this gene is inactivated are eyeless. The same gene controls eye development in flies, frogs, and Frenchmen. Deep, deeper, and deepest: homology goes all the way down to the gene, and the framework of common descent makes sense of it all.

Humans are sometimes born with a tail. Whales are sometimes born with tiny hind limbs. Chickens can grow teeth. Darwin pointed to the existence of these so-called *rudimentary organs* in all sorts of creatures, and claimed that common ancestry would predict the progressive loss of certain structures in certain types of organism. Yet the basic plans for these lost organs remain buried deep within every successive individual. Many animals carry vestiges of structures they no longer use or need. Blind fish that live in caves still carry all the genetic and developmental machinery needed to build eyes. Chickens have the machinery to make teeth. Whales can still make hindlimbs, and humans can still make tails. Common ancestry accounts for blind cavefish that have turned off that particular developmental program, and common ancestry accounts for genetic eruptions, such as chickens with teeth, whales with legs, and humans with tails. If every organism shares a common genetic plan, then the codes for various forms persist through successive generations, sometimes switched on, sometimes switched off.

A consilience: common descent explains the strange similarities in the development of very different animals and the fact that so many organisms display peculiar and seemingly unnecessary features.

The evidence accumulates. Fish have gills, which develop from structures called gill arches that give rise to gill slits. Humans don't have gills, nor do any other mammals, but all mammals have gill arches, and those gill arches give rise to slit-like structures that never open up. Mammalian gill arches form jawbones instead. Pigs have tails, and humans have just about everything you need to make a tail (such as a tailbone), but the tail never (or rarely) develops.

Why would an animal start to make gills or a tail and then stop? Evolution's explanation is that as a species changes, it doesn't have the luxury of clearing out the old structures while the new structures are being formed. It's more like upgrading a car's engine *while the engine is still running*. Evolution is, accordingly and famously, a tinkerer, not an engineer (Jacob, 1977). Evolution does not design new organisms, it tinkers with, makes slight modifications to, what is already there.

What is the evolutionary explanation for this? Evolution tells us it is easier for species to work around unnecessary features than it is to remove them. In the case of embryos, the genetic instructions for development are passed on from fish to species that branched off from fish, including pigs and humans. In pigs and humans, the instructions for the development of gills and webbed feet are present but ignored. Evolution acts in such a way that the development of gills and webbed feet in pigs and humans no longer occurs, but these ancient but obsolete genetic instructions are still present.

The bottom line: the common set of instructions that guide development is a clue to common descent.

GENETICS

The newest line of evidence supporting evolution comes from the field of genetics. DNA is the molecule within each cell containing genetic information and instructions used in the development and functioning of all living organisms. Common metaphors for DNA are a blueprint or a code. DNA contains instructions on how the individual organism develops and functions. For example, there is a section (a "sequence") in the DNA instructions that directs the functioning of the eye, and this section contains the particular instructions that direct the eye to develop and function properly. A DNA sequence is a chain of nucleotides (which scientists represent by letters) that contains genetic instructions. Adenine, cytosine, guanine, and thymine (or A, C, G, and T) are the nucleotides (or letters) of which DNA sequences are composed. Every living thing on Earth uses these four nucleotides to spell out its genetic instructions. From humans to dogs, salmon to salamanders, and bacteria to bananas, these four nucleotides are the language in which genetic instructions are encoded.

In 1859, when Darwin made his case for descent with modification, there was scant knowledge of biochemistry and no knowledge of the molecular details of inheritance. Although the modest monk Gregor Mendel's pioneering work on genetics occurred at about the same time, it was unknown to Darwin (and to everyone else until the turn of the twentieth century). Since then, the relatively young field of molecular genetics has generated a vast trove of data that is elegantly explained by common ancestry. The explanatory success of common descent in accounting for comparative genetic phenomena underscores the fertility of the original explanation.

In using genetics to study evolution, scientists compare and contrast the different DNA sequences among species. There are many similarities in the DNA sequences not only between humans and primates (we share 97 percent of our genes with monkeys), but also between humans and bacteria, between humans and butterflies, and between humans and bananas (roughly 50 percent of the human DNA sequence is shared with the banana!).

A genome, to borrow a metaphor from Francis Collins, former director of the Human Genome Project, is an information repository something like a set of encyclopedias. The medium is DNA, and each volume of the set is a chromosome (humans have 23 pairs of chromosomes). Each chromosome contains thousands of genes, which are paragraphs of coded information that are decoded in the process of making particular proteins (such as hemoglobin or a digestive enzyme). The paragraphs vary in length and are sometimes interrupted by stretches of noncoding DNA. The alphabet is A, C, G, and T (the nucleotides adenine, cytosine, guanine, and thymine), which combine into DNA sequences.

When techniques for reading DNA sequences were developed, biologists began to amass information about genomes and the secret codes they contained. While initial studies focused mostly on the genes themselves, genomes contain vast amounts of nongene information, pages and pages and pages of it, in which the gene paragraphs are embedded. More on that later. These studies revealed the deep homologies we just examined, and showed that organisms believed to be closely related based on anatomy and/or the fossil record also have similar gene sequences. Organisms considered more distantly related have sequences that are less similar.

Sequence differences correlate with descent and not with function: whales, being mammals, have genes that are more similar to cow genes than they are to fish genes even though whales and fish live entirely in the water. Bats and birds both fly, but bats, being mammals descended from other mammals, have genes that are more similar to mouse genes than they are to bird genes. In other words—and this is important—analyses of gene sequences have revealed patterns of similarity that are uncorrelated with biological features (having fins, flying with wings, being single-celled). Instead, the patterns correlate with lines of biological descent. The earliest observations of gene sequences made in the early days of molecular biology are nicely explained by common ancestry.

The advent of large-scale sequencing of entire genomes, including the historic announcement in 2001 of the sequencing of the human genome, has created an enormous and ever-expanding compendium of genomic sequences from organisms throughout the tree of life. We can read vastly more than a paragraph here and there, as those initial studies did—genomics has given us an entire library full of encyclopedias, with all those pages of mysterious nongene information included. Looking through these encyclopedias, biologists see marks of descent with modification on every page. Let us consider three examples of these marks:

1. The existence and location of pseudogenes.
2. The existence and location of virus-inserted sequences.
3. The location of movable genetic elements.

A *pseudogene*, as the name implies, is a genomic paragraph that looks a lot like a gene but has been inactivated by mutation so that it no longer functions to direct the building of a protein. Like a map of Eastern Europe from the 1988 *Encyclopedia Britannica*, a pseudogene is an obsolete chunk of information in an otherwise functional compendium of information. Animal genomes, including the human genome, are chock full of pseudogenes. For example, humans (like other mammals) are able to smell through the action of olfactory receptors, which are encoded by a large family of similar genes. Humans (like other mammals) have about a thousand different olfactory receptor genes, but more than 60 percent of them are pseudogenes. This is a human-specific state of affairs and explains why we don't make good bloodhounds. Other mammals carry around olfactory receptor pseudogenes, too, but humans have a lot more of them. So nonhuman animals typically have more refined senses of smell. The existence of a pseudogene is an oddity that is reasonably explained by descent with modification, especially when we consider that our genomes have no mechanism for deleting nonfunctioning genes. In other words, genes occasionally get deactivated without getting edited out of the genome. That shouldn't be too surprising; after all, genetic diseases like cystic fibrosis are caused by broken genes that are still carried in the human genome.

Pseudogenes are also in the same location (in the genome) as their functional homologues in other species. In other words, when comparing the mouse encyclopedia with the human encyclopedia, we find that the olfactory receptor paragraphs are in the same volume, on the same page, in mice and in men, *whether or not the paragraphs have been inactivated*. This remarkable fact is explained by common descent: the mouse encyclopedia and the human encyclopedia are both copies of encyclopedias derived and passed on from a common mammalian ancestor. We carry within our every cell a tremendous number of genes, sitting in the same places as they sit in our fellow mammals, in the same places they sat in our common ancestors, many of which have simply been shut off. Had they been switched on, we might be human bloodhounds.

Another example in the genome that shows the mark of descent with modification is the existence and location of *virus-inserted sequences*. HIV is the most famous member of a family of viruses that specializes in copying themselves directly into a host's genome. These viruses, called retroviruses, have signatures that are easy to detect. Mammalian genomes contain tens of thousands of these signatures, and comparison of different genomes reveals these signatures in the same genomic location in closely related species. We know about these viruses because every now and then they come back to life and start infecting people again. And we know they don't insert themselves in the same place each time. If two species share the same signature in the same genomic location, this implies that the virus inserted itself into the common ancestor of those two species. So the best explanation of a viral signature in the same genomic location in, say, a gorilla and a squirrel monkey is common ancestry.

Our final example that shows the mark of descent with modification is the location of *movable genetic elements*. First named "jumping genes," movable genetic elements are pieces of a genome that can hop around. They were considered heretical when Barbara McClintock first described them in corn. We now know she was right (she won the Nobel Prize in 1983, 35 years after first describing jumping genes). These fascinating chunks of DNA are now called, less fetchingly but more academically, "transposable elements." Many animal genomes are nearly overrun with various types of transposable elements. Almost half of the human genome is made up of these things. Like retroviruses, these wayfaring pieces of DNA write their characteristic signature in the genome. Like retroviruses, they don't land in the same place each time. That means that when we see a distinctive signature of a transposable element sitting in the same genomic spot in a whale and in a cow, we find our most reasonable explanation by pointing to common descent: a common signature was passed on to the whale and cow by a shared ancestor.

Common descent explains otherwise inexplicable phenomena, such as the exact positions of retroviruses or jumping genes in the genome, as well as the similarities within the genomes of apparently disparate creatures.

CONCLUSION

The evidence from the *Book of Nature* accumulates, coincides, conciliates (to use our opening metaphor) around the theory of common descent, descent with modification, or, as we would call it, evolution. The fossil record, biogeography, comparative anatomy, embryology, and genetics all point to a single best explanation: evolution by natural selection.

Just as the *Book of Scripture* requires a *hermeneutic*—principles of interpretation that guide our understanding of the text—so, too, the *Book of Nature* requires a hermeneutic. In our discussion of the Genesis creation narratives, we relied on the principles of interpretation developed by Augustine. In reading the *Book of Nature*, we have relied on the consilience of inductions as our interpretive principle. I suspect a consilience of inductions is an effective principle for understanding both books. The best interpretation of the *Book of Scripture* will very likely unite a diverse set of Biblical texts in a mutually supportive, unifying, and illuminating way.

In this detailed discussion, we see that a large amount and variety of evidence from the *Book of Nature* supports a very old earth, the natural production of species, and the very late entry of humans. Only by bringing the *Book of Scripture*, which tells us *that* God is the Creator, together with the *Book of Nature*, which tells us *how* God creates, can we gain a better and deeper understanding of God the Father, Almighty, Maker of heaven and Earth.

Chance and Creation

THE MONKEY TRIAL

Stanley Kramer's 1960 movie *Inherit the Wind* was nominated for four Academy Awards and was called "a rousing and fascinating motion picture" by *Variety*, the entertainment-trade magazine. As rousing and fascinating as the motion picture may be, this fictionalized account is a far stretch from the events the film is loosely based on—the Scopes Monkey Trial, the 1925 case in which the state of Tennessee charged John Scopes with teaching evolution in a public school. Scopes was charged with deliberately violating Tennessee's antievolution statute, which stated that "it shall be unlawful for any teacher to teach any law that denies the story of the Divine Creation of man as taught in the Bible, and to teach instead that man has descended from a lower order of animals." Although the Scopes trial was the first legal case to receive national radio coverage, what really happened has been obscured. Many believe that this trial is where evolution finally triumphed over religion, a viewpoint reinforced in the 1960 film. In reality, evolution and religion were but minor players in the Scopes Monkey Trial.

The Scopes trial began as a publicity stunt to draw a crowd to the small town of Dayton, Tennessee and aroused such enthusiasm that the event has been captured in a half-dozen television and motion pictures. The trial, like the movies, was staged: the lawyers were celebrities, and Scopes' students, who were encouraged to testify against their well-liked teacher, were coached in their testimonies; peddlers sold refreshments, and monkeys roamed the streets (Larson, 1997). John T. Scopes, a well-liked football coach who taught math and science, was an easy target and a willing victim; town leaders had recruited him as a defendant. His "crime," which he couldn't recall ever having actually committed, was teaching evolution. He was just a sideshow, anyway, to the attorneys William Jennings Bryan and Clarence Darrow. Scopes himself never spoke at the trial.

Prosecutor William Jennings Bryan, although portrayed as an anti-intellectual fundamentalist, was a prominent figure in the Democratic Party and an active member of the American Association for the Advancement of Science. None of his arguments attacked science in general. Bryan argued that the theory of evolution (still in its early stages) was not yet proven and should not be conveyed as though it were. Bryan relied heavily on scientific evidence, citing gaps in fossil records and the rather large and obvious differences between primates and humans (not yet accounted for by the theory of evolution). He further stressed the importance of the majority's right to influence what is taught to their children, especially in cases where children's traditional beliefs were being discredited. Although Bryan was poised for a good fight, he was thoroughly unprepared for a dirty fight by an unprincipled opponent.

Clarence Darrow was well-known for his radical beliefs and his tendency to find fault with traditionally accepted moral principles. He was famous for defending two cold-blooded college-aged murderers, who in search of adventure plotted and committed the successful slaughter of a 14-year-old boy. Darrow argued in favor of life in prison over the death penalty, suggesting that it was Nietzschean philosophy and the boys' Darwinian ancestral instincts at fault in this tragedy, rather than the thrill-seeking killers themselves. He argued, "Is there any blame attached because someone took Nietzsche's philosophy seriously and fashioned his life on it? The University is more the blame than he is...it is hardly fair to hang a 19-year-old boy for the philosophy that was taught him at the University" (Weaver, 1995: 39). Despite his eagerness to blame the university curriculum for the murder of an innocent boy, he fiercely advocated the importance of academic freedom during the Scopes trial. Finally, Darrow held Christian belief in contempt claiming it to be foolish and ungrounded.

At the heart of the 1925 trial was the recently passed antievolution bill barring the teaching of human evolution in the Tennessee public schools. Southern Protestants interpreted the teaching of evolution as a direct attack on the Christian faith. Others feared evolution's effects on society. Human eugenics, the practice of weeding out unfavorable traits from the human population, seemed directly aimed at the weak and powerless; defenders of eugenics claimed natural selection—survival of the fittest—in support of social engineering.

The trial began quite civilly. At the start of the trial, Bryan was far from unreasonable in his assessments of evolution and contemporary science. Bryan conceded several plausible aspects of evolutionary theory, on one occasion admitting that the six "days" of creation vastly exceeded a literal span of 144 hours. Moreover, at the time of the trial, many Christians claimed that the teaching of evolution was compatible with the Bible, although Bryan, and many other Christians, did not. Although Darrow's initial strategy was to prove that there was no conflict between Christian teachings and evolution (so Scopes was not a blasphemer), he opted for a more radical approach: prove the Bible false.

Straying from the actual case, Darrow and Bryan engaged—as lawyer and witness—in a verbal war between atheism and religious fundamentalism. Darrow called Bryan to the stand as a biblical expert and pressed him on controversial passages in the Bible: passages regarding Adam and Eve, the historicity of the great flood, and the infamous passage from the book of

Joshua where the sun is purported to have "stood still." Darrow's atheist and antisupernatural scorn were blatantly obvious. Scopes himself never said a word.

It should be noted that Darrow lost the trial and Scopes was fined one hundred dollars. The sentence was eventually thrown out on a technicality.

The Scopes trial has been misinterpreted as an all-out war between science and religion—a war in which science reigned victorious. Nothing could be further from the truth. At best it was a debate between one religion (Christianity) and a not yet fully vindicated scientific hypothesis (evolution); it quickly degenerated into a debate between atheism and fundamentalism. It also involved issues such as secularism, modernism, biblical interpretation, states' rights, individual rights, eugenics, and so on. Casting the Scopes trial as a simple conflict between science and religion omits these subtleties and complexities. It's easier to caricature history, debates, and issues (and use them for one's own ideological ends) than to understand them in all their multifarious and muddy glory.

Many contemporary Christians share Bryan's fears when he said, "I object to Darwinian theory, because I fear we shall lose the consciousness of God's presence in our daily life if we must accept the theory that through all the ages no spiritual force has touched the life of man and shapes the destiny of nations" (Larson, 1997: 39). We find Christians today, like Bryan, hoping that evolution will be proven untrue, believing that they need to preserve room for God's creative handiwork. The most impressive, well-funded and highly organized effort in this regard is the so-called intelligent design (ID) movement.

Scopes II: The Dover Panda Trial

Questions regarding God's function in the creation of the world and the role of theological explanations in the school system are as relevant in America today as they were 80 years ago. In 2005, a number of parents whose children attended schools in Dover, Pennsylvania, challenged the school system for requiring that *Intelligent Design* (ID), the theory that the origin of life and some complex features of living things are best explained by an intelligent cause (not an unguided or undirected process like natural selection), be taught as an alternative to evolutionary explanations for the origin of life. The school district itself did not advocate teaching ID as an alternative to evolution, but they did advocate reading a statement mentioning ID to students in biology classes. Sometimes referred to as "Scopes II," the trial concerned another concerted effort to reject a completely evolutionary account of the origin of living things and to create room for an intelligent designer. Then-President George Bush lent his weight to the debate by endorsing the teaching of ID to America's high school students. Unlike the Scopes trial, pandas figured more prominently than monkeys.

ID is offered as a scientific solution to the current gaps in explaining life's origins and its complexities by natural selection alone. ID's critics claim that, despite its scientific pretensions, ID is little more than creation science clothed in contemporary garb. Creation science affirms the Biblical account of creation quite literally, believing in a series of direct actions that God created each individual species. Creation science usually affirms a literal six-day creation and, consequently, a very young earth as well. Creation science is, in spite of its name, more religion than science. The Supreme Court had earlier ruled that creation science was a religion, so the teaching of creation science in public schools violates the US Constitution's ban on government support for any religion.

The Dover parents who objected to ID being taught in their schools believed that it was deceptive for teachers to present ID as a *scientific* alternative to evolutionary theory. ID, they contended, was a disguised attempt to sneak creation science in on their children; ID is creation science by another name. In December 2005, Judge Jones ruled in favor of the concerned parents—since ID resembles creationism more than a valid scientific theory, he declared the presentation of ID in school classrooms unconstitutional.[1]

How did we get from Scopes I to Scopes II? Or better, how, as evolution came to be overwhelmingly accepted by scientists, did creationism creep back into the classroom? Since this is not a history book, I won't speculate on these historical matters. However, since this *is* a science and religion book, it is worth considering the most recent public expression of this debate. In particular, it is worth considering the case for and against ID. Here we find, once again, a genuine battle over religion and the sciences of origins.

INTELLIGENT DESIGN

In his book *Darwin's Black Box*, biochemist Michael Behe offers what he believes to be scientific evidence—irreducible complexity—in support of an intelligent designer. *Irreducible complexity* holds that certain biological systems are too complex to have evolved, one step at a time, from simpler predecessors. Irreducible complexity refers to a system in which certain functions can neither be removed nor reduced without the collapse of the entire system. Behe defines an irreducibly complex system as one "composed of several well-matched, interacting parts that contribute to the basic function, wherein the removal of any one of the parts causes the system to effectively cease functioning" (Behe, 1998: 39) A light bulb, for example, is irreducibly complex—remove the filament or the bulb or the wires that transport the electricity to the filament or the vacuum—and the light bulb cannot function; it takes all of these features together for the light bulb to function; the loss of any single part results in the collapse of the entire system. While Behe generally accepts the idea of evolution, he claims that the existence of irreducibly complex biological systems (such as blood-clotting or the flagellum of the *E coli* bacterium or the human eye) are simply too complex to have arisen through evolutionary processes. An intelligent designer must have inserted itself at this point to create such complex processes or parts out of nothing.

Darwin himself was keenly aware of the difficulties of explaining "organs of extreme complexity" by natural selection. He found the human eye especially troubling. He confessed in a letter to a friend: "About the weak points I agree. The eye to this day gives me a cold shudder...." In *The Origin of Species* he wrote: "To suppose that the eye with all its inimitable contrivances for adjusting the focus to different distances, for admitting different amounts of light, and for the correction of spherical and chromatic aberration, could have been formed by natural selection, seems, I freely confess, absurd in the highest degree" (Darwin, 1859: ch. 6). Could a step-by-step process like natural selection have produced something so complex as the eye? Is such a supposition "absurd in the highest degree" (and so a reason to reject natural selection)? As critics were wont to remind Darwin, we should expect wings to have survival value only when fully formed – half a wing is worse than no wing (because creatures with half a wing, unable yet to fly, would be much slower in running than similar creatures without half-wings and so would be more likely victims of predators). So there seems no plausible step-wise process, in which the intermediate species are likely to survive, for the creation of wings. Darwin would write of another complex organ: "The sight of a feather in a peacock's tail, whenever I gaze at it, makes me sick!"[2]

When we read Darwin's comment about the eye in its fuller context, we see just how such a step-wise process might have gone:

> To suppose that the eye with all its inimitable contrivances for adjusting the focus to different distances, for admitting different amounts of light, and for the correction of spherical and chromatic aberration, could have been formed by natural selection, seems, I freely confess, absurd in the highest degree....Reason tells me, that if numerous gradations from a simple and imperfect eye to one complex and perfect can be shown to exist, each grade being useful to its possessor, as is certain the case; if further, the eye ever varies and the variations be inherited, as is likewise certainly the case; and if such variations should be useful to any animal under changing conditions of life, then the difficulty of believing that a perfect and complex eye could be formed by natural selection, should not be considered as subversive of the theory (Darwin, 1859: ch. 6).

Darwin goes on to describe light sensitive cells in simple animals that progress to more eye-like elements in more complex animals, suggesting a possible evolutionary path for the development of the eye. Confirmation of such a step-wise natural process of the creation of the eye was, of course, just a hope in the nineteenth century. At this point, Darwin's theory was more promise than fulfillment. Evolutionary theory was in its infancy and did not yield all of its secrets immediately.

Behe and other ID defenders contend (against Darwin) that there are irreducible complexities (organs of extreme complexity) that could not possibly have arisen through evolutionary processes. Darwin's hope is, they say, Darwin's delusion.

Behe's argument begins with evolution's inability to explain the origin of organic life from inorganic matter. The spontaneous generation of the living from the nonliving, of the bios from the prebiotic, *is* a genuine problem for evolutionary theorists. In fact, the gap between living and nonliving is vastly greater than, say, the gap between amoeba and anteaters. As Richard Robinson puts it: "Give biologists a cell, and they'll give you the world. But beyond assuming the first cell must have somehow come into existence, how do biologists explain its emergence from the prebiotic world four billion years ago?" (Robinson, 2005: 396) The widely cited Urey-Miller experiments of the 1950s claiming proof that life originated by lightning striking a prebiotic soup have been decisively refuted. As physicist Fred Hoyle puts it: "In short there is not a shred of objective evidence to support the hypothesis that life began in an organic soup here on Earth" (1983: 23). Are we led, thereby, to an intelligent designer at least to provide that initial spark of life?

Barring supernatural explanation, the question, "How did life begin?" remains unanswered. Evolution has it that we adapted from a series of less complex ancestors. But where did those first ancestors come from? What ignited that first spark of life? This is one of the unanswered questions that incite people to put forth arguments for ID. The late English astronomer Fred Hoyle once suggested that because life is so vastly improbable, it could not have arisen by chance. He contends that life on Earth began as a result of the importation of viable bacterial cells from space aliens (of course, this leads one to ask: how did life begin on their planet?). An omnipotent God who intentionally gets the ball rolling seems no more outrageous than a spaceship of aliens who shower life on Earth's surface. Let us concede the problem and move on to Behe's next step in his argument.

Behe then invites us into the biochemical world that Darwin could not have seen because the microscopes in his day were too primitive; but we can now see into what was for Darwin a black box. In this microscopic world we observe the cilia and flagella by which cells are propelled, we see blood-clotting proteins, and the production of antibodies by the immune system. These highly complex systems, he argues, could not have been produced by evolution. If they were missing just one of their many parts, they would not function; such nonfunctioning cells would collapse under their own weight. So these systems could not have evolved in a step-by-step Darwinian fashion. If natural selection works on small mutations, one component at a time, it can't produce processes that require the simultaneous mutation of several, interrelated components. A functioning flagellum, for example, requires the precise cooperation of perhaps hundreds of distinct proteins. How could natural selection, then, produce a complex flagellum by assembling the components one at a time? Behe contends that it couldn't and so ID is called on to account for evolution's failures. "Life on earth," Behe writes, "at its most fundamental level, in its most critical components, is the product of intelligent activity" (Behe, 2001: 254).

While many Christians have come to the defense of ID, so too, curiously, have some atheists. In his book *Seeking God in Science: An Atheist Defends*

Intelligent Design, Bradley Monton describes the dangers of defining science in a way that excludes ID or anything else that relies on supernatural causes or processes. An atheist himself, Monton does not believe in ID, but he states that there is evidence in favor of ID that should not be ignored. Prominent atheist philosopher Thomas Nagel has also suggested that ID may have some merit (Nagel, 2012). Like Monton, Nagel does not believe that the biological evidence should compel one to embrace ID, but he concedes that the evidence available is strong enough to keep ID on the intellectual table. Nagel is skeptical of the claim that traditional evolutionary theory tells the whole story regarding human life. The evolutionary account raises several questions regarding how life came into existence from lifeless matter—the transition that preceded the process of biological evolution. Loosely endorsing ID as a potential scientific theory, Nagel states, "God, the purposes and intentions of God, if there is a god, and the nature of his will, are not possible subjects of a scientific theory or scientific explanation. But that does not imply that there cannot be scientific evidence for or against the intervention of such a nonlaw-governed cause in the natural order" (Nagel, 2008).[3]

ID is rejected by some religious believers primarily because it looks like just one more god-of-the-gaps type of argument. According to god-of-the-gaps arguments, belief in God is rationally permissible only if invoking God solves a problem or fills a gap in our scientific knowledge. According to this view, the quasi-science of a god of the gaps is on a par with scientific hypotheses such as gravity and atoms. Like gravity and atoms, God is rationally acceptable only if God is the best available explanation of some data. The problem with god-of-the-gaps arguments is that if science should discover a natural explanation of the phenomena in question, then there is no need to postulate a god to explain them.

Consider some historical examples. God has been invoked as a scientific hypothesis to explain a wide variety of natural phenomena such as rain, thunder, and floods. Now, of course, we attribute rainstorms and related phenomena to purely natural (if hard to predict) processes. Prior to the seventeenth century, God was thought to be the ultimate cause of the motions of planets and stars. As natural laws came to the fore (such as the principle of inertia and laws of motion), the explanatory role of God diminished. Although cosmologists such as Kepler, Galileo, and Newton believed that God played an essential role in the continual governance of the cosmos, God's routine activity as the mover or pusher of the planets gradually receded in the minds of most scientists. By the end of the eighteenth century, Laplace, the leading mathematical astronomer of his day, declared that God was no longer mathematically necessary to explain the motion of the planets. Likewise, Darwinian natural selection offered a viable natural explanation of the existence of biological species that were once believed created in an instant by God; so Paley's invocation of a god of the biological gaps disappeared.

As god-of-the-gaps arguments have been offered, God has gotten progressively squeezed out of the gaps. The god of the gaps is the incredible shrinking god.

Even under the best of circumstances, arguing from gaps to God is little more than a confession of ignorance.[4] And even invoking God cannot turn ignorance into knowledge.

Suppose you are eating a late dinner at someone's house and you hear a loud, inexplicable sound coming from one of the upstairs bedrooms. Your host tells you not to worry—it's just a ghost. Not believing in ghosts, you scoff. "No, really," your host insists, "it is a ghost. We sealed off the room with caulk, so we know it's not the wind. We had a plumber fix the pipes, so we know it's not the plumbing. We had an exterminator chase out all of the animals, so we know it's not rodents." Your host continues to explain how he had eliminated all of the natural hypotheses that you considered. Should you, therefore, accept the ghost hypothesis? I think not. While it's true that a ghost would explain the noise, a wide variety of other things would as well—goblins, for example, and gods, but also natural causes that neither you nor your host are aware of. If you don't believe in ghosts, it is better just to confess your ignorance and wait for a more plausible, natural explanation.

It is, likewise, better for the theist to confess her ignorance of the natural causes of irreducible complexity or of organs of extreme perfection and wait for biologists to develop more plausible, natural explanations. As Charles Coulson, the first Oxford professor of theoretical chemistry writes: "When we come to the scientifically unknown, our correct policy is not to rejoice because we have found God; it is to become better scientists" (Coulson, 1953: 16).

In response to Behe's claim that irreducible complexities have no scientific explanation, scientists have indeed developed several such natural explanations. Consider, for example, bacterial flagellum, the icon of irreducible complexity. Biologists have offered a plausible explanation of the step-by-step evolutionary process that produced flagella. So what about blood coagulation and eukaryotic cilium? Surely we need an intelligent designer to explain them? We can expect similar discoveries – if not now, then in the future – of all of ID's "irreducible" complexities: just give biologists some time to unravel nature's secrets.

THEISTIC EVOLUTION

Theistic evolution holds both that God is Creator (a supernatural claim) and that species evolved through natural selection (a natural process); that is, God created the world through the natural processes of evolution. How can one consistently believe that God is the Creator and that the world and all that it contains were created by natural, scientifically explicable, processes?

When standing at the brink of the Niagara Falls, a viewer sees wondrous beauty that, to her mind, can only be attributed to God. One can, at the same time, attribute the grandeur of the Falls to a series of glacial recessions, collections of compressed sediments, the gravitational forces pulling down on a large body of water, and so on. Nevertheless, peering over the edge of the waterfall, some viewers cannot shake their awareness of a divinity who created the spectacular sight with the intention of beauty. Again, this is not to deny that the Falls emerged from a series of natural, geological processes. God's intention to make his creation beautiful is compatible with God's use of natural processes to create what he intended.

Theistic evolutionists believe that a careful reading of the *Book of Scripture* teaches that God is the creator of the heavens and the earth and a careful reading of the *Book of Nature* teaches that the means of creation was evolution. The Book of Scripture and the Book of Nature perfectly coalesce.

Before God and evolution get too cozy, we must remind ourselves that evolution is a very chancy process. There are at least two sorts of random occurrences that are required for the existence, of say, *Homo sapiens*—favorable mutations and changes in the environment.

Favorable mutations, variations, must occur at just the right time for species to adapt to a changing environment. The vast majority of mutations, random as they are, are not beneficial to a species—only a vanishingly small number of mutations are beneficial. Think of the negative connotations associated with *mutant*—a weird, often ugly, creature who doesn't fit in—and you get the sense that mutations are not always favorable. Since most mutations harm rather than help an individual, that individual is not likely to "fit in" with its environment. If so, that variation is unlikely to be passed on to succeeding generations.

Imagine the first living single-cell. If a single, favorable variation had not occurred at precisely the right time for that cell, as the earth got warmer, say, life on Earth could have ended once and for all, never to be repeated. If species don't acquire variations that enable them to adapt to changing environments, they might simply go extinct. This has already happened to 95 percent of the species that have ever existed.

Now think of all of the favorable variations that were required to move from that original, single-celled species to *Homo sapiens*. It is astronomically improbable that all of the favorable variations necessary would have randomly occurred at precisely the right times. Of course, we know that they did. But, it seems, even God himself must have been holding his breath waiting for precisely the right random mutation to occur at just the right time.

At least one random event seems to have been required if human life was possible—the great extinction of 65 million BC. Climate change was one likely culprit exacerbated, perhaps, by the impact of a seven-mile wide asteroid off the coast of the Yucatan in Mexico. The environment changed so suddenly that all of the dinosaurs were wiped out in one fell swoop. Without the extinction of dinosaurs, the existence of large mammals would have been impossible.[5] Large mammals would have been fair and easy game for the T rex or velociraptor. Had large mammals evolved before the extinction of dinosaurs, the end result would have been a lot of fat dinosaurs (and no large mammals). Without them, human existence as we know it would likewise have been impossible.

So, how did God do it—given these chancy events?

While natural selection itself is not a method of chance (it selects for survival value), what it selects from *is* a matter of chance—random mutations. Random mutations supply the fuel that fires the evolutionary machinery. Without mutations, individuals within a species would have roughly the same characteristics; none would be any better than another in terms of skill in avoiding predators or attractiveness in coaxing mates. It's only when mutations occur—making some individuals slightly faster or able to smell better—that natural selection kicks in, lending its endorsement to the favorable trait. Without mutations, natural selection is empty. But, and here's the God and creation problem, mutations are *random*. How can a random process be compatible with God's intentions to create plants and animals, and then humans (in His image)? If the process is random, how could God have known what he was going to get? How could God have guided a series of random events?

Let us press the problem of creation and randomness. Most Abrahamic theists believe that God intended not only the creation of humans but also the birth of this or that human including themselves. That is, God's purpose was not only for the creation of free, rational, moral agents (i.e., humans) but also for the existence of Luis Oliveira, Liang Hao, Abbas Yazdani, and Noralynn Masselink. Again, if mutations are random, how could God possibly have foreknown, let alone intended, the creation of beings *like* you and me (let alone you and me)?

Biologist Douglas Futuyma contends that chance undermines belief in a creator. He writes: "By coupling undirected, purposeless variation to the blind, uncaring process of natural selection, Darwin made theological or spiritual explanations of the life processes superfluous" (Futuyma, 1998: 5). Even Omnipotence can't make plans based on chance. In the words of late Harvard paleontologist George Gaylord Simpson, "Man is the result of a purposeless and natural process that did not have him in mind" (1967: 345). If chance, so the argument goes, then no super-intending God.

Is it possible to rationally believe in a creator given the random nature of evolution?

BIOLOGICAL RANDOMNESS

Biological evolution is the change in organisms over time via random mutation. Mutations occur at the level of genes that combine in new ways so as to produce new structures or patterns of behavior in an organism. But, biologists remind us, mutations are not caused by the organism's needs; mutations just happen—they are, again, random. In fact, the vast majority of mutations are detrimental to the fitness of the organism. Most mutations are destructive to cells and individual organisms; they make the individual slower (perhaps by increasing head size or decreasing leg strength), for example, or more susceptible to disease. But every once in a while a mutation occurs that produces a favorable trait. So, for example, a species comes to acquire a thumb-like digit that helps it to grasp bamboo (pandas), or a longer neck that helps it reach food higher up in the trees (giraffes), or the ability to swim in water even though it's a bird (penguins). But the mutations didn't occur *because* the panda needed a thumb, or the giraffe needed a longer neck or the penguin needed swimming lessons—they just happened. Randomly.

When biologists speak of "random mutation" they do not imply ignorance of the probability that certain mutations will happen at certain times, nor do they claim that it is impossible to predict the likelihood of particular types of mutations as compared to others. In fact, some mutations are known to occur more readily than others. *Random mutation,* as understood by the biologist, is that *the pattern of mutations in a given population of organisms is not affected by the "needs" of those organisms; mutations are "blind" to the good of the organism.* Mutations are random because their causes are not the needs of the affected individuals.

While mutations are random in the sense that they are blind to the needs of the species, they are not random in a number of other significant ways. "For example," says Dawkins, "mutations have well-understood physical causes, and to this extent, they are non-random" (Dawkins, 1996: 70). If mutations are produced by well-understood physical causes, then God could have used those well-known physical causes to produce precisely the variations necessary to bring about the creatures that he intended to create. If "randomness" just means, as biologists strictly define it, "neutral to the needs of an organism," then there's no problem for thinking of God working through random processes *in this sense.* God could ensure, then, that mutations occur (through natural processes) as needed.

God could use His knowledge of the relevant physical processes to produce certain variations that are then, in the right God-controlled or God-predicted circumstances, selected and passed on to future generations. These favorable variations continue to accumulate over long periods of time to produce exactly the species that God intended to create. Randomness, in the biological sense, creates no problem for God's ability to create, through natural processes, what God wanted to create.

Random = Unpredictable

"Randomness" is often defined in terms of unpredictability; *a random process is one in which an individual outcome cannot be predicted with certainty.* If mutations are random in the sense of being unpredictable, then how could God have known which mutations would have occurred for natural selection to act upon?

Coin tossing is useful for illustrating an important distinction between random processes. Consider Albert, who is equipped with a high-resolution camera and an ultrafast computer. Suppose Albert's instruments can gather all the relevant data—initial position of coin on finger, initial velocity, rotation of the coin, air currents, features of the surface of the coin and the landing surface, and so on. With this data and his highly advanced computer, Albert can generate a fail-safe prediction within a few milliseconds of the toss. What was previously unpredictable has become predictable.

The Albert example shows us that we need to distinguish two kinds of unpredictability: unpredictability *in principle* and unpredictability *in practice*. *A process is unpredictable in principle if no knower under any circumstances could accurately predict the outcome of the process.* Such a process would mean that even if one knew all of the relevant initial conditions and all of the relevant physical laws, one could not predict the outcome. If a process is unpredictable in principle, then even God could not predict the results of that process.

A process is unpredictable in practice if there is no known method for accurately predicting the results of the process but if such a method is possible. Unpredictability in practice arises from ignorance of the initial conditions and/or natural laws, and/or a lack of equipment that could assist an accurate prediction. Predicting the results of a process may involve too much information and require more sophisticated information-processing tools than we now possess. For human beings, for now at least, a coin toss is a random process because we lack the practical ability to predict the outcome; it is for us practically impossible to predict at this point. But perhaps coin-tossing will yield its mysteries; perhaps an Albert will come along who can, with the right equipment, make accurate predictions of coin-tossings. There are surely some processes that are unpredictable *to us now* which, with increased knowledge, will one day become perfectly predictable. And presumably if there is a God, he already possesses sufficient information so that everything that is unpredictable in practice *to us* now, is predictable to God.

If mutations are random merely in the sense of being unpredictable in practice (to humans now), then it might still be possible for God to purposely use an evolutionary process. A divine superknower might be able to predict, from the initial conditions and natural laws, precisely which mutations would occur. While the results of the processes involved in genetic mutations may be forever unpredictable to us, they could still be predictable to God. According to this sense of random (random only to finite knowers), God would have no problem intending to and then creating human beings in general and Luis, Hao, Abbas, and Noralynn in particular.

Is Reality Really Random?

The vast majority of physicists claim that certain quantum phenomena are unpredictable in principle—not even God could predict this or that quantum event. The classic case is the decay of a radioactive atom. Although we can very accurately predict what will happen to a large collection of radioactive atoms (giving rise to the knowable half-life of a particular type of radioactive atom), no one, not even God, could predict what will happen to a single radioactive atom. As far as physicists can tell, this process is random in principle; there is no possible process for making an accurate prediction.

The above claim was qualified with "as far as physicists can tell." It's possible that the One True Physical Theory (unbeknownst to us but not to God) could make radioactive decay completely predictable. If so, the processes involved are predictable in practice and, of course, predictable to God. And if predictable to God, he could work through them to knowingly create human beings through evolution by natural selection.

Consider a computer that generates random numbers. From the perspective of human beings, the generated number is unpredictable. However, the computer uses a process, a program, that generates the numbers. If one were knowledgeable about the program and completely aware of the conditions under which it was operating, one could perfectly predict each generated number. So what appears completely unpredictable to humans is easily predictable given sufficient knowledge. The same may go for God: even if, after all human inquiry is completed, aspects of reality appear random to human beings, they might nonetheless be completely predictable to God. Indeed, there may be a completely predictable (to God) higher reality within which our unpredictable (to us) reality fits; reality as it appears contains some unpredictable (to us) processes that are controlled by God in ways we could never understand.

Within the context of evolution our cognitive limitations should not be surprising: surely our cognitive faculties, if evolutionarily produced, would be good at those sorts of beliefs/activities necessary for our survival but not so good at things distant from survival such as high-level mathematics and theoretical physics. Another way to put this: while we may be good at understanding things the size of mates, predators, and enemies, we are not likely to be so good at understanding the very small or the very large. So tiny fractions and multiple infinities should prove hard to grasp (and they are), and atoms and galaxies should prove hard to grasp (and they are). And we should firmly believe that, like the visible light spectrum, perhaps only a thin portion of reality is accessible to us given our cognitive equipment (and it is). We shouldn't too hastily concede that we know or don't know whether reality is or is not, at bottom, random.

Unpredictability may be nothing more than human ignorance and finitude; there may be nothing that is random from God's perspective. And if reality is not unpredictable, then God could plan with certainty that natural processes would produce the results that God intended.

GOD, CHANCE, AND PURPOSE

If reality is random in the strongest sense—that is, if reality is unpredictable in principle (again, even to God)—how could God be creator? Let us assume that mutations are random in the strongest possible sense—mutations are unpredictable in principle. Could God direct the evolutionary process or intend the creation of human beings if it were, at bottom, random in this strong sense? No matter how much God peered into the future, no matter how hard he squinted, he could not have seen which mutations would occur. So, he could not have known with certainty which species natural selection would produce. How could God have used evolution, natural selection, and random mutations to create the beings he intended?

God as Riverboat Gambler

A skilled gambler walks into a riverboat saloon, sits at a table with no idea who he is playing or which cards each player is holding. Over the course of the evening, he loses a hand or two, makes little money on certain hands, and walks out with all of the money from each of his opponents. The skilled gambler was successful because, while he couldn't predict the outcome of any single hand, he could predict, given his vast knowledge of the probabilities, that he would emerge the winner.[6]

God, like the riverboat gambler, may have sufficient knowledge of the probabilities of possible mutations. While a single mutation may be unpredictable, a series of mutations might converge sufficiently for God to manage the natural developmental processes of life. While a single flip of a fair coin might be random, a series of coin flips is not (it will converge on 50% heads and 50% tails). So even if a single mutation is random, a series of mutations might converge sufficiently for God to use knowledge of the convergences to superintend the natural developmental processes of life. A one-shot random process could not be expected to yield purpose. But goal-directed guidance may be possible through knowledge of convergent sequences of mutations. While lacking the certainty of a deterministic system, God might still be able to make "good bets" and so intend the outcomes of his God-created natural, random processes. On this view, God is so finely attuned to the probabilities, he can be certain he'll walk out a winner.

This overstates things a bit. Even with perfect knowledge of all of the relevant probabilities, God *might* walk out a winner. If we think in terms of poker, I think it's certain that God would walk out a winner. No human being could manage probabilities and bets the way God could. But evolution is not poker. God might know enough to get *roughly* what God wants, but the gaps in God's knowledge leave open the possibility that God might not get *precisely* what God wants. For example, God might get something like cabbages and something like human beings, but, given that he's working with probabilities that are out of his control, God cannot guarantee cabbage or, more importantly, Luis Oliveira, Liang Hao, Abbas Yazdani, and Noralynn Masselink.

The unpredictability of mutations implies that even God could not have known *exactly* what creatures would evolve. Even so, it is possible that he could have had some idea of what *types* of creatures would arise. Given his knowledge of the initial conditions and natural laws, God could have known that the process of evolution would produce rational beings. Kenneth Miller, a prominent Christian biologist, contends that evolution is so inherently unpredictable that God could not have known that human beings like us would have arisen. Although God may not have known that they would look or act exactly like us, he could have known that these creatures would at least have free will, consciousness, and self-consciousness. Such a creature might not be a *Homo sapiens*, "it might be a big-brained dinosaur, or it might be a mollusk with exceptional mental capabilities. My point is that I think eventually under the conditions that we have in this universe you would get an intelligent, self-aware and reflective organism, which is to say you'd get something like us. It might not come out of the primates, it might come from somewhere else."[7]

Consider a related example. God might know that if individuals get near water, water creatures, say with fins and a bullet-like body, would evolve (without knowing if they'd be sharks or whales or penguins). Or, God might have known that if individuals get up into the heights and press against the wind, flying creatures would evolve (without knowing if they'd be eagles, insects, or flying squirrels). So, too, God may know that as mammal sizes get larger, the need for cooperation and community would create the "evolutionary space" that highly advanced intelligence (moving into self-consciousness and free will) would fill (without knowing if that space would be filled with Luis Oliveira, Liang Hao, Abbas Yazdani, and Noralynn Masselink).

God as Riverboat Gambler requires a modification of one's views of divine providence. If God must rely on probabilities, he could know only very roughly what sorts of creatures *might* evolve without knowing precisely which ones *would* evolve. He could know that human-like creatures would evolve (free, rational, moral agents), without knowing if those creatures would be Luis Oliveira, Liang Hao, Abbas Yazdani, and Noralynn Masselink.

God as Chess Master

Suppose we consider God as something akin to a chess master. A chess master can't predict her opponent's moves but the chess master will know exactly how she will respond whatever move her opponent makes. That is, the chess master will know, in advance, how to get the result she wants by complete knowledge of her responses to every one of her opponent's possible moves. Response seems not quite the right term; in a sense, she is *pre*sponding to her opponent's moves, although she will have to make her move in time (and so, when it occurs, it appears to be a response). No matter what her opponent does, the chess master will use it to her advantage and produce her inevitable checkmate. So, too, God may have programmed the physical laws and initial conditions to *pre*spond to every contingency. For example, if mutation *a* occurs, God programs in that *X* will occur (to get his desired result), and if mutation *b* occurs, God programs in that *Y* will occur (to achieve his desired result). No matter what happens, God has already programmed in all of the alternate plans for achieving his purposes. If God is Omniscient, then God will know of every possible contingency and be able to plan accordingly. If God is Omnipotent, God is able to adjust the initial conditions and natural laws to accommodate those contingencies and achieve his purposes.

Imagine (to change the metaphor more than slightly) a hungry mouse, which has been placed in a laboratory maze. It smells cheese but is not sure how to get to it. With so many turns and blank walls, it is impossible for the mouse to know where to go. But suppose the scientist has designed the maze so that each pathway in the maze converges on the cheese at the end of the labyrinth. The scientist cannot predict with certainty how the mouse will respond at each juncture. However, the scientist can know, given his knowledge of hungry mice and the setup of the situation, that the mouse will find the cheese. He can't predict the precise path, but he can predict the outcome. He's set up the situation so that no matter what the mouse chooses, he'll end up chomping on cheese.

Likewise, on the Chess Master model, while God may not be able to predict the outcome of each random mutation, it is possible that God could know the various relevant natural tendencies and set up the world with a variety of built-in responses (*pre*sponses), knowing fully well what the ultimate outcome will be—Luis Oliveira, Liang Hao, Abbas Yazdani, and Noralynn Masselink.

God as Santa Claus

Every year Santa makes his annual trip around the globe dropping off presents—based on a precise naughty/nice metric—under the Christmas trees of countless boys and girls. While the children don't know exactly what each box will look like, they know that each box contains a present. The box is irrelevant—it's just a container for a present. The requirement for the box is simply that it be a suitable container—the sort of thing into which the present can fit—but that's about it. The exact shape, size, color wrapping and bow are irrelevant. After all, what makes a present a present is what's *in* the box.

Perhaps what makes humans uniquely human is not their particular body (not being just this tall or wide, or having that color of hair or skin), but what's in the body—a soul. According to this view, God may not have known exactly which sorts of bodies would evolve, but he did know that some body or other would evolve, one that would be capable of sustaining a soul. If God could know that rational beings would evolve (without knowing their precise shape or size), God could then insert God-created souls into them, thus creating human persons. God as Santa Claus doesn't know exactly what each box will look like, but he knows there will be a box (a body capable of housing a soul) and he knows which present he'll put in a box (a unique soul). God knew that he would create you (by inserting your soul into the appropriate body) but not exactly what you would look like.

God as Santa Claus could know that bodies capable of distinctly human capacities (free will, consciousness, and self-consciousness); that is, bodies capable of supporting or interacting with souls would emerge through the evolutionary process, again without knowing exactly what they would look like. God then inserted the soul of Luis Oliveira, Liang Hao, Abbas Yazdani, and Noralynn Masselink, the soul that makes them the individual persons they are, into appropriate containers, thus creating Luis Oliveira, Liang Hao, Abbas Yazdani, and Noralynn Masselink.

The God of the Philosophers

This final alternative for divine creativity given unpredictable mutations affirms the timelessness that is attributed to the so-called God of the

Philosophers. Discussions of God and evolution generally assume that God is inside of time and has to gaze as best he can into a hazy crystal ball to see the future. If reality is unpredictable in principle, then some things about the future cannot be known from present conditions (even for God). If God is in time and reality unpredictable in principle, then the future can't be known with certainty even to God.

But what if God is not in time? What if God is outside of time?

The God of the Philosophers is the God of abstract, unlimited perfection: God is omnipotent, omniscient, immutable, morally perfect, and eternal. The attribute of eternity means that God is outside of and therefore not bound by time. A better term for this position is *timeless eternity*. According to this view, there is no before or after for God; God exists in the eternal now (everything is in the present for God).

Classical Western theism has long held that God exists outside of time. While God's relationship to time is difficult or impossible for humans to grasp, the implication for the present discussion is significant: reality may be unpredictable in principle but God knows the results of random processes with certainty. God does not know by calculation. But even if there are physical processes that are unpredictable in principle—even if God himself could not have predicted their outcome, given knowledge of the initial conditions and natural laws—God knows both the processes *and* outcomes now.

According to this view, if God were fully apprised of the initial conditions and natural laws, he could not have predicted the existence of a single species. So what? This would present no problem for the God of the Philosophers because he does not know "the future" by virtue of predicting it. He knows "the future" by willing it. Since God transcends time, he knows and wills at one and the same time the initial conditions, the physical laws, the random mutations, the current environment, *and* the produced result (say a new species). And he knows the result not by predicting it (which is impossible given randomness) but by willing it.

Here's a way to think about this. A timeless God creates everything—past, present, and future—all at once. So God at once creates the heavens, the earth, and all they contain—from the first amoeba to currently existing humans—*now*. For God, humans are certain because they exist in God's now. So even though God couldn't have predicted the existence of Luis Oliveira, Liang Hao, Abbas Yazdani, and Noralynn Masselink from that first amoeba, he nonetheless ensures their existence not by predicting but by simultaneously willing the evolutionary process that would produce them (in all of its glorious randomness) *and* the result of that process—Luis Oliveira, Liang Hao, Abbas Yazdani, and Noralynn Masselink.

CONCLUSION

How can someone believe in a creator God given the truth of evolution? Young earth creationists and ID theorists say you can't. So you have to choose: faith or science? In all fairness to ID theorists, they do claim the decision is between science and science, but their "science" conceals a deep and intractable faith agenda. Evolution does create a problem for God's achieving God's purposes through an essentially random process. But there are at least four possible models for God acting in the world—God as Riverboat Gambler, God as Chess Master, God as Santa Claus, and the God of the Philosophers[8]—which combine God's creative powers with unpredictability in a variety of ways. If there is a God, then it's possible that God created the world for a purpose. Evolution is not, by definition, blind, pitiless chance.

CHAPTER 8

The Evolution of God?

THE GOD HELMET

Imagine surfing the net and stumbling upon an advertisement in Gadget Universe for a "God helmet," which promises to get you in touch with your god within, reduce your blood pressure, and help you lose 20 pounds of unwanted fat. Results are guaranteed within the safety of your own home—no need to get up early on Sundays for church and no need to give alms to the poor (although the God helmet is $1795, "a bargain at any price but if you act now, you can get it for three easy payments of $595 plus $39.95 shipping/handling"). Ignoring the "snake oil salesman" sign going off in your head, you order your own God helmet. Quivering with excitement when it is finally delivered, you tear the box open, place it on your head, and plug it in. Very soon you fall into a deep, relaxing trance where, for the first time in your life, you feel at one with the universe.[1]

You might scoff at this imagined scenario, but the God helmet is already a reality. Michael Persinger, neurophysiologist at Laurentian University in Ontario, Canada, has developed his own God helmet, clinically called a "transcranial magnetic stimulator." This simple device emits an electromagnetic field that stimulates sectors in the frontal lobe of the brain, creating feelings of an out-of-body experience, oneness with the universe, and a felt presence of the Other. In brief, and not to put too fine a point on it, the God helmet electro-stimulates an experience of God.[2]

The roots of the God helmet are found in neurological studies that use neuroscanning technology to noninvasively study "the spiritual centers of the brain." The physiological benefits of sustained meditation and ritual practices have long been known: lower blood pressure, enhanced immune system (so fewer diseases and less illness), reduced anxiety, and weight loss. But the brain–body–spirit relationship is a mystery that has only recently been scientifically probed. For example, studies of Buddhist and Catholic mystics reveal, despite doctrinal differences, activity in the same areas of the brain—the parietal lobe. The parietal lobe is typically involved with orienting and identifying objects (including one's self) in space and time. When mystics are in a deep meditative state, activity in the parietal lobe is dramatically decreased, generating feelings of boundlessness and timelessness.

Regardless of religious belief, one loses one's sense of an individual self, and of location in space and time; one feels union with God. This, evidently, is the brain on God.

The study of the brain on God, dubbed "neurotheology," aims at understanding the neurophysiological basis of religious experience, meditation, ritual, and religious belief. How is the brain involved in mystical, religious, and spiritual experiences? While some religious believers may find neurotheology threatening, humans are, after all, mind–bodies that are deeply intertwined. Therefore, religious experience must be mediated by mind. If mind–brains are likewise interrelated, religious experiences and beliefs will be processed in the appropriate quadrant(s) of the brain. Just as there are visual and hearing modules of the brain, so too there will be god-modules. So far, no problem. This is just what we should expect of physiologically constituted (even if spiritual) beings such as ourselves. For humans, spirituality will always be embodied.

But neurotheology carries in its wake the threat of reducing God, the Alpha and the Omega,[3] to alpha waves in the brain; that is, God is nothing more than electromagnetic brain stimulations—God exists *solely* in our minds. Prominent philosopher Paul Thagard claims: "Mounting evidence in neuroscience and psychology requires the abandonment of many traditional ideas about the soul, free will, and immortality" (Thagard, 2010: xii). Some neurophysiologists can scarcely conceal their excitement at explaining God away once and for all: "God cannot exist as a concept or as reality any place else but in your mind" (Newberg, 2001: 37). Has neurotheology shown God to be just a phantom floating about in our brain?

Let's temper this excitement with a dose of scientific reality. In spite of all of its promise and bluster, there is precious little evidence to support the claim that we're hard-wired to believe in God. Consider the meager evidence that neurophysiologists Andrew Newberg and Eugene d'Aquili, who enthusiastically pronounce God's sole existence in our mind, adduce in favor of a God neuron: "We must now turn to the normal functioning of 4 tertiary association areas and to their relationship to the limbic system. We postulate that these areas, under certain conditions, may be involved in the genesis of various mystical states, the sense of the divine, and the subjective experience of God" (Newberg, 1993). The use of numbers and technical terms can't conceal their exaggerations: *postulating* something that *may* be involved (*under certain conditions*) in religious experience scarcely amounts to hard scientific evidence. The proclamation of God as brain spasm is premature.

A similar cautionary tale followed the publication of Dean Hamer's *The God Gene: How Faith Is Hardwired into Our Genes* in which Hamer claimed that human spirituality is an adaptive trait, and that he had located the gene responsible for this trait (VMAT2). The "God gene" codes for the release of certain intoxicating brain chemicals that, when released, produce spiritual feelings. In *Time's* sensational cover story, "Is God in Our Genes?" behavioral neuroscientist, Michael Persinger, proclaimed: "God is an artifact of the brain."[4] Upon closer examination, though, it became clear that Hamer had little evidence to support his startling claim—an unreplicated study here, a few anecdotes there, sprinkle in some shoddy statistics and *voilà*, you've got the god gene. The problems run deeper: science has no explanation of how any gene (or the brain for that matter) produces any bits of behavior or conscious experience. We haven't discovered a gay gene (which Hamer also claims to have identified), a thrill-seeking gene, a musicality gene and not, for god's sake, a god gene. After a scathing critique of the book in *Scientific American,* Carl Zimmer suggested changing the title to *A Gene That Accounts for Less Than One Percent of the Variance Found in Scores on Psychological Questionnaires Designed to Measure a Factor Called Self-Transcendence, Which Can Signify Everything from Belonging to the Green Party to Believing in ESP, According to One Unpublished, Unreplicated Study.*

What about that God helmet, then? Doesn't it prove that there's a god-spot in the brain? Despite Persinger's claims to an 80 percent success rate in producing spiritual experiences, attempts to scientifically replicate Persinger's study have come to naught. Perhaps the power of suggestion, not electro-magnetism, produced the spiritual high. Richard Dawkins, seeking a spiritual experience if not enlightenment, embarked on a pilgrimage to Persinger's laboratory. After he was fitted with the God helmet and seated comfortably in a silent, dark room, his temporal lobes were electro-massaged. But he didn't see God or have a spiritual high. He was not one with the universe and failed to transcend his self or body. He experienced no euphoria. He didn't even experience relaxation or pleasantness. Nothing (but not nothing-ness). If you were thinking of investing in a God helmet, hoping for a quick and easy path to enlightenment, better just to save your money.

God As Nothing But

Neurotheologians have sought in vain to show that God is nothing but a brain spasm, a figment of the human imagination. According to the creators of the God helmet, God-spasms (religious beliefs) are the products of perfectly natural electromagnetic processes. Come up with the natural explanation of the origin of religious belief and you eliminate the need for a supernatural explanation. But, so far, they have failed to come up with a natural explana-tion. But wait, wait. More natural explanations of religious belief are on offer. According to philosopher Daniel Dennett, God is nothing but an evolution-arily induced figment of our imagination. Science, according to Dennett, has shown us that *God is a collective illusion or a delusion* fobbed off on us by our genes (Dennett, 2007). He's not alone in this judgment. Biologist Richard Dawkins, in *The God Delusion*, claims that God is, no surprises here, a delu-sion: "The irrationality of religion is a byproduct of a particular built-in irra-tionality mechanism in the brain" (Dawkins, 2006: 214). Both Dennett and Dawkins hold that something about our cognitive makeup, something about the human mind, makes us susceptible to god-beliefs. Once the natural (and irrational) cognitive processes that forge belief in God are uncovered, belief in God, lacking all rational foundation, will slowly wither away.

Here's a way to think of it. Children naturally believe what their parents tell them. Their parents tell them there's a Santa Claus, and they lack the rational powers to resist the suggestion of their parents. So they believe in Santa Claus. God is like Santa Claus.

"He's making a list, checking it twice, gonna find out who's naughty or nice," so goes the popular Christmas song. This part of the song could apply equally well to Santa or to God. Santa and God both care about the moral successes and failings of human beings and are completely in the know about who's naughty or nice. Both have the ability and desire to do something in response to and even encourage improvement in the naughty/nice ratio: Santa by dispensing presents on Christmas day, God by dispensing judgment. These are striking similarities, but they share an even more striking dissimilarity: while no (sane) adult believes in Santa, most believe in God (in the United States, over 90%); it's relatively easy to be cured of Santa beliefs; on the other hand, God-beliefs are, like the common cold, harder to shake.

Dennett views this as both lamentable and ludicrous: "The kindly God who lovingly fashioned each and every one of us and sprinkled the sky with shining stars for our delight—that God is, like Santa Claus, a myth of childhood, not anything a sane, undeluded adult could literally believe in" (Dennett, 1995: 18). Even though belief in God is only for the insane or deluded, Dennett concedes that the God-delusion is contagious. The God delusion is, like God, omnipresent: people around the world and throughout time believe in God.

Consider how belief in Santa Claus withers away. Parents tell gullible young children that Santa visits every house in the world showering presents on good boys and girls. When the older child learns that the cause of her belief in Santa was a fabrication, one created and sustained by gullibility, she stops believing in Santa. Suppose, following Dawkins and Dennett, we come to believe that our brains very naturally fabricate god-beliefs. Would that show that it's time for humanity to grow up and stop believing in God?

HUME'S NATURAL EXPLANATION OF RELIGION

Dawkins and Dennett follow in a long line of thinkers who claim to have pried the lid off the mind and peered inside to identify the true, nongod, cause of religious belief. By plumbing the psyche, they reveal the secret springs and levers that produce beliefs in gods. Just beneath the surface of belief in Omnipotent Love lurk murky motivations and selfish urges. Systematic and nearly universal self-deception sustain the illusion that reason or religious experience support belief in God. Dawkins and Dennett have rolled away the stone to reveal God the Delusion. But they didn't get there first; they apprenticed at the feet of the masters of suspicion: Sigmund Freud and Karl Marx. Freud and Marx claim to have uncovered the ignoble origins of religious belief and hence to have unmasked its untruth. The four of them—Dawkins, Dennett, Freud, and Marx—share a common intellectual ancestor: David Hume.

Psychologist Sigmund Freud believed that humans are fundamentally constituted by drives or instincts. A variety of these natural instincts manufacture god-beliefs. For example, Freud contends that religion is nothing more than the projection of human properties onto unfeeling and hostile nature in the hope that ultimate reality (God) is father-like. With uncharacteristic understatement he writes: "We find reality generally quite unsatisfactory." So we create a "God" who tames and personalizes nature; unable to tolerate the belief that reality is conspiring against us, we are driven by our insecurities and impotence to believe that reality is on our side, cares for us, and rewards us for our sufferings. Religion, according to Freud, is a kind of immaturity for those who can't face up to the frightening realities of nature (Freud, 1927).

Karl Marx criticized religion as a tool for maintaining the status quo of oppression, by urging the working class to accept the conditions of oppression in this life in exchange for the hope of something better in "heaven." Religion, the opiate of the masses, dulls the pain of injustice, which inhibits the oppressed from pursuing justice.

Freud and Marx concur that natural but ignoble forces—envy, resentment, fear, sexual drives, and so on—conspire to produce belief in gods; these beliefs are produced neither by God nor by reason.

Like Dawkins, Dennett, Marx, and Freud, Hume (1711–76) judged most religious beliefs irrational yet was curious about why so many apparently rational people could believe in them. If not reason, then what natural forces drive people to belief in God? In order to understand Dawkins's and Dennett's critique of religion, let's consider Hume and his arguments.

A character in Tom Stoppard's play *Jumpers* declares of the modern atheist: "Well, the tide is running his way, and it is a tide that has turned only once in human history. There is presumably a calendar date—a moment—when the onus of proof passed from the atheist to the believer, when, quite suddenly, secretly, the 'noes' have it."[5] Philosopher Stephen Cahn locates that calendar date in the 1779 publication of David Hume's *Dialogues Concerning Natural Religion* (Cahn, 1988: 63). Because of that book, Hume is widely perceived as undermining any possible rational defense of belief in God. With theism lacking a foundation in reason, atheism becomes the live alternative: the "noes" have it. It will just take time for everyone to see that Hume has indeed turned the tide of history.

David Hume was so attracted to philosophy while a university student (at the tender age of 11 or 12) that he feigned study of the law all the while poring over the great Greek and Roman philosophers. When overstudy of philosophy threatened his health he, as one might expect, tried his hand at the business of importing sugar. When business failed to hold his attention, he returned to his first love to write one of the great classics of philosophy, *Treatise of Human Nature*. Although he expected it to revolutionize philosophy, instead it "fell deadborn from the press." The tide may have started turning but it would turn rather more slowly than Hume had hoped.

Hume is a curious tide-turner for atheism. Although even unto death his religious views were unclear, followers and critics alike have been eager to ascribe beliefs to him (usually their own). His self-composed, fill in the blank epitaph is typically unrevealing: "Born 1711, Died [—]. Leaving it to posterity to add the rest." He was certainly a critic of many religious beliefs—beliefs in miracles and life after death, as well as the excesses of Catholicism and Calvinism—so much so that "murmuring zealots" accused him of skepticism and atheism his entire life. Yet denying some Christian beliefs is not tantamount to affirming atheism, and he almost certainly believed in some sort of god (Gaskin, 1988). Nonetheless, he has become the patron saint of modern atheists who eagerly attribute their own beliefs to Hume. If nothing else, this much is certain: David Hume—skeptic, atheist, agnostic, theist, whatever—wrote a lot about religion.

Hume's discussion of religion revolved around two topics: "As every enquiry which regards religion is of the utmost importance, there are two questions in particular which challenge our attention, to wit, that concerning its foundation in reason, and that concerning its origin in human nature" (Hume, 1957: Intro). Consider the first, the foundation of religion in reason: Hume has been credited with demolishing religion once and for all (Google "Hume" and "demolish" or "demolition" and you'll find thousands of citations in support of this dubious claim). Dennett and Dawkins concur: Hume demolished religion. The second topic is the natural origin of religious belief; that is, how can we understand religion as a natural phenomenon? Here's a way of putting the second question: if religious beliefs are irrational, how is it that so many (apparently rational) people acquire and maintain them?

Hume did not conceive of himself as the demolisher of all things religious. About the first topic, he writes: "Happily, the first question, which is the most important, admits of the most obvious, at least, the clearest solution. The whole frame of nature bespeaks an intelligent author; and no rational enquirer can, after serious reflection, suspend his belief a moment with regard to the primary principles of genuine Theism and Religion" (Hume, 1957: 21). Hume's claim that genuine religion finds rational support makes one wonder, of course, what Hume meant by "genuine religion." Many claim that Hume's profession of rational religion was disingenuous; after all, in 1697, Thomas Aikenhead was hanged in Edinburgh for professing atheism. But Hume seemed content to let charges of atheism swirl around him (without fear for his neck). While Hume clearly rejects the more robust beliefs of, say, Christians and Muslims, as rationally unfounded, he seems to have affirmed a much more minimal theism of a supreme intelligence that creates the world. His affirmation of faith may have been something like: "I believe in God the Creator, the sorta mighty."

His personal beliefs aside, here is Hume's question: What has moved so many people in so many different places at so many different times in history to believe in God?

Most primitive peoples, people of the hunting and gathering variety, had precious little time left over for philosophizing: rational reflection on the whole of nature. Yet they nearly universally believed in gods. So, it seems, there must have been some other cause of their belief than reasoned reflection.

So Hume wonders: What is it that disposes human beings to beliefs in gods? Religion, Hume contends, arises from the very ordinary human passions of hope and fear, particularly in "the anxious concern for happiness, the dread of future misery, the terror of death, the thirst of revenge, the appetite for food and other necessaries" (Hume, 1957: 166). Our fears, when combined with ignorance of the true causes of natural processes, contribute to beliefs in invisible intelligent powers. He writes: "No wonder, then, that mankind, being placed in such an absolute ignorance of causes, and being at the same time so anxious concerning their future fortune, should immediately acknowledge a dependence on invisible powers, possessed of sentiment and intelligence" (Hume, 1957: 30).

Hume would concur with John Dewey, who wrote: "There can be no doubt... of our dependence upon forces beyond our control. Primitive man was so impotent in the face of these forces that, especially in an unfavorable natural environment, fear became a dominant attitude, and, as the old saying goes, fear created gods" (Dewey, 1998: 409). Hume's guess about the natural origin of religion would only very recently find confirmation. Recent work in the cognitive and evolutionary psychology of religion sounds remarkably Hume-like. It is precisely to this research that Dawkins and Dennett appeal in support of their claim that God is a delusion.

BELIEVING IS NOT SEEING: THE DEATH OF OLD-SCHOOL EMPIRICISM

Hume is doubly relevant to this discussion. He is not only the intellectual godfather of Dawkins and Dennett (beating them to the punch by some two hundred years), he also defended old-school *empiricism*—the claim that *all knowledge comes through our senses*. Empiricism, following Aristotle, holds that there is nothing in the mind which is not first in the senses. Every genuine item of human knowledge is acquired through seeing, hearing, touching, tasting, or smelling: seeing is believing (better, "Believing is seeing"). The mind, prior to the acquisition of sensations is, to use John Locke's quaint phrase, a blank slate; experiences enter in and write clearly on that slate. The mind, to start my own quaint metaphor, is an empty cup waiting for experience to fill it up. According to old-school empiricism, there are no innate ideas—we are not born with mental tools (concepts or categories) through which we understand experience. In fact, all of our mental tools arise through sensory experience (and reflection on experiences). We enter the world mentally naked—with an empty mind–brain. While the Dawkins–Dennett naturalistic critique of religion has a great deal of current cache, old-school empiricism has gasped its last breath.

One day I was walking across my campus and saw someone walking toward me from afar. After quickly identifying the person, I yelled out, "Hi, Eddy." Receiving no reply, I charged forward, indignant. But when I got closer, I saw that the person whom I had greeted so enthusiastically was not Eddy and was, in fact, someone I had never seen before. Embarrassed, I mumbled something indistinct and slunk off in the other direction. My embarrassment is of little interest, but what I saw is: cognitive science suggests that I *saw* Eddy. My senses received various bits of incomplete sensory information that approximated Eddy. Some cognitive modules in my mind operated on those, filling in various details, producing a vision of Eddy. My mind was not the passive receptacle of sensations assumed by old-school empiricism, it was an active contributor to my perception!

Old-school empiricism has been decisively refuted by recent developments in cognitive science. Cognitive science is a relatively new discipline that unites psychology, neuroscience, computer science, linguistics, and philosophy in the study of the operations of the mind/brain. It is concerned with how the mind processes information—how information is acquired, stored, retrieved, ordered, and used. The scientific study of the thinking mind has considered many functions and capacities of the mind, including perception, attention, memory, pattern recognition, concept formation, consciousness, reasoning, problem-solving, language-processing, and forgetting. Cognitive science refutes old-fashioned empiricism: we have inbuilt cognitive systems, faculties, or modules that process information and produce immediate, nonreflective beliefs. Our minds are not (and never were) blank slates (Eysenck, 2010).

In short, cognitive science studies how the mind works. It considers a host of fascinating questions, such as: How do we get information about the world? What is that information like? How is that information processed by our minds? What is the view of the world that the mind produces? Cognitive science holds that our minds come equipped with a set of cognitive faculties that actively processes our perceptions and shapes our conceptions of the world. Our cognitive faculties actively receive and mold our experiential input into output beliefs about the world. We take in a little bit of data, our mind actively processes it, and out pops the world (or, more precisely, our conception of the world).

Old-school empiricists claim that our mental faculties don't "add" to our experience. If this were true, though, we should be skeptics about nearly every important area of human inquiry. In a nutshell, the skeptical problem is that our experiential input (present moment, finite, fleeting) is insufficient to support our belief/knowledge output: the world (past, present, future, enduring, other persons, etc.). We have minimal experiential input and massive informational output (Sternberg, 2012: 21, 193–205, 212–13). Even if we were to use logic and mathematics to order our experience, the world presented to us in our finite experience would pale in comparison to the infinitely rich and vast world we believe in. Our own experience provides a paucity of information incapable of supporting our knowledge of the world. Think of the world: it extends into the distant past and proceeds into the unforeseen future; its physical dimensions are both inconceivably vast and microscopically tiny; it includes people, some of whom lived long ago and far away, and it includes me, a being who is conscious and self-conscious and who persists through time. Now think of your own puny experiences: could they, when supplemented with the rules of logic and mathematics, produce this vast world (or, more precisely, rational beliefs about the world)? Even if we were to add the experiences of others to our repository of information, we would be incapable of inferring to the vast world. Fortunately, where experience and logic alone must fail, we are equipped with cognitive faculties that contribute substantially to our beliefs about the world (Greco, 2000).

BORN TO BELIEVE

Numerous experiments in cognitive science reveal that in spite of our beliefs about the thoroughness of our experiences, perceptual inputs provide only fragmentary sketches of the world around us that are in turn "colored in" by various cognitive tools or modules. Research in this area demonstrates that sensory experience underdetermines our beliefs about the world around us.[6] For example, studies in so-called change-blindness show our remarkable inability to attend to more than a single item within our visual experience; various items in our visual experience, those we are not attending to, are not impressed upon our minds (as old-school empiricism claims). Though real and part of our visual sensations, we simply ignore most of what we experience. In addition, dramatic changes in what we experience are totally missed by our mind (and then we seamlessly incorporate the new sensations with the old ones) (Simons and Levin, 1997, 1998; and Simons, 2000).

What, in addition to our five senses, are some of these cognitive faculties?

The Memory Faculty

Consider your belief that you ate bread for breakfast. Since that belief concerns the past, you can't see, hear, touch, taste, or smell the bread. If you were an old-fashioned empiricist, you should be skeptical of that belief. Fortunately for us, we have a memory faculty that is as much a part of the human constitution as our five senses.

Theory of Mind (ToM)

How do you know that other people exist? And by this I mean *persons*—things like you with thoughts, feelings, and desires. The character Data, from *Star Trek: the Next Generation,* was not a person. He had the body of a person but he lacked the characteristic inner life so essential to being a person. Poke Data as many times as you like and, not being a person, he will never feel pain; reject him, and he will never feel sad. He may elicit pain behavior (by yelling "Ouch!" and moving his arm) or sadness behavior (by crying) but, not being a person, he can't feel pain or sorrow. How do you know that there are any other people in the world besides you? How do you know that all the "people" in the world are not just so many more Datas—cleverly constructed robots with excellent makeup jobs? How do you know that behind all those person facades lie persons—individuals with thoughts, desires, and feelings? You can't experience another person's feelings; you can't see another person's thoughts (even if you were to cut off the top of their head and peer into their brain); even Bill Clinton can't really feel another person's pain. Yet thoughts, desires, and feelings are all essential to being a person. So you can't tell from the outside or just by looking, so to speak, if someone is a person. I can know that *I* am a person because I experience my own thoughts, feelings, and desires. But I can't see or feel, because I don't have any access to your inner-experience, if you or anyone else is a person. So if old-school empiricism were true, we could never believe in the existence of any other persons. Cognitive science has shown that our belief in other persons—in their inner self—is produced by a cognitive faculty called, not surprisingly, "Theory of Mind" (Baron-Cohen, 2000). While we can't see other minds, we nonetheless have a built-in mental detector.

Belief in the Past

So far, we've listed and discussed memory and ToM; what other cognitive faculties do we have? We also believe that there is a past. This may seem odd, but this belief is assumed in every historical belief that we have; for example, that Caesar crossed the Rubicon or that the Chinese invented gunpowder. I couldn't possibly have any sensations or experiences of Caesar in a boat or any ancient Chinese inventor, so if I had to rely solely on my senses, such beliefs would be irrational. Bertrand Russell once asked, "How do you know that you weren't created five minutes ago with your memories intact?" And while this may seem a silly philosophical question, it does show the limits of our sensory knowledge. Lucky for us, we are cognitively disposed to reliably form beliefs about the past. All this assumes that there is a past—that the world was not created five minutes ago—an assumption that cannot be based on any present experiences.

The Uniformity of Nature

Even in science, that formidable fortress of experiential and experimental confirmation and refutation, one must simply accept without proof the uniformity of nature. That is, one must assume that the future will be like the past and that laws hold everywhere in the universe, not just in our local domain. Science makes generalizations about the behavior of everything everywhere based on a finite set of extremely limited experiences. We couldn't possibly have experiences or sensations of those parts of the universe that exceed our senses (we cannot see everything in the universe). In addition, the future likewise exceeds our experiential grasp. We can pile finite experiences on top of finite experiences, but we will never be able to infer anything about *every* object *everywhere* (without assuming the uniformity of nature). The practice of science would be impossible without our natural cognitive ability to generalize from a paltry, finite set of data to everything everywhere at every time: past, present, and future.

We have an inborn tendency or disposition to believe what we remember, that there are other persons, that there is a past, and that the future will be like the past. What is significant about these cognitive faculties is that they could not be justified by or derived from our five senses. Without them, though, we would have precious little knowledge of the world.

Reason Is Overrated

One more point—a psychological point of some philosophical significance: the vast majority of beliefs produced by our cognitive faculties, by our innate tendencies to believe, are formed in us *immediately*, without reasoning to them or inferring them from other beliefs ("immediate" implies that they are not mediated by or derived from other beliefs) (Clark, 1990). Cognitive scientists call such beliefs *intuitive* or *nonreflective*. With nonreflective beliefs, we don't slowly reflect on a body of data, then make a careful inference about which belief is best supported by the data. Nonreflective beliefs are produced in us instantly, as it were, by the direct operation of the relevant cognitive faculty. We don't reason to such beliefs; if anything, we simply trust them and use them to build up our knowledge of the world and to live our lives. We remember that we had bread for breakfast, we believe in the past, we hold that the future will be like the past, and we assume that there is an enduring world independent of our present experience of it. We couldn't possibly *reason to* most of our beliefs about the world based just on our five senses (Greco, 2000; Plantinga, 1993).[7]

Of course, not all of our beliefs are immediate or nonreflective. Some beliefs are acquired and maintained because of other beliefs we hold. After hearing testimony at a trial, one might infer that the defendant is guilty. After weighing the evidence, one may come to believe that green tea improves health. Scientific theories (such as beliefs that there are electrons or that $E = mc^2$) are often accepted after conducting certain experiments or after the observational evidence has been carefully examined. But acceptance of scientific theories assumes a great deal that can't be proven (even Einstein assumed the uniformity of nature and the truths of mathematics), and most of us believe most scientific theories simply because someone told us (perhaps by reading them in a book).

Here's a way to look at it: we are creatures. Creatures are finite, limited, dependent, and, typically, fallible. We can't reason up from our fives senses to the world. Try as we might, it just can't be done. Old-school empiricism is wrong. We creatures depend on our naturally outfitted, inborn cognitive equipment to help us grasp reality.

Born Believers: The Cognitive Science of Religion

For most of the twentieth century, anthropologists, assuming that cultural groups are radically different, were keen to seek out those differences.

For example, while some cultures are scared of mice, others eat them alive (where part of the culinary delight is, upon biting, hearing that one last squeak). Some people delight in watching cats lowered alive into a fire on stage, others keep them as pets and treat them like children. That's just cats and mice (and just four different cultures). Check out any twentieth-century anthropology book and you'll see vast differences among cultures. However, studies in cognitive science show that, in spite of these apparent differences, humans share a great many fundamental beliefs. How could that be given the vastness of time and space that separate human beings?

The cognitive science answer goes as follows: Humans share roughly similar beliefs because we have similar minds (that is, we have similar cognitive faculties). Our common biological heritage produced relatively similar minds—evolutionary forces shaped minds with virtually identical cognitive equipment. When those minds are put to work in roughly similar environments, they produce roughly similar beliefs. Given fairly similar environments, humans are presented with roughly the same challenges to their survival (the needs for food, say, or mates). So evolutionary processes equipped humans with similar cognitive faculties and, when those faculties are applied to their specific (yet fairly similar) challenges, we should expect to find similar beliefs. Beneath vast surface cultural differences we find very real and deep similarities both in cognitive processing and in the beliefs these processes produce. Therefore, virtually every person in every culture possesses all of the cognitive faculties mentioned above and so will have similar (but not identical) beliefs: belief in persons, memory beliefs, belief in the past, and so on.

Some of these other common cognitive faculties are involved in the origin and development of religious beliefs. The cognitive science of religion has given us good reason to believe that we have a natural, instinctive religious sense—a god-faculty.[8]

Agency-detecting Device

Suppose you're walking in the woods and see bent blades of grass all pointing in the same direction, and you instantly form the belief that there's a food source nearby (a rabbit, say, or a deer). Or perhaps while strolling on the beach, you see a foot-shaped indentation in the sand and immediately believe that another person (a possible mate or an enemy) or even a food source had walked there. Or you're sound asleep and hear a sharp, strange noise in your home, and you sit up quickly, believing there's an intruder in your house. These and countless similar instances are evidence that human beings come equipped with a cognitive faculty (sometimes called *an agency-detecting device [ADD]*) that generates beliefs about agency—the belief that something or someone has the ability to act.

This ADD is activated sometimes with just the slightest stimulation. When stimulated, our ADD immediately (that is, nonreflectively or non-inferentially) produces beliefs in an agent—a being who can act (perhaps to harm us or even to help us). The evolutionary advantage of agency detection is obvious: without such immediate beliefs/responses to certain motions (rustling bushes) or sounds (things going bump in the night), we might end up as food for a predator or the victim of an enemy. Reflection would usually prove detrimental to our well-being. Imagine if our primitive ancestors had relied on thoughtful reflection: "Hmm, that was a loud and possibly scary noise, now wasn't it? I wonder what could have caused it? The wind, the plumbing, or a lion? No, [sticking a finger out the window] it's not windy, so it couldn't have been the wind. Plumbing hasn't been invented yet. Must've been a lion. Yep, that's it, a lion." By the end of such a reflective process that primitive philosopher would have ended up as lion lunch.

"Better safe than sorry" is the standard operating procedure of ADD. Responding quickly to dangerous situations has added health benefits: if your philosophy were "slow and steady" and you were to rely on careful reflection, you likely wouldn't win the race; in fact, you'd likely wind up dead. So our evolved ADD is highly sensitive—we instantly respond without rational reflection to the slightest provocation. Psychologist Justin Barrett has given a widely accepted name to this disposition: the *hypersensitive agency detection device* (known better by its acronym, HADD).

Evolutionary processes selected cognitive faculties that produce *immediate* response/beliefs without the aid of reflection precisely because of the urgency of these sorts of situations. Like lungs and hearts, nature has equipped us with automatic cognitive processes that are essential to our survival.

Theory of Mind Revisited

After HADD detects agency, another cognitive faculty, which cognitive scientists call the *Theory of Mind* (*ToM*), quickly kicks in and attributes beliefs, desires, and purposes to the postulated agent. ToM hardwires our social awareness: it moves us to consider, contemplate, believe in, and even feel the presence of conscious minds. ToM takes us from the simple belief that there's an agent who acts, to an agent who acts *mindedly*, that is, with intentions or purposes. The attribution of intentions or purposes to agents is useful: if we believe an agent has a purpose (to eat us, steal from us, mate with us), we not only act or react, we can plan. Suppose you are walking through a dark alley and you see someone lurking in the shadows. You will likely attribute intentions to that agent—is he or she there to help or harm? Based on your beliefs about his or her intentions, you adjust your actions accordingly.

ToM may have developed so that humans could better negotiate their tricky relationships with human competitors. We could not function socially without ToM. The better humans became at detecting purposes, the better they became at anticipating the plans of nearby human competitors and then acting accordingly. But ToM seeped from beliefs about humans into beliefs about nonhuman agents. It spread everywhere. We not only see human faces, we see, as anthropologist Stewart Guthrie writes, faces in the clouds (Guthrie, 1995).

The God-faculty

HADD and ToM not only produce beliefs in animals and embodied enemies (and friends), they also produce belief in gods. If ordinary people can't
explain their own experiences, they might find themselves immediately
believing in extraordinary persons: supernatural beings, including ghosts,
angels, or gods. Really big events such as floods and thunder may require
really big agents. When HADD gives way to ToM, big reasons are assigned
to big agents for the big things they do. We attribute adequate powers and
purposes to the causes of great events: only a very powerful, minded agent
could cause such extraordinary events (and for extraordinary reasons). So we
attribute super qualities—super powers and super knowledge, for example—
to the causes of super events.

In these sorts of circumstances, HADD produces god-beliefs immediately, and ToM attributes intentions to the postulated super agent. For sake
of shorthand, *we shall call ToM, taken together with HADD, the god-faculty.*
For the formula-friendly (and to the horror of cognitive scientists):

$$HADD + ToM => God\text{-}beliefs^9$$

Such HADD-produced god-beliefs include a host of beliefs in extraordinary human-like beings including, for example, fairies, elves, witches, and
demons. For our purposes, we will call such beliefs "god-beliefs," or just
"God."

Belief in God, then, is a natural belief produced by our inborn cognitive
faculties.[10] If a belief is natural, it does not imply that the belief is true; we
also each have a natural disposition to believe we are better than average, and
it can't be true that everyone is better than average. So a naturally produced
religious belief is not, thereby, a true religious belief.

Being equipped with HADD and ToM does not mean that everyone
believes in God; a natural, instinctive belief could be overridden by, say,
the influence of unbelieving parents or a government that institutionally
enforces atheism. Or one might be naturally inclined toward religious belief
but reject it perhaps due to experiences of suffering. But the cognitive science
of religion does claim that in the right circumstances, even among atheists,
god-beliefs will find their way into one's thoughts. From angry exclamations
of unfairness aimed at the god one does not believe in to the prayers of a
soldier in heated battle ("there are no atheists in foxholes"), the god-faculty
continues to assert itself. The dramatic rise in religious belief in post-Maoist
China suggests that the god-faculty reasserts itself with just the slightest cultural encouragement (or removal of cultural discouragement).

God: The Evolutionary Problem

Consider the most seriously committed religious practitioners—priests and
monks. Priests and monks spend a great deal of their time in ritual activities,

not hunting and gathering. The buildings that they use for their ritual practices, usually constructed at vast expense to their communities, neither store grains nor house animals. Finally, they are often celibate; in the days of old, they may have overseen virgin sacrifices. Priests and monks are evolutionary problems.

Although natural selection favored HADD and ToM, surely it opposed religious beliefs. Religious beliefs are evolutionarily *costly*—celibacy is hardly the secret to evolutionary success. Evolution favors traits that help an individual live long enough to reproduce and so pass on its genes to succeeding generations. Whatever inhibits reproductive success is an evolutionary problem. Religious practices should have been selected out—they are an evolutionary problem.

While extraordinary religious practices such as celibacy and the sacrifice of virgins hinder reproductive success, even more ordinary religious practices seem evolutionarily maladaptive. In times of scarcity, which were most times for our primitive ancestors, ritual sacrifices of highly valuable commodities such as grain and animals were inconducive to survival. Because they take time away from hunting, gathering, and reproducing, worship and prayer are costly. Religious beliefs and practices are evolutionarily costly.

How, then, could such costly practices have become common, natural, even normal? Why weren't costly religious beliefs mercilessly excised by the razor of natural selection?

Most evolutionary accounts of religion hold that religious beliefs and practices in themselves have no survival value (Atran, 2002). However, the *faculties* that produce such beliefs—HADD and ToM—did and do have survival value: they developed to help us fight or flee predators and enemies, and to anticipate our adversaries' purposes, and, among many other things, to find and secure mates. But god-beliefs and practices don't help us fight, flee, feed, or reproduce; so, *they* don't have survival value.[11]

While HADD and ToM *were* produced by evolutionary processes, god-beliefs, very likely, were not: god-beliefs are little more than accidental, "unintended" byproducts of HADD and ToM. While HADD and ToM were "intended" to produce predator, mate, and enemy beliefs, they also happened to produce god-beliefs. Because HADD and ToM helped humans to be successful in avoiding predators and foiling enemies, their side-effect god-beliefs were not (or perhaps could not be) selected out. The evolutionary benefits of HADD and ToM outweighed the costs of religious beliefs. The bottom line: belief in gods is an accidental or byproduct belief.

Byproducts

Traits that are *byproducts*, not direct consequences of natural selection, are not uncommon.[12] Natural selection seeks adaptive traits, ones that improve one's reproductive success (by increasing the chances of producing offspring). But such traits are sometimes accompanied by another trait that is not adaptive, one that on its own would never have been selected. For example, the redness of blood is a byproduct of hemoglobin's ability to store oxygen (hemoglobin turns red when oxygenated). The wrinkles on your knuckles are byproducts of your evolutionarily successful ability to bend your fingers. Byproducts are accidental, nonadaptive extras; they are not adaptive traits.

A *byproduct belief*, then, is a belief that is a byproduct of faculties designed for the production of other sorts of beliefs. If all of the above is correct, religious belief is a nonadaptive byproduct belief—and a costly one at that. What started off as a perfectly good predator and enemy-detector, mate-seeker, or food-finder went awry, so say Dawkins and Dennett, in the production of belief in gods. Without rational reflection to rein in the god-faculty, it turned from evolutionarily expectable people and predator beliefs to beliefs in gods who "explain" the weather, motions of the planets, success in hunting or growing crops, good and bad fortune, disease, and even death.

Religious beliefs are like the redness of blood and knuckle-wrinkles— neither essential nor intended by evolution; religion is nothing more than an accidental, unintended byproduct of perfectly natural processes.

Explaining God Away?

If this standard evolutionary account of religion—belief as byproduct—is correct, what follows about the status or rationality of religious belief? Could an accidental, byproduct belief be anything but irrational? Doesn't the cognitive science of religion show that evolutionary forces, not a supernatural being, cause religious beliefs? And those forces intended to get us attuned to predators, enemies, and mates, not gods. If any beliefs should be produced, they should concern animals or humans. But the god-faculty ran rampant, producing extravagant and unintended beliefs in ghosts and gods. So as we've seen, Dennett claims that the god-faculty is a "fiction-generating contraption" (Dennett, 2006: 120); Dawkins is no less dismissive: "The irrationality of religion is a byproduct of a particular built-in irrationality mechanism in the brain" (Dawkins, 2006: 184). Or as Yale psychologist Paul Bloom puts it, religion is "an incidental byproduct of cognitive functioning gone awry" (Bloom, 2005). According to Dawkins and Dennett, evolutionary, natural explanations of religious belief make supernatural beliefs irrational; the evolutionary psychology of religion doesn't just explain God, it explains God away.

Natural versus Supernatural Explanations

Some argue that the rational underpinning of religious belief is removed when a natural explanation for religious belief is discovered. So Matthew Alper, author of *The God Part of the Brain,* claims that "[i]f belief in God is produced by a genetically inherited trait...this would imply that there is no actual spiritual reality, no God or gods, no soul, or afterlife" (Alper, 2000). Identify the natural explanation, and a supernatural explanation is superfluous. For example, if one believed in God because one believed that God brought the sun and the rain, then learning that physical processes account for the weather patterns would pull the rug out from under one's belief in God. If there's a perfectly acceptable natural explanation for some phenomenon, there's no need for a supernatural explanation.

This sort of argument assumes that a supernatural God could not have used natural processes to accomplish God's purposes. Does the discovery that belief in God is produced by natural cognitive processes preclude a supernatural explanation of belief in God? Could there be two noncompeting, even complementary, explanations of the same phenomenon?

Suppose you were traveling through space and, on the far frontier, discovered writing in the stars that said, "Made By God." Startled, you begin to think, in the face of this powerful evidence, "Wow, the universe *was* made by God!"

Sulu, your physicist, is intrigued but unconvinced. She cosmologically calculates, starting at the Big Bang and extrapolating from the laws of physics, that the "Made By God" sign was an expectable result of perfectly natural processes. So she concludes: "Nothing special here. This sign was not God-produced, it was produced by natural processes." The natural explanation, she contends, eliminates the supernatural explanation.

You note the obvious: a supernatural God could have used God-designed natural processes to make the sign, "Made By God." A natural and a supernatural explanation could both be true.

If it's possible for a supernatural God to use natural processes to accomplish God's purposes, then it's possible for God to intend for religious beliefs to be produced by (supernaturally designed) natural processes. By pointing out the natural explanation then, one has not thereby precluded a supernatural explanation. After all, God may have created through evolutionary processes a faculty that makes humans aware of God. Religious beliefs are processed through our naturally produced, ordinary cognitive faculties. No surprise there. But then showing that natural processes are involved would not thereby show that the god-beliefs are a delusion. As philosopher Alvin Plantinga writes: "To show that there are natural processes that produce religious belief does nothing to discredit it; perhaps God designed us in such a way that it is by virtue of those processes that we come to have knowledge of him" (Plantinga, 2000: 145).

Science and Simplicity

Sulu the scientist, after listening patiently, objects: "Sure, it's possible that there be both a natural and supernatural explanation of exactly the same phenomenon, but it's not necessary to accept the supernatural explanation once a natural explanation has been discovered. God might have caused the sun and rain by natural processes, but it's not necessary to believe in a God that did so. And God might have erected the 'Made By God' sign, but why go beyond what is necessary to believe? I accept the principle of simplicity: we should believe only what is required to explain the data. If we have a complete natural explanation of some phenomenon in question, then there's no need to look beyond that for an additional but unnecessary explanation. While a supernatural explanation of natural processes is possible, one should not bring in the supernatural unless it is rationally required. To paraphrase Occam's razor: don't multiply explanations beyond necessity. One *should not* because one *need not* appeal to the supernatural."

Sulu gives you pause, but then you realize that she is simply being a scientist. You, however, were not being a scientist. You did not offer God as a scientific theory, as the best or the simplest scientific explanation of the data. You didn't offer God as a theory at all. You concede that the scientist should preclude *scientific* appeals to the supernatural from the practice of science. The scientist, you believe, should simply be silent, as scientist, about whether or not there is (or is not) a complementary supernatural explanation of the data. You just found yourself believing in God.

Moreover, you remind yourself that you don't believe in other persons because they have been proven to exist scientifically or because they are the simplest explanation of person-like behavior. It's simpler to believe that only you exist (and that other persons are just figments of your imagination). If only you exist, then there's only one thing. What could be simpler? If you were to rigidly believe in the simplest hypothesis, you wouldn't believe in other persons, or the external world, or the past or the future. Outside of the laboratory, you don't take simplicity as your guide to truth. So you don't avoid hugging your wife when you see her because there's no scientific proof that she's a person (and you only hug persons), you just find yourself hugging the person you love and believe in.

Appeals to simplicity, as important as they are to the practice of science, need not and should not dictate beliefs outside of the laboratory. Simplicity, scientific theorizing, the best explanations—these are all irrelevant to *your* judgments about persons, the past, and God.[13]

THE UNRELIABILITY ARGUMENT

One might think that the god-faculty cannot produce justified religious beliefs because it is not reliable. Dawkins claims that a built-in irrationality mechanism produces beliefs in a multiplicity of gods, ghosts, angels, fairies, demons, and so on. The god-faculty produces too many false and contradictory beliefs to be trustworthy. So the god-faculty, like wish-fulfillment or the "I am better than average" faculty, can't produce rational beliefs.

But the god-faculty is not a special, dedicated cognitive faculty. It's just a couple of our very ordinary faculties, including ADD and ToM. And ADD and ToM are reliable.

While most of us today lack finely honed hunting or fighting skills, we are still good at agency detection. We hear a knock on the door or hear the squealing of tires and believe that we have a visitor or that someone is driving nearby. You see paw prints in the ground or bite marks in your lettuce and believe that a rabbit has invaded your garden. Of course, sometimes upon hearing a sharp noise downstairs we jolt out of bed with the firm *but false* belief in an intruder. Or we might jump up with heart racing when we mistake a stick for a snake. But ADD's sensitivity does not diminish its general reliability.

Our attribution of intentions via (ToM) is likewise reliable. We couldn't function in the human world without fairly accurately attributing intentions, beliefs, desires, feelings, and purposes to other people. I hear your loud exclamation when pricked with a pin and believe you are in pain. I see you cry and believe you are sad. You tell me you are fine but I read the anxious expression on your face.[14]

Of course, we see faces in clouds and attribute intentions to sun, wind, and rain. But such false attributions of agency, while giving us pause, do not diminish ToM's general reliability.

The bottom line: ADD (even though it's hypersensitive) and ToM *are* reliable. And it's difficult to imagine that Dawkins and others think they aren't.

But, to press Dawkins's and Dennett's point, we need to remember that ADD is hypersensitive. Even the most religion-friendly understanding of the god-faculty must concede that it produces a lot of kooky and false beliefs. It doesn't lead ineluctably to Yahweh, for example; it is more likely to produce beliefs in lesser "gods." The god-faculty frenetically produces belief in gnomes, ghosts, and goblins as well as angels, ancestors, and aliens. Such a wacky diversity hardly inspires confidence in a faculty that produces so many false beliefs. So maybe ADD and ToM are reliable in ordinary contexts— in the presence of enemies, friends, predators, and food—but not in the extraordinary contexts that produce zany "god" beliefs. How can we trust the god-faculty in these sorts of areas?

Consider our visual faculties. They work well in the right circumstances— if the lighting is good and if we are close enough to the objects being perceived. But if it's dark or dim, or if we're far away, vision produces all manner of false and fuzzy perceptions. Perhaps something similar goes for ADD and ToM. In the presence of people and predators, or given people or predator clues (like bent grass or footprints in the sand), they produce generally true beliefs. But in less optimal circumstances, they produce wildly crazy beliefs. Dawkins and Dennett, then, can be taken as claiming that while ADD and ToM are reliable in their very ordinary contexts, the god-faculty is unreliable in the extraordinary contexts where it produces many loony beliefs.

Response to Unreliability

How might the theist respond to the charge that the god-faculty is unreliable and so produces irrational beliefs? Let us consider a parallel argument involving our moral faculty.

Suppose that Dawkins and Dennett had argued instead that we have an evolutionarily produced moral faculty which, like the god-faculty, is unreliable. It's not hard to see how a similar case could be made. After all, the moral faculty *has* produced zany beliefs such as widow burning, infanticide, cannibalism, and female genital mutilation. Given such wacky and incompatible output beliefs, we can't trust the moral faculty that produced those beliefs. So moral beliefs are unjustified or irrational.

But is this the only or even the best way to think of the moral faculty?

Consider a transplant doctor at a hospital with five patients in desperate need of organ transplants; one needs a heart, the other a liver, another a kidney, another a face, and another a set of lungs. Into the hospital walks a healthy man with precisely those organs needed by each of the five patients. Is it morally acceptable for the doctor to kill the healthy man in order to harvest his organs to save the lives of the other five? You almost certainly and instinctively answered, "No!" In so doing, your moral faculty was engaged and nonreflectively produced your response.

Harvard psychologist Marc Hauser believes that humans have just such a built-in moral faculty, one that produces judgments of right and wrong (Hauser, 2006). This common moral faculty operates unconsciously without rational reflection, producing judgments of right and wrong immediately. Hauser considers the moral faculty a "universal toolkit" for building specific moral systems. Just as each child comes into the world equipped with a brain wired for the acquisition of language, so each of us is born equipped for the acquisition of morality. Morality, Hauser argues, "is grounded in our biology."

What, then, is included in our universal moral grammar? The Golden Rule–"Do unto others as you would have done unto you"—is found everywhere. Prohibitions against murder, rape, and other types of aggression are also universal. No doubt there are more universal prohibitions, but let's just consider the prohibition against murder.

Even though there's a universal rule that says, "Don't kill people," there's often disagreement about who counts as a person. US President Theodore Roosevelt, for example, denied full personhood to Indians: "I don't go so far as to think that the only good Indians are dead Indians, but I believe nine out of ten are, and I shouldn't inquire too closely into the case of the tenth." It's just this sort of belief that excused the genocide of the Indian in the conquering of the West. Jews, blacks, and, for that matter, barbarians (noncitizens) in general have been considered nonpersons and with horrific results—as nonpersons, they are not protected by the prohibition against murder. While we're at it, there is a tremendous variety of "non-persons" who have been unprotected by the prohibition against murder—babies (in societies that practice infanticide), fetuses (where abortion is accepted), and old people (euthanasia). With all this killing, one might start thinking that there couldn't possibly be a universal prohibition against murder.

But, and here's the key point, in every society, it is wrong to murder persons. Citizens in societies that permit killing Jews, blacks and barbarians are mistaken about what constitutes a person. They are mistaken about a factual belief—who is a person?—not a moral belief. The moral faculty is reliably delivering a true belief—"Don't murder," but people are mistaken about those to whom the principle applies. Something besides the moral faculty produced the mistake.

How much agreement should one expect of beliefs produced by the moral faculty? Agreement on the most basic prohibition, for sure. Likewise, we should expect that disagreement about a host of surrounding culturally influenced beliefs will produce vastly different and culturally specific expressions of that basic prohibition. Of moral norms more generally, moral philosopher Chandra Sripada writes: "There are certain *high-level themes* that one sees in the contents of moral norms in virtually all human groups—themes such as harms, incest, helping and sharing, social justice, and group defense. However, the *specific rules* that fall under these themes exhibit enormous variability" (Sripada, 2008: 330). Cultures will take on various moral principles because the prohibition against murder is embedded in a set of culturally specific beliefs. Indeed the precise form of the prohibition will be shaped by culture.

While one finds a plethora of culture-specific rules, they orbit around deeply profound, higher-level moral themes that are delivered reliably by our moral faculty. Despite the wide variety of culturally specific beliefs, the moral faculty is, I believe, truth-aimed.

Suppose we think of the god-faculty along the lines of the moral faculty. Rather than thinking of the god-faculty as unreliable, perhaps like the moral faculty it produces very rudimentary, deep and even true beliefs in the divine/moral dimension of reality. Perhaps it is moving humans toward a true belief in a supreme transcendent and morally providential being. Along the way, the god-faculty will, influenced by culture, produce a wide variety of divergent beliefs. Since those beliefs are products of the god-faculty *and* human culture, unreliability can't be chalked up to the god-faculty alone. Left to its own devices it would produce primitive and imprecise but roughly true beliefs about a transcendent moral providence.

I haven't proven that the god-faculty in extraordinary circumstances is roughly reliable. I have only shown that like the moral faculty it might be. Moreover, the so-called unreliability of the moral and god faculties may be due to cultural influences, not to the faculties themselves. If there is a god (who is morally provident) and if there are moral truths independent of human beliefs and culture, then the god and moral faculties are likely reliable. But noting that we have such faculties and that they sometimes produce false beliefs is not sufficient to show that they are unreliable. False beliefs could be the result of cultural influences, not the faculties themselves, and the faculties could produce universally true, deep, and important beliefs.

CONCLUSION

I have not argued that the cognitive science of religion supports rational belief in God. I have not argued that God is the best scientific explanation of the god-faculty and/or of widespread religious beliefs. I have argued, against Dawkins and Dennett, that having such an evolutionarily produced god-faculty does not undermine the rationality of religious belief. Learning about the origin of religious belief does not undermine the justification of religious belief. The evolutionary psychology of religion neither proves nor refutes God's existence: it's neutral with respect to the rationality and irrationality of belief in God.

Here's how I'd look at the god-faculty if I were an atheist: "So, that's why so many people believe in God." And here's how I'd look at the god-faculty if I were a theist: "So that's how God created us so that people would believe in him." But realizing there is a god-faculty and conjecturing about its evolutionary origins won't and can't settle either God's existence or the rationality of belief in God.

CHAPTER 9

Evolution and Ethics

EXPLAINING EVERYTHING

Evolution, German biologist Ernst Haeckel wrote in 1868, is "the magic word by which we shall solve all the riddles that surround us" (Haeckel, 1901). For those eager to rid the world of God, morality is sometimes viewed as the final frontier. It's easy, so the story goes, to explain the natural world, including curiously strange human animals, through natural, evolutionary processes. But it's not so easy to explain nonnatural properties like good and bad, or meaning and purpose in natural terms. Good and evil transcend the physical world and so suggest a supernatural source of morality. So the search is on for a natural (i.e., nonsupernatural) foundation for morality. Find the natural foundation for morality, and God is banished from the world altogether.

The time has come, E. O. Wilson trumpeted, "for ethics to be temporarily removed from the hands of the philosophers and biologicized" (Wilson, 1975: 562). Seeking to divorce ethics from God (or any transcendent source or warrant), Wilson hopes "that if we explore the biological roots of moral behavior, and explain their material origins and biases, we should be able to fashion a wise and enduring ethical consensus" (Wilson, 1998b). A biologicized ethics would be based on the evolution of various traits, because "true character arises from a deeper well than religion" (Wilson, 1998a: 245). But can ethics survive biologicization—can it be grounded in evolution alone? Can ethics be divorced from a transcendent or religious foundation? In short, can evolution really solve *all* of the riddles, including the riddle of morality?

Evolutionary ethics is the attempt to root or ground human morality in evolution. It's not an initially promising prospect. After all, how could survival of the fittest serve as the foundation of morality? While there are some surprising resonances between human and animal cooperation some of which are suggestive of human morality, evolution can't fully solve the riddle of human morality. But why would we expect evolution to be the solution to everything? After all, evolution cannot solve the riddle of making a perfectly cooked three-egg omelette. But so what? Just as evolution doesn't have the right ingredients to cook omelettes, it doesn't have all of the right ingredients for cooking up human morality.

Neither of the two most common caricatures of evolutionary ethics is well-informed or justified. The first, the Selfishness View, usually offered by critics of evolutionary ethics, holds that evolutionary ethics would favor selfishness of a particularly sexual variety or Social Darwinism, which holds that we shouldn't provide social supports for those who are seen as not being directly useful to a society. Some even embrace eugenics, which involves the cleansing of the human race of unfit members. The second caricature, the Romantic View, offered by overly optimistic defenders of evolutionary ethics, naively and romantically extends endearing and prosocial animal traits and behaviors to human behaviors.

According to the Selfishness View, evolution is a curious hook on which to hang morality. After all, evolution, if it values anything at all, values survival and those traits conducive to survival, that is, those traits that help individuals fight, feed, flee, and reproduce. What ethical guidelines could there be for such activities? For fighting, there could be rules for boxing, and for feeding, etiquette. Fleeing is more of a freestyle event than a rule-governed activity. And then there's reproducing! Men might find in evolutionary ethics just the rationalization for serial monogamy that they've long been seeking; Hugh Hefner, founder of the *Playboy* enterprise and de facto leader of the hedonism movement, could be evolutionary ethics' leading thinker and *Playboy* magazine its Bible. Dr. Cecil Jacobson, aka "The Sperminator," the fertility specialist who fertilized at least 15 eggs with his own sperm and has at least 23 offspring (he had eight children with his wife), should be recommended for sainthood. Mother Teresa, however, who ministered to the downtrodden and took a vow of celibacy, is the apotheosis of evolutionary evil; she not only woefully failed to pass on her genes, but she also perpetuated a group of people that nature would otherwise have excised from the race of life. And Hitler may have been mistaken about the weaker race, but his enthusiasm to properly people and advance the master race was a stroke of evolutionary genius.

Little wonder that T. H. Huxley—"Darwin's bulldog"—recoiled at the thought of basing ethics on evolution (natural selection): "The ethical progress of society depends, not on imitating the cosmic process, still less in running away from it, but in combating it" (Huxley, 1894: 183).

In contrast, the Romantic View holds that human evolution was not the individualistic, competitive picture just presented, but rather a cooperative, altruistic endeavor. Cooperation—not competition—is the key to survival. Given this, humans should look to the ant and the ape as moral models, not to St. Hugh and St. Adolf. We find in the ape just the "You scratch my back (and pick my lice) and I'll scratch your back (and pick your lice)" sort of altruism necessary for humans to flourish in community. The Proverbist was thus wise to commend the ant: "Go to the ant, you sluggard; consider its ways and be wise" (Proverbs 6:6 NIV). Despite being a "walking battery of exocrine glands," the ant is genetically wired for communal living in a harmonious, socially stratified colony, laboring heartily for the good of the whole. If only the Proverbist had also known the truth about the grasshopper. Google "sociobiology AND grasshopper" and you will find the expected article or two on ejaculate size and courtship behavior of grasshoppers, but you will also find warm and fuzzy articles about maternal investment and males hanging out together in the same bush. The unlikely Portuguese man-of-war, with its different species of zooids freely swimming together in colonial harmony, is the evolutionary exemplar of multiculturalism. Mammals survive better if they can just learn to get along. Nature, it seems, is velvet-gloved, not red in tooth and claw. It must be conceded that some cooperative animals partake of some decidedly uncooperative behavior. The starved lioness, who generally cares for her own newborn, may dine on her offspring (she sometimes can't stop at just the umbilical cord). Goldfish and pike eat their own young as well. Ants take other ants as their slaves. Some termites lick their queen to death when she is no longer fertile. But, according to this view, if we would but follow the kindly ant and his ilk, we would walk the moral straight and narrow.

The best of evolutionary ethics finds itself somewhere between these extremes of selfishness and Social Darwinism, on the one hand, and the Romantic View of altruism and cooperation, on the other. Evolutionary ethics finds within prehuman ancestors some of the basic ingredients of human morality. For example, we can see social instincts in mammals, ones that mimic altruism. We will first consider the nature of morality and then various ways that evolutionary ethicists have sought to explain human morality.

THE NATURE OF MORALITY

A mother, hearing her baby stir in the middle of the night, fights her deep desire for sleep and, anticipating her baby's needs, tears herself from her warm bed and feeds her infant. A grandfather sets up a trust fund to provide college tuition to all of his grandchildren. A neighbor joins a local watch group to ensure the safety of the neighborhood. A woman volunteers six hours per week at a local soup kitchen. A soldier throws herself on a grenade to save the life of her fellow soldiers. A person, moved by the plight of Sudanese refugees, makes a sizeable donation to the Red Cross.

These model cases of morality share features that we can draw upon in our attempt to gain an understanding of the nature of morality. We will use these examples to consider two dominant approaches to the understanding of morality: the duty/rule approach and the virtue approach.

The Duty/Rule Approach

Before studying morality, you might have thought the primary subject matter of ethics is rules or duties like "You shall not kill" or "You should keep your promises." According to such a conception of morality, you fulfill all of your ethical responsibilities simply by following all of the rules. Good people are good rule-keepers. In the previous examples, the dutiful mother, grandfather, neighbor, citizen, and citizen of the world are moral models.

One sees one's duties, learns of the situations in which they apply, and then acts in accord with duty.

The sphere of action includes not only one's self, kin, or neighbors but also the world; moral duties are *universal* and in two senses. First, they apply to everyone in relevantly similar circumstances. Second, they extend to everyone regardless of relationship, race, creed, color, or geographical location. In the first case, moral duties are binding on everyone—one can't make exceptions for one's self, thinking that one is somehow above the law. While we may have a natural inclination to favor kin, we nonetheless have duties to everyone. A Buddhist teaching puts the matter: "As a mother even at the risk of her own life watches over her own child, so let everyone cultivate a boundless love toward all beings." Duties extend beyond the realm of family and friends to the world. It is an open question whether or not parents, in their role as parents, have a duty to care for their own children before they care for the children of others. But if we restricted our sense of right and wrong to kith and kin, the world would be a dangerous place indeed.

One final clarification or consequence of our ordinary understanding of duties: We typically think that *moral judgments are objectively true.* Consider, for example, "Slavery is bad," "People have a right to life, liberty, and happiness," and "Hitler was wrong to kill the Jews." If someone were to disagree, they'd be wrong—their beliefs would be false. And if moral beliefs are true or false, then there are moral facts that make these beliefs true or false. Just as the fact that grass is green makes the belief that "Grass is green" true, so, too, some moral fact makes the belief "Hitler was wrong to kill the Jews" true. Our duties are not simply matters of opinion or expressions of one's tastes or desires. Think of the following progression: "You say potato, I say po-tah-toe; you like potatoes but I prefer tomatoes; you think murder is bad but murder makes me glad." The first two are clearly matters of taste; they are expressions of the preferences of the person speaking (and so are subjective). But there's something wrong with a person who takes delight in murder or thinks it good. There's surely something more to murder's being wrong than that it's not my personal preference. The duty not to murder is surely neither subjective preference nor taste—it is objective.

Duty-keeping needs some clarification. A person could be a duty keeper but still not be morally good. For example, Andrew Carnegie, one of the most famous names in philanthropy, was a ruthless scoundrel. Carnegie, the great steel magnate, betrayed his best friend, ignored his wife and children, abused and underpaid his workers, and turned his back as union-busting government officials shot and killed striking workers who were rightly demanding decent working conditions and a living wage. Yet we now know of Carnegie only for his generosity—Carnegie Mellon University, Carnegie Hall, three thousand public libraries, and organizations devoted to the pursuit of world peace. By the time of his death, he had donated over $350 million of his $450 million fortune (in 2014 dollars, multibillions). While he was certainly generous, he was no saint. He gave away his vast sums of money, he revealed to friends, so that people would forget that he was a vicious villain who purchased his fortune with human blood and tears. His acts, while good, were poorly motivated. What was defective about his motivation is that he was generous not for the sake of his beneficiaries but only for his own sake. He performed good actions only to improve his reputation, not to improve the lives of those he helps.

What would be a good motivation for doing one's duty? A *good motivation is one that primarily desires the good of the person or persons that one is helping and not one's own good.* And sometimes there's cost involved—one desires the good of the other, sometimes at one's own expense. The expense may be money, time, sleep, pleasure, or even life itself. The usual name for such a good motivation is *altruism.* Altruism involves not only acting for another's benefit but also desiring or intending another's benefit; the altruist not only helps another, but she also *wants* to help another. The mother who wearily but gladly feeds her child in the dark of the night, the woman who secretly works at a soup kitchen, the soldier who throws herself on the grenade, and the man who quietly writes the check to help the Sudanese—when motivated primarily to benefit the other, all of these actions are motivated by altruism.

The Virtues Approach

Some moral philosophers reject a duties approach to morality. Plato and Aristotle, for example, believe that being good is not primarily a matter of being good rule-keepers. According to them, *ethics is primarily about the formation of character.* The primary question is not, "What rules should I follow?" but *"What sort of person should I be?"* Their answer is: one who is self-controlled, courageous, just, and wise. Such virtues are character traits, and although they do not precisely specify any actions, they are dispositions which move one to act in certain ways in certain situations. When a just person is put in a situation that demands justice, she will act justly. And, in the proper situation, the wise person will act wisely. According to this approach, right actions flow from a good character.[1] The kind parent rouses herself for her hungry child, the generous person writes the big check when faced with people in need, the self-sacrificial person volunteers her time, and the courageous person lays down her life for her friends.

Virtue is an *inner moral strength* that helps one to respond appropriately to the challenges in life. The virtues, which one develops over the course of one's life, are what make one fully human. The virtues are part of what it means to be a full, fulfilled, or flourishing human being. In Africa's Yoruba culture it is claimed that a human being is not fully human simply by virtue of being born of human parents. The vices—gluttony, for example, or sloth, anger, or cowardice—are, on the other hand, dehumanizing.

Both the duties/rules approach and the virtues approach to ethics assume that morally valuable choices are free choices and so assume that human beings have free will. Freely chosen altruistic acts are morally good, while forced acts, even with good consequences, are either morally bad or neutral.

Altruistic acts—acting for the benefit of another—are a problem for evolutionary ethics. How, in the competition for scarce resources, could evolution, which seems to value the survival of the individual, produce traits that benefit another? If our nature developed from an individualistic, competitive process that prizes sexual success, how could we become self-denying, social, or altruistic?

HUMAN NATURE

We descendents of animals are, well, animals. Our humanity is, at least partly, our animality. We may have come from dust, but it was animal dust from which we came. We are more closely related to chimpanzees than they are to their nearest cousin, the gorilla. If we want to find the roots of human nature, then we need look no further than our prehuman ancestors. And so we look to the great (we hope) apes.

Because we are not chimpanzees, we can't make any simple generalizations from chimpanzee nature to human nature. We may share 99 percent of our genes with chimpanzees but that 1 percent difference is whopping.[2]

Some of our moral and social skills and concepts are rooted in our animal ancestry. Some sense of morality, no doubt primitive, emerged as *Homo sapiens* emerged from *Homo erectus*. Mary Midgley writes: "Morality cannot be viewed as a thunderclap, occurring along with the instant invention of language at the moment of the sudden and final emergence of the human race" (Midgley, 1978: 175).

But, once again, we are not chimpanzees. Even Dawkins seems unable to abide the thought. In *The Selfish Gene*, he defends the thesis that all biological entities are merely receptacles for selfish genes: "We and all other animals, are machines created by our genes" (Dawkins, 1976: 2). Selfish genes, not biological individuals, are the ultimate constituents of biological reality, says Dawkins. They control their host's destiny and shuck their host body off at death only to be reincarnated in a new and better vessel. With regard only for their own destiny, they don't care a whit for their host. One's genetic destiny is to thrust one's genes into next year's new and improved model. So Dawkins writes: "We are survival mechanisms—robot vehicles blindly programmed to preserve the selfish molecules known as genes" (Dawkins 1976: ix).

But, evidently, the "we" doesn't include us. Dawkins shrank from the thought that human beings are simply the sum total of their selfish genes. Apparently drawing upon that whopping 1 percent, he asserts that "we have the power to turn against our creators. We, alone on earth, can rebel against the tyranny of the selfish replicators" (Dawkins 1976: 201). After arguing that natural selection is an irresistible force, he asserts that humans can resist that irresistible force (and so takes it all back). Although we are survival mechanisms, we are not simply the sum total of our genetics and environment. And therein lies the gap into which Dawkins inserts human freedom.

One might have thought that selfish genes would produce selfish organisms but such an inference, Dawkins rightly informs us, does not follow.

Genes can be selfish while their hosts can be empathetic and even downright decent (as long as empathy and decency improve reproductive success). There aren't, after all, genes for selfishness. Genes simply act for their own benefit (and not for the benefit of their host). While our nature is partly animal, we are neither selfish animals nor selfish gene machines.

How might evolutionary seeds have been watered and cultivated to produce human morality?

The Evolution of Cooperation and Compassion

Evolutionary ethics finds incipient "moral systems" within those traits or prosocial emotions that developed in social animals. As cooperation proved successful against the competition, *social instincts* developed to increase cooperation (and thus to more successfully compete). Individual competitors found they did better when they joined a team. And, as we all know, when one is part of the team, one must abide by team rules. Self-interest must give way, at least partly, to other-regard. As our biological ancestors progressed from cells to mammals, forms of cooperation increasingly emerged.

Although *cooperation* has its costs—cooperation/sharing may require foregoing a feeding or reproductive opportunity—it also has its benefits. Examples of cooperative benefits abound in the natural world: bees that share information about the location of recently visited flowers; Mexican Jays that both protect and indiscriminately feed any child in their flock; ant and termite colonies that are highly organized; and South American vampire bats that share their blood with the less fortunate.

Care for offspring is also evident in prehuman ancestors. Increases in mammalian body mass and lifespan are correlated with fewer offspring that require more and lengthier care. Mammalian advancement thus brings with it increased parental investment. Primordial cells care little for their minions, and fish pay little attention to their offspring after they are squirted out of their bodies. But mammal infants demand and receive a great deal of quality time from their parents.

Finally, more advanced mammals apparently experience primitive forms of *empathy*. Animal empathy likely first developed in the mammal parent toward her child. Elephant mothers, for example, are devoted to their offspring. If they should lose a child, their grief is palpable and long-lasting. Consider Joyce Poole's poignant reflection on an elephant's three-day vigil over her still-born baby: "As I watched Tonie's vigil over her dead newborn, I got my first very strong feeling that elephants grieve. I will never forget the expression on her face, her eyes, her mouth, the way she carried her ears, her head, and her body. Every part of her spelled grief" (Poole, 1997: 95). Some researchers report that elephants weep. The portions of the brain that are active when humans experience social loss (the anterior cingulated cortex) are likewise active when advanced mammals experience social loss. Animal empathy isn't restricted to kin. Jules Masserman discovered that rhesus monkeys forego food if they know that by securing food, another monkey would suffer an electric shock (Masserman, 1964). Many monkeys chose hunger to avoid administering the painful stimulus. One monkey nearly starved to death, refusing to eat for 12 days, rather than inflicting pain on another monkey.

So we find in our mammalian ancestors the seeds of cooperation, parental care and investment, and empathy. But we have not yet established human morality. Morality, after all, is other-regarding; it demands that we move beyond self and even child to the world. Although in the animal world there are a few curious and notable instances of regard for those outside of one's kin or clan, they are few and far between. How could human morality have moved beyond in-group cooperation and parent-child empathy to love of neighbor?

Here's how a more complete evolutionary story might go. Morality has developed because humans have evolved prosocial actions and emotions that incline an individual to act for the common good of their kin. As cooperation trumped competitive strategies, early human and "proto-human" societies developed structured kin groups and even clan groups. As selection forces operated on these clans, empathy toward nonrelated clan members developed. Since these clans were often in direct and indirect competition with other clans, intraclan competition would be discouraged and intraclan coopera-tion encouraged. As civilization progressed, clans became less shielded from competitor clans and, as a result, the rules for who counted as part of the "clan" increasingly became less stringent. Thus we humans were evolution-arily equipped for the task of helping our nonkin "brothers and sisters."

THE ALTRUISM DILEMMA

The seeds of a Darwinian dilemma were planted in the previous sections. Our primitive ancestors, if they are the gene machines that Dawkins imag-ines, are unlikely candidates for genuine, other-regarding moral sympathies and actions. Other-regarding behavior improves the other's reproductive suc-cess, not one's own. Empathy and decency can go only so far if empathetic and decent individuals aren't better at reproducing. Apathetic and indecent individuals seem destined to prey upon the empathic and decent, removing empathy and decency from the gene pool. Advantage: immorality.

Evolution is not a team sport: evolution's bloody truth is that biological creatures are in the competition of life not only with other species but also with members of their own species. There may be advantages to being on a team, but natural selection awards prizes to individuals (or their genes), not to teams. Given this view, Huxley proclaims: "Life was a continual free fight, and beyond the limited and temporary relations of the family, the Hobbesian war of each against all was the normal state of existence" (Huxley, 1888). Little wonder Huxley thought evolution infertile ground for ethics.

Yet we seem to find in nature other-benefiting traits such as empathy, sterile workers, maternal care, and warning calls. The honey pot ant's sole task in life is to hang upside down, filled with sugar water, waiting to be tapped to slake the thirst of the queen. Wolves hunt in packs and kittens huddle together against the cold. There is a great deal of cooperative behavior in nature. Are such cooperative traits likewise altruistic?

The answer to this question, to fall back on a familiar philosopher's ploy, depends on what we mean. If we mean by altruism simply "actions that benefit others," then such traits are clearly altruistic. If this be altruism, though, then the boxer crab that holds the anemone in its claws to use its stinging tentacles to ward off predators would be a closet altruist because even the anemone gets to eat the crumbs from the crab's table. And "cleaner fish" (wrasse) which eat the parasites off of the gills and mouth of larger fish (grouper) would be thereby altruistic (rather than just hungry). And so too, certain Brazilian trees and plants would be altruists because they evolved pockets suited to the lair of various ants; and those ants, which ate the larvae of insects harmful to those trees, would likewise be altruistic. But there's surely more to altruism, at least the kind humans find morally desirable, than simply benefiting another organism.

Biological altruism is stronger: *biological altruism is when an organism's behavior benefits other organisms at a cost to itself.*

Altruism, biologically defined, seems to violate the very forces that drive evolution. Natural selection countenances no traits or behaviors that do not benefit the individual. But altruism involves traits that do not benefit the individual (and are evolutionarily costly to the individual). Therefore, if evolution, then no altruism. Darwin himself was troubled by the thought of an exclusively other-benefiting trait, which he believed "would annihilate my theory, for such could not have been produced through natural selection." Wilson acknowledges that altruism is "the central theoretical problem of sociobiology: how can altruism...possibly evolve by natural selection" (Wilson, 1975: 1).

Other-regarding behaviors, with no self-benefit, are simply inexplicable on orthodox Darwinian evolutionary theory. Michael Ghiselin reminds: "If natural selection is both sufficient and true, it is impossible for a genuinely disinterested or 'altruistic' behavior pattern to evolve...Scratch an 'altruist,' watch a hypocrite bleed" (Ghiselin, 1974: 247). If underneath biological "altruism" we find a selfish gene, we may not have found altruism at all.

We know of sterile honeybees that sting intruders and then die, birds that (literally) stick their neck out for their flock and screech as an enemy approaches, and bonobo apes that leap into the fray to defend a mate in a brawl. Are these altruistic animals? Biological altruism comes in at least three flavors: kin selection, reciprocity, and group selection. Let us consider them individually to see if they resolve the altruism dilemma.

Biological Altruism: Kin Selection

J. B. S. Haldane, the great British polymath of the 1920s and 1930s, exclaimed through the suds of his beer, "I'd jump into the river to save two brothers and eight cousins," thus introducing the theory of *kin selection*—that organisms may have good reason to be altruistic to their relatives. William Hamilton worked out the details of this theory in 1964. He convincingly argued that kin selection is an influential mechanism of natural selection. Its central idea is that while an individual may not be able to inject its own genes into the next generation, its kin—its brothers and sisters, cousins, aunts, and uncles—may be able to do that for it. The theory of kin selection is based on the insight that the "key to evolutionary success lies in improving [one's] gene ratios"; and since relatives share one's genetic material, "help given to relatives in itself rebounds to the favor of one's own reproductive interests" (Ruse, 1986: 220). Darwin himself suggested "that selection may be applied to the family, as well as to the individual" (Ruse, 1986: 237). Since relatives share one's genetic material, helping relatives can help one get one's genes into future generations. Kin selection is the "We Are Family" understanding of altruism.

Kin selection is demonstrated by Hamilton's Rule, which states that "a trait of helping others at some cost to the individual can be expected to be favored if $rB > C$, where r is the degree of genetic relatedness to the individual, B is the benefit to the recipient, and C is the cost to the individual" (Joyce, 2006: 20). A sacrificial behavior would be evolutionarily warranted only if the cost to the actor is less than the benefit to the recipient, times the degree of genetic relatedness. Hamilton's nifty rule predicts that one may lay down one's life for one's brother and sister (who carry half of one's genes), or, but less likely, for several of one's cousins (who carry 1/8 of one's genes), or (even more unlikely) one's second cousin. One can drown satisfied, knowing that one's genes are being carried on in other vessels. In one fell swoop, kin selection explains honey pot ants, screeching birds, sterile bees, and gallant bonobos. If one can get one's genes propelled into future generations by screeching at an advancing enemy (even if one is torn apart limb by limb and then eaten), or by stinging an intruder and then dropping dead to the ground, then one is evolutionarily successful.

Hamilton's rule also predicts that one will not lay down one's life for a friend, and certainly not for an enemy. While a prairie dog might stick its head up and bark loudly to warn the colony of an invading coyote or hawk, transport it to a distant colony and it won't risk itself for unrelated prairie dogs.

Kin selection is thin altruism—it explains actions that benefit one organism at the expense of another but only for blood relatives. To understand the limits of kin-selection as altruism, consider the spadefoot toad, famous for its spade-like toe on its hind feet that it uses to dig its underground burrows. A few spadefoot tadpoles morph into cannibals with a discriminating palate: their serrated beak draws tadpoles into their mouth but if they should taste their own kin, they spit them out. In so far as kin selection is altruistic at all, limiting benefits to kin is thin altruism indeed.

Moreover, kin selection is disanalogous to moral altruism. While an organism's behavior benefits other organisms at a cost to itself, kin selection concedes no actions that are not done for the benefit of one's genes. Kin selection seems more like genetic egoism than moral altruism. Every action is done for the benefit of the gene. The organism and its kin serve the gene.

If genes are calling the shots, it seems more like gene selfishness than other-regarding altruism.

If sacrifice on behalf of kin ensures the gene's distribution into future generations, then biological "altruism" is explained. But don't look behind the curtain. The only thing you can pull out of the kin-selection bottle is a disguised selfish genie.

Biological Altruism: Reciprocity

If we wish to explain a thicker, more expansive altruism, one closer to moral altruism for humans, we will have to do better than kin selection. It's easy to see how we might love our genetically related kin as ourselves (since they are cracked mirrors of our biological self), but how can we love our genetically unrelated neighbor as ourselves? Since we are competing with them for food and mates, their success could mean our failure.

Reciprocity or reciprocal altruism—"You scratch my back, I'll scratch your back altruism"—offers an explanation of biological altruism to nonkin. Reciprocal altruism refers to acts that are sacrificial in the short term but that provide a benefit to the helper at the same or another time (Trivers, 1971). *A does something for B, hoping that B will (perhaps at a later time) reciprocate the action and help out A.*

Consider two examples. A benevolent bat shares its regurgitated blood with a starving bat in hopes of a future sharing in its own times of scarcity. Since vampire bats can live for only a few days without food and failing to find blood is not uncommon, the sharing of an excess of blood saves bats from starvation. Likewise, grouper don't eat "cleaner fish" (wrasse) even though swallowing them might seem natural and expected. In their mutually beneficial relationship, the larger fish looks after the welfare of the "cleaner fish" (e.g., by warning them when they are about to swallow). Such interactions are mutually beneficial and always with an anticipation of future reward. Hence, reciprocity is sometimes called "mutualism."

With vampire bats, when sharing is not reciprocated, sharing stops. Tit for tat confirmed. Or not: while many greeted bat-sharing with great excitement, subsequent and more careful study showed that bats favor kin (but sometimes get confused).

While defenders of reciprocity insist that this is genuine biological altruism, it's not so clear. Biological altruism, recall, is when the actions of one organism benefit another organism *at a cost to oneself.* With reciprocity, there's an initial down payment, but there's no net cost to the organism that performs the apparently altruistic action. Mutually beneficial behavior, reciprocity, is not genuine altruism.

Biological Altruism: Group Selection

Group selectionists hold that group selection has, along with kin selection and reciprocity, pushed humans along on the path to cooperation.[3] In reciprocal relations the sacrificial aspect is only apparent or short term. Group selection holds that certain individuals' behavior can be fitness-sacrificing through and through. If evolution functions at the group level, natural selection could favor fitness-sacrificing behavior that is good for the group. This is the "It Takes a Village" understanding of altruism.

Group selection holds that groups with genuinely altruistic cooperation have fitness advantages over groups of selfish individuals. There are, as we've noted, cooperative benefits, benefits that redound to members of groups— the sharing of goods, more possible mates and shared care of children. Perhaps key to the human social evolutionary story is the ubiquity and power of competition between groups. Given often deadly competition between groups, those groups that can rally their members together in genuine self-sacrifice are more likely to defeat less cohesive competing groups. The altruistic traits that bind groups together thereby provide a selective advantage over other groups. Altruistic groups—those with members disposed to lay down their lives for their friends—are likely to out-survive selfish groups. If altruistic groups outcompete (out-survive and out-reproduce) selfish groups, then the altruistic traits that draw those groups together will be passed on to their off-spring. Thus, there is a selection advantage to developing genuinely altruistic traits that hold groups together, especially in times of want and war.

Dawkins, a harsh critic of group selection, concedes that groups often do better than individuals. Consider his metaphor from rowing: "One oarsman on his own cannot win the Oxford and Cambridge boat race. He needs eight colleagues...Rowing the boat is a co-operative venture." He goes on to note: "One of the qualities of a good oarsman is teamwork, the ability to fit in and co-operate with the rest of the crew" (Dawkins, 1976: 38).

Group selection suggests a resolution of the altruism dilemma by explaining how genuinely altruistic behavior could prove reproductively successful. Living in a group that is genuinely committed to your welfare, while you are genuinely committed to theirs, is a better plan for survival than the alternatives. Members of a selfish group are less likely to survive in competition with altruistic groups. If altruistic groups have a selective advantage over competing nonaltruistic groups, altruistic group members will have improved prospects of survival and reproduction. Therefore, group selection explains the evolution of altruism by natural selection.

Even supposing that group selection effectively and plausibly explains the evolutionary origin of in-group moral altruism, we have not thereby explained morality. The moral demand is not merely to be kind to members of one's own group; we are to be kind to all human beings. Group selection may foster kindness within one's group but it has a dark side: it likewise fosters nastiness toward those outside one's group. The ties that bind are also the ties that divide. Evolution by group selection might explain tribalism or nationalism or patriotism, but it cannot explain kindness to and justice for those outside of one's tribe.

Group selection is doubly defective. Since group selection operates on groups, those traits conducive to successful group solidarity will be valued evolutionarily. But the good of a group cannot be the standard of moral goodness; a whole host of otherwise immoral traits and practices would or could be favored by group selection. For example, genocide, racism, elitism, cannibalism, fascism, homophobia, and nationalism seem just the sorts of things that successfully bind groups together. Just because something is good for a group does not mean that it is morally good. There must be some objective moral value, independent of survival value and even group survival values, by which to judge human behaviors.

Biological Altruism and Human Morality

Evolution should be seen as equipping human nature with some of the basic tools necessary for the development of morality—prosocial emotions such as sympathy and parental care. It has also equipped humans with rationality. If humans evolved to the point where free will could emerge, then another moral ingredient is added to the mix. If ethics is about the fulfillment of human nature, as virtue ethics holds, then it is our evolved nature that is in need of fulfillment. And evolution can explain how we developed a moral sense: a set of cognitive faculties that enable us to grasp moral truths.

Morality sometimes demands that our primary motivation is the good of another person. It requires us to be just to all people, regardless of their membership in our family or tribe. While evolution may have created sympathy, kin, and even group love, it is difficult to imagine it creating deep and sometimes costly regard for those outside of our family or tribe. If altruism is essential to morality, evolution has not solved the riddle of morality.

With kin selection we get biological altruism for the sacrificer but not for the gene that moved the sacrifice; and we get biological altruism only for kin and not for nonkin. With reciprocal altruism we get something like a primitive, animal version of *apparently* other-regarding behavior. But tit for tat implies that no actions are ultimately done at a net cost to the individual; this scarcely rises to the level of altruism. We're better off simply using the terms "kin selection" and "reciprocity" without gussying them up by adding "altruism" to the mix. If altruism requires actions that are primarily for the good of another (including non-kin) with a cost to oneself, then there is no obvious nonhuman model of altruism in kin-selection and reciprocity. Group selection, if feasible, would extend the domain of other-regarding behavior, but leave one morally circumscribed by one's tribe.

What is the kind of altruism to which humans should aspire?

Recall Andrew Carnegie: we learned from Carnegie that moral altruism is not simply acting for the benefit of another and not simply acting to benefit another at a cost to one's self. Carnegie was missing the key motivational component in moral altruism: he was motivated to improve his reputation, he was not motivated by regard for other people. Moral altruism requires that one be motivated to act primarily for the good of the other and not for some benefit to oneself. Sympathy, compassion, and love lie at the heart of moral altruism. An altruist may gain some direct or indirect benefits for her actions—she may gain praise, friendship, gratitude, increased self-esteem, and she may even win The Nobel Peace Prize. But when acting altruistically, her motivation is not primarily praise or prizes. Given the centrality of other-regarding motivations to altruism, biological "altruism" is misnamed—there are no cases of "biological altruism" in which an individual is motivated to act for the good of the other. Wrasse, ants, bats, and bonobos lack the motivational component essential to moral altruism.

Evolution may have jumpstarted our movement in the direction of sympathetic, other-regarding behavior. We have been evolutionarily shaped for prosocial behavior and for the virtues, emotions, and values that hold groups together. We should expect to find both kin selection and reciprocal altruism operative in human interactions, and we do. We feel more affection for and perform more other-regarding actions for our own kin than for other members of our species. It takes an extraordinary effort to show the same regard for nonfamily as we show for our family. Loving your neighbor as yourself is vastly more difficult than loving your own family members as yourself.

We should also expect to find human examples of reciprocal altruism. And, again, we do: taxes, capitalism, and the returning of favors illustrate reciprocal altruism in the human realm.

We should expect to find in-group loyalty and devotion and we do: patriotism, racism, tribalism, and so on. Some of this, of course, is both powerful and good. Some, as noted, is not.

Our biological instincts to favor kin and community may be telling us something true about the moral life. Parents have greater obligations to their children than they do to their neighbor and to the stranger. Family first is the moral message, but when your house is in order, move out into the world. And given the importance of community to human flourishing, moral obligation then extends out into your neighborhood, tribe, city, or nation. If your tribe or nation is flourishing and you have available resources, your moral obligation then extends to the stranger and beyond your nation to the world. Evolution explains why we are better with the first two (family and tribe) than the third (the rest of the world). Sadly, as we in the West have grown fat, we have not proven as eager to help the stranger as our brother. We have not loved our neighbor as our biological self (or our genetic relatives).

Conclusion

Evolution's inability to explain all of human morality should not be a matter of deep concern. Natural selection is not the answer to every riddle. That's because it isn't suited to explain everything. It's a potent and fertile theory, but it's not meant to explain gravity, the strong nuclear force, cooking the perfect meatloaf, or Beethoven's Fifth. It's not so much that evolution tried to explain gravity or the strong nuclear and was found wanting; it's that natural selection is just not the right explanation for those sorts of things. As with meatloaf, evolution lacks the right ingredients. And it lacks the ingredients to fully explain human morality. But, again, so what? Why should it solve the riddle of everything?

We may find analogs in the biological world but the analogs are not human morality. Humans did not come into being from nothing, so there's an evolutionary path traceable from our prehuman ancestors to human beings that tells the story of how we developed the basic tools necessary for grasping morality. The evolutionary story of the development of morality—one of kinship relations, cooperation, and community—tells how human morality got its start. But human morality moves us way beyond kith and kin.

Two analogies may help here. The ability to distinguish sounds was surely evolutionarily advantageous. But we don't get the whole of music from this biological instinct, and it's a big leap from this biological instinct to Beethoven's Fifth. The ability to count was evolutionarily driven and some chimps can count. But we don't get the calculus from our mammalian predecessors. Animal music and mammalian counting are distant and dim analogs of Beethoven's Fifth and the calculus. It took a prodigious use of distinctly human reason and creativity—building on centuries of human reflection, cultural refinement, and experimentation—to produce Beethoven's Fifth Symphony and the calculus.

Human morality is a lot more like the calculus and Beethoven's Fifth than counting and distinguishing sounds. Like math and music, morality goes way beyond what we find in our mammalian ancestors. It seems unlikely that evolution could provide much more than the most rudimentary building blocks of morality. Given that human morality is so much more than what is attainable via kin selection, reciprocity, and group selection, the development of human morality may, unlike math and music, require an additional foundation or source. Like music and mathematics, human morality requires at least a great supplement of reason: it also requires free will, and maybe even God.

CHAPTER 10

God and the Good Life

A DAWKINSIAN WORLD

Richard Dawkins claims that the world that science discovers has "no design, no purpose, no evil and no good, nothing but blind, pitiless indifference" (Dawkins, 1995: 133):

> In a universe of blind physical forces and genetic replication, some people are going to get hurt, other people are going to get lucky, and you won't find any rhyme or reason in it, nor any justice. The universe we observe has precisely the properties we should expect if there is, at bottom, no design, no purpose, no evil and no good, nothing but a blind, pitiless indifference.

The bottom line of a *Dawkinsian world*: while the natural world, the world of physics, is replete with extension, duration, numbers, atoms, asteroids, quarks, and pains and pleasures, it is singularly devoid of good and bad. Give a complete scientific description of a bullet passing through the head of a young child—initial velocity, size of entry wound, size of exit wound, loss of blood—and you have nowhere found the evil.

The world that science presents, the sum-total of Dawkins's world, is a world without good or evil. In the world of facts, value is nowhere to be found. Take God out of the equation and morality is hard to come by.

Plato needed the transcendent Form of the Good, and the prophet and priest needed the will of God to make room in the cosmos for objective good and evil. Some contemporary philosophers flee from God but run into the arms of a godlike but nonexistent Ideal Observer who transcends human contingency—those peculiar particularities and limitations that so prevent us less-than-ideal observers from seeing beyond our and our kin's own gratification—to determine the Good for all and for all time. Expand the world to include the transcendent, and good and evil easily find their place. But cast your net into the natural world, the world of fact, and see if you can dredge up value.

Given these constraints, can we pull goodness out of the evolutionary hat (in a Dawkinsian world)? Can evolution, or better, evolution emptied of the eternal, provide the content and foundation of morality?

MORAL FICTIONS

In a Dawkinsian world—a world with "no design, no purpose, no evil and no good, nothing but a blind pitiless indifference"—morality is, to borrow a quaint phrase from philosopher J. L. Mackie, "queer" (Mackie, 1977). Objective moral values would be "queer" in a Dawkinsian world because they are unlike everything else in the world (indifferent, nonmoral facts).

Queerness multiplies. We firmly believe that our moral judgments are objectively true—that when we claim that slavery is wrong or that we have a right to liberty and happiness, there is something that makes our judgments true. Such judgments are not simply matters of human preference, desire, convention or utility. If the institution of slavery were to maximize desire satisfaction or utility, it would still be wrong. Independent of human beliefs and desires, something makes it wrong. Let us call the something that makes things right and wrong, *moral facts* (be they God's will, Plato's forms, or an essential human nature). Since there is no objective value in a Dawkinsian world, it is a mistake to think of our moral judgments as objectively true. If there are no objective moral facts, none of our moral judgments is true. Our deeply held belief that our moral judgments are true is mistaken.

Moral judgments, judgments about what one ought to do, also have what Richard Joyce calls practical clout (Joyce, 2006). The *practical clout* of a moral judgment lies in the fact that *moral judgments seem inescapable and authoritative*. The practical clout of a moral judgment involves the idea of moral authority: a built-in reason to comply with the moral demand. This notion of authority distinguishes moral judgments from other principles, like rules of etiquette, (e.g., "You ought to use utensils" and "Wash your hands after using the restroom"). Moral judgments have an authority that rules of etiquette do not. Practical clout involves inescapability and authority, which captures how we view and use moral judgments.

Can evolution tell a convincing story of the development of inescapable and authoritative moral judgments? Kinship selection and reciprocity led humans to behave in helpful ways. To further lead people to act helpfully, natural selection may have favored the trait of making moral judgments. Morality provided humans with the idea that they ought to help others, even to the point of self-sacrifice. Prosocial emotions can motivate cooperative behavior; moral judgments add additional oomph by persuading humans that they *ought* to do so.

Joyce argues that this story is ultimately unconvincing because we are mistaken about moral judgments: in a Dawkinsian world, there are no moral facts. *Evolution does not vindicate morality; it debunks morality.*

Given a lack of moral facts, one might be tempted to abandon moral discourse altogether. Joyce rejects this option in favor of *fictionalism*. He believes that moral discourse cannot be gotten rid of without serious, perhaps even disastrous consequences and so maintains that moral discourse must continue even if there are no truths to hold the discourse together. The moral fictionalist recognizes the benefits of moral discourse, claiming that it is practically useful, all the while maintaining that there are no moral truths. Moral discourse can "bolster self-control," because it imbues actions with either a "must-be doneness" quality or a "must-not-be-doneness" quality (Joyce, 2001: 181). If you think there is an objective moral fact about, say, gluttony, *and you believe it,* then you are less likely to succumb to your chocolate temptations. Moral beliefs inoculate us against temptation.

Joyce argues that as denizens of a Dawkinsian world, we are increasingly aware that our moral beliefs are untrue. Nonetheless, it makes practical sense to continue using moral discourse as a useful fiction even though right and wrong have been drained of their meaning. Ruse and Wilson concur: "Human beings function better if they are deceived by their genes into thinking that there is a disinterested objective morality binding upon them, which all should obey" (Ruse and Wilson, 1986: 179).

Fictionalism Rejected

The problem with fictionalism is that moral thought and moral language have utility and power only when they are actually believed. If people were to come to believe that morality is a useful fiction, it would lose its power to motivate people toward moral behavior. In Dostoevsky's *The Brothers Karamazov*, Smerdyakov claims, "If God does not exist, everything is permitted." This quotation has often been taken to imply Dostoevsky's belief that morality is essentially dependent upon God; hence, if there is no God (nothing to make value judgments true), then there is no right or wrong and everyone may do as he or she pleases. Dostoevsky may also have had something else in mind. He might have meant that if God does not exist, human beings will lose their motivation to be moral. Remove the divine judge and human beings will simply do as they please.

Consider an analogy. When my son was 7 years old his teacher ruled his class with an iron fist. She laid down rules for proper conduct that all of the students in her classroom learned well. If asked, each could recite the rules without hesitation and each would endorse the rules as essential to the proper functioning of the class. But when the teacher left the room, chaos ensued. The students believed the rules, but absent the rule-maker and judge, they broke them. When his teacher left the room, to paraphrase Dostoevsky, everything was permitted.

Moral fictionalism puts us in a teacher-leaves-the-room sort of situation. Inescapability and authority walk out with the teacher. Once objective ethical value departs, we lose moral motivation. Lacking moral motivation, we might more self-consciously select strategies that improve our evolutionary fitness but pay no heed to our fictional moral sense. Robert Wright wonders whether "after the new Darwinism takes root, the word moral can be anything but a joke" (Wright, 1994: 326). Remarkably, he goes on to claim: "But I do believe that most people who clearly understand the new Darwinian paradigm and earnestly ponder it will be led toward greater compassion and concern for their fellow human beings. Or, at least toward the admission, in moments of detachment, that greater compassion and concern would seem to be in order" (Wright, 1994: 338). One might wonder how morality's being a joke could be thought to inspire greater compassion and concern and not a more dogged, individualistic pursuit of one's own desires. Ruse is more candid: "The simple fact is that if we recognized morality to be no more than an epiphenomenon of our biology, we would cease to believe in it and stop acting upon it. At once, therefore, the powerful forces which make us co-operators would collapse" (Ruse, 1991: 508). Such a view would be demoralizing: one would lose one's motivation to be moral.

MOTIVATING MORALITY

On the assumption that we've evolved into rational, self-interested, and prosocial persons, what might motivate us to be moral? What view of the world, a non-Dawkinsian world, might comport better with our deeply held convictions about moral truths and their authority to motivate morality? Can theism undergird morality in a way that is both inescapable and authoritative?

If we are restricted to benefits attainable in this earthly life, it is not always in our best interest to be moral. Indeed, it may be in our best interest to lie, cheat, or steal (if we can get away with it), if there is no next life with which to contend. If only this-worldly benefits are available to us, then morality might be perceived as an obstacle to our own interests. Happiness is not directly proportional to virtue in this earthly life. Happiness is sometimes inversely proportional to virtue (in this life). This is not hard to see with moral demands so severe that no earthly benefit could accrue to oneself for their performance: the giving up of one's life for one's child, say, or a lifetime of sacrifice for one's severely mentally disabled child; remaining in a deeply troubled marriage for the sake of one's children; speaking up when someone else is falsely blamed, even though assuming responsibility may prove costly to oneself; caring for an elderly parent with Parkinson's.

Even less demanding duties—to declare all of your income on your tax returns, not to overbill to cover your deductible when making a claim to your insurance company, not to exceed the speed limit or run a red light while running late for an important meeting, or to return the extra money that the salesperson mistakenly gave you for change—are contrary to your own interests (assuming you can violate these duties with impunity). In evolutionary terms, exploitation may be more beneficial—that is, may better promote genetic fitness—than altruism. Robert Wright explains: "People sometimes lie, cheat or steal...and they may behave this way even toward people who are nice to them. What's more: people sometimes prosper in this fashion. That we have this capacity for exploiting, and that it sometimes pays off, suggests that there have been times during evolution when being nice to people wasn't the genetically optimal strategy" (Wright, 1994: 215).

Although we are self-interested, altruism, being motivated by and acting for the interests of others, is a moral demand. The highest moral state of the individual is not only doing the right thing but doing it out of genuine sympathy for the other. Altruism is genuine only when it arises primarily out of concern for others and not out of a desire to attain one's own benefits—like winning the Nobel peace prize, having a great reputation, or even getting into heaven (or avoiding hell). Moral motivation cannot lie simply or even chiefly in intending benefits for oneself.

It is not difficult to see the moral defectiveness of a selfish motivation. One might act in a manner that is perceived as kind, self-sacrificial, patient or generous; but one's motive is selfish if one desires only one's own benefit. Just as we would properly judge as base the person who is generous simply to get into a public office, so too we would properly judge as base the person who is moral simply to gain God's favor or eternal bliss. The other, who has indeed benefitted from such actions, has been used as a tool, as a means to our end.

Selfishness debases apparently other-regarding actions and diminishes the moral value of such actions. The altruistic demand of the moral life includes not only other-regarding *behavior* but also the proper concern, desire, or feelings for the other.

How can theism properly motivate the moral life without degenerating into selfishness?

Let me proceed by way of example. Suppose one is considering both whether to have children and how one should behave toward them. Consider the selfish parent-to-be. She will have children only because she supposes they will bring her happiness, perhaps to satisfy her desires for holding small, cuddly things or to give her something to boast to her friends about or to financially provide for her in her old age or because she is lonely and can't make any adult friends. She may be good to her children but only as a means to her own happiness.

Now consider the altruistic parent-to-be. She will have children both for her own sake and for the sake of the child. She will surely want the child and the benefits of child-rearing but will primarily desire the good of the child itself. She may have talents, finances, opportunities, or a whole hunk of burnin' love that are better shared than kept to herself. Her behavior toward her child will be self-sacrificial and altruistic, not primarily because of the benefits that accrue to herself. Her devotion to her child is motivated primarily by her desire for the good of the child itself.

But the altruistic parent also reasonably hopes that her sacrifices will create an environment of security, freedom, honesty, peace, joy, fun, and reciprocal love that will redound to herself as well. The parent gives and gets, thus creating a healthy environment both for the child and for herself. Deprive a parent of the hope that doing her duties toward her child will result in a greater good both for the child and for herself and that parent will be demoralized. Deprive parents in general of such hope, and the project of parenting will be quickly abandoned. The self-sacrifice demanded of the parent requires that the parent believe that her actions will ultimately result in achieving an apex of well-being for both her child and herself.

What I've said about parenting can be extended to other members of one's moral community as well. Becoming virtuous or doing one's duty must be properly and primarily motivated by genuine concern for the other. This does not, however, require one to abandon all self-interest. One should hope that one's moral efforts contribute to a community of mutual satisfaction in which every person both desires and seeks to attain the good of the other. We should strive toward a community devoted to the welfare of each of its members.

Self-interest neither can nor should be eliminated. If we have evolved to be part animal-like, part god-like, we should expect fully moral human motivation to include both self- and other-regard. Fortunately, self-regard is not inconsistent with genuine altruism. It is possible, as it is for the good parent, to primarily desire the good of the other and to nonetheless desire one's own good. One can and should hope to bring about a situation of maximum desire-satisfaction both for others and for oneself.

In order not to be demoralized, the life of virtue or duty can't be seen as an obstacle to my happiness. That is, I must believe that my pursuit of your good is likewise conducive to my good (and so not all cost to me). The moral motivation of rationally self-interested people requires the *hope* that everyone's desires, including mine, can be mutually satisfied. What, precisely, should be our hope? What should we hope for if we wish to properly motivate the moral life?

Here, once again, is the problem: there is no necessary connection in this life between devotion to virtue and human desire-satisfaction. If restricted to this-worldly benefits, wickedness may be the best policy to secure human happiness. But, mere creatures that we are, becoming virtuous cannot be seen as an obstacle to attaining happiness. We cannot reasonably adjudge that our interests are better served by immorality.

What rationally self-interested beings need, therefore, is hope that there is a next life in which virtue results in happiness. There must be a next life, in which virtue and happiness embrace, if justice is to prevail. It should motivate us because we will believe that our best but invariably puny efforts to flourish will not be in vain. Deprive us of that hope, and we will believe that since the moral struggle cannot be won it is not worth fighting. Better to gain all of the this-worldly benefits—pleasures and avoidance of pains—that one can for oneself.

But should we hope for a better world simply to gain our own happiness? Aren't we led back to selfishness once again? Here the demands of virtue are clear and, as is emphasized by most theists, our own interests cannot be completely satisfied unless and until they include the interests of others. The fulfilled human being seeks the good of others. The life of virtue demands that we consider not only our own interest but also the interests of others. If one desires the interests of others, isn't one being selfish? Here the reply seems obvious—wanting the good of others is the opposite of selfishness: it is altruism at its finest.

The life of virtue is acquired by ridding ourselves of unwarranted and exclusive devotion to ourselves and taking on the interests of others (while not denying a healthy self-interest). In so doing, one finds one's deepest desires satisfied—to know and to be known, to care for and be loved by others, to take delight in the joys and grieve at the sorrows of another (who likewise grieve and rejoice with oneself).

Virtue is the reward, so to speak: when virtue and justice embrace, an ideal community of people is formed, one which genuinely delights in and seeks one another's good. Mutual satisfaction of our deepest human desires ensues.

The moral life that I have been describing suggests a double source of desire satisfaction. First, the virtuous person secures the satisfaction of her other-regarding desires. Second, as a member of a community devoted to her happiness as well, the virtuous secures the satisfaction of her own desires as well.

If we are to take the moral demand seriously, to sacrifice our happiness and even life itself for the good of another, then rationally self-interested persons must believe that it is possible to attain virtue and happiness in the next life. These are precluded in a Dawkinsian world.

Theistic belief unites the altruistic imperative of the moral life with the attainment of human happiness. Neither virtue nor human happiness is guaranteed in this life. If they are attainable, there must be postmortem existence where virtue is consonant with happiness. If either virtue or happiness through virtue are not attainable, then the motivation to strive for them is diminished. Restricting ourselves to this-worldly goods, therefore, is demoralizing: the moral life is not sufficiently motivated and one might more reasonably choose the life of wickedness. Motivating the moral life, therefore, rationally demands hoping for a next life in which virtue is attainable within a community of likeminded people and intrinsically issues forth in happiness.

Does God Make Us Good?

We have offered a theoretical argument that a theistic world can rationally motivate morality but that a Dawkinsian world cannot. In a Dawkinsian world good and evil are queer, and morality a useful fiction (one that can be dropped if it should suit our needs). Let us consider the question more practically. Does God motivate people to be moral? In short, does God work? Divine commands are surely inescapable and authoritative. And, when backed up by threat of punishment and reward, rationally compelling. But, does God actually make us good? Dennett denies this premise:

> Perhaps a survey would show that as a group atheists and agnostics are more respectful of the law, more sensitive to the needs of others, or more ethical than religious people. Certainly no reliable survey has yet been done that shows otherwise. It might be that the best that can be said for religion is that it helps some people achieve the level of citizenship and morality typically found in brights [holders of a naturalistic worldview]. If you find that conjecture offensive, you need to adjust your perspective. (Dennett, 2006: 55; my addition)

Against Dawkins and Dennett, as a matter of fact, religious beliefs are unusually successful at fostering human cooperation and motivating morality (and nonreligious beliefs are not).

Empirical support for the altruistic and cooperative benefits of religious belief is enormous. Rich Sosis demonstrated that nineteenth-century religious communities were much more likely to survive than secular communes; on average, religious communes lasted four times as long as secular communes (Sosis, 2000). Sosis and Bressler found that among the kibbutzim in Israel, the religious ones had considerably higher levels of cooperation than secular ones and that religious males were far more altruistic than secular males (Sosis and Bressler, 2003). Dominic Johnson's survey of 186 societies around the world found that the likelihood of supernatural punishment involving moralizing "high gods" is favorably associated with cooperation (Johnson, 2005).

Why is religious belief conducive to altruism and cooperation? Jonathan Haidt and Selin Kesebir define moral systems as "interlocking sets of values, practices, institutions, and evolved psychological mechanisms that work together to suppress or regulate selfishness and make social life possible" (Haidt and Kesebir, 2010). Religious beliefs typically involve just the sorts of entities and practices that suppress selfishness and make social life possible. In addition to general moral teachings against selfishness—love thy neighbor as thyself—religious systems usually involve nonhuman personal agents with the concern for and powers to create the moral cooperation necessary for longstanding group cohesion. A personal, supernatural being is either the source of morality or the companion of goodness. Most importantly, this being is conceived of having the powers to deter antisocial behavior.

The general problem for cooperation is called the *free-rider problem*. It may be evolutionarily advantageous to be a member of a cooperative community with all the benefits of cooperation, but even better to be selectively immoral when it is to one's advantage. So, in the paradigm case, the free-rider takes advantage of everyone else paying their fare to ride the bus but fails to pay their own fare; they are, literally, free-riders. There are countless ways to be free-riders on the cooperation created by moral good will: cheating on taxes (and getting the benefits of living in a tax-paying society) or in one's business dealings, not working as hard, stealing from grain stores, and so on. As long as punishment is unlikely (because punishment detection and enforcement are costly), free-riders can gain benefits for themselves with relatively little cost to themselves or to society.

Supernatural punishment solves the free-rider problem with little or no cost. Religious beliefs and practices can increase the costs of defection to the point that it would be irrational to free ride. In addition to human punishments, the threat of supernatural punishment dramatically ups the moral ante. With superknowers and superpunishers, free-riders are ensured both detection and punishment. Since supernatural agents serve as legislators, police, judges, and punishers, there is little cost to keeping the peace. Cheaters will be caught and punished. The punishments may, but need not be, in the next life.

Empirical studies support the claim that cooperative behavior increases as the belief in or fear of detection increases. Jesse Bering discovered that 3-year-old children were much less likely to open a forbidden box when told that an invisible agent, Princess Alice, was in the room (Bering and Parker, 2006). Azim Shariff and Ara Norenzayan showed that atheists and theists alike were significantly more generous, honest, and helpful when primed with God concepts (Shariff and Norenzayan, 2007). Religious people are much more likely than the nonreligious to engage in behaviors that benefit others at a personal cost when religious thoughts are freshly activated in their mind. In one experiment that involved giving money anonymously to a stranger, simply adding eyespots to the computer background dramatically improved giving (Haley and Fessler, 2005). Another experiment showed that drawing eyes on a collection box used to collect funds for drinks in university lounge increased payment (Bateson, Nettle and Roberts, 2006). Being watched decreases selfish behavior; being watched by God (who not only knows but punishes) even further decreases selfish behavior.

But it takes even more than being watched to dramatically increase unselfish behavior. Mere religious belief, or fear of detection, may keep one from cheating, but only deep and sincere religious belief as reflected in regular religious practices are morally transformative. Recent empirical research has shown that, for example, regular church-goers have a number of interesting, statistically significant, and positive moral traits. Religion, as a source of moral behavior, is demonstrably superior to unbelief.

Can religions deliver what they promise, to make people morally and spiritually better? Recent research has shown that religious conviction is superior to nonreligious motivations to morality and is empirically verified as better at motivating morality. In short, religion supports morality.

While religious beliefs sometimes channel intolerance and violence, they also tame our vicious and selfish nature. Studies show that religious believers in the United States are generally more moral than their secular counterparts. While the health and longevity benefits of being part of a religious community have long been known, the moral benefits of being in a religious community are just as well attested.

Arthur Brooks, the Louis A. Bantle Professor of Government Policy at The Maxwell School of Citizenship and Public Affairs at Syracuse University, concludes that active religious believers are vastly more generous than nonbelievers. Drawing upon hard data from the 2005 National Bureau of Economic Research, the 2000 Social Capital Community Benchmark Survey, the 1996–2004 General Social Survey, the 1998–2001 International Social Survey Programme, and many others, his analysis, in *Who Really Cares?* shows a striking moral difference between religious and secular Americans. Consider this, he asks:

Imagine two people: One goes to church every week and strongly rejects the idea that it is the government's responsibility to redistribute income between people who have a lot of money and people who don't. The other person never attends a house of worship, and strongly believes that the government *should* reduce income differences.

Knowing only these things, the data tell us that the first person will be roughly twice as likely as the second to give money to charities in a given year, and will give away more than *one hundred times* as much money per year (as well as fifty times more to explicitly nonreligious causes). (Brooks, 2006: 10)

The religious believer is vastly more likely than the secular person to, among many other things, volunteer, give blood, or loan money to friends and family (and to do so more generously). Even subtracting money given to and time volunteered at religious institutions, religious believers are still much more generous with their money and time. On any metric of generosity, the religious person trumps the secular person. Brooks concludes: "Religious people are more charitable in every measurable non-religious way—including secular donations, informal giving, and even acts of kindness and honesty—than secularists" (Brooks, 2006: 38).

Critics of religion often claim a religious bias either in favor of a theocratic imposition of a severe religious morality or a ghettoistic avoidance of a wicked public square. Religion tempts its proponents to triumphalism or tribalism. Religion, on this view, is the root of nearly all political evil.

Yet study after study suggests that religion, at least in the West, often plays a pivotal role in fostering precisely those norms, disposition, skills, and relationships that democratic theorists tell us are essential to active citizenship.

In recent work on the development of what might be termed *civic capacities* (such as voluntarism), studies have shown that houses of worship in the United States are the most important seedbeds for developing leadership, communication, and other "civic skills" that are crucial in modern democracies. In addition, religious people are engaged in more civic activities. Such findings ought to be heartening to democratic theorists who emphasize the importance of an informed and attentive public.

There is also a generally positive association between levels of religiosity and the possession of "social capital," that is, those dispositions and networks that foster collective decision-making. In his *Bowling Alone,* Harvard political scientist Robert Putnam argues convincingly that dispositions, such as interpersonal trust and reciprocity, are crucial to effective political and economic institutions. Religious institutions are key venues for the development of those kinds of dispositions. The power of religion is so pronounced that Putnam himself has raised the concern publicly that declining religious participation rates among younger people might have toxic effects on healthy civic life in the United States.

Americans who are actively religious are considerably less prone to alcohol and drug abuse and therefore are physically healthier and live longer than their nonreligious counterparts. Health and religiosity, both of which are enjoyed by the actively religious, are the best predictors of happiness in the elderly. People with deep faith and involvement in faith communities recover more rapidly from the blows of life such as divorce or the death of a loved one.

In addition to the health and longevity benefits of happiness, there are moral benefits: religious people, like all very happy people, are much more likely to be loving, forgiving, trustful, and helpful.

Are such psychological and sociological claims at all relevant to questions of the existence of god? If the lives of religious believers are in accord with the nature of ultimate Reality, a Reality that is loving and good, one might reasonably expect the lives of religious believers to be increasingly loving and good. Being properly aligned with the moral structure of the universe should prove morally empowering. If religious believers avail themselves of genuinely salvific or morally transformational processes–through divinely inspired writings, divine grace, divine rituals, or divine assistance–then we might expect transformed behavior. Not perfection, of course, because religions are often the mostly keenly aware of the corrosive effects of sin, but moral improvement, surely.

Religious critics, who trot out horrific anecdotes such as the September 11th terrorist attacks and female genital mutilation, ignore the goods delivered by religion. In addition to generosity and honesty, as noted above, religious belief has historically delivered many other great goods. Consider Christian involvement in the eradication of infanticide, gladiatorial games, and slavery. Granted, slavery wasn't abolished for centuries, but very early on Christian slave owners were admonished to treat their slaves with compassion, and their slaves were considered, unlike in pagan belief systems, equals in the eyes of God. What about religious involvement in poverty and famine relief, and the general kindness shown by the believer toward her children, neighbor, or even a stranger (not to mention widows, orphans, and prisoners)? In the West, institutions such as hospitals, universities, orphanages, and alms barns all owe their creation to Christians.

Natural rights were considered to be given by God, and equal rights arose in a milieu that affirmed the priesthood of all believers. The rule of law arose in a culture committed to a Lawgiver. Human dignity arose within a culture that progressively grasped what it meant to be created in the divine image.

The scientific revolution emerged through the work of Christian scientists such as Copernicus, Galileo, and Boyle. How do we weigh the artistic goods of Michelangelo, Da Vinci, and Bach?

Finally, for God's sake, what about potlucks?

Deeply religious groups have much higher levels of trust, cooperation, and sharing than nonreligious groups, especially in difficult or trying times. The behaviors of people who have religious beliefs—say, those who believe in god or God or gods—but who are not religiously active are virtually indistinguishable from those with no religious beliefs at all. So while Princess Alice and eye drawings may prevent peeking and paying the buck one already owes, the best foundation for honesty, generosity, and charity seems to be deep and profound religious belief supported by *active participation* in religious rituals and communities.

Conclusion

Belief in God is morally advantageous because it motivates rationally self-interested people to be moral. Moreover, only if there is a next life in which virtue is attainable and happiness expected can one be properly motivated to be moral. Belief in a superknower who exercises a kind of moral providence dramatically increases prosocial behavior.

If this moral argument were the sole reason offered in defense of theism, belief in God would be held on poor grounds indeed. We might concede the truth of this argument and simply be *demoralized*. The sober truth might just be that it is sometimes in my best interest to be wicked.

But suppose we were to locate this debate within the context of a larger theistic argument in which we were able to demonstrate that theism is roughly equal in explanatory power to naturalism. In such a case, the moral advantages of theism might tip the scales in favor of belief in God. No doubt there are other pragmatic advantages to theism as well concerning, say, the meaning of life or the grief suffered when loved ones die. These pragmatic advantages may provide additional reasons to believe in God. All things being equal, it is surely more reasonable to accept an explanatory theory that has more moral and pragmatic advantages than its competitors. As for motivating and undergirding the moral life, theism has the advantage.

CHAPTER 11

In Search of the Soul

THE INVENTION OF THE SOUL

We can date the invention of the soul to that fateful night of November 10, 1619. Snowbound in a room in Ulm, Germany, Rene Descartes squeezed his frigid body into a stove, fell asleep, and dreamed vividly and wildly. He entered the stove a body but exited a soul. The human soul, Descartes learned in his dream, directs the mechanical, material body like a puppetmaster her puppet. The nonphysical soul pulls the strings and the physical body sings and dances in response. The soul is the captain, the body the ship. The soul is a nonphysical or metaphysical ghost, the body is the machine that it haunts. The soul is the essentially human—it's what makes me me—and the body is only incidentally connected to me and can be shucked off, without loss of self, like a fingernail, flake of skin, or lock of hair. I am, Descartes wrote, "a thinking thing"—a soul, not a body.

Descartes's division of the mind from the body—"Cartesian dualism"—freed us from our bodies and so liberated us from the tyranny of cause and effect in the material world; and although worms destroy our bodies, yet in our souls shall we see God. In one fell swoop, Descartes preserves freedom and proves immortality (against the rising tide of materialism and atheism). By transporting us—our soul—into the metaphysical (spiritual) world, we are thus freed from the grasp of the law-governed physical world.

Upon waking from his dream, Descartes pilgrimaged to the Holy House of Loreto in thanksgiving for this divine blessing.

Although the cold drove Descartes into that stove and out a blessed man, it would prove his final undoing. Having been persuaded by Queen Christina of Sweden to go to Stockholm, he found himself taking daily winter walks to the palace at 5 a.m. to tutor the Queen in math. The Swedish winters combined with breaking his lifetime habit of not getting out of bed before 11 a.m. left him tired and weak. After just a few months, in 1650, he died of pneumonia.

While Descartes considered his bright night of the soul a divine gift, William Temple (Archbishop of Canterbury from 1942–44) called it "the most disastrous moment in the history of Europe" (Temple, 1964: 57). One wonders why Temple used such strong language: whatever happened in that stove, how could it have been worse than, for starters, the Holocaust, slavery, or either of the two world wars? Secular philosopher, Gilbert Ryle, heaped scorn on Cartesian dualism—the claim that humans are composed of two parts, the material body and the immaterial soul. He caricatured Descartes's view as "the ghost in the machine" and dedicated his most famous book to ridiculing it (Ryle, 1949). Daniel Dennett rejects the radical separation of mind and body as profoundly antiscientific. Christian and atheist alike, then, have joined forces, hoping to eliminate once and for all the woeful, yet enduring, Cartesian blight on Western civilization.

As you may have guessed, the above legend is only partly true but widely repeated. Descartes dreamed, for example, in a stove-heated room, not in a stove. He did not invent the soul or even the idea of the soul. The roots of mind–body dualism are found in most religions, in many philosophies, and even in common sense. Some of the central metaphors of the Descartes legend, especially those that suggest a radical separation of mind and body, find their origin in Plato. One finds intimations of mind–body dualism in the Judeo–Christian tradition in which God creates humans by breathing into their dust-formed nostrils the breath (spirit) of life (Genesis 2.7). Finally, Descartes explicitly rejected the view that the mind is in the body as a pilot is in his ship.

It's not our purpose to set the record straight concerning the Descartes legend (although we'll return to Descartes later). Instead, we will look at the vexed matter of the relationship of mind and body from the perspective of science and religion. Descartes, for example, claimed that he was defending the Christian view of the mind–body relation. He also believed that his conception of the human person as a body–soul composite allowed room in the chain of cause and effect (that governs planets, for example, and machines) for such essential religious beliefs as human freedom. His view also grounded his hope for life after death.

Pervasiveness of Mind–body Dualism

When we think about what it means to be human, we are keenly aware of physical bodies that walk, see, touch, and talk. When we look in a mirror, we see a reflection of our extended fleshy structure. When we step on a scale, the numbers communicate to us that our bodies have a specific weight. Our bodies can sparkle and shine, and they can bruise and burn. When we stare into the mirror, or step on the scale, or apply a band-aid, we are aware of our bodies. Our bodies seem like an important part of being human.

But that's not all there is to human existence. Sometimes when we look in the mirror, we not only see our reflection, we *imagine* looking quite different than we actually do. Occasionally, when we step on a scale, we *desire* the numbers to be a little lower than they actually are; so we *plan* to exercise. When our bodies are burned or bruised, we *experience* pain in a way that no one else could by simply looking at the wound or hearing an account of what happened. Thus, when we look in the mirror, step on a scale, or apply a band-aid, we are aware of more than just our bodies. Our awareness—our ability to desire, plan, and imagine, or to consciously experience pleasure and pain—is mental stuff, not body stuff. Mental stuff (consciousness) lead many to believe that, in addition to a body, something like a mind or soul exists, one that is the subject—the "I" or the self—of our consciousness.

The depiction of an individual as both a body and a mind suggests a dualistic perspective of the human person. Regarding the nature of human persons, *substance dualism* holds that both *an immaterial mind and a material body exist as distinct, separate, individual substances.* Dualistic perspectives are the most common, and perhaps even the most *commonsensical* way of understanding the nature of humankind. Psychologist Paul Bloom argues that belief in dualism is innate (inborn) in all humans and so is not learned (Bloom, 2004).

Descartes and Plato were clearly substance dualists. According to substance dualism, the mind exists, and is of the utmost import to being human; in fact, the mind (soul, spirit) is the part of us that makes us human. It cannot be eliminated (without me ceasing to be me). The mind cannot be explained away, and it cannot be reduced to the brain or chemical properties of the brain.

It's easy to see why the mind resists being reduced to the brain (explained fully in terms of chemical or neuronal processes) or at least why mental properties seem clean contrary to physical processes. Consider your visual sensation of, say, Albert Einstein. If a neurologist were to cut open your brain, he might see gray matter but he wouldn't see an image of Einstein. Or suppose you got cut on the forearm and are now in pain. While portions of the brain would be active (suppose an electroencephalogram records the firings of neurons in your hypothalamus), and a neuroscientist may be able to identify the chemical processes involved, neither the brain activity nor the chemical processes are the pain itself. C-fiber firings are not the pain, and chemical processes are not the pain. Pain is a feel (or a feeling) that is qualitatively different from the physical processes associated with it. Try as you might, you would search the brain in vain for the pain. Physical properties, or the properties of physical or chemical processes, are quite different from mental properties. While scientists have shown many *correlations* between the mental and the physical, there's not a single successful *reduction* of the feeling of pain or a visual sensation to brain processes (i.e., a complete explanation of pain in terms that eliminate the mental). The mental is qualitatively different from the physical. So, perhaps, the mind is not reducible to the brain.

Records of dualism extend as far back as Zarathustra who, around 6000 BC, maintained that reality was divided into two different elemental energies: Good, that is reason (associated with the soul), and Evil, a bodily energy (Trimble, 2007: 11). Similarly, Greek philosopher Plato divided reality into two separate realms, the intelligible world (good) and the material world (not so good). Plato argued for the soul's independence from the body, and he highlighted the disparity between the intelligible and material worlds as evidence of the soul's immortality as well as its ability to exist and possess knowledge in a disembodied state. These forms of dualism often denigrate the body and celebrate or valorize the immaterial soul or mind (and its ultimate release from the body in which it is imprisoned). The immortal soul, according to Plato, is trapped or imprisoned in and by the mortal and passional body.

CHRISTIANITY AND DUALISM

Various scriptural passages suggest that the ancient Hebrews and early Christians accepted some form of substance dualism. According to the early Hebrews, and many Christians today, the human being is comprised of two parts: the material body and the immaterial, God-breathed soul. Genesis 2.7 states, "The Lord God formed the man from the dust of the ground and breathed into his nostrils the breath of life, and the man became a living being." This passage suggests that the human body (i.e., a physical thing that is purely constituted by matter) is not itself a human person. Rather, it takes the "breath of life" to transform a body into a human person. This passage suggests that body and soul have separate origins, properties, and compositions.

Although Old Testament terminology regarding the soul is disputed, the Hebrews believed in the disembodied existence of the deceased in Sheol. Sheol was first conceived of as a temporary loading dock for the dead. It was said to have existed somewhere underground and hosted those who await the resurrection in a state of disembodied conscious existence. Sheol also sometimes indicates the *permanent* resting place of the wicked (i.e., Hades, hell). In Matthew 10.28, Jesus advises his disciples to "fear not them which kill the body, but are not able to kill the soul: but rather fear him which is able to destroy both soul and body in hell."

Many Christians have accepted a dualistic view of human persons, embracing the belief that the human person will continue to exist as a soul or spirit after their earthly death (even as their bodies degrade in the grave). The body returns to the dust from which it came while the soul rises up to meet God: "And the dust returns to the ground it came from: and the spirit returns to God who gave it" (Ecclesiastes 12.7). Many Christians believe that after a person dies, their earthly body decays in the ground while *they* live on in a disembodied state for a time until they are reunited with a new, resurrected body.

In the Roman Catholic tradition, Pope John Paul II explicitly affirmed mind–body dualism: "It is by virtue of his spiritual soul that the whole person possesses such a dignity even in his body. Pius XII stressed this essential point: If the human body takes its origin from pre-existent living matter, the spiritual soul is immediately created by God."[1]

THE SCIENCE OF THE MIND

The West's love affair with mind–body dualism ended abruptly on September 13, 1848 when an explosion shot a 3 foot 7 inch, 13.25-pound iron rod through the brain of Phineas Gage. Gage, the 25-year-old foreman of a railroad blasting crew, was using the rod to tamp gunpowder into a hole in the rock. But when the rod struck stone it caused a spark and the resulting explosion propelled the 1.25 inch diameter rod up and through his left cheek and out the top of his head; the rod landed 20 yards behind him. Gage was not killed, living more than a decade longer. The damage to his brain, however, caused a complete transformation in Gage's character. The previously kind, affable, and gentle Gage became impulsive, unreliable, quarrelsome, irreverent, and disrespectful. His personality change was so radical his friends said, "Gage is no longer Gage." So great was the change, his bosses refused his pleas to return to his job. He would later find gainful employment as a human curiosity at Barnum's American Museum in New York.

Gage "proves" that the mind (soul/spirit) does not float free of the brain/body *a la* Descartes's legend. Impacts on the brain are impacts on the mind/soul/spirit. What happens to the brain, happens to the mind. Maybe, the thought occurs, the brain *is* the mind.

When I was a student I knew a man who was a sweet, gentle Christian. He later sustained a closed head injury in a snowmobile accident. When he emerged from his three-week coma, his personality was thoroughly changed. He was no longer sweet and gentle, and he was no longer a Christian. He had become, through a bump on the head, a bitter, angry atheist. If radical mind–body dualism were true, a bump on the head would not affect beliefs, emotions, and attitudes. The mind, after all, free floats in the nonphysical world and is connected to the body uni-directionally—the mind rules the body but is unaffected by the physical stuff of the brain. And if faith is essential to salvation, how could this man's eternal destiny hang upon a bump on the head?

Depending on the location of a brain lesion, an individual may lose the ability to form new memories, or comprehend elementary speech patterns. Some injuries prevent patients from being able to identify colors or even the faces of their family members (Churchland, 1988: 143–44). Neuroscientists, in so-called localization studies, have even been able to locate which part of the brain is activated when an individual is undergoing a certain psychological event or experience. They can locate *where* we remember, feel, or desire. A team of psychologists discovered that when patients experienced the loss of a loved one, there was marked activity in the prefrontal cortex and the anterior cingulate cortex. Other studies have shown that long-term psychological dysfunctions, such as depression, can alter the size of the hippocampus and even change the shape of the brain altogether over a significant period of time (Green, 2005: 15–17). Our psychology, therefore, is intimately linked to our brain and its processes.

We can locate thoughts and feelings within the brain. A sneaking suspicion arises: my wet, gray matter—the brain—is me, the source of my feelings, thoughts, and desires. There is no "I" that commands my body like the captain of a ship. There is no soul that is oblivious to the stormy seas that shake and rattle my brain.

MATERIALISM: THE MIND IS THE BRAIN

Contemporary science has declared war on the mind. Cognitive scientist Stephen Pinker states, "Cognitive neuroscience, the attempt to relate thought, perception, and emotion to the functioning of the brain, has pretty much killed [the soul]" (Pinker, 1999). Harvard biologist E. O. Wilson contends that science has searched the nooks and crannies of the brain and come up empty handed: "The brain and its satellite glands have now been probed to the point where no particular site remains that can reasonably be supposed to harbor a nonphysical mind" (Wilson, 1998: 99). The announcement of the elimination of the soul—echoed by myriad scholars in various scientific fields—is one to which atheist Richard Dawkins haughtily adds, "Good riddance" (Dawkins, 1999).

Those who reject the immaterial mind, *materialists*, believe that the only things that exist are material entities and physical processes. *Reductive materialism* is the view that the relationship between the body and the so-called mind is that the "mind" is completely reducible to the brain or brain processes.[2] Francis Crick, who with James Watson co-discovered the structure of the DNA molecule, is a reductive materialist. He embraces the "Astonishing Hypothesis" that "the 'You,' your joys and your sorrows, your memories and your ambitions, your sense of identity and free will, are in fact no more than the behavior of a vast assembly of nerve cells and their associated molecules. As Lewis Carroll's Alice might have phrased it: 'You're nothing but a pack of neurons'" (Crick, 1994: 3). Such scientists and philosophers claim that "studies show" that the mind is *nothing but* the brain or the mental is *nothing but* physical processes that go on in the brain and central nervous system. According to this view, mental states are identical to physical states in the brain.

Rejecting immaterial substances such as minds or souls, materialists hold that the human person is completely definable in terms of the body's physical components and the physical processes these components undergo. Philosopher Daniel Dennett, in *Consciousness Explained,* claims that "there is only one sort of stuff, namely matter—the physical stuff of physics, chemistry, and physiology—and the mind is somehow nothing but a physical phenomenon. In short, the mind is the brain" (Dennett, 1991: 33).

The materialist brands the typical, commonsensical ways of thinking about the mind or soul—beliefs, thoughts, feelings, souls—as "folk psychology," quaint but outdated ways of understanding mental phenomena. Materialists deny that we really have any beliefs, feelings, or desires. In the materialist's world, folk descriptions of mental phenomena are to be translated into strictly physical terms and then eliminated altogether. In the hands of reductive materialists, the mind and mental phenomena are redefined using concepts such as "behavior," "brain processes," and "function." The belief that honey tastes sweet is nothing but chemical processes x, y, and z in the brain. The feeling of pain is more than *caused* by a particular formation of neurons in the brain, it *just is* a particular formation of neurons in the brain. Every mental state is reducible, without remainder, to a physical state. The mental is the physical.[3]

Reductive views attempt to explain (away) the mind in terms of the brain and central nervous system. Scientists, when considering competing explanations, don't want to multiply entities beyond necessity (this is called "Ockham's Razor"). Materialism would reduce the number and kind of terms we use to describe humans. In an attempt to make this idea clear, philosopher Dale Jacquette writes, "If we can explain an eclipse of the moon without assuming that there are demons who cloak or devour it, then Ockham's Razor requires us to eliminate the concept of demon from our theory of the moon's eclipse" (Jacquette, 1994: 35). If the mental can be fully accounted for in terms of the physical, then Ockham's razor would require the elimination of nonphysical souls or minds. Souls go the way of demons, ghosts, and goblins.

Daniel Dennett explains reductionism as it applies to human persons:

> Some people are gentle and generous others are ruthless, some are pornographers and others devote their lives to the service of God. It has been tempting over the ages to imagine that these striking differences must be due to the specific features of some extra thing (a soul, or mind) installed somehow in the bodily headquarters. We now know that tempting as this idea still is, it is not supported in the slightest by anything we have learned about our biology in general and our brains in particular. The more we learn about how we have evolved, and how our brains work, the more certain we are becoming that there is no such extra ingredient. We are each made of mindless robots and nothing else, no nonphysical, nonrobotic ingredients at all. (Dennett, 2003: 3)

Materialism seeks to fully explain the mind in terms of neurophysiological processes. The brain sends messages to other body parts through neurons and other special cells. Neurons transmit information by firing electrical charges to different parts of the body, triggering sensation and motor skills.

Philosophically, dualism faces a problem not faced by materialism: how could an immaterial soul cause a material body to move? We know how a rock might break a window or how a hand might throw a rock—that is, we know how one material thing can cause another material things to move. But, try as we might, we can't break the window just by thinking it; we can stare at the window, think intently about wanting it broken, furl our brow and think even harder, but we won't break the window by thinking. Sticks and stones may break bones, but just thinking about them won't. The mental can't have, it seems, that kind of affect on the physical.

Descartes, in a letter from Princess Elizabeth of Bohemia, is aware of this issue. Princess Elizabeth asks him to tell her "how the human soul can determine the movement of the animal spirits in the body so as to perform voluntary acts...For the determination of movement seems always to come about from the moving body's being propelled" (Anscombe and Geach, 1954: 274–75). Being propelled requires contact between two objects (like a pool ball moving when struck by another pool ball). But a fluffy soul, one that exists outside of space and time, can't come in contact with a hard, enduring body, and thus cannot move it. All physical effects have physical causes. According to this principle, physical events cannot be explained by mental events, substances, or properties.

If the mental cannot affect the physical, it would be impossible for a mind to relate causally to a body. Philosopher Jaegwon Kim frames the problem like this: how do "two substances with such radically diverse natures, one in space-time, with mass, inertia, and the like and the other lacking wholly in material properties and not even located in physical space, stand in causal relations to each other" (Kim, 2001: 32). Causal relations depend on spatiotemporal interaction. Causal interaction between mental and material substances is impossible because they have opposing essential natures. The body is essentially spatial, the mind is essentially nonspatial. Just as the soul can't weigh 175 pounds or turn red when embarrassed, it also can't be here or there. If the soul can't be located in space, it cannot interact with the body. Interactions must take place somewhere and souls can't be somewhere.

Christian Materialism

Christian materialism holds that persons are material beings without souls.[4] Christians who endorse materialist—nondualist—conceptions of persons claim that dualism was a Greek intrusion into the Christian tradition. The biblical view, they contend, is *Hebrew holism*, which is a kind of materialism about human persons—humans are not made of both material stuff and spiritual stuff, they are material stuff only (from the dust of the earth) but, given their unique capacities (consciousness and self-consciousness), humans are often referred to metaphorically in nonmaterial ways (as souls or spirits). But, according to the Bible, humans are not literally body–soul composites (the Greek view). They are thoroughly materially constituted. Instead of a dualist (mind–body) view of persons, they claim that the Bible supports a monistic—single stuff—view of the constitution of persons as purely material. Christian materialists contend that the brain and not the soul thinks, feels, and desires. Or better, I, a fully physical being, think, feel, and desire.

Christian materialists interpret passages of the Bible that appear to endorse a separate soul or spirit as referring to the whole person, not to an immaterial substance. While the Bible may say, "My soul cries out to the Lord," that does not mean that my anguished immaterial soul orders my material mouth to open and then engages my vocal chords to produce a crying noise. Rather, I, in my anguish, cry out to the Lord from the very depths of my being. There is no supervising soul instructing the body. According to Christian materialists, the Christian tradition got it wrong by forcing Greek thought onto biblical texts. The importation of souls into Christian theology imposed a foreign, even pagan, view of human persons on the Bible itself.

Christians who are materialists about persons are not materialists about ultimate reality.[5] They are firmly committed to a dualist structure of ultimate reality: reality is composed of two sorts of stuff—matter and spirit. The world (all that is not God) is material while God is Spirit.

However, they believe that human persons, though created in God's image, are composed of just one sort of stuff—matter. Take away our bodies (or remove all of our body parts), and there is nothing left over, there is nothing left of us.

A Philosophical Problem for Materialism

In spite of its widespread acceptance by most contemporary philosophers, neuroscientists, and many religious thinkers, materialism about persons appears to leave something out. Philosopher Colin McGinn puts it this way: "The more we know of the brain, the less it looks like a device for creating consciousness: it's just a big collection of biological cells and a blur of electrical activity—all machine and no ghost."[6] How could we possibly get mind, or mind-like properties or things, out of bits of matter?

To illustrate this point, philosopher Frank Jackson introduced the thought experiment known as "Mary's Room." Consider the following

> Mary is a brilliant scientist who is, for whatever reason, forced to investigate the world from a black and white room *via* a black and white television monitor. She specializes in the neurophysiology of vision and acquires, let us suppose, all the physical information there is to obtain about what goes on when we see ripe tomatoes, or the sky, and use terms like "red", "blue", and so on. She discovers, for example, just which wavelength combinations from the sky stimulate the retina, and exactly how this produces via the central nervous system the contraction of the vocal cords and expulsion of air from the lungs that results in the uttering of the sentence "The sky is blue."...What will happen when Mary is released from her black and white room or is given a color television monitor? Will she *learn* anything or not? (Jackson, 1982)

The question of whether or not Mary will learn something new when she finally *sees* color seems quite clearly, "Yes." Materialists, however, answer Jackson's question with a resounding, "No!" They claim that, should Mary know all of the physical elements of color and the neurophysiological processes involved with seeing color, she will learn nothing new when she actually sees color herself.[7]

In spite of protestations to the contrary, reductive materialism seems incapable of accounting for the subjective quality of what it is like to *experience* mental phenomena; it seems to leave out the felt qualities of our sensations. Indeed, one of the most devastating shortcomings of materialism is that *third-person physical descriptions* (of chemical processes or neuronal configurations) cannot, in principle, adequately represent *first-person subjective experiences or states*—the feel of a feeling, the sensation of a color, the sadness of an emotion. Feelings, sensations, and emotions refuse reduction.

Third-person data, or data about behavior and brain processes, are what can be observed and known from the outside, so to speak, by a third person. Typical third-person data might be: "He looks hungry," or "She appears sad," or "The pre-frontal cortex has an increase in activity associated with her report of being in pain." First-person data, or data about subjective experience, are how or what I feel, what I desire, or what I see, and so on. Typical first-person data would be my feeling hungry, my being sad, or my being in pain. It's hard to see how to reduce my being sad, for example, to "She appears sad." Dale Jaquette contends that reductionists are "denying the obvious." He argues: "It has been said that there is nothing more obvious or better known than the contents of our immediate mental states. They are right before us and available for the most detailed inspection whenever we choose, though we can sometimes make mistakes in describing them" (Jacquette, 1994: 58). Mental phenomena seem indispensible; a complete theory of mind must account for them.

Materialist explanations, at least so far, have not, and maybe cannot, offer an objective, scientific, third-person account of the subjective feeling of pain or the sensation of the color red. Substance dualist John Foster states: "It is hard to see how any set of propositions about behavior, functional organization, physiological makeup, environmental circumstances, or anything else that might feature in the chosen reductive analysis, could suffice to specify how it feels to the subject to be in pain, or to be having a certain type of sensory experience, or to be in the grip of a certain type of emotion, or to be in any other mental state of an experiential kind" (Foster, 2001: 21). The problem of first-person subjective states resurfaces. Cognitive science is at this point unable to explain (let alone explain away) thoughts, feelings, or desires.[8]

RESURRECTING CARTESIAN DUALISM

Let's recall and develop the elements of the Cartesian substance dualism myth. Properties are neatly divided into those that are mental and those that are physical, and each set of properties requires suitable substrata. Mental properties (such as being in pain, feeling sad, or believing) can be properly ascribed only to a mental substance, and physical properties (such as size and spatial location) can be ascribed only to a physical substance. Accordingly, mind and body are separate entities. For Descartes, the substance that supports the mental properties is the soul, or the immaterial mind. As an immaterial substance, the Cartesian soul has no parts and does not take up space. The physical body, on the other hand, exists in space, and is the subject of such properties as shape, length, weight, and height. Although the physical body is not a thinking thing, it is through the material body that the soul makes direct contact with the physical world. But human persons are essentially thinking beings—souls. Thus, the Cartesian legend holds that the physical body is a contingent, expendable feature of a person.

Critics of this Cartesian legend reject the claim that mind and body are completely different stuff. This "abyssal separation between body and mind" is, according to Antonio Damasio in *Descartes' Error*, Descartes's error. Descartes failed to recognize the interdependence of mind and body (Damasio, 1994: 249–50).

Science, so it seems, is on Damasio's side. Studies in neuroscience and biology reveal that our minds and brains are intricately intertwined, and that mind is dependent on brain. For example, the use of alcohol and drugs can affect our mental stability. The physical deterioration of certain areas of the brain can lead to drastic changes in personality. The removal of some parts of the brain can result in loss of certain skills, memories, and sensations. The mind's functioning is directly connected to the functioning of the brain.

Let us quickly save Descartes from his detractors, not because we care so much about Descartes but because his views are instructive for understanding the issues involved in the mind–body relationship. Although Descartes thought that soul and body were distinct entities, he believed that soul and body were nonetheless causally interrelated. They are so integrally related that mind and body form a "unitary whole," a "substantial union."[9] He writes: "Nature also teaches me, by these sensations of pain, hunger, thirst and so on that I am not merely present in my body as a sailor is present in a ship, but that I am very closely and, as it were, intermingled with it, so that I and the body form a unit" (Descartes, 1993: Med. VI). Descartes was a holist about persons—we are a tightly interwoven mind–body unit. A human person is not a conglomeration, like oil and water, of two contrary and unmixable substances. A human person is a mind–body unity with mind and body in mutual interaction.

The mind, Descartes thinks, is causally connected to the body in such a way that our intentions, desires, and thoughts cause the movements of our body in and around the world. Why not? Our mental desires, intentions, and conscious decisions seem to influence many of our physical actions. When we intend to slow a moving vehicle, we press our foot on the brake pedal. If we desire to eat a donut, we reach our hand into the box and grab our favorite one. The influence also runs in the other direction—with bodily events causing mental events. When we take a big gulp of hot cocoa after playing in the snow, the physical action of drinking burning liquid triggers the mental event of pain. Looking at the snow (with one's eyes) causes visual sensations of whiteness. A whack on the head can give a person a headache and even change their beliefs and emotions. Mind affects body, and body also affects mind.

The radical separationist view attributed incorrectly to Descartes at the opening of the book and at the beginning of this section is not a plausible version of mind–body dualism. "Cartesian dualism" was neither endorsed nor defended by Descartes. Perhaps Plato was a Cartesian dualist. Descartes was not. There are no current Christian defenders of Platonic dualism. No Christian thinker now believes that the mind is imprisoned within the body, that the body is bad, that the soul is immortal, that the mind alone captains the body, or that the mind is so abyssally separate from the body that it cannot be affected by bodily or brain events. The soul, in contemporary Christian thought, is not the ghost in the machine. Cartesian dualism may be an error but it's not Descartes's error, and it's not an error embraced by contemporary Christian thinkers.

CONTEMPORARY CHRISTIAN DUALISM

Colin McGinn claims that, "The trouble with theistic dualism is that it vastly exaggerates the gap between mind and brain. The mind is far more dependent on the brain than the theory acknowledges" (McGinn, 2000: 88). Christian dualists are neither oblivious to nor disdainful of the very important insights of the science of the mind. Let us consider the views of two contemporary Christian dualists, Richard Swinburne and William Hasker.

Richard Swinburne holds that the mind and the body are two separate entities, and that the mind cannot be reduced to or completely explained in physical terms. Yet, according to his *soft dualism,* during one's normal earthly life, the soul is dependent for its functioning (having a mental life) on the functioning of the body. Soul and body are interdependent. He argues against materialism by presenting mental phenomena—sensations, thoughts, purposings, desires, beliefs—to show that they are distinct from physical phenomena such as public behavior or particular brain events. That is, first-person subjective experiences are fundamentally different from third-person descriptions. Against hard-core dualism, he argues that the body is an essential part of a human person.

While Swinburne denies that mind and brain are identical, he does recognize the close relationship between them. According to Swinburne, a human person consists of two parts—body and soul—not just soul. Of the soul part, Swinburne states it "is the necessary core which must continue if I am to continue, it is the part of the person which is necessary for his continuing existence" (Swinburne, 1986: 146). Swinburne believes that the soul is the essential *part* of the person, but he does not concede that the soul is the *only* part that makes up the person. Swinburne also contends that the body is part of the human person as well. He states that "my arms and my legs are parts of *me*...The person is the soul together with whatever, if any, body is linked temporarily to it" (Swinburne, 1986: 146). Recognizing the close relationship between mind and brain, Swinburne claims that a normal soul functioning requires a body.[10] Swinburne writes: "The brain gives rise to a man's mental states—his beliefs, including his apparent memories, and his desires, their expression in public behavior, and his characteristic pattern of unintended response to circumstance" (Swinburne, 1986: 147). Swinburne recognizes the importance of the brain, and recognizes that, for the human, a functional mind relies on a functional brain. There is no abyssal separation between mind and body in Swinburne's soft dualism.

William Hasker defends *emergent dualism* in which the mental emerges from the physical, that is, consciousness and mental properties appear when body and brain have evolved to the appropriate level of complexity. As an example of emergent properties, when the right amounts of hydrogen and oxygen, two gases, are combined, in the right way, an entirely new substance with entirely new sets of properties emerges. Add a gas to a gas and you get a thirst-quenching liquid. So, too, Hasker holds that when the wet matter of the brain evolves to an appropriate level of complexity, a mind emerges, one which permits thoughts, feelings, and desires (minded activities). Not only do mental properties emerge from the material brain, but an "emergent individual"—the mind—emerges as well (Hasker, 2001: 116). On this view, neither the mind nor mental properties is reducible to physical substances or properties (just as water and its properties are not reducible to hydrogen and oxygen and their properties), despite the fact that they emerge from them.

Hasker uses the analogy of a magnetic field to illustrate the process and power of emergence. A magnetic field is something above and beyond the magnet itself. The magnetic field cannot be *reduced* to the magnet itself. An extremely intense magnetic field has within it the power (via gravity) to hold together, even in the absence of the magnet that created it (Hasker, 2005: 81). According to emergent dualism, while the mind is an independent entity, it is not an entity that is inserted from the outside as substance dualism suggests. Brains and minds are neither hostile nor independent. Rather, they are tightly linked in a persistent "monogamous" relationship. If mind emerges from matter, it's not hard to imagine that some changes in the supporting matter could and would produce changes, sometimes profound, in the mind.

Soft and emergent dualisms lie somewhere between Platonic dualism and materialism. Christian dualists, like Hasker and Swinburne, believe that their views make the best sense of the biblical picture of persons, the resurrection of the dead, and the undeniable results of neuroscience. They also throw in a dash of serious philosophical reflection on the nature of the mental and the physical. Hasker reminds us of an important aspect of philosophical discovery: "[if a] theory should be 'realistic' about the results of the sciences, it should also be 'realistic' about the phenomena of the mind itself" (Hasker, 2001: 115).

CAN THE MENTAL AFFECT THE PHYSICAL?

How could material and immaterial substances possibly interact? If minds were not located in space, how can there be a place *where* interactions occur.[11] Furthermore, how *immaterial* substances could even have contact with, let alone influence, *material* substances is difficult to conceive.

The possibility of causal interaction between the soul or mind and the body has not been a conceptual problem for Christians—they have a model for such interaction in divine creation. Christians believe that God, though a spirit, can bring about events in the material world. Mind not only moved matter into the heavens and the earth, it created matter ex nihilo. Christian theism assumes God's ability to interact with the physical world. God, like the soul, is a nonspatial, immaterial substance. Since Christians have little trouble with the concept of an immaterial substance that influences physical events and substances, they have little trouble conceiving of the mind influencing the body. This is not an *argument* against the causal interaction problem. But it would show the irony of a Christian rejecting substance dualism on account of the causal interaction problem.

CONCLUSION

The mind–body problem has not been resolved. We presented two options—materialism and dualism—as well as reasons for favoring and rejecting both. At this point, there is no decisive reason—biblical, philosophical, or scientific—to favor one view over the other. While science may seem to be nudging us in the direction of materialism, materialism seems incapable of providing an adequate account of mental phenomena. While the Christian might hold that her worldview includes the supreme example of the mental causing the physical (God creating the world), she has not yet offered an account how this is possible. Whichever you choose, materialism or dualism, you are left with something important that is fundamentally unexplained—how the mental causes the physical or how the mental could arise from the physical. Which mystery do you choose?

What hangs on this debate? I suspect not much. While the Christian tradition has overwhelmingly endorsed mind–body dualism, its only relevant universally binding statement on the matter seems clearly to oppose only Platonic dualism (where the soul continues on after death without a body) and to support an essential connection of our humanity to our body. The Apostles' Creed, sometimes called "the Creed of Creeds," states very simply, "I believe in the resurrection of the body." Christian materialism, soft dualism, and emergent dualism are all firmly committed to the resurrection of the body.

APPENDIX: THE ILLUSION OF FREE WILL?

Virtually every religion is committed to free will. We must be free to make significant moral choices, to freely carve out our own character, and, perhaps most importantly, to love and serve God (or to follow the Dao or the eightfold path). Freedom is also assumed in moral responsibility. In the punishment of evildoers, we assume that they could have done otherwise and so hold them responsible for their free but reprehensible choices. Freely choosing badly, according to many religions, gets one assigned to the flames of hell. Finally, free will is assumed in everyday life—we are free to choose our spouse, our career, our destiny. Take away that freedom and we seem considerably less than human: puppets hanging on the strings of our past.

Major news sources, from the *Times* to the *Telegraph*, proclaim that free will is an illusion. "We certainly don't have free will," says leading British neuroscientist Patrick Haggard in the *Telegraph*.[12] Who can argue with a leading British neuroscientist? "I'm just a machine," he defiantly proclaims. In the *New York Times Magazine*, Jeffrey Rosen, declared the death of free will (and associated views of moral responsibility and punishment).[13] In *USA Today*, biologist Jerry Coyne declared that scientists, especially neuroscientists, have shown that free will is an illusion. You may have thought that you chose your hair style, socks, or a bagel, but you haven't. He writes:

> You may *feel* like you've made choices, but in reality your decision to read this piece, and whether to have eggs or pancakes, was determined long before you

were aware of it—perhaps even before you woke up today. And your "will" had no part in that decision. So it is with all of our other choices: not one of them results from a free and conscious decision on our part. There is no freedom of choice, no free will. And those New Year's resolutions you made? You had no choice about making them, and you'll have no choice about whether you keep them.[14]

Free will is an after-the-fact rationalization of a fully, physically caused action. Neuroscientists, who understand how the brain works, have declared free will, our sense or feeling of choice between competing appealing options, an illusion.

The sorts of claims that Coyne and others make against free will smack of science and so make it seem that science, once again, conflicts with a significant religious doctrine—freedom of the will. Let's look at one of these arguments, namely Coyne's, to see if it holds up. His primary argument, he says, is simple:

We are biological creatures, collections of molecules that must obey the laws of physics. All the success of science rests on the regularity of those laws, which determine the behavior of every molecule in the universe. Those molecules, of course, also make up your brain—the organ that does the "choosing." And the neurons and molecules in your brain are the product of both your genes and your environment, an environment including the other people we deal with. Memories, for example, are nothing more than structural and chemical changes in your brain cells. Everything that you think, say, or do, must come down to molecules and physics.

The argument seems to go as follows: we are completely physical creatures and are thus, ultimately, governed by the laws of physics. Just as the regularity of the laws of physics determine every physical event in the universe, so, too, the laws of physics determine every one of your actions ("choices").

Lest you think I exaggerate about our being completely physical with completely determined choices, he offers an analogy to make his point: "Our brains are simply meat computers that, like real computers, are programmed by our genes and experiences to convert an array of inputs into a predetermined output." Meat computers—given the input, the output is fully determined by the hardware and software. We are no more free than carbon-based computers. Just as my computer must display 72 when I push 8 and then x and then 9 and then =, so, too, I must do thus-and-so (and nothing else), when my "buttons are pushed" in a particular situation. Coyne is not alone in these declarations. Neuroscientist Sam Harris likewise proclaims: "You seem to be an agent acting of your own free will. The problem, however, is that this point of view cannot be reconciled with what we know about the human brain."[15]

If Coyne is right, we are meat puppets whose strings are pulled by the laws of physics. But is he right? Has contemporary science shown that the laws of physics entirely determine every event? *Determinism* is the thesis that the future is entirely determined by the interaction of the past and the laws of physics. Is the world deterministic? During the eighteenth, nineteenth, and early twentieth centuries, most philosophers and scientists thought that it was. But most contemporary physicists think that determinism is false, that at least some of the laws of physics are probabilistic rather than deterministic.

Let's set this issue aside. Notice also the above quotation from Coyne says nothing about free will. How exactly does the (supposed) truth of determinism show that we have no free will? As follows:

> [L]et me define what I mean by "free will." I mean it simply as the way most people think of it: When faced with two or more alternatives, it's your ability to freely and consciously choose one, either on the spot or after some deliberation. A practical test of free will would be this: If you were put in the same position twice—if the tape of your life could be rewound to the exact moment when you made a decision, with every circumstance leading up to that moment the same and all the molecules in the universe aligned in the same way—you *could have chosen differently.*[16]

Free will, defined here as the ability to decide between two options, is sometimes called "the ability to do otherwise." Coyne's denial of free will, then, holds that all of our actions are determined, that we could not have done other than what we are compelled to do.

Many philosophers argue that the inference from 'determinism is true' to 'we can't be free' is too quick. *Compatibilism* is a view that holds that the truth of determinism is compatible (hence the name) with free will and responsibility. Compatibilists holds that as long as a person does what he or she wants to do, and is not coerced or forced by outside forces, that person is free. On this view, what a person wants or desires could be entirely determined by that person's genetic makeup and how that person was raised (the person's environment). Nonetheless, if a person's actions are determined by her desires and not by outside forces, her choices are free. So if one's deepest desire is for vanilla ice cream and no one is holding a gun to one's head, the choice of vanilla ice cream is free. This is true, according to the compatibilist, even if the individual's desire for vanilla ice cream was caused by the laws of physics.

There are subtleties here, as one might imagine. Suppose a crazy neuroscientist created in a person a strong desire for vanilla ice cream. Such recreations of a person's ordinary desires might be considered a kind of coercion and the choice of vanilla ice cream not free. Or suppose one develops a malignancy in the brain that creates an unassailable desire for vanilla ice cream. Again, that would be a form of coercion and the action would not be free. But in general, compatibilists claim that what is contrary to freedom is compulsion or coercion, not determinism. Thus they'd reject the second step in Coyne's denial of free will.

Compatibilism has religious forms, the most famous of which is Calvinism, which holds everything that happens is willed by God. Putting Calvinism and Coyne together we get the following: If God is the ultimate cause of the laws of physics, and if everything that happens is dictated by the laws of physics, then God is the ultimate cause of all human actions. Insofar as someone is moved by their own desires, their own heart, that person is, according to Calvin, free. So even though in his almighty power God renews the wills of those he loves "determining them to do good," they nonetheless do so freely. All human actions are determined, ultimately by God, and yet, if they are also in accord with what one desires, they are free. Calvin's view might best be called "compatibilism"—the view that all human actions are caused or determined but some are free. Free acts are those that one wants to do (even though one's wants are determined). We may be meat puppets, but at least we are God's meat puppets (and hence free).

Those with a more robust conception of free will and moral responsibility may find the Calvinist solution sophistic or worse as it seems to make God the author of evil. So let's consider another view.

Libertarianism affirms free will, but denies that free will is compatible with determinism. While not all libertarians are mind–body dualists, many are. Some scientists who deny free will think that it would require something like a soul, some part of us that isn't subject to the laws of physics (but something which we don't have). Coyne, for instance, writes:

> To assert that we can freely choose among alternatives is to claim, then, that we can somehow step outside the physical structure of our brain and change its workings. . . . That's a claim that our brains, unique among all forms of matter, are exempt from the laws of physics by a spooky, nonphysical 'will' that can redirect our own molecules.[17]

Neuroscientist Patrick Haggard, no friend of free will, defines free will in "the spiritual sense," one that requires a soul, or, as he calls it, "a ghost in the machine."[18] If we are mind–body composites, then only our brains are governed/caused/determined by the laws of physics. Our minds, and so, we, are not governed by the laws of physics. If there is a part of us—our sou–mind–self—that is free from slavery to the laws of physics, then it's possible for us to be self-initiators of our own free actions. We can be agents of our own actions, free from the dictates of physics. In the case mentioned by Coyne, our mind-soul-self might initiate an action (in the brain) and then initiate a conscious choice (in the brain) a short time thereafter. Both could be freely instigated by our mind-soul-self. While Coyne, Haggard, and Harris don't believe in an immaterial soul, there's nothing in science that shows that there is no such thing as a soul (and it's hard to see how it could). If we have souls, then it's possible for us to be free.

Souls may not be popular these days—among neuroscientists, anyway, meat puppets are preferable to ghosts in machines—but popularity among scientists is not evidence against something. Have the neuroscientists proven that the physics that governs matter, also governs all human actions? Let's clear away some confusions.

Part of the evidence neuroscientists claim for the illusion of choice is that our bodies seem primed to act long before the conscious part of our brain is engaged. For example, brain scans show that, when pushing a button on the left or right side of a computer, parts of our brain are engaged many milliseconds before the subject was aware of *deciding* to push the left or the right button. A recent study by neuroscientists Soon, Brass, Heinze, and Haynes "found that two brain regions encoded with high accuracy whether the subject was about to choose the left or right response prior to the conscious decision."[19] How far before? As far as ten seconds.

Many neuroscientists claim the data from these sorts of experiments show that what we experience as free will is really an illusion. Evolution, they argue, has effectively shaped us so that we act quickly and without conscious deliberation and then evolution added on a mechanism to produce a conscious belief (the experience of "the choice") as a much later tagalong (but one that does not figure causally in the action). Evolution, thank goodness, has primed us to act quickly without the slow and ineffective interference of conscious deliberation.

Has neuroscience killed free will? Let's look at a bit more closely at the inferences involved.

Suppose that the brain events involved in conscious "deciding" are preceded by other brain events of the sort that the neuroscientists are discovering. Suppose, given the choice between vanilla or chocolate ice cream, my brain starts moving my hand to the vanilla ice cream half a second before the part of my brain that consciously "decides" in favor of vanilla is engaged. It looks as though my brain moved me to the vanilla, I didn't decide or freely choose the vanilla. The order of action seems to be: My brain moves me toward the vanilla, I form a conscious belief, "I want the vanilla," and then I choose the vanilla. The conscious belief seems not to figure at all in the action.

Philosopher Al Mele offers a number of compelling reasons to think that the data don't support various claims about the nature of choice that figure in these arguments. Suppose that we concede that in these sorts of cases, human actions are not consciously decided; the "decision" came too late to enter into the causal process involved in the action.[20] It doesn't follow that we don't have free will. Even if many or most of my choices are caused by activities in my brain that don't involve choice, it doesn't follow that I am unable to freely choose this or that sometimes on some occasions. After all, I don't freely decide to breathe or when my heart beats, but conceding that many or most of my actions are not free does not imply that none is free. The defender of free will needn't hold that *all* human actions are free, just that *some* are free. Those that are free, are those about which a decision is made, and then the decision causally factors into the action. Unless neuroscientists show that this is impossible, they have not shown that free will is impossible.

But have the neuroscientists shown that even the choices in question aren't free? The brain regions that Soon et al. measure are predictive of the conscious choice only 60 percent of the time, which isn't much higher than the 50 percent that could be achieved by just guessing. So it's rash to conclude that any decision was actually made at the earlier time. Perhaps the neural activity involved means that the subject is more likely to select the button on the left than the button on the right. But free will isn't threatened by our having a preference, tendency, or inclination to act in one way rather than another. The neuroscientists haven't shown that they aren't measuring preference or inclination rather than action decision.

Furthermore, the ability of the neuroscientist to predict with a much higher degree of accuracy—perhaps even 100 percent—wouldn't mean that human actions are not free. I hate beets and anyone who knows me can predict with 100 percent certainty that, given the choice between beets and vanilla ice cream, I wouldn't choose beets. I will choose ice cream over beets of my own free will (I could do otherwise—I *could* choose beets—but I won't). Free will does not require that I make choices inconsistent with my character or desires. I may have made a different choice. It is possible that I choose beets even if 100 percent of the time I choose vanilla ice cream instead of beets. The ability to predict actions does not by itself show that they are not free. One would have to show that I could not have chosen otherwise.

Is free will an illusion? So far the scientific evidence against free will is either exaggerated or irrelevant. The data are often presented with more certainty and less ambiguity than is warranted. If mind–body dualism is true, then free will is possible because humans are free from the tyranny of physics. If compatibilism is viable, humans can be free. But even if you reject mind–body dualism, the claims that science has proven that free will doesn't exist are vastly overstated.

CHAPTER 12

This Most Beautiful System

Is God Unnecessary?

In 1687, Isaac Newton wrote: "This most beautiful system of the sun, planets and comets, could only proceed from the counsel and dominion of an intelligent and powerful being. This Being governs all things, not as the soul of the world, but as Lord over all."[1] In 1801, the French mathematical astronomer Pierre-Simon Laplace (1749–1827), "the Newton of France," was called to the palace to discuss celestial motion with Emperor Napoleon. Napoleon valued conversations with the best practitioners of natural philosophy. But Laplace worried Napoleon. Laplace, the greatest mathematical astronomer of his day, had fine-tuned Newton's mathematical formulas that described the orbits of the planets. According to Newton's pioneering but imprecise formulas, God was occasionally required to enter into the celestial system to give the planets a boost. Without a divine shove, the planets would, like moths to a flame, spiral into the sun. While God was not continuously required by physics to keep the planets moving (as previously required in Aristotelian–Ptolemaic astrophysics), God's assistance was necessary every now and then to give them a boost. Like Aristotle's quaintly outdated physics, Newton's updated physics required God as a scientifically necessary hypothesis: for Newton, good physics was also good theology.

During the next 150 years (from 1650 to 1800), astronomers made increasingly precise observations with better mathematical tools. By 1800, the laws of physics (refinements of Newton's laws) no longer required God's occasional intervention to motivate those lazy planets and prevent their fiery demise. Given the principle of inertia and Newton's revised laws of gravity, the planets would go on their merry way forever—no God required. When Napoleon was informed of Laplace's work, he was dismayed to find no mention of God. When the troubled Napoleon asked Laplace where God fit into in his grand scheme, Laplace replied, "Sire, I have no need of that hypothesis."

This story is, like many stories in this book, fiction mixed in with fact. It is true that Laplacean physics excluded supernatural forces in its explanation of the movement of the planets, but Laplace never said that God is an unnecessary hypothesis. The only known record of this conversation is in the diary of William Herschel, the greatest observational astronomer of his day (and the discoverer of Uranus). Herschel writes:

> The first Consul [Napoleon] then asked a few questions relating to Astronomy and the construction of the heavens to which I made such answers as seemed to give him great satisfaction. He also addressed himself to Mr Laplace on the same subject, and held a considerable argument with him in which he differed from that eminent mathematician. The difference was occasioned by an exclamation of the first Consul, who asked in a tone of exclamation or admiration (when we were speaking of the extent of the sidereal heavens): "And who is the author of all this!" Mons. De la Place wished to shew that a chain of natural causes would account for the construction and preservation of the wonderful system. This the first Consul rather opposed. Much may be said on the subject; by joining the arguments of both we shall be led to "Nature and nature's God." (Lubbock, 1933: 310)

Herschel's modest summation of the discussion with Napoleon is that both he and Laplace are committed to "Nature and nature's God."

Teasing out Laplace's exact religious views is not easy. It's likely that Laplace was uncomfortable with the Church's official view of the cosmos. By 1800, the Church still had not affirmed Copernicanism (the theory that the planets revolve around the sun) as a physical fact, and it wouldn't do so for another 20 years. Although Laplace was a lifelong Catholic, he may have attended mass only to appease his wife. He was skeptical of the reliability of the gospels, believed most religions to be mythical, and did not care for the power and ambition of the Catholic Church. But skepticism about a human religious institution is not the same as denial of the existence of God. He very likely believed in some sort of deity. But we can't be sure.

No modern science and religion book could call itself complete without (inaccurately) repeating the Laplacean mantra, "I have no need of that hypothesis," implying that science has no need of the God hypothesis. Even if Laplace didn't say it, his quote is essential for the culturally dominant story that claims that as science progresses, the need for God diminishes.

THE GREAT DISAPPEARING DEITY

The deepest intellectual battle is not between science and religion (which, as we have seen, can operate with a great deal of accord), but between *naturalism* and *theism*—two broad philosophical (or metaphysical) ways of looking at the world.[2] Neither view is a scientific view; neither view is based on or inferable from empirical data. Metaphysics, like numbers and the laws of logic, lies outside the realm of human sense experience. So the issue of naturalism versus theism must be decided on philosophical grounds.

Metaphysical naturalism is the view that *nothing exists but matter/energy in space–time*. Naturalism denies the existence of anything beyond nature. The naturalist rejects God, and also such spooky entities as souls, angels, and demons. Metaphysical naturalism entails that there is no ultimate purpose or design in nature because there is no Purposer or Designer. On the other hand, *theism* is the view that *the universe is created by and owes its sustained existence to a Supreme Being that exists outside the universe.* These two views, by definition, contradict each other.

Some take scientific advancements as favoring naturalism. They believe that scientific findings increasingly make the existence of God unnecessary or superfluous. Scientifically, we no longer need the existence of God to explain the physical things that happen in our universe.

Belief in God may have been reasonable when the natural world was mysterious, before the advancement of modern science, back when we had no idea about how the physical world worked. Back then, God was routinely called on to explain, for example, the motions of the planets. But now we know that planetary motion is explained by the principle of inertia under the direction of the law of gravity. Gravity, not God, explains the motions of the planets. God was also called on to explain the geological shape of planet earth: divine creation, followed by the flood of Noah, shaped the mountains and canyons. But now we know that mountains and canyons are shaped by the movement of the earth's crust, as well as by wind and water. Plate tectonics and erosion, not God, explain the shape of our planet. Finally, God was called on to explain the existence of biological species— through supernatural selection, the earth's many species exist. But now we know that *natural* selection is involved in the origin of species. Evolution, not God, explains why the world has so many different species. Now that we understand the science of planetary motion, geological processes, and the origin of species, we know that God is no longer necessary to explain these phenomena. Few educated people believe that God lowers his shoulder to shove planets around or dips his hand into the dirt to scoop out mountains or literally breathes life into dust. Why believe in God if there is nothing left for God to do?

Science might be consistent with the existence of God, but that doesn't mean science gives us any reason to think that God exists. Science may not be contrary to God, but science surely seems to render God impotent or irrelevant.

How can we make progress on the debate between naturalism and theism? In this chapter we discuss the Fine-Tuning Argument, which holds that the conditions necessary to produce and sustain life in our universe are so "fine-tuned" that they suggest a designer or God.

EVIDENCE AND EXPECTATION

Before discussing this argument, we need to consider how we will weigh the evidence in favor of theism or naturalism. We will use a common and plausible method, called *the expectation principle.* The following example illustrates how this principle works. Suppose you are the parent of a young child, one prone to reckless behavior with sporting equipment. While sitting inside your home, you hear a loud noise. You know your child is playing outside, near your garage, with a tennis racquet and ball, and the sound you heard was shattering glass. Your child walks in, and you ask what happened. He sheepishly looks down and replies, "Nothing." Unconvinced, you think to yourself, "Dang it, he did it again. Evan just broke the garage window!" When you formed that belief, you were using the *expectation principle.*

The expectation principle helps us choose between competing hypotheses. Employing this principle, we ask, "Under which hypothesis would one more likely *expect* the data to be true?" In our example, the data favors the hypothesis that Evan broke the garage window over the hypothesis that "nothing" happened, because the Evan hypothesis is confirmed by the data. If Evan had broken the garage window, you would expect the sound of shattering glass. If nothing had happened, you wouldn't. Given the data, you have good reason to believe that Evan broke the garage window.

Many hypotheses could adequately explain any set of data. That is why the expectation principle must be paired with another principle, one that requires that hypotheses under consideration have *some likelihood of being true, independent of the data.* Imagine that Evan says the window broke because an alien spacecraft flew through it. While this hypothesis would lead you to expect the data, it is not a viable hypothesis. You don't reject the alien spacecraft theory because it is not as good an explanation as the "Evan did it" hypothesis. While both are equally good at explaining the data, you reject the alien spacecraft hypothesis because it has no likelihood of being true independent of the data; it lacks plausibility.

We determine the initial plausibility of hypotheses by judging them against our general background knowledge—our basic beliefs about what exists and how things work in the universe. So while a small alien spacecraft would fully explain the broken window, it fails the likelihood test because it doesn't match up with our understanding of reality. Most otherwise perfectly good hypotheses (one's that would lead us to expect the data)—aliens from outer space, ghosts, and goblins, vast international conspiracies—are eliminated at the outset because we rightly judge them to be initially implausible. A ghost would fully explain the creaking noises and apparent screams coming from your attic, but if you think, as I do, that there are no ghosts, you will look elsewhere for an adequate explanation.

Some otherwise very good explanations will not be able to convince those who have already decided that a given hypothesis is too implausible for serious consideration. If you reject the existence of God at the outset, you won't consider any evidence in God's favor. Only if you grant God some initial plausibility, can new evidence make it reasonable to believe in God.

The story of the origins of the universe starts with a primordial explosion commonly known as the Big Bang. The universe exploded into existence about 14 billion years ago when an infinitely dense region (called "the singularity") exploded, and out burst all the matter of the universe, shooting in every direction like pellets fired from a shotgun. Gravity, then, drew those caroming "pellets" together to form atoms, stars, and galaxies. One galaxy developed sufficiently to include a solar system, and in that system was our planet Earth, which, when sufficiently cooled, produced the waters out of which life first crawled.

Early on, the Big Bang theory had many critics and dissenters. Prominent among them was astronomer Fred Hoyle. What is notable about Hoyle's reluctance to accept the Big Bang is the extent to which this was motivated by his background views about the nature of ultimate reality. Hoyle was an atheist, and believed that his *steady state model of the universe*—the view that the universe is roughly the same everywhere and at all times (and so has no beginning or end)—fit much better with atheism. The Big Bang model, Hoyle thought, fits much better with theism. This he found troubling. Hoyle believed that theism would find more support from a universe with a beginning than atheism would.

Hoyle's suspicion seems right: if the universe has a beginning, then it looks like a creation. And if the universe is conducive for life, then it looks like it has a designer.

The Fine-Tuning Argument

Over the last 50 years, scientists have discovered that the physical laws, constants, and initial conditions that govern our universe are highly structured and precisely adjusted—fine-tuned—for the existence of life. Scientists have been surprised and even stunned to learn of the fragile prospects for the existence of life. Cosmologist Martin Rees summarizes what was necessary for everything to come together to produce life: "Any universe hospitable to life has to be 'adjusted' in a particular way. The prerequisites for any life of the kind we know about—long-lived stable stars, stable atoms such as carbon, oxygen and silicon, able to combine into complex molecules, etc.—are sensitive to the physical laws and to the size, expansion and contents of the universe" (Rees, 2003: 376). Had one or perhaps a few of these prerequisites deviated just the slightest, a life-conducive universe could not have emerged.

The fine-tuning argument says that because the possibility of a life-permitting universe existing is so small, our universe, with its precise initial conditions and laws, must have been fine-tuned by God. Astronomer George Greenstein writes: "As we survey all the evidence, the thought insistently arises that some supernatural agency—or, rather, Agency—must be involved. Is it possible that suddenly, without intending to, we have stumbled upon scientific proof of the existence of a Supreme Being? Was it God who stepped in and so providentially crafted the cosmos for our benefit?" (Greenstein, 1988: 26–27). We will look at just a few (of the more than 20) examples of some of the precise conditions necessary for life: the scale of the universe, the force of gravity, and the production of carbon.

The Scale of the Universe

Given that our planet is just a blip on the cosmic map and that we are but a blip within that blip, some may at first be skeptical about our significance in the cosmos. After all, the universe is so big, surely our existence is too insignificant to merit any special consideration. Carl Sagan once wrote, "Lost somewhere between immensity and eternity is our tiny planetary home. In a cosmic perspective, most human concerns seem insignificant, even petty" (Sagan, 1980). While awareness of our insignificance in relation to the vast cosmos may cause despair or dread, it need not preclude metaphysical and theological speculation. In fact, the immensity of the universe is a surprisingly good thing.

The universe could have been any number of different sizes and shapes. It might have existed for only a very short period of time and it may have been very tiny; it could have been approaching its sweet sixteenth birthday and it may have fit inside a grapefruit. Instead it is very old, about 14 billion years old, and unimaginably vast, estimates range from 85–160 billion light years wide. And it's expanding every day at velocities approaching the speed of light (hang on to your hat).

British particle physicist and theologian John Polkinghorne explains why the vastness of our universe is a good thing: "While such immensity can sometimes seem daunting to the inhabitants of what is effectively a speck of cosmic dust, we should not be upset, because only a universe at least as big as ours could have lasted the 14 billion years required to enable human beings to appear on its scene. Anything significantly smaller would have had too brief a history" (Polkinghorne, 2009: 51). According to Polkinghorne, all the essential things we need for life—stars and carbon and planets and evolution—take lots and lots of time. Anything less and we wouldn't be here. It took 380,000 years for the first atoms to form, 500–750 million years for the first stars, a billion years for the first galaxy, and 9 billion years for our solar system. The same vastness that causes our feelings of insignificance actually makes it possible for us to feel anything, or even to exist, at all.

The Force of Gravity

Imagine all of the subatomic particles of the universe in a violent explosion, their teensy selves propelled at astronomical speeds into the lonely darkness. But instead of falling to the ground, exhausted, these particles found one another and formed communities of atoms, molecules, substances, stars, galaxies, planets, and people. In order for this to occur, the initial explosive forces, which conspired against the reformation of its constituent parts, would have to be overcome by an even more powerful force in order to attract the particles to one another to form into the stars, galaxies, and planets necessary for life. Without gravity, the pellets would have exited their chamber and traveled to the outer reaches of space alone, with no hope of ever coming into contact with another pellet.

Gravity is the attractive force that draws bodies in the universe together. Love may make the world go round, but gravity pulls worlds together in the first place. For the lovelorn, take heart: everybody is attracted to you (and fret not about your weight—the more you weigh, the more attractive you are).

Gravity, like the scale of the universe, is also finely tuned. This force is represented by the gravitational constant, G ($6.67 \times 10^{-11} \text{m}^3 \text{ Kg}^{-1}\text{s}^{-2}$). If G had been weaker, it would not have had the strength to overcome the initial explosive forces of the Big Bang and bring particles in the universe together, forming stars and planets. If G had been slightly weaker, stars would have been too cool for nuclear fusion, and, as a result, many of the elements needed for life chemistry would never have formed. On the other hand, if G were stronger, the universe would have collapsed in on itself too quickly for life to evolve. Had it been slightly stronger, stars would have been too hot and would have burned too rapidly to produce the chemicals necessary for the creation of life; our life-prospects would have gone up in smoke.

According to the philosopher of physics Bradley Monton, "the range of life-permitting gravitational forces is only about one part in 10^{36} of the total range of forces" (Monton, 2009: 79). You can see why scientists have been so impressed. The odds of gravity falling within that range are incredible. Thus, gravity is precisely fine-tuned for the formation of stars, galaxies, and planets. If we held constant all the other fundamental laws of the universe, any change in G would have had devastating consequences for the development of life.

The Production of Carbon

We may prize diamonds and gold, but the more humble carbon is the building block of life. Carbon is essential to our existence. Because of carbon's remarkable chemical properties (it is uniquely able to bond both with itself and with many other elements), it is able to form the very special molecules that comprise organic life. Miners know where to dig for gold, but where does one dig for carbon? The answer is stars, the furnace of life. These diamonds in the sky are the source of carbon-based life. Although Jane Taylor's 1806 nursery rhyme wondered about those twinkling, twinkling little stars, we can thank twentieth-century astrophysicists for the answer. Today we know that the first stars were fiery balls composed of the most basic elements—hydrogen and helium, elements manufactured just after the Big Bang. The cosmos couldn't do too much with just hydrogen and helium. Life depends on many more elements, especially carbon. Other life-essential elements—elements smaller than iron but larger than helium— are manufactured through fusion processes in the interior ovens of stars. During supernovae explosions, these elements are spread throughout the cosmos. Strange as it sounds, we are made from stardust.

The production of carbon, then, depends on the existence of stars. The existence of stars depends on even more cosmic fine-tuning. Let us consider just one: *the strong nuclear force*, the strongest physical force in the universe. This superforce binds the nuclei of atoms together. The protons in the nucleus of atoms are positively charged so, like the positive ends of magnets, they repel one another. Without the strong nuclear force, the repulsive forces of these electromagnetically charged protons would tear apart the nucleus of atoms. More precisely, nuclei could never have formed. Change this force even a little, and life would not have been possible. If, for example, the strong force had been just 10 percent weaker, protons and neutrons would not be able to bind together at all, making nuclear fusion impossible. Since stars are fueled by nuclear fusion, this would have rendered the production of carbon impossible. No carbon, no life. On the other hand, if the strong nuclear force were slightly stronger, stars would burn a great deal faster. Since life took billions of years to evolve, it is probable that if the strong nuclear force had been just 4 percent stronger, stars would have burned out long before life had time to evolve.

And Even More Fine-tuning

Scientists have collected over two-dozen cases of fine-tuning. If, in what follows, you don't understand every detail or concept, don't worry, you're in good company. I certainly don't understand all of this, and I'm not sure many physicists do either. They certainly don't yet understand how everything hangs together. But you can get the main point without understanding each and every detail.

Mathematical physicist Roger Penrose claims that given *the principle of entropy*, the increasing unavailability of some energy to do work, the amount of usable energy required to produce our universe must be unusually precise. If the initial state of our universe had been random, it would have been a high-entropy disaster and could not have resulted in the universe we find today. He estimates that the likelihood of the universe having enough usable energy to produce life-sustaining universes at the time of the Big Bang is phenomenally small: 1 part in 10 to 10^{123}.

The cosmological constant measures the gravitational pull exerted from empty space (a vacuum-like space–time devoid of matter but full of non-material "stuff"). The cosmological constant is associated with a kind of "anti-gravity" that seeks to pull apart what gravity would pull together. The cosmological constant, at less than 10^{-120}, is very, very close to zero. In the battle between gravity and antigravity, the cosmological constant must be fine-tuned to sustain conditions conducive to life. What would have happened if the cosmological constant were not, for all practical purposes, zero? If the cosmological constant had been −1, the universe would have expanded and collapsed in just 10^{-43} seconds. In this universe's brief life, nothing life-producing could have happened. By contrast, if the cosmological constant had been +1, the universe would have expanded forever at an exponentially absurd rate. Atoms would have been ripped apart as the universe doubled its size in just a fraction of a second, making life impossible. Change the cosmological constant slightly and a life-permitting universe is impossible.

While cosmologist and astrophysicist Martin Rees and philosopher Robin Collins both trim the evidence for fine-tuning down to six examples, their lists include different examples—another indication of the plethora of evidence. In Rees' list we find the importance of numbers such as "D = 3", the specified number of macroscopic spatial dimensions in our universe, and "ε = 0.007," which defines how firmly atomic nuclei bind together. Collins includes the smallness of the cosmological constant as well as the difference between proton and neutron mass. The point, and we will belabor it no further, is that although we have looked closely at only four examples, the claim that the universe is finely tuned for life is supported by an impressively large body of evidence. Had any of these figures varied more than just slightly, the universe would not have been capable of producing life.

Roger Penrose, as noted, estimates that the likelihood of our universe having just the right amount of usable energy at the time of the Big Bang to produce a life-sustaining universe is 1 part in 10 to 10^{123}. The minuscule size of this number is nearly impossible to comprehend. I can understand 1 part in 2 (or one-half), 1 part in 52 (the chance of drawing the ace of spades from a deck of cards), 1 part in 600,000 (the chance of getting struck by lightning), or even 1 part in 3 million (the chance of winning the lottery—much less than getting struck by lightning!). But 1 part in 10 to 10^{123} boggles the mind. The notation, 10^3, refers to a 1 with three zeroes after it, or "one thousand." The notation, 10^6, refers to a 1 with six zeroes after it, or "one million." We get those. But we don't even have a name for 10^{123} (a 1 with 123 zeroes after it), much less a name for 10 to 10^{123} (a 1 with 10^{123} zeroes after it). In fact, to even write down the numeral is impossible. "Even if we were to write a 0 on each separate proton and on each separate neutron in the entire universe—and we could throw in all the other particles for good measure—we should fall far short of writing down the figure needed," says Penrose of his discovery (Penrose, 1989: 233). To get some idea of the practical impossibility of that number, consider that there are 10^{80} electrons in the observable universe.

Imagine you have an old-fashioned, very touchy, black and white television with dial controls. Imagine further that there is only one channel in the world and that you are thousands of miles away from where it is being broadcast. You have two further difficulties: a lousy antenna and two-dozen dials. In order to lock in that one channel, each of the 24 dials needs to be precisely set. If a single dial is just a smidgen off, you will get no reception. The probability that all of the dials would be tuned just right to bring in that one station is astronomically tiny. The difficulty of receiving this distant television signal gives you some sense of the fine-tuning involved. Our universe is very much like this situation, but the probability that each of the constants and initial conditions is precisely fine-tuned for the existence of life is even smaller.

Perhaps our existence was the result of precisely planned tuning.

With the probability of winning a $200 million lottery at 1 in 1 billion, it wouldn't be reasonable to bet a buck that you will win. But 1 in a billion is practically money in the bank compared to the 1 part in 10 to 10^{123} chance that our universe would be life-permitting. I wouldn't bet the farm on those odds.

Explanation and Expectation

The fine-tuning of our universe for life, what Rees calls "a seemingly special cosmic recipe," has elicited several possible responses. The principal explanations of our finely tuned universe are:

- The universe came out of nothing
- A single universe exists out of chance
- A single universe exists out of necessity
- A multiverse exists (many, many universes and no God)
- God created a single universe
- God created a multiverse

Let us now apply the expectation principle to the primary question at hand: Which of the competing hypotheses should lead us to expect our life-conducive universe?

Out of Nothing?

Laurence Krauss's, *A Universe from Nothing: Why There Is Something Rather than Nothing,* offers a sensational new answer to the old question of his subtitle—the universe comes from nothing (Krauss, 2012). In case you miss his not so subtle point—the universe didn't come from God. "The universe," as MIT physicist Alan Guth says, "might be the ultimate free lunch." Krauss is no slouch. He is a theoretical physicist who specializes in the origins and nature of the cosmos (cosmology) and is Foundation Professor and director of the Origins Project at Arizona State University; he also wrote *The Physics of Star Trek.* How could the Foundation Professor and Director of the Origins Project and author of *The Physics of Star Trek* come to believe that an entire universe came from nothing?

The ancient Greeks thought that you could only get nothing from nothing. Something from nothing? Impossible! They even had a phrase for it, one widely repeated in classic arguments for the existence of God: ex nihilo, nihil fit. Out of nothing, nothing comes. If there ever was a time when there was nothing, there couldn't be anything now.

What did the Greeks mean by nothing? I suppose they meant something like, well, nothing (hard to think of a better term). But let me try some others: the absence of everything, what's in a vacuum, empty space, what's left when you take away everything, no thing or things (not even one). Nothing.

Krauss rejects ex nihilo, nihil fit because he thinks modern physics demands it. In fact, he thinks that getting something from nothing is not only not impossible, it is not even difficult (Krauss, 2012: xiii), and it may even be necessary. In an interview he claims: "Not only can something arise from nothing, but most often the laws of physics require that to occur."[3] Krauss thinks of the universe as the ultimate card trick ("inflationary prestidigitation")—a universe pulled out of the sleeve of nothing. But unlike most card tricks, Krauss claims, it's not a trick—something from nothing is real.

Can we really get something from nothing? I'm a philosopher by profession and I concede that there are very few statements that philosophers agree upon. Philosophers generally agree on the law of noncontradiction: no statement can be both true and false at the same time and in the same relationship. But I can't think of much of anything else. Except this: ex nihilo, nihil fit. Out of nothing, nothing comes. They agree that if you start with nothing, even if you wait a really long time, you'll get nothing. Take a big box of nothing, dump it into a blender, mix it up, and you get nothing. Open up a large can of nothing, add water, and you'll have a can of water (but not water plus something else, just water and nothing else). Start with nothing, stir in some gravity, and you get nothing. Ex nihilo, nihil fit is as good as it gets for philosophers.

Strauss, however, thinks the ancient Greek notion of nothing needs to be replaced due to discoveries in contemporary physics. What I called "empty space" isn't really empty—so-called empty space is filled with mass and energy, which, according to quantum theory, produces the particles that make up stuff. He writes: "The laws of quantum mechanics imply that, on very small scales, for very short times, empty space can appear to be a boiling, bubbling brew of virtual particles and fields wildly fluctuating in magnitude" (Krauss, 2012: 97). "Nothing," according to Krauss, ain't what it used to be. "Nothing" is a boiling brew of virtual particles and energy. The universe, along with us, emerged from "density fluctuations" from the "quantum fluctuations" in this "quantum nothingness" (Krauss, 2012: 98).

Krauss insults those who disagree and stick to that good old-time definition of "nothing." He writes: "But therein, in my opinion, lies the intellectual bankruptcy of much of theology and some of modern philosophy. For surely 'nothing' is every bit as physical as 'something,' especially if it is to be defined as the 'absence of something.' It then behooves us to understand precisely the physical nature of both of those quantities. Without science, any definition is just words" (Krauss, 2012: xiv). Most definitions are, for better or worse, just words. Of course, it's a free country and people can define a word in any way they like. For example, I might have written a book titled, *Finding the Married Bachelor*, and then, halfway through informed you that I had abandoned the ancient Greek definition of bachelor as "unmarried male," opting instead for "married male." Or I might have "found" a unicorn by which I mean "two-wheeled cycle," not the old-fashioned "horselike animal with a single horn." Krauss's definition of "nothing" transforms it into something. Again, he's free to define words as he likes, but it sure seems like he's cheating. A paragraph after he calls space "empty" (which, recall, he defines as a boiling, bubbling brew of virtual particles and fields wildly fluctuating in magnitude) he calls it "otherwise empty space." In the next paragraph he says that the universe results from these quantum fluctuations "in what is essentially nothing." The book should have been titled, *A Universe from Something*.

We don't get something from nothing (nothing as most of us understand it). We get something (the stuff of stuff) from something—a boiling, bubbling brew. So he doesn't reject ex nihilo, nihil fit because he doesn't really hold that something came from nothing (in the old-fashioned, quaint sense of the word). He doesn't really think that *nihil* is nothing. *Nihil*, we now know because physicists tell us, is something—a boiling bubbling brew of mass and energy. One might then reasonably wonder, where does that boiling bubbling brew come from?

His argument proceeds from those virtually undetectably particles to the universe as a whole: "I then go on to explain how other versions of 'nothing'—beyond merely empty space—including the absence of space itself, and even the absence of physical laws, can morph into 'something.' Indeed, in modern parlance, 'nothing' is most often unstable. Not only can something arise from nothing, but most often the laws of physics require that to occur." But, then, there isn't nothing, really, on this view. There are, after all, the laws of physics. Where do they come from? From nothing?[4]

Back to that free lunch. How does Krauss claim we get a universe from nothing? He writes:

> This is an example of something that Guth coined as the ultimate free lunch. Including the effects of gravity in thinking about the universe allows objects to have—amazingly—"negative" as well as "positive" energy. This facet of gravity allows for the possibility that positive energy stuff, like matter and radiation, can be complemented by negative energy configurations that just balance the energy of the created positive energy stuff. In so doing, gravity can start out with an empty universe—and end up with a filled one. (Krauss, 2012: 92)

This original empty space is highly structured, first by gravity. But gravity cannot be decoupled from energy. By $E = mc^2$, energy can be transformed into matter. Then gravity can transform matter into the galaxies that provide the home for humans. If the original empty space is structured by the law of gravity that is essentially connected to energy, you've really got *something* there. Not nothing.

In short, for Krauss, nothing is not really nothing. Krauss's quantum vacuums are highly structured somethings. So the world does not come from nothing. The somethings it comes from—that bubbling soup of energy and mass or the laws of physics or gravity/energy—make one wonder. Where do they come from? Surely not from nothing (ex nihilo, nihil fit).

Chance?

Perhaps, in the case of our universe, we were just lucky. If the values of the fundamental constants, laws, and conditions of our universe had to be some specific set of numbers, and if any set of numbers is as likely as any other, then perhaps we just lucked out. Maybe our universe was simply a lucky roll of the dice.

Chancy events happen all the time: people win the lottery, they are struck by lightning (sometimes multiple times in one life!), and some die of uncommon diseases. Many of these things are incredibly rare and unpredictable, yet none of them seems to call out for a special explanation. So the mere fact that an event is unlikely does not mean it requires or demands a special explanation. Rather, unexpected events that seem to demand a special explanation are those that are *particularly surprising*.

Particularly surprising, unexpected events need to be explained, while unsurprising, expected (even if unpredictable) events do not. It is these latter events for which chance is, frequently, a perfectly adequate explanation. I don't know exactly how to define "particularly surprising," so let me proceed by example. If I randomly draw an ace of spades from a deck of cards, this is somewhat but not particularly surprising, and so no special explanation is required (in this case, one that appeals to chance). But, if I am playing poker and my opponent regularly deals herself four aces, this *is* particularly surprising and requires a special, nonchance explanation.

John Leslie offers a very powerful analogy. Suppose you have been convicted of a crime and sentenced to death by firing squad. The laws of the land specify that on your execution day, ten soldiers—expert marksmen all— will simultaneously fire multiple rounds at you as you stand in front of a brick wall. Your execution day comes, and you stand, teeth clenched, as shots ring off. Amazingly, however, you are not killed, not even grazed! After this ordeal you are released and left to contemplate just what happened (Leslie, 1989: 13–14).[5]

While one expert marksman might occasionally miss one of his shots, the likelihood that all the marksmen will miss with all their shots is incredibly low. Your immediate reaction to surviving is that the situation must have been rigged; someone must have fixed the situation so that the marksmen would intentionally miss. Unless it was rigged, it is hard to see how all the marksmen would misfire. Being spared death when all of the expert marksmen miss their mark is particularly surprising and demands a nonchance explanation. A particularly surprising event is inexplicable by simple appeal to chance.

The Chance hypothesis needs to reject the claim that the fine-tuning of our universe is particularly surprising. But fine-tuning is particularly, even astoundingly, surprising. The universe is precisely governed by factors that permit the existence of life, but those features could so easily have been skewed, resulting in a sterile universe. Nonetheless, physicist and Nobel laureate Frank Wilczek has been quoted saying: "The universe appears to be just one of those things" (Berlinski, 2008: 139). If it's just one of those things, then it's not particularly surprising and no special, nonchance explanation would be required. Is the universe, as Wilczek claims, just one of those things? Thrown in among old shoes, stale bread, a broken umbrella, and homely dogs, a universe fit for life is oddly out of place. Our universe resists being just one of those things. If it's not just one of those things, if it is both unexpected and particularly surprising, then chance fails as an explanation.

Let's examine just how hard might it be for chance to produce a fine-tuned universe. The process of acquiring our universe's 20-some fine-tuned features by chance would look something like winning "Cosmic Poker."

Consider this example. Suppose you watch me shuffle a complete deck of cards ten times. I hand the deck of cards to you and let you shuffle them several times. Then I draw the cards one at a time from the top of the deck to the bottom. As I show them to you, we see that they come out in perfect order—ace through king, spades through clubs through diamonds through hearts. What should you believe?

While it's certainly possible that they came out in that order by chance—it is, after all, one of the possible results of a random process—it would not be reasonable for you to believe that. The probability that the cards would be in order is 1 in 10^{68}. That's

$$\frac{1}{806581751709438785716606368564037669752895054408832777824000000000000}$$

Of course, that's the probability of any order not just the highly ordered one that resulted. But even though various orderings are equally probable, shuffling is a randomizing process, not an ordering process. Multiple shuffles lead one to expect a disordered set of cards, not an ordered set. A highly ordered set is suspiciously like, as Hoyle states, "a put-up job." And that is what you should believe if the cards came out in perfect order—that a being with intelligence and ability played a trick. Highly surprising and remarkably ordered events, like the card example, should lead one away from chance explanations toward a personal explanation—an explanation in terms of a person with sufficient intellect and powers.

Our even more highly surprising and remarkably ordered universe precludes a chance explanation. The existence of life, one might reasonably think, is in the cards.

NECESSITY?

The Chance hypothesis fails because the fine-tuning of our universe appears to have been exceptionably, unfathomably unlikely. The fine-tuning of our universe is only unlikely if it were possible that the fundamental constants, laws, and initial conditions of our universe could have been different than they are. But what if these values could not be anything but the way they are? Some have argued that the assumption that these values could have been different is false; our universe is the way it is *out of necessity*. If this is the case, then there is nothing surprising about those life-conducive values. According to the Necessity view, these values couldn't have been otherwise.

Is it reasonable to explain the universe's fine-tuned features by appealing to necessity? By *necessity*, we mean that it *could not have been different than it is*. So 2 + 2 is necessarily 4 (and couldn't be 6, *pi* or infinity); and squares necessarily have four corners and four sides (and couldn't be three-sided). I, like many other things, have most properties contingently (they might have been different than they are). Even though I am 5'10", I might have been 7'10"; and I used to weigh a lot less than I do now (and I hope to weigh less in the future). My height and weight are not necessary; they could have been different than they are.

Could our universe have been different than it is? Are the physical constants of our universe more like 2 + 2 = 4 and squares or more like me and my height?

The Necessity hypothesis claims that the constants, laws, and initial conditions of our universe *must* have the values they have and, as a result, the only universe that can exist is our universe. It is a mistake, on this view, to presume that these values and conditions could have been anything other than what they are. The universe we have, with its life-permitting laws and conditions, is the only universe in the cards. Richard Dawkins, commenting on the laws and initial conditions of our universe, says that "Hard-nosed physicists say [they] were never free to vary in the first place" (Dawkins, 2006: 144). On this view, natural laws are like the laws of logic. Just as it is impossible for two plus two not to equal four, so too it was impossible for there to be any other physical laws, constants, and initial conditions.

Is the Necessity view a plausible explanation of the fine-tuning of our universe? It passes the first condition of the expectation principle: if the view were correct, we would expect the fine-tuning features of our universe. However, the Necessity view fails the second condition: the antecedent likelihood test. The laws of physics are not, for all we can tell, like the laws of logic. The laws of physics and the initial conditions of a universe admit of a wide range of possibilities. We have no independent reason to accept and every reason to deny that our universe is the only possible universe: there are too many ways the world could have been. Nothing in logic and mathematics, the most general of our general background knowledge, indicates that our universe is the only possible world. This universe, as best we can tell, simply cannot exist out of necessity. The claim of the necessity of physical laws has not been demonstrated, but merely asserted. Without a compelling argument, it looks like little more than a confession of faith.

"It seems then," says Paul Davies, "that the physical universe does not have to be the way it is; it could have been otherwise" (Davies, 1992: 169). The universe and all that it contains does not exist out of necessity. It might not have existed and it might have been very different from the way it is. The way it is is remarkably, surprisingly, and contingently life-conducive.

THE MULTIVERSE

Let's imagine that everything about the firing squad scenario is the same, except for one detail. This time, after you are released following the failure of your execution, you learn that you were not alone in your predicament. Rather than being the only convict facing a firing squad, you learn that an infinite number of convicts had faced an infinite number of firing squads. If this were the case, then the fact that the entire cadre of marksman missed you might not be that surprising. If there is an infinite number of convicts standing in front of an infinite number of firing squads, then you might expect that some of the firing squads will miss their target without intending too. Upon learning that you were one of an infinite number of convicts fired upon, you might reasonably surmise that your survival was not suprising.

With an infinite number of tries, the extremely unlikely becomes likely. T. H. Huxley expressed this idea when he allegedly claimed that given an infinite amount of time at a keyboard, monkeys would randomly type the complete works of Shakespeare. Likewise, given an infinite number of universes, we might reasonably expect a universe conducive to the existence of a Shakespeare.

Martin Rees claims that this is like "an 'off the shelf' clothes shop: if the shop has a large stock, we're not surprised to find one suit that fits. Likewise, if our universe is selected from a multiverse, its seemingly designed or fine-tuned features wouldn't be surprising" (Rees, 2003: 214). Of course, our universe *is* surprising, so surprising that some claim the existence of an infinite number of universes. Disturbed by the fact that our universe's singularity was so improbable, some physicists began to speculate that perhaps ours is not the only one. Our entire history, Rees claims, "could be just an episode, one facet, of the infinite multiverse" (Rees, 2001: 158).

Multiverse theories attempt to explain the appearance of fine-tuning in our universe by postulating the existence of many universes, each with different physical parameters. The idea is simple: if there are lots and lots of universes, then we might expect that one, or a few, of these universes will be conducive to life. Our universe would not be particularly surprising, and no divine explanation would be necessary.

The Squeeze-Bang Model

One of the earliest multiverse theories was the oscillating universe or squeeze-bang model. Originating in the 1920s, this model was based on the idea that our universe is part of a larger sequence. Each big bang, resulting in a universe of sorts, is followed at some point by a big crunch or squeeze, where the current universe collapses back in on itself as a result of gravity. The whirling energy from this big crunch causes a successive big bang and...*voila!* A new universe is born. This oscillating universe cycles forever, with each new universe arising like the mythical phoenix erupting out of the flames only to be reborn from its own ashes. If this were the case, our universe would be one of perhaps infinitely many. In such a sequence, a big bang that results in a universe fit for life would be unsurprising. With infinitely many tries, the improbable is probable; a universe fit for life is bound to pop up eventually.

Despite its initial promise, however, most scientists have abandoned the oscillating universe model. The most glaring difficulty it faces is that an oscillating model must have been quite fussy about the types of universes that it produced. Why? Because there are three types of universe that would have resulted in the cessation of the oscillating universe. Had a big bang actually produced one of these three, the whole process would have ceased full stop.

The first cycle-stopping universe would be one that collapses without enough internal oomph to produce another big bang. The production of such a universe would have ended the cycle with a crunch and a whimper (that is, no bang).

The second type of cycle-stopping universe may be a great deal like our own which, to our best guesstimate, will expand forever. If gravity isn't sufficiently powerful to overcome the initial explosive forces, a universe will expand forever. If a universe expands forever, to infinity (and beyond), it can't recollapse for subsequent universe attempts. A big bang but no squeeze.

The third type of cycle-stopping universe involves the second law of thermodynamics, which asserts that we are in a state of increasing entropy; as time goes on, usable energy decreases and the universe becomes more chaotic and disorganized. Put simply, the universe is running out of steam; it is not an Energizer bunny—it cannot keep going and going and going and going. Without available energy, life would be impossible. Joseph Silk has calculated that in just 10 to 100 tries, entropy would have drained the universe of available energy making life impossible.

We can't know which of the three cycle-stopping universes is most likely. We don't know how entropy would be affected by the shift from world to world. But the bottom line is clear: a cycle-stopping universe would very likely have arisen at some point long before our own universe could have graced the cosmic scene. Therefore, it's not reasonable to believe that the squeeze-bang process could have had enough tries to produce a life-conducive universe.

Concurrent Universes

Is there a view of the production of new universes that avoids the problems of the oscillating model? Instead of a series that temporally precedes our universe, perhaps there is a large number of universes that exist concurrently with our own. While this idea may have been around in science fiction for some time, its scientific origins date back to the 1950s in the work of American physicist Hugh Everett (Byrne, 2008). Everett hypothesized that every quantum event branches into new realities or worlds. In less technical terms: when reality faces a decision, it actualizes both. On this view, at some point after the big bang, the universe splits—again and again and again—into separate worlds. Consider yourself—the observer of quantum phenomena: subsequent "yous" likewise branch into each new reality. There is an infinite number of "yous," each with its own unique history, existing in an infinite number of concurrent branching worlds. If you're tired of the same old you, there's a new you every quantum moment. This quantum-branching idea sounds crazy, but it is grounded in a useful interpretation of quantum theory.

Another picture holds that there are inflationary universes that spawn new universes forming as bubbles, which in turn spawn more new universes, ad infinitum (Linde, 1994); let us call these newly spawned universes "bubble-babies." Here's an image of the bubble-baby universes: imagine a balloon being blown up with a bubble forming in a weak spot. This bubble expands and then is cut off from the original balloon. As it expands, another bubble forms in another weak spot that is then cut off and continues expanding, and so on and on. The formation of new universes gives a bubble that does not eat up the old universe, which itself keeps expanding outside the bubble. Each generation of universes keeps growing, but inside it new bubble-baby universes keep forming. It seems as though the second law of thermodynamics—that our universe is running down—would preclude this sort of process continuing forever: with energy no longer available, this process would limp to a halt. But perhaps the laws of thermodynamics get jump-started anew with each universe formation. Perhaps. Although there is, as of yet, no evidence to confirm this theory, it is premature to say this inflationary view is physically impossible.

Perhaps black holes give birth to new universes: as matter is sucked into a black hole it is squirted out the other end as a newly forming universe. Some have even conjectured a method for producing test-tube universes: by imploding a bit of matter in a laboratory, one could create a black hole and, in its womb, a baby universe.

Multiverse hypotheses abound and it is beyond the scope of this chapter to evaluate the scientific merits and demerits of each of them. We can, however, evaluate multiverse theories as an explanation of the apparent fine-tuning of our universe. Despite their differences, these theories share much in common. In each of these models the laws of physics differ in each universe. Our universe's specific combination of laws and constants is just one of many existing combinations. While the vast majority of multiverses are life-prohibiting, because there are so many different combinations, the fine-tuned constraints of *our* universe are not a surprise.

When it comes to explaining the fine-tuning of our universe, multiverse hypotheses are perhaps the biggest competitor to a God hypothesis. Despite their recent popularity, they have been subjected to a great deal of scrutiny since their inception. Even enthusiast Martin Rees states that "all these theories are tentative and should be prefaced by something akin to a health warning" (Rees, 2001: 158). What is it about these theories that prompts doubt?

Multiverse Theory Evaluated

Ironically, one of the biggest objections to multiverse hypotheses is an objection rather similar to one levied by atheists against the belief in God. Many atheists have claimed that because God is said to exist outside of the bounds of space and time, it is unclear how we could have any evidence for God's existence and, as a result, be justified in the belief that God exists. Multiverses face a similar objection. The universes postulated by multiverse theories exist in regions of space–time completely disconnected from and inaccessible to our universe. Since these universes are unobservable and untestable, it is unclear how there could be any direct scientific confirmation of these other universes. We are completely ignorant of multiverses and may remain so forever (Ellis, 2011; Polkinghorne and Beale, 2009: first appendix).

Further, multiverse theories might not be a good explanation for fine-tuning even if we grant their existence. The problem is that multiple universes, by themselves, cannot guarantee the existence of a life-conducive universe. Unless an uncountably huge number of universes exist, a fine-tuned universe is not likely. Earlier we considered how the probability of a life-sustaining universe might be something like 1 in 10 to 10^{123}. If this were the case, there must be nearly 10 to 10^{123} universes for us to expect our universe. So unless a multiverse hypothesis can justify at least nearly that many universes it violates the expectation principle.

But even if an *infinite* number of universes exist, that fact, on its own, would provide no reason to expect life-conducive universes (Collins, 2007). For all we know, the mechanism, the physical laws, that churns out different universes might generate only universes that are inhospitable to life.

A mathematical example can help to illuminate this point. An infinite series of numbers does not guarantee that an even number will be produced (the series could be the set of odd numbers). Infinity alone does not guarantee any specific number whatsoever. It would be a mistake to think that an infinite number of universes would guarantee any specific universe whatsoever, including life-conducive ones like ours.

Consider those Shakespeare-loving monkeys again. In the early 2000s, researchers at Plymouth University in England set the Shakespearean task for six Sulawesi crested macaques. When the primates were first left alone with computers they bashed their machines with a stone. Although they developed an inordinate fondness for the letter S, they failed to produce a single word. In fact, their favorite computer-related activity was defecating on the keyboard. It's not clear that monkeys could produce the complete works of Shakespeare, even given an infinite number of them banging on an infinite number of computers for an infinite length of time.

The point: lots of random tries does not guarantee any results. So, too, having lots of universes does not guarantee a life-conducive universe. Whatever physical processes produce multiple universes might get stuck on the letter S, endlessly producing an infinite number of bland and sterile universes.

So not just any multiverse theory and not just any infinite set of universes will do. The physical theory in question must provide some reason for thinking that life-conducive universes could be generated. If "the universe generator" could generate only bland, nonlife-conducive universes, then we haven't eliminated the surprise in finding our life-conducive universe.

God and Multiverses

Are we led, therefore, to God over the multiverse? Perhaps simplicity considerations, which are part of our background knowledge for assessing the initial likelihood of hypotheses, favor the God hypothesis. Martin Gardner, for example, contends that the simplicity of a single creator is preferable to the messiness of multiverses. He writes: "The conjecture that there is just one universe and its creator is infinitely simpler and easier to believe than that there are countless billions upon billions of worlds, constantly increasing in number and created by nobody" (Gardner, 2001). David Berlinski argues, while the atheist must appeal to a multitude of unlikely events and entities, "the theologian need only appeal to a single God lording over it all and a single universe—our own" (Berlinski, 2008: 153).

Should we follow Gardner and Berlinski and reject the multiverse theory in favor of the God hypothesis? I think the answer is no. What moves or will move physicists to accept a version of the multiverse theory is the theory's ability to explain a vast, disparate, and otherwise inexplicable body of data. Acceptance will come only when this theory finds some sort of experimental or observational support (conceding the difficulties with unobservable worlds). If the multiverse theory should become accepted science, it will be part of a theory that is testable and observable—even if the multiverse portion of the theory is not. So while it may be highly speculative and lacking evidential support now, it might become part of widely accepted science. Stephen Barr, particle physicist and Catholic, says, "It seems to me very stupid for religious people to go around and attack ideas like the multiverse because they think it somehow hurts a religious argument. It may turn out someday demonstrable that it's true, and it'll backfire on them."[6]

Rather than squeeze God into the gap of current scientific ignorance, only to be squeezed out should multiverse theory find evidential and experimental support, the theist should remain open to the possibility of multiverses and ask if there is anything in their theology that might lead them to expect or accommodate multiverses.

If you think the existence of one universe requires a special, even divine, explanation, surely a multitude of universes will require a special, even divine, explanation. The question, "Why is there something rather than nothing?" is no less puzzling if it's rephrased in multiverse fashion, "Why is there everything rather than nothing?" Multiple universes multiply the riddle of existence. Contemporary physicist and Christian Gerald Cleaver is comfortable with the idea of a multiverse and thinks it shows "a much deeper understanding of the whole story of creation." Cleaver writes, "With the multiverse, the human perception of reality has grown and expanded by previously unimaginable orders of magnitude. With the dawning of the multiverse paradigm, Christians are thus able to perceive the creative nature of God on a scale and vastness as never before."[7]

Consider the following example. Suppose upon your return from a trip to the grocery story with your penniless, 4-year old child, you discover that she is carrying her favorite candy bar, say (in honor of Martin), *Reese's*. You are surprised to see that she has a *Reese's* knowing that you never paid for it. You suspect petty theft. When queried about the origin of the *Reese's*, your daughter explains: "There's nothing special about the *Reese's* because I have twenty other candy bars." Then she supplies a multicandiverse by withdrawing 20 other, non-*Reese's*, candy bars from her pockets. The multicandiverse does not eliminate your surprise at your daughter's possession of her favorite candy bar; indeed, the multicandiverse only increases your anxiety that your daughter is a thief (and not just a petty one).

So, too, multiplying universes neither eliminates the surprise that we find ourselves in one suited for life, nor does it reduce the need for a special, perhaps even divine, explanation.

The theist, of the Judeo–Christian–Muslim variety, can easily accommodate multiverses within her theology. This theological tradition affirmed what has been called *the great chain of being*, which holds the following beliefs. There is more goodness in a thing the more it is like God, the highest reality. So sentient creatures are more valuable than nonsentient creatures, cognitive creatures more valuable than merely sentient creatures, and so forth. An entire scale of existents can be ranked according to the possession of progressively more valuable properties from the lowliest of rocks up through amoebas, plants, and animals, into human beings and finally to God. Medieval theologians thought that God, out of his goodness, had created beings to occupy every possible niche from microbes to man.

The multiverse theory suggests that "everything" has a vastly greater scope than the medievals could have imagined. God out of his goodness may indeed have created everything—every possible kind of thing in every possible kind of universe. God may not only love the world, God may love every world. The multiverse might be the ultimate expression of divine goodness and creativity.

THEISM OR NATURALISM

Naturalism, which denies the existence of any supernatural forces or beings, leads us to expect nothing at all, let alone our finely tuned universe. An infinite number of hypotheses are equally likely given naturalism. A universe of one steel ball or two steel balls, or only helium, or with a stable, unexploded singularity. . . . ad infinitum, are all equally likely given the hypothesis of naturalism. Naturalism, having no preferences, has no universe preferences. So naturalism does not lead us to expect a finely tuned universe like ours. As far as we can tell, our universe appears to be preferred; it looks as though a life-sustaining universe was in the cards. Using the expectation principle, if we take the fine-tuning data as evidence, theism is vastly preferable to naturalism. Given a belief in the initial plausibility of theism, then the evidence of fine-tuning confirms theism over its major competitor, naturalism.[8]

Theism leads us to expect a universe like ours with people like us. If there is a God who wishes for creatures like us (free, rational, moral beings capable of worshipping the divine), then we would expect a universe like ours. Our universe looks, for all intents and purposes, like it was expected, even designed, with us in mind. Frank Tipler, one of the first and best physicists of fine-tuning, writes: "When I began my career as a cosmologist some twenty years ago, I was a convinced atheist. I never in my wildest dreams imagined that one day I would be writing a book purporting to show that the central claims of Judeo-Christian theology are in fact true....I have been forced into these conclusions by the inexorable logic of my own special branch of physics" (Tipler, 1994: Preface). According to the expectation principle, theism is vastly preferable to naturalism given the fine-tuning data as evidence. If you judged theism initially plausible, then the evidence of fine-tuning could confirm your belief over its major competitor, naturalism.

The argument from fine-tuning is far from open-and-shut case: it cannot demonstrate or conclusively prove God's existence. The atheist or agnostic might think that the initial likelihood of theism is quite low, so low that even though fine-tuning constitutes powerful evidence, it doesn't make theism an overall compelling position. But this shouldn't trouble theists. While the nontheist's judgment about the initial likelihood of God's existence may rationally settle the matter for her, it doesn't settle the matter for those with different judgments of the initial likelihood of God's existence. Our assessment of the likelihood that God exists, prior to considering these arguments, will greatly shape where we ultimately end up. For those who are inclined toward God's existence, the arguments we've considered may rationally push them from agnosticism to theism, or, may strengthen and support their already held theistic belief.

CHAPTER 13

Judaism and Evolution

God's Gift of the Jews

Ashkenazi Jews, who make up 80 percent of the Jews in the world today, have, on average, the highest IQs of any ethnic group in the world. While Asians are often touted as the smartest people in the world, Ashkenazi Jews as a group average 115 on an IQ test—eight points higher than Asians and dramatically higher than the world average of 79.1. Ashkenazin skills in verbal reasoning, comprehension, working memory, and mathematics are simply astounding—the group averages 125 on an IQ test of verbal reasoning. Since 1950, 29 percent of Nobel Prizes have been awarded to Ashkenazi Jews, who represent a mere 0.25 percent of the global population. Did God choose the Jews because they were so brilliant or because, as legend has it, they were the best story-tellers?

A list of the greatest physicists of the twentieth century would be woefully incomplete without Jews; 26 percent of all Nobel Prizes in Physics have gone to Jews. Niels Bohr helped us understand the nature of the electron. Richard Feynman expanded our understanding of quantum electrodynamics. Murray Gell-Mann discovered a new quantum property—strangeness—and a new subatomic particle—the quark. John von Neumann pioneered discoveries in game theory and modern computing, as well as advanced the field of quantum mechanics. Wolfgang Pauli developed the Pauli exclusion principle and hypothesized the existence of neutrinos. Steven Weinberg took the first step toward unifying the fundamental forces of the universe. Robert Oppenheimer and Edward Teller worked together on the Manhattan Project to develop the first atomic bomb. And, towering above them all, Albert Einstein, he of $E = mc^2$ fame, is perhaps the greatest scientist of all time. No wonder then, when I was teaching at a Christian college, a university physicist asked me how we could have a physics department without Jews!

This sounds like an auspicious start to a chapter of a book on science and religion. There appear to be striking similarities between twentieth-century physics led by Jews and the scientific revolution led by Christians. Perhaps we are experiencing a renaissance of science and religion, with the children of Moses leading us into the Promised Land.

But we're not. By and large, these Jews are ethnically Jewish but not religiously. They are secular scientists who just happen to be Jews. They would not consider themselves Jewish scientists, any more than they'd consider themselves German or American or Danish scientists. Neither their religion nor their nationality figures in their scientific work or their conception of themselves as scientists. They're just scientists. They are secular, atheistic, and sometimes downright hostile to religion. Weinberg, an avowed atheist, told a *New York Times* interviewer in 1999, "With or without religion, you would have good people doing good things and evil people doing evil things. But for good people to do evil things, that takes religion." Yet he says his work on the origin of the universe, the Big Bang, may offer "some comfort to those who believe in supernatural creation." Still he claims that science and religion are in conflict or, at least, in serious tension (Weinberg, 2008). For his part, he chooses science. Feynman rejects belief in God as well: "The theory that it's all arranged as a stage for God to watch man's struggle for good and evil seems inadequate." And while Einstein said that God does not play dice and repeatedly invoked God in relation to his work, he spoke only metaphorically. His belief in God amounted to little more than a cosmic religious feeling. Yet, while critical of a personal God who was involved in human affairs, Einstein was deeply religious, had a sense of awe at the order of the universe, and had a keen sense of mystery (Isaacson, 2007).

Nearly to a man, these scientists think that science is in conflict with belief in a personal God who works miracles in the world. They believe in a world strictly governed by mathematical laws, a world that leaves no room for supernatural intervention. You might find a deist here or there—a person who believes that God created the inviolable laws of nature but who does not get personally involved in the world (this God answers no prayers, exercises no providence, effects no salvation, and works no miracles)—but mostly you'll just find atheists or agnostics.

There is some suggestion of an indirect connection between religion and science in the work of Bohr.[1] Bohr was influenced early on by the writings of Søren Kierkegaard, a famous nineteenth-century Christian philosopher. Kirkegaard suggested that a fully flourishing human life went through various stages—from a life of pleasure, to a life of duty, to a life of faith—but moving through these stages is neither automatic nor inevitable. In order to move through these stages one must make a free leap of faith from one stage to the next. In physics, Bohr hypothesized that electrons are able to stay in their orbits, and not collapse into the much heavier nucleus of an atom, because they contain packets, or quanta, of energy. These quanta of energy come in discrete units, so electrons could only be at, say, levels 1 or 2 or 3 (not levels ¾, or 1.5, or 2.75); add one unit of energy and the electron "jumps" to the next full level; reduce a unit of energy and the electron "jumps" down precisely one full level. Given an increase of energy an electron takes a Kierkegaardian *leap* to the next quantum level (Loder and Neidhardt, 1996). This alleged connection is highly speculative and offers no clear connection between Jewish belief and Bohr's quantum view of electrons. That's about as good as it gets for an alleged science-religion connection with these folks.

What, then, is the Jewish view of the relationship between science and religion? In order to get a clear view of this, we will have to ignore most of these famous Jewish scientists and consider what some reflective Jews have written about their religion and its relation to science.

EXPULSIONS AND RETURNS

While issues in science and religion go back millennia, they mostly come into focus during the scientific revolution in Western Europe. Prior to the scientific revolution, as we've seen, natural philosophy (which would eventually morph into what we now call "science") included a great deal of theology and philosophy. Moreover, prior to the scientific revolution, the idea of God was used to explain wide swaths of natural phenomena. Because God was believed to be the Creator and Sustainer of the world, his existence explained the order and motion of the cosmos. God created each of the animals individually, taking just a few hours to create them. Noah's cataclysmic flood explained the structure of a very young earth—mountains and valley, rivers and oceans. Theology, the Queen of the Sciences (*scientia*), reigned alone at the top of all human inquiry; everything else—philosophy and natural philosophy—served theology as handmaidens. As the scientific revolution began to topple theology from its throne, science would become an autonomous and authoritative discipline.

So where were those high-IQ Jews when the science-religion discussion started heating up? Where are the Einsteins and Gell-Mans of the scientific revolution? Sadly, everywhere and nowhere. In 1492 Columbus sailed the ocean blue, but that year also marked the expulsion of the Jews from Spain. They could either convert to Christianity or leave the country. If they decided to evacuate, they had to leave their property and possessions. If they stayed but didn't convert, they were killed. They had already been expelled from England (1290) and France (starting in 1306), and from most of Europe. Quite simply, widespread anti-Semitism drove the Jews out of Europe, the hotspot of the scientific revolution. They were not allowed to return to England until 1655, and then only sporadically and under restrictive conditions. Being repeatedly driven from place to place, being forced to sell everything and depart within months, and having no secure place to lay their heads, the Jews could not effectively study natural philosophy. Jews didn't contribute to the scientific revolution because they had no place at the table (or in the laboratory or observatory). Issues regarding science and religion are unlikely to arise in a group that is forced into poverty and a nomadic life. Survival, not science, was at the top of their to-do list.

The Jews weren't left completely without a voice during that period. Some very fine Jewish thinkers reflected on the new natural philosophy and Jewish attitudes toward it. As you can imagine, Jewish opinions, as with Christian opinions, ranged rather widely. Let us consider two representative but diverse thinkers, David Gans and Tobias Cohen. But first, let us develop some understanding of the Jewish tradition.

TRADITION, TEXTS AND INTERPRETATION

Unlike the Christian tradition, there were no councils that codified the Jewish faith into a set of creedal statements like the Apostles or Nicene Creed. So it is difficult to precisely define orthodox Jewish belief. Nonetheless, Judaism's greatest philosopher/theologian Rabbi Moshe ben Maimon ("Maimonides" also known as "The Rambam") provided just such a definition of Judaism in *Shloshah Asar Ikkarim*, the "Thirteen Fundamental Principles" of the Jewish faith. Maimonides held that these 13 principles constitute "the fundamental truths of our religion and its very foundations." We can do no better to attain an understanding of Judaism than briefly outline his Thirteen Principles of Jewish Faith:

1. Belief in the existence of the Creator, who is perfect in every manner of existence and is the Primary Cause of all that exists.
2. Belief in G-d's unity.
3. Belief in G-d's noncorporeality (and that He is unaffected by any physical occurrences).
4. Belief in G-d's eternity.
5. The obligation to worship G-d exclusively and no foreign false gods.
6. The belief that G-d communicates with man through prophecy.
7. Belief in the primacy of the prophecy of Moses our teacher.
8. Belief in the divine origin of the Torah.
9. Belief in the immutability of the Torah.
10. Belief in G-d's omniscience and providence.
11. Belief in divine reward and retribution.
12. Belief in the arrival of the Messiah and the messianic era.
13. Belief in the resurrection of the dead.

Many Jewish congregations recite these Thirteen Articles, as an affirmation of faith, every day after the morning prayers in the synagogue.

The Thirteen Principles assert the sacred authority of the Torah, the authoritative text of Judaism. Immediately, we find a diversity of opinion within the Jewish tradition. Some understand "Torah" to refer to the Five Books of Moses (the first five books of the Hebrew Bible: Genesis, Exodus, Leviticus, Numbers, and Deuteronomy). Others believe that Torah includes the entire Hebrew Bible (which Jews call "the Tanakh" and Christians call "the Old Testament"). Still others believe that Torah refers to the entire body of Jewish law and teaching. Jews also accept an oral Torah, which explains the meaning of the texts in the Torah and how to apply the Laws in Torah to life. The oral Torah, developed by rabbis,[2] is known as the Talmud. And, no big surprises here, subsequent tradition developed commentaries on the Talmud.

The source of the Torah's authority is that God delivered the Torah to Moses (and so is the ultimate author of Torah). One should, consequently, faithfully accept without question these divine deliverances. But, as noted,

since the Torah can be difficult to understand, the wisdom of God-inspired
Sages was collected in the Talmud. Again, one should faithfully accept without question such divinely guided deliverances. So the Torah and Talmud
were considered two equal founts of Jewish authority.

Sounds nice and neat. You've got the Torah, God's word, and the Talmud,
the key to unlocking the Torah. Should be easy, then, for Jews to reach a
common understanding of God's word. But such matters are seldom so nice
and neat.

If you put three rabbis in a room and ask them a question about Torah,
you'll get three different answers. If you ask a single rabbi what a passage from
Torah teaches, the rabbi might stroke his beard and say, "Well, hmmmm,
Rabbi Schlomo said *x*, and Rabbi Tzvi said *y*, and Rabbi Akiva said not-*x*
and not-*y*." And so, even though you've consulted a single rabbi, you now
have three very different opinions on the understanding of Torah. There is a
famous rabbinic story about disagreements on interpretations of Torah:

> For three years there was a dispute between Beit Hillel and Beit Shammai,
> the former asserting, "The law is in agreement with our views," and the latter
> contending, "The law is in agreement with our views." Then a *bat kol,* a voice
> from heaven, announced, *Eilu v'eilu divrei Elohim Chayim,* "These and those
> are the words of the Living God," adding, "but the law is in agreement with
> the rulings of Beit Hillel."
>
> Since both "*Eilu v'eilu* are the words of the Living God," what entitled
> [the members of] Beit Hillel to have the law fixed according to their rulings?
> Because they were kindly and modest, they studied their own rulings and
> those of Beit Shammai, and were even so humble to mention the words of Beit
> Shammai before their own.[3]

These *and* those are the words of the Living God. This interpretation *and*
that very different interpretation are the words of the living God. This story
is often cited in support of varying yet plausible interpretations of Torah.
The Sages themselves concede the possibility of divergent but valid interpretations of the Torah. In the Talmud it is stated that there are 70 faces of
Torah.[4] Indeed, to the outsider, the Talmud sometimes looks like little more
than a batch of enthusiastically expressed contradictory opinions.

Most Jews are willing to live with the tension of unresolved and even irre-
solvable interpretations of the Torah. Of course, not all Jews are willing to
live with varying yet plausible interpretations of Torah; some assert that *only*
their view is the word of the living God.

Let us now return to how Gans and Cohen treated the issue of the new
science in relation to their Jewish beliefs.

JEWS AND THE NEW SCIENCE

David Gans (1541–1613) might be the one Jew who actually participated
in the scientific revolution, though his credentials in this regard are slight.
Born in what is now Germany, he spent his adult life in Prague where he

met, observed, and conversed with astronomers Johannes Kepler and Tycho Brahe. Brahe conscripted him for some assistance (mostly translation work), but Gans did no original astronomical work of his own. Gans' *Magen David* (1612) was the first book in Hebrew that mentions the work of Copernicus. Although aware that traditional Jewish interpretations of the Bible supported an earth-centered cosmology, Gans wrote: "In this domain, the human mind is completely free to discover the theory which seems to be in conformity with its own logic" (Neher, 1977). Gans noted that the discrepancy between Copernicanism and earth-centered *interpretations* of the Bible is not the same as a discrepancy between Copernicanism and *the Bible itself*. What Copernicanism calls into question is a widely accepted interpretation, not the Bible. While Gans defended Ptolemy's earth-centered system, he cryptically remarked that through the work of Tycho and Kepler things were going to change. Gans also hoped that by working closely with non-Jewish astronomers, he could offer a model of Jewish-Christian cooperation on very general natural theology (knowledge of God gained from the study of nature), theology shared by Christians and Jews alike. Sadly Gans' second-rate astronomy had little influence either on his contemporaries or on subsequent generations of Jewish and Christian thinkers. Perhaps even more sadly, his model of tolerance was never replicated.

On the other side of the science-religion spectrum, we find Tobias Cohen (1652–1729). The dominant view of his time, encouraged by rabbis, was that one should devote oneself to the study of God's *word* (where one could discover the truth), and one should not devote oneself to the study of God's *world* (where one could not discover the truth). This view of human capacities to grasp the truth—optimism about Torah study and pessimism about natural philosophy—persuaded many bright Jewish students to take up the study of Torah and not waste their time on natural philosophy. While Gans was open to discovering natural knowledge of God through the study of the heavens, Cohen thought that knowledge of the heavens had been revealed to the biblical sages, Abraham and his children, and so could be best studied in the Torah.[5] Just by studying the Bible itself, one could reach an understanding of the cosmos and the earth. Cohen referred to Copernicus as "the firstborn of Satan," believing that Copernicus's sun-centered system was inconsistent with the view authoritatively developed and defended in the Jewish tradition.

Cohen was a partial exception to his own strictures on human thought. He was trained in medicine, going on to serve as personal physician to five sultans of the Ottoman Empire. His massive work, *Ma-aseh Tuviyah*, considered theology and natural philosophy in one volume, and medicine in another. His would become the most influential Jewish work on natural philosophy and medicine.

This brief diversion through the scientific revolution explains why Jewish thinkers generally avoided natural philosophy. Even if they had been interested in the study of natural philosophy, anti-Semitism by and large prevented their participation. Jewish attitudes toward natural philosophy varied from openness about the new astronomical sciences to complete skepticism about the human ability to grasp important truths independent of God's word. The former attitude was defended by Maimonides, so let us move back in history to the greatest of all Jewish thinkers.

MAIMONIDES

No discussion of Jewish thought would be complete without reference to Maimonides (1138–1204), Judaism's greatest philosopher and theologian. Gans seems to follow in Maimonides' footsteps when he claimed that while the Torah is authoritative, the opinions of rabbis who are commenting on the Torah (in the Talmud) are not. Maimonides' monumental and systematic *Mishneh Torah* effectively undermined the authority of the Talmud. His hope was that by reading the *Mishneh Torah* alongside the Torah, one might know how to act in every situation in life; one wouldn't need to consult the considerably more obscure Talmud.

Maimonides was born in Spain and then was driven out of the country under threat of conversion to Islam or death. His family took refuge in Morocco, traveled a bit in the Holy Land, and then ended up in Egypt. He read Greek philosophers in Arabic and absorbed science and philosophy from the Islamic culture that surrounded him. He trained in Torah as a rabbi, studied medicine, and served as court physician to the Sultan Saladin of Egypt. In short, he was exposed to and grew to respect the best of Greek, Jewish, and Muslim philosophy and natural philosophy. Little wonder that he would famously proclaim: "Listen to the truth from whoever says it."

Maimonides sought to bring insights from both natural philosophy and philosophy to his understanding of Scripture. Understanding the world that God created could both illuminate passages of Scripture and eliminate heretical understandings of the Bible. The study of the natural world, natural philosophy, therefore, is religiously significant. One should use that truth as one seeks to understand the Torah. Since all truth is God's truth, Maimonides took truth from whomever and wherever he could find it—the Greeks, the Muslims, astronomy, and so on.

Maimonides was a rationalist who defended reason over tradition as the final authority over Jewish belief and practice. His preference for reason opened up the Jewish world to the "foreign sciences." If texts in the Torah were found to be in conflict with a truth discovered by reason, the text should be interpreted figuratively or metaphorically. Maimonides was generally disposed toward a figurative reading of Scriptural texts. For example, he famously opposed literal readings of passages that ascribe human attributes to the divine—those that claim that God had a body or spoke (like a human, with a tongue and voicebox). So he allowed truths established by reason to likewise open up the reader to understanding the figurative, true meaning of texts.

In his most famous philosophical treatise, *Guide for the Perplexed*, Maimonides argued that it is fitting and proper to depart from the opinions of the rabbis, and follow the reasoned judgment of Gentile scholars, in matters of astronomy. For example, he rejected the rabbis' estimates of astronomical distances: "You must, however, not expect that everything our Sages say respecting astronomical matters should agree with observation, for mathematics were not fully developed in those days; and their statements were not based on the authority of the Prophets, but on the knowledge which they either themselves possessed or derived from contemporary men of science" (Maimonides, 2006: 3.14). They were offering their own opinions, not reporting the "dicta of the prophets." They were not, therefore, offering Scripture itself, or even an authoritative understanding of Scripture, and so, their belief could be rejected. Moreover, some early sages believed that due to principles of motion, the sun and stars produced loud noises as they orbited the earth. Maimonides claimed that later sages abandoned that false belief and concludes: "for speculative matters everyone treats according to the results of his own study, and everyone accepts that which appears to him established by proof" (Maimonides, 2006: 2.8).

Natural philosophy, then, can correct the sages' generally accepted understanding of Torah. We can put this into a general principle: If rabbinic teachings can be shown to conform with reasoned truth, they can and should be accepted. But if not, such rabbinic statements, even those in the Talmud, are merely individual opinions, not Torah, and should be rejected.[6]

Contemporary Jewish Approaches to Science and Religion

The texts of books that are shared with the Christian Bible are roughly the same as those in the Torah. So we'll find similar issues relating the worldview of the ancient Hebrews with the worldview of modern science. For example, the Genesis account affirms creation in six days, all of the animals in a single day, and the creation of humans from the dust. On Rosh Hashanah, the Jewish New Year, Jews celebrate the ensoulment of Adam; upon blowing the shofar, they say: "*Hayom Harat Olam*—today is the birthday of the world." By tracing human ancestry back to Adam (born 5,766 years ago), one can deduce a very young earth: add six days to Adam's birthday, and you've got the beginning of the world (5766 years + six days). A natural reading of many texts reveals an earth-centered cosmos. In Chapter 10 of the book of Joshua, for example, we read that the day lasted longer because God held the sun in place (God did not stop the earth from rotating). All of the issues we considered in earlier chapters in relating the Bible to science—Ptolemy vs. Copernicus, the age of the earth, evolution, etc.—we can find in relating the Torah (and Talmud) to science.

Perhaps the best single contemporary case to raise science-religion issues is evolution. As noted in previous chapters, most traditional readings of the Book of Genesis, including most traditional rabbinic readings, assert that about 6,000 years ago God created the world in six days and created Adam from the dust and Eve from the rib of Adam. As noted in previous chapters, contemporary science rejects most of that story. We will start with a consideration of the views of Natan Slifkin, known as "the Zoo Rabbi," who argues that Darwinian evolution is compatible with religion. Then we will consider his detractors who claim that evolution contradicts and compromises core truths of Torah and the Talmud and so must be rejected; humans are not, as Slifkin alleges, modified monkeys created by a random process. They are image bearers of God created by divine fiat. This debate offers a sense of the science–religion discussion in contemporary Judaism.

The Zoo Rabbi

Natan Slifkin, born in 1975 in England, is an Orthodox rabbi famous for his attempts to reconcile contemporary science with Torah. Trained in rabbinical studies, Slifkin began to consider the relationship between Torah and the animal kingdom. This led to the development of the Zoo Torah program, which at various major zoos uses Torah as an aid to wildlife education, and wildlife education as an aid to understanding Torah. Slifkin makes two controversial claims. First, the cosmology of Torah should not be understood literally, and second, the views of the rabbinic sages in the Talmud are not infallible, especially when it comes to scientific matters. In this he follows Maimonides who claims, for example, that Genesis 1 should be interpreted metaphorically as referring not to literal days but to a hierarchy of creation and that rabbinic pronouncements in the Talmud can be rejected because they don't have the high and sole authority of Scripture itself.

Slifkin positively embraces Darwinian common descent: "Rabbi Simcha Zissel Ze'ev…argued that Rabbi Salanter was such a refined human being that nobody who encountered him could have entertained the idea that he evolved from a monkey. But those who have studied biology and anthropology—the science of human origins—find compelling reason to believe this" (Slifkin, 2006: 317). He contends that Darwinian evolutionary processes are God's means of creation: "It is abundantly clear from all this that the randomness of Darwinian evolution poses no theological problem whatsoever. Judaism has no problem with processes that appear to be random, and in fact it sees them as an ideal means via which God dynamically exerts His will" (Slifkin, 2006: 293). Contrary to a literal interpretation of Torah, Slifkin holds that the universe is billions of years old, that God created through Darwinian processes, and that humans descended from primate ancestors. These are or should be clear, he thinks, to a mind attentive to reason and experience, and to a person faithful to God.[7]

Three of his books have been declared heretical—as inconsistent with Torah—by distinguished ultra-Orthodox[8] rabbinic authorities. What, then, has created such a controversy in the Jewish community?

One can understand the initial sources of discomfort in Slifkin's approach to understanding reality. Slifkin, affirming Maimonides' "take truth from wherever you find it," calls himself a rationalist, which he defines according to these three tenets:

- *Rationalists* believe that knowledge is legitimately obtained by man via his reasoning and senses, and should preferably be based upon evidence/reason rather than faith, especially for far-fetched claims.
- *Rationalists* value a naturalistic rather than supernatural interpretation of events, and perceive a consistent natural order over history—past, present and future. They tend to minimize the number of supernatural entities and forces.
- *Rationalists* understand the purpose of mitzvos [commandments of the Jewish law], and one's religious life in general, primarily (or solely) as furthering intellectual/moral goals for the individual and society.[9]

Rationalism, which prizes reason over unreflective faith and tradition, is contrasted with mysticism, which is skeptical of the mind's ability to arrive at significant truths independently of revelation. Mystics believe that God's direct miraculous activity is the dominant source of creativity in the world, especially in the ancient world and in the messianic age to come. Finally, mystics view following God's commands as a kind of magical means of manipulating the spiritual forces, of which there are many, in the universe.[10]

Slifkin, following his reason and senses, contends that the universe and all that it contains resulted from divinely ordained natural processes over the course of billions of years. As a scientist, then, one should restrict oneself to consideration of the natural processes that brought about stars, galaxies, planets, animals, and the human animal. Even life itself, Slifkin argues, arose naturalistically, through very natural and gradual processes, without direct appeal to God; God did not "zap" things into existence. God used God-created laws to bring about his creation. God is like a cosmic engineer: he can design and then build into nature all of the laws that are necessary to bring about precisely what God wants to create. Unlike Microsoft, God does not have to continually issue patches to correct for unforeseen programming errors. This forms the basis of one charge of heresy against Slifkin—the claim that it is against Torah and the sages of the Talmud to believe that the universe is billions of years old.

How can one square science's claim that the universe is billions of years old with Torah's claim that it was created about 6,000 years ago? Slifkin follows Maimonides down the path of metaphor and away from the ancient rabbis' more literal interpretation of the creation story in Genesis 1. In his Introduction to *Guide for the Perplexed*, Maimonides writes:

> Now, on the one hand, the subject of Creation is very important, but on the other hand, our ability to understand these concepts is very limited. Therefore, God described these profound concepts, which His Divine wisdom found necessary to communicate to us, using allegories, metaphors, and imagery. Our Sages put it succinctly, "It is impossible to communicate to man the stupendous

immensity of the Creation of the universe. Therefore, the Torah simply says, 'In the beginning God created the heavens and the earth' (Gen. 1.1)." Thus they pointed out that the subject is a deep mystery. It has been outlined in metaphors so that the masses can understand it according to their mental capacity, while the educated take it in a different sense. (Maimonides, 2006: Introduction)

Given the great difference between Creator and creature, and our limited ability to grasp the Creator, God must stoop down and speak to us using concepts that we can grasp. These concepts are not adequate to their subject, the Almighty. So God, in order to communicate essential truths to the uneducated masses (that is to nearly everyone in the ancient world), had to use language that they could grasp. He had to accommodate himself to the thought patterns of the day and age. Taking those ancient thought patterns or concepts as literal would diminish our understanding of what God intended to communicate about the creation.

Just as the statement, "the hand of God" is not literally true (God does not have a hand or a body), neither is the statement that God created the world and everything in it in six, 24-hour days. Although the Talmud generally commends literal interpretations, Slifkin finds precedent for nonliteral interpretations in a Talmudic text that claims that the entire book of Job is nonliteral. There was no historical Job who lost everything; the book of Job is simply a parable (but it nevertheless still communicates God's truth).

Slifkin also finds clues internal to the text, clues that indicate that "day" should not be taken literally. Consider Genesis 1.5:

And God called the light "day," and He called the darkness "night:" and it was evening, and it was morning, one day.

"Day" in a single verse means both "the time of light" (morning) and "evening and morning." In Genesis 2.4 we read that God made the heavens and the earth in one day (not on six successive days, as stated in Genesis 1). So "day," within the context of Scripture itself, can have many meanings. Moreover, Slifkin notes that a day is literally one full revolution of the earth on its axis with sunlight appearing at dawn and disappearing at dusk. But the sun wasn't created until the fourth day. Again, we find an internal clue that "day" couldn't mean a literal, 24-hour day. If to God a day is as a thousand years (Psalm 90.4), that is, an indefinitely long period of time, then each day of creation represents an indefinitely long period of time.

Rabbi Slifkin's biggest reason for rejecting six literal 24-hour days of creation is because this explanation cannot be squared with science. If he has to choose between science and an antiquated view of Torah, Rabbi Slifkin rejects the antiquated view of Torah. But, again, rejecting an interpretation of Torah is not tantamount to rejecting Torah. Using God's world to understand God's word is not to denigrate the authenticity of God's word. Rejecting the authority of a rabbi, is not the same as rejecting the authority of God.

What, according to Slifkin, is the authoritative teaching of Torah on Genesis 1? If the teaching has nothing to do with how God created the world, what *does* it have to do with? Slifkin's interpretation of Genesis assumes, first and foremost, that the Torah is a work of theology and morality, not physics and biology. So he does not look to the opening chapters of Genesis for information about how and when God created the world. Rather, his allegorical interpretation of Genesis holds that these chapters are intended to teach who is the Creator and who are the Creatures. Who is God, then, and who are we? And what is our place in Creation?

Consider an analogy with the Song of Songs—a book of the Bible that is ostensibly about a lover and his beloved (with some rather steamy allusions), one which never mentions God. Early in the first-century CE, debates raged about the appropriateness of the inclusion of this lusty book in the Hebrew Bible. Yet it was included and is read on Passover, one of Judaism's highest and holiest religious celebrations. The most widely accepted interpretation of the Song of Songs is allegorical. The Song of Songs on the surface is about man–woman love, but theologically and morally it is really about God's love for Israel. Rabbi Akiba, accepting this allegorical interpretation in the early first-century CE, would go so far as to call the Song of Songs the holiest book in the Bible. When one is tempted to think that God has abandoned his chosen people, the Song of Songs reminds them that Israel is still God's beloved.

Following Maimonides, as well as some influential rabbis and some portions of the Talmud, Slifkin has developed and defended an allegorical interpretation of Genesis 1 that could not, in principle, conflict with contemporary science. It couldn't conflict because his interpretation makes no scientific claims. Understood as a moral and theological treatise, the early chapters of Genesis are simply the wrong genre to contradict any teachings of science. Science and Torah occupy entirely separate spheres—Gould's nonoverlapping magisteria. By using reason and the senses to understand God's world, Slifkin, again following Maimonides, claims to have developed a fuller and richer sense of the Creator and his Creation.

The Literal Interpretation of Torah

Given the diversity of the tradition, we can be sure that there are at least three understandings of the relationship of contemporary evolutionary theory to Torah. We have already considered the separationist view of Slifkin—Torah and science are in two, nonoverlapping spheres of inquiry and so cannot contradict one another. Slifkin is also a kind of integrationist—he brings contemporary science to bear both on his understanding of Scripture and his understanding of the Creator and his Creation. Let us conclude this chapter with contemporary Jewish thinkers who claim that there is a conflict between Torah and evolutionary theory and who resolve the conflict in favor of Torah. Science and Scripture, according to these thinkers, can and do conflict in the case of evolutionary theory and the life of faith demands submission to Torah and a rejection of science.

A recent survey of 176 Orthodox Jewish college students about evolution and related issues showed the students, *especially science students*, to be decidedly antiscience.[11] Only 8 percent of them believe that evolution correctly explains the origin of life, and only 6 percent believe that humans evolved from apes. Interestingly, only 2 percent of science majors accept evolution and believe that humans evolved from apes. Seventy-three percent of those surveyed believe that the universe is roughly 7,000 years old, and 90 percent think that all current land animals descended from those that were on Noah's ark. Again, a greater percentage of *science majors* than nonscience majors believe in a young earth.

Jews in the Orthodox tradition accept both the written Torah and the oral Torah, the Talmud, as authoritative. Both are considered divinely inspired and, therefore, infallible. The oral Torah provides the interpretive key to unlocking the mysteries of the written Torah. So Orthodox Jews cannot reject, as a matter of faith, the teachings of either the written or oral Torah. The Torah and Talmud teach that God created humans by special divine fiat 5,766 years ago on the sixth day of the universe. One embraces an old earth and evolution only on pain of heresy. Indeed, some Orthodox Jews believe that it is forbidden even to read a book that defends evolution.

If the Talmud is authoritative and offers interpretive principles for understanding the Torah, a well-known Talmudic principle seems to prohibit nonliteral interpretations of Torah: "a verse does not depart from its literal (or plain) meaning." This is surely too strong—as noted, Torah clearly contains a great deal of metaphorical and figurative language, and within the Talmud we find interpretations of texts that depart from their literal or plain meaning (such as the book of Job or the Song of Songs). When, then, should one depart from the literal meaning of a text? The Orthodox answer seems to be only when the Talmud requires it.

Some Orthodox thinkers are skeptical of the human ability to attain knowledge independently of the Torah and Talmud. In Slifkin's terms, these sorts of thinkers are mystics (who likewise reject Maimonidean rationalism). So when the infallible Talmud infallibly interprets the infallible Torah, one is not permitted to deviate on the basis of fallible human inquiry. Science, as a fallible human enterprise, couldn't possibly compete with knowledge of Torah derived through the Talmud. As Orthodox physicist Naftali Berg writes: "All scientific theories by definition are tentative. They are not absolute. Our job is to investigate those theories that are consistent with Torah" (Silman, 2002). Science, therefore, could not and so should not be called upon to help us understand Torah. A science-informed deviation from Torah would be heretical.

Some Orthodox Jews employ scientific arguments that are similar to Christian creation scientists. They contend that there is a lack of transitional forms in the fossil record, that there is no evidence of a new species evolving from a preexisting species (we can see animals getting bigger or insects changing colors, but we've never witnessed the emergence of an entirely new species), that there is insufficient time for all species to have evolved by random mutation, and that you can't get order from chaos (entropy counts against evolution).

Let us consider one representative and famous book rejecting evolution, Lee Spetner's *Not By Chance: Shattering the Modern Theory of Evolution*. Spetner is an MIT-trained physicist who taught quantum mechanics and electromagnetic theory at Johns Hopkins University, Howard University, and the Weizmann Institute. After moving to Israel in 1970 his interests shifted to evolution, which he subsequently rejected as unsupported by the evidence (and, I suspect, as inconsistent with the Torah). His own views are a combination of microevolution and the Talmud.

Spetner's central argument against macroevolution—that entirely new species could be produced through small random mutations—is probabilistic. As mentioned previously, when biologists say that a mutation is *random*, they mean that it is neutral with respect to the needs of the species. Ducks didn't mutate webs because nonwebbed birds needed to accommodate themselves to a watery environment, and fish didn't grow fins because non-finned water creatures needed to steer or propel themselves better in water. Mutations are random—they are not responsive to the needs of creatures. In fact, most mutations are detrimental to the good of the creature that possesses them. While a pair of wings might be really useful, the mutation of a single wing would likely make a creature go in circles, and the mutation of wing nubs would slow a creature down. Predators are very likely to devour most creatures born with a mutation (if the mutation permits survival at all). A few, very few mutations prove beneficial to the creature that possesses it. If so, that creature may survive longer or be more attractive to mates and so pass on that favorable trait to succeeding generations. So much for random mutations.

Now to the probability argument: if mutations are rare, if mutations are random, if favorable mutations are rarer still, and if only some favorable mutations are passed on to subsequent generations, then the creation of a new species is statistically impossible. Taking figures from the relevant scientific literature, Spetner makes the following calculation. He gathers from the scientific literature that getting a new species would take about 500 steps (separate mutations). Next he calculates the probability of getting all 500 steps to occur successfully in a row. He argues that since the probability of getting a single favorable mutation is $1/300,000$, the probability of getting 500 favorable mutations in a row is $1/300,000$ multiplied 500 times. Thankfully, he does the calculation for us: the probability of a new species is 2.7×10^{-2739}! If his calculations are correct, then getting a single new species via random mutations is statistically impossible. Moreover, getting every species is, well, more impossible. He claims there just aren't enough favorable mutations and not enough time to produce new species.[12]

If mutations are nonrandom (perhaps creatures have an inbuilt mechanism that is favorably responsive to changes in their environment), then speciation might be possible. Spetner, then, suggests a way in which a certain form of evolution might be consistent with a literal reading of Torah. Drawing on

Talmudic resources, Spetner contends that all living creatures derive from God's original creation of 365 beasts and 365 birds.[13] Moreover, he claims Talmudic authority for the necessity of animals to evolve. With nonrandom mutations, all living creatures evolved from the original 730.

While Spetner rejects contemporary evolutionary theory as nonscientific (not supported by the empirical evidence), he offers his Talmudic view, along with his suggestions about nonrandom mutations, as the view best supported by the evidence. His mixture of the Talmud and micro- (and possibly macro-) evolution, is an example of the integration of science and religion. Most ultra-Orthodox Jews and many Orthodox Jews, however, oppose evolution and choose Torah.

Conclusion

We have considered only two views from two branches of Judaism—Orthodoxy and ultra-Orthodoxy and their consideration of evolution. There are other, more liberal, branches of Judaism—Reform and Conservative—which don't hold such high views of the authority of Torah and Talmud. Their members are historically and temperamentally more inclined toward evolution. I have selected Orthodox believers because people of the book are more likely to face serious science and religion issues than people who aren't overly committed to an authoritative text. When a book is believed to be divinely inspired, to offer infallible information, and apparently to speak to matters that science apparently speaks to (e.g., the age of the earth and the creation of species)— that may require a fundamental rethinking of the relationship of one's beliefs with science. Most Orthodox believers see science and religion in conflict and resolve the conflict in favor of Torah. Slifkin's views are part separation, part integration. Spetner's views turn out, surprisingly, to be integrationist (although he rejects most scientists' understanding of evolution).

Taking a book to be divinely constituted and authoritative raises serious questions for believers in the book, many of which have been raised in this chapter. If it's an ancient book, in what sense is the worldview of the ancient world optional and in what sense is it required for subsequent believers? How does religious language work—must God accommodate himself to inadequate human concepts in order to communicate important truths? In a book with a variety of literary genres, how does one tell if a passage should be interpreted literally, metaphorically, or allegorically? Does one need an infallible tradition to settle the interpretation? Is the book intended to teach, say physics and biology, or is it only intended to teach theology and morality? What authority does tradition have on understanding the book? And what should one's attitude be toward an infallible book and fallible science? Finally, if God revealed himself in two books—nature and Scripture—how should understandings from the two books be put together?

Let us conclude with a passage from the Talmud, which represents the characteristically open view that most Jews have toward Torah interpretation: "Any dispute that is for the sake of Heaven is destined to endure; one that is not for the sake of Heaven is not destined to endure. Which is a dispute that is for the sake of Heaven? The dispute(s) between Hillel and Shamai. Which is a dispute that is not for the sake of Heaven? The dispute of Korach and all his company."[14] The Talmud defends noble disputes— those that are for the sake of Heaven; if not noble, it will not endure. Only time will tell, then, if the dispute between Jewish evolutionists and Jewish nonevolutionists is a noble one.

CHAPTER 14

Islam and Evolution

WHAT IS ISLAM?

I start this chapter in a manner quite different from previous chapters—without a catchy hook. Although the central theme of the book is science and religion, it behooves us given these troubled times to, from the very beginning, counter the urge to judge 1.5 billion Muslims by the actions of a relatively few radical fundamentalists. We need to resist our natural tendency to form opinions based on bad things rather than good things: we typically let a single, and often unrepresentative, bad thing outweigh a bevy of good things in our judgment of people and groups.[1] Since we're going to encounter some bad things in our discussion of Islam and evolution—name calling, fatwas, and death threats—we need to counter those with the many and deep good things of Islam. So we pause, right at the beginning, to understand Islam.

Osama bin Laden is not the voice of Islam. A 2008 Gallup Poll of Muslims in 35 countries worldwide showed that 93 percent of Muslims favor peace (disturbingly, 7 percent don't—though not all of the 7 percent condone terrorism).[2] Let us treat those prejudices against Islam as helium-filled balloons and release them into the sky as we seek to understand Islam itself (and Muslims themselves).

Perhaps the most characteristic Islamic belief is uncompromising monotheism: there is one unsurpassable, divine being, Allah.[3] Allah communicated through a host of prophets beginning with Adam and proceeding through, to name a few, Abraham, Moses, David, Ishmael, and Jesus. God's final and definitive revelation, one that reaffirmed the monotheistic message of the previous prophets, was revealed by God to the Prophet Muhammad in the early seventh-century AD. Muhammad, whose full name is Muḥammad ibn 'Abd Allāh ibn 'Abd al-Muṭṭalib ibn Hāshim, then preached the essence of that final revelation, "God is One," and proclaimed submission or surrender as the only pathway to God ("Islam" means "submission"). In order to become a Muslim, a follower of the teachings of Islam, one must simply say "there is no god but Allah, and Muhammad is Allah's Messenger" (in Arabic, "*La ilaha illa Allah, Muhammad ur-rasoolu Allah*").

Allah's revelation to Muhammad, recorded in the Quran (which means "the recitation"), are considered by Muslims to be the very words of God. While the Quran is the foundational, authoritative religious text for Muslims, a collection of texts second in authority is the Hadith, which contain the sayings of or reports about Muhammad (which he was determined should remain separate from the revelation of God).[4] Although the Quran assumes the truth of portions of the Hebrew Bible and Christian Scriptures, it, unlike those texts, contains very little narrative (and very little information about the life of Muhammad); the Quran is essentially a book of moral and spiritual guidance. To get a taste of the Quran, consider the seven-line opening chapter (Surah) of the Quran:

> In the name of God, the Lord of Mercy, the Giver of Mercy!
> Praise belongs to God, Lord of the Worlds,
> the Lord of Mercy, the Giver of Mercy,
> Master of the Day of Judgment.
> It is You we worship; it is You we ask for help.
> Guide us to the straight path:
> the path of those you have blessed, those who incur no anger
> and who have not gone astray.[5]

These verses, repeated in daily prayers and weekly prayer services for over a millennium, affirm Allah's mercy first, but also God's guidance and sovereignty. The phrase "In the name of Allah, the Most Gracious, the Most Merciful" is repeated billions of times every day. While many might question whether or not Islam is a religion of peace, Islamic ritual is grounded in a firm and regular reminder of Allah's Grace and Mercy.

Muslims believe that human beings are created to love and serve the One True God as revealed through the prophets. The central Muslim beliefs can be summarized in the following six articles of faith:

1. *Oneness of God*. A Muslim believes, first and foremost, in One God, Supreme and Eternal, Infinite and Mighty, Merciful and Compassionate, Creator and Provider.
2. *Messengers of God*. A Muslim believes in all the messengers of God, including Adam, the first Prophet, along with Abraham, Ishmael, Moses, Jesus and Muhammad, the final Prophet.
3. *Revelations and the Quran*. A Muslim believes in all Scriptures and revelations of God, including the Torah, the Psalms, and the Gospels. The Quran is the final testament in this series of revelations, comprising the direct words of God, revealed through the Angel Gabriel, to Muhammad.
4. *Angels*. A Muslim believes in angels, purely spiritual and splendid beings that are charged with a specific duty.
5. *Day of Judgment*. A Muslim believes that at the end of the world, the dead will rise to a fair judgment. Everything we do, say, make,

intend, and think will be brought up on the Day of Judgment. People with good records will be welcomed to Paradise, and people with bad records will be cast into Hell.

6. *Predestination.* A Muslim believes in the Power of a Wise and Compassionate God to plan and execute His plans.

A life of devotion to Allah requires the Five Pillars of Islam, which are:

1. *Shahadah*: Profession of one's faith that there is no God except Allah, and Muhammad is His Messenger.
2. *Salah*: Prayer five times a day (usually facing Mecca).
3. *Zakat*: Almsgiving of 2.5 percent of one's total net worth to the poor and needy.
4. *Sawm*: Fasting and self-control during the holy month of Ramadan.
5. *Hajj*: Pilgrimage to Mecca at least once in a lifetime if one is physically and financially able.

These Six Articles and Five Pillars combine to establish the identity of Muslims, in spite of many other differences, through time and across the globe.

The righteous—those who are faithful to Allah to the end, those whose good deeds outweigh their bad ones—will attain a blissful, eternal paradise. The wicked, on the other hand, are bound over to hell. As stated in the Quran: "Every soul will taste death and you will be paid in full only on the Day of Resurrection. Whoever is kept away from the Fire and admitted to the Garden will have triumphed. The present world is only an illusory pleasure" (3.185).

Islam's two major branches—the Shi'a and the Sunni—initially divided over the proper succession, and hence authority, of its leaders. Sunnis believe that the Muslim community properly selected a leader after Prophet Muhammad's death. Shi'as, on the other hand, believe that the Prophet appointed his son-in-law, Ali, by divine will, to be his successor. Iran's Ali Khamenei, who succeeded the Ayatollah Khomeini, is the current *Vali-e Faqih* (Supreme Leader of the Islamic Republic) and is considered by some a descendant of Muhammad's son-in-law, Ali. The Sunni-Shi'a divide raises the following issue: is leadership/authority by divine appointment or community agreement? While this basically political difference would yield some theological differences (and a great deal of social strife), Shi'as and Sunnis are united in accepting the supreme authority of the Quran and the Five Pillars of Islam.

Aside from Islam's monotheism and Five Pillars, there is, as one might expect of a 1500-year-old religion with over a billion adherents, widespread doctrinal disagreement among Muslims. Muslims agree on the nature of God, the most basic practices (the Five Pillars), and the afterlife; beyond that, there is wide variability in Muslim's beliefs. Understanding the Quran, written in Arabic, requires an understanding of the text and its language in its seventh-century context. Disagreement about text interpretation, especially whether or not a particular text should be understood literally or figuratively, is directly relevant to a discussion of the science of origins. Unlike Christianity, Islam has no universal or binding creeds or statements of faith; unlike Roman Catholicism, it has no Pope and no authoritative centralized authorities or councils to determine matters of faith and practice. Sunni Islam, to which the majority of Muslims subscribe, has no official religious hierarchy. Muslim views have also been influenced by the cultural diversity within Islam, a globe-spanning religion that finds majority populations in countries as diverse as Middle Eastern monarchical Saudi Arabia and Southeast Asian democratic Indonesia. Muslims in the United States are very different from Muslims in the Republic of Kazakhstan (whose citizens labored under institutionally enforced atheism during their Soviet phase). By and large, the majority of Muslims do not adhere to rulings of any particular scholar or group of scholars. The question, "Who speaks for Islam?" is a profound and vexing one.

A Religion of Peace?

Again, although peace is not of central concern to the theme of this book, it requires consideration so that Islamic views on science and religion get a fair hearing. One might think, given representations of Muslims in the media, that Islam is inherently violent. If Islam is believed to be inherently violent, one might not give Muslim thinkers the attention they deserve. Since many have formed opinions of Muslims based on the actions of a few suicide bombers, the question, "Is Islam a religion of peace?" merits consideration. So bear with me, as we bring theological, sociological, and political matters into the discussion before proceeding to a consideration of Islam and science.

Quranic verses cited in favor of peace and religious tolerance include the following:

- "On account of [his deed], We decreed to the Children of Israel that if anyone kills a person—unless in retribution for murder or spreading corruption in the land—it is as if he kills all mankind, while if any saves a life it is as if he saves the lives of all mankind. Our messengers came to them with clear signs, but many of them continued to commit excesses in the land." (5.32).
- "There is no compulsion in religion: true guidance has become distinct from error, so whoever rejects false gods and believes in God has grasped the firmest hand-hold, one that will never break. God is all hearing and all knowing." (2.256)
- "People, We created you all from a single man and a single woman, and made you into races and tribes so that you should recognize one another. In God's eyes, the most honored of you are the ones most mindful of Him: God is all knowing, all aware." (49.13)[6]

Such verses, along with many others, offer a Quranic foundation for peace, compassion, liberty, and tolerance, all within a context of social, ethnic, and theological diversity.[7]

These verses come from the authoritative text of Islam, but what do Muslims themselves actually believe? A fascinating glimpse of Muslim views on faith and politics can be gleaned from the Pew Research Center's 2013 survey of Muslims in non-Western countries.[8] Pew researchers conducted a remarkable 38,000 face-to-face interviews in more than 80 languages in 37 different countries, from Azerbaijan all around the alphabet and back again to Afghanistan.

The democratic impulse is truly alive and well among Muslims around the world. The majority of Muslims in 31 of 37 countries prefer democracy over a strong ruler. In some countries—Ghana, Tajikistan, Lebanon, Kosovo, to name just a few—the number of people on the side of democracy is overwhelming: 87 percent of Ghanaian and 81 percent of Lebanese Muslims, for example, favor democracy. Muslims are also strongly in favor of religious freedom. In nearly every country, Muslims were overwhelmingly supportive of the claim that it is good that others are free to practice their faith. This suggests that religious persecution of Christians and Jews in Muslim-majority nations is in the hands of a small minority. The view of the vast majority in most of these countries affords great hope for religious liberty around the world: in 33 of the countries surveyed over 75 percent of all Muslims are supportive of religious liberty and tolerance.

Finally, Muslims are concerned about religious extremism in general and Islamic extremism in particular. In the 22 countries where the question—"Is suicide bombing justified?"—was asked, only six countries reported more than 15 percent advocating suicide bombing. Since the moral objection to suicide bombing is that it kills innocent civilians, it is worth noting that while most US citizens condemn suicide bombing, US military interventions in Muslim-majority countries have killed vastly more innocent civilians in the twenty-first century than all suicide bombers put together.

When all of the data on democracy and liberty are added to data collected about American Muslims,[9] one thing rings loud and clear: Muslims around the world are in favor of peace, harmony, liberty, and tolerance. The stereotype of the Muslim terrorist must finally be laid to rest—this is the view of a very small minority. Those in the West should stop judging Islam in the light of this small minority.

And yet, worldwide, we have seen many instances of (Muslim) terrorism since 9/11. If Islam is a religion of peace, what motivates these mostly young men to violence? The Gallup Poll cited in the opening paragraph suggests that Muslims are motivated to violence not primarily on theological grounds but on political grounds. The political motivations are, for the most part, fear of Western domination (which can be cultural as well as economic) and occupation. A culture that values chastity and marriage, for example, can justifiably fear the Western intrusion of extramarital sex and pornography.

The US thirst for oil, civilian deaths in Iraq,[10] and US support for Israel over Palestine have exacerbated Muslim concerns about occupation.

Let me mention just one more source of Muslim animus. The US drone policy has done more to radicalize Muslims than any Muslim cleric. The ubiquity of drones in various parts of Afghanistan, Pakistan, and Yemen inflicts severe psychological harm on those who live nearby.[11] One might think that inflicting severe psychological harm on our enemies well justified. But enemy combatants are a tiny minority of those harmed by drones. Although we have been assured that our drones don't hit civilians, the majority of drone victims are innocent civilians.[12] While drones have killed many "high-value" enemy combatants, they have also killed 40 civilians here, 35 there, who knows how many over there. It would take a dozen or more Boston Marathon bombers to equal the civilian destruction of a single US drone strike. Although the most obvious cost is incurred when an innocent person is maimed or killed, the constant humming of drones that might at a moment's notice release their deadly cargo has driven children indoors and into nightmares.

Muslims, therefore, legitimately fear economic and cultural colonialism, on the one hand, and the deaths of countless innocents in wars and drone strikes, on the other. None of us, Christian or Muslim, Western or Middle Eastern, has completely clean hands. Let us, then, judge one another by the best of our religion, not by the worst.

Enough sociopolitical digression. Let us return to a discussion of Islam and evolution.

THE GOLDEN AGE

It is a time when one culture, supported by its signal religion, is vastly intellectually superior to other cultures, cultures likewise supported by their signal religions. The world is at war—a war of religions with the fear of death for those who do not convert. Content to remain in their state of darkness, the ignorant and uncivilized barbarians resist the civilizing force of the more progressive religion. The time: the eighth to fourteenth century. The place: Europe, the Middle East, and portions of Asia. The progressive religion/society: Islam. The barbarians: Christians.

By the end of the eighth century, Islamic empires covered much more land than that covered by the Roman Empire at the height of its glory. During the so-called Dark Ages, which were indeed mostly dark for Christians, Islamic science was a shining light. Between the eighth and the fourteenth centuries, Muslim rulers, encouraged by their faith and by religious leaders, lavished huge sums of money on the advancement of knowledge. Caliph Harun al-Rashid, the founder of Baghdad's library, zealously sought out every book in the world. This massive library, the House of Wisdom (*Bayt al-Hikma*), would establish Baghdad as a center, perhaps *the* center, of learning in Islam's so-called golden age. Al-Rashid commissioned the acquisition and translation of ancient texts; the knowledge hidden within them for centuries was voraciously gobbled up. The motto "Seek knowledge even in China"[13] inspired a search for knowledge wherever it could be found (regardless of its source).

With their mathematical discoveries and forays into experimental science, Muslim scientists set the foundation of the seventeenth-century scientific revolution. Let us very briefly consider two Golden Age scientists and their significance to the scientific revolution.

Ninth-century Persian mathematician Muhammad al-Khwarizmi (c. 780– c. 850), from whose name we get the term "algorithm," is considered "The Father of Algebra." Working in Baghdad's House of Wisdom, he produced the first textbook of algebra, *Kitab al-Jabr*; algebra received its name from al-Khwarizmi's book. Al-Khwarizmi also introduced the Arabic numbers (which were, in reality, Hindu) to the West.[14] The scientific revolution simply would not be possible without algebra.

Modern astronomy was inspired by the increasingly accurate astronomical observations and calculations of Arab astronomers who were motivated by the need to accurately determine the beginnings of Ramadan and of prayer times. The House of Wisdom can be credited both for funding the work of astronomers and for the prestige it assigned to astronomical research. Ibn al-Haytham (965–c. 1040), also known as Alhazen, is considered the father of modern optics. In his writings, one finds a clear defense of key elements of the modern scientific method: the careful observation of physical phenomena and consideration of their mathematical relationship to theory. His *Al-Shukūk 'alā Batlamyūs* (*Doubts Concerning Ptolemy*) was the first to call into question the adequacy of Ptolemy's astronomical system.

From mathematics to the scientific method, seeds of the scientific revolution were sown in Islam's Golden Age. It could be truly said at that time that "the ink of a scholar is more holy than the blood of a martyr."

If we journey from the thirteenth century to the twenty-first century, we find an entirely different Muslim attitude toward science.

DEBATE AND DEATH THREATS

In 2011, in the midst of his weekly sermon, Imam Usama Hasan found himself constantly interrupted by members of his congregation (which had been infiltrated by a group of about 50 protestors).[15] Hassan, a senior lecturer in engineering at Middlesex University and Imam of the Masjid Tawhid, a mosque in East London, had come before his congregation on a near weekly basis for the past 25 years to lead Friday prayers. On this day in 2011, when he suggested that evolution was compatible with Islam, audible grumbling could be heard. As he proceeded, the grumbling resolved into verbal exclamations. One person yelled, "Have we descended from apes? Yes or no?" "Answer the question," they demanded, "It's a simple question." When Hasan replied, "Yes," chaos ensued. "Where is the sheik?" they shouted. "The sheik will make it clear!" After 25 good years, based on a single sermon, he heard someone call out for his execution.

In response to Hassan's affirmation of evolution, Abu Zubair of the conservative Muslim organization Islamic Awakening released a video[16] in which he asserted that, "The call to evolution is a call to *kufr* [disbelief] and apostasy from Islam." He cited the ruling of the Saudi scholar Muhammed Ibn al-Uthaymeen who contends that a person who unrepentantly teaches evolution "should be stopped by any means necessary even if it means his execution." While apostates "must be executed," Zubair cautioned that private individuals should not take the Hasan matter into their own hands.

Imam Hasan recanted his support for evolution.

How, one might wonder, did we get from the Golden Age of Islam, an age in which Muslim/Arab scholars rivaled the world in science, medicine, and philosophy, to the contemporary situation that includes fatwas and death threats for endorsing Darwinism.

The Muslim Reception of Darwin

Shortly after the first public presentation of Darwin's theory in 1858, the remaining Muslim empires were "dismantled and nearly the entire Muslim world was colonized" (Iqbal, 2007: 11–12). The Ottoman, at one time a vast empire that encircled southeastern European, the Middle East and northern Africa, had seen its former territory and vassal states colonized and its sphere of influence shrunken dramatically to the Anatolian peninsula. In 1853 Tsar Nicholas I of Russia proclaimed the Ottoman Empire, "the sick man of Europe." The once mighty Mughal Empire, stretching at its height across the Indian subcontinent, was a shadow of its former self when it fell under British rule in 1858. Iran, the center of the former Safavid Empire (which was once known as "Persia") was never officially colonized but was politically and economically dominated by Russia and Britain.

Muslims living under colonial occupation/domination were considered little more than savages and infidels in desperate need of the civilizing influence of European-Christian culture. Europeans were patronizing and condescending, believing themselves to be the superior race with the divinely ordained obligation to civilize inferior races. Finally, European powers were exploitative, profiting from the raw materials and immense population of the countries they colonized.

Science was considered just one more means of asserting European and Christian "superiority" and Arab, African, and Persian (and Muslim) "inferiority." The European "scientific revolution" was viewed by some Muslims as little more than support for the technology used to create "weapons of terror."

Darwin's theory arrived in this colonized and patronized Muslim world as an imperialistic European import. Muslims, therefore, approached Darwinism with an understandable wariness of European ambition and culture.

By the nineteenth century, precious few Muslims were equipped to fairly evaluate the work of Darwin. Islamic science had fallen far from its glory days.[17] After a centuries-long decline, science in the Islamic world was virtually nonexistent. The demise of their empires was accelerated by their resistance to modernization and their subsequent inability to resist the technologically superior Europeans.

Finally, Darwin's views arrived in Muslim countries in fits and starts, and even then with very oblique, distant relations to the original text/ideas. A Muslim student likely learned about Darwinism, as he did anything from the West, from a Christian missionary teacher. We can imagine the transmission as follows: Missionary Smith, whose native language was not Arabic, communicated ideas derived from an English-language essay by, say, Pastor Jones, which amounted to Pastor Jones' second-rate comment on or criticism of the *Origin* (with little or no familiarity with the *Origin* itself). We have Darwin as appropriated by Jones, as appropriated by Smith, and as "translated" by Smith from English into Arabic (or Turkish). One might expect something to get lost in this translation. The *Origin of Species* itself was not published in Arabic until 1918, and then only the first six chapters. Again as one might expect, ignorance and caricature of Darwinism were not uncommon.

Misunderstandings multiplied when European or Europe-friendly transmitters and translators allied Darwinism with their own agendas. When issues of racial and religious superiority are tossed into this already unstable mix, the possibilities of misunderstanding are mind-boggling. Sprinkle on colonialism and exploitation, and you have a recipe for disaster. For example, Darwin's alleged insistence on progress (caricature) was offered as support for European models of education and civilization for primitive and benighted Arabs (condescension and colonialism).

Darwin was not presented to Muslims in culturally neutral mathematical formulae. Darwinism did not enter the Islamic world naked and unashamed—it came wrapped in heavy cultural clothing. Nonetheless, Muslim responses varied greatly, from wholesale acceptance to outright rejection. One might expect a wide diversity of opinions from a religion as diverse as Islam, and there were. The early debate over Darwinism, such as it was, was left largely to scholars. Early on, a few Muslim scholars affirmed the compatibility of Islam and evolution.[18] Those who rejected it typically thought, without vitriol, that it was incompatible with the Quran (Iqbal, 2009). Let us consider two important nineteenth-century thinkers, Hussein al-Jisr and Jamal Al-din Al-Afghani, who were among the first to critically consider Darwinism.

Hussein al-Jisr (1845–1909), from Tripoli, defended Darwinism, arguing that it could be reconciled with the Quran. His 400-page treatise, fetchingly titled *al-Risalah al-Hamidiyah fi haqiqat al-diyanah al-Islamiyah wa-haqiqat al-shari'ah al-muhammadiyah* (*A Hamidan Treatise on the Truthfulness of Islam and of the Shariah*), was a highly technical work dealing with modern evolutionary theory from the perspective of Islamic theology and logic (Elshakry, 2011). In response, Sultan Abdulhamid, the Ottoman Sultan whom the *Treatise* is named after, awarded al-Jisr the Sultan's Prize for his contribution to Ottoman scholarship. In this exercise of faith Al-Jisr offered a rational defense of Islam, with the theory of evolution as his testing ground. Al-Jisr lived and learned in a putrid stew of European imperialism. Western scholars and missionaries allied imperialism with vicious attacks on Islam: Muslims were portrayed as backward and benighted savages. Al-Jisr sought to decisively counter these accusations in his *Treatise*.

Al-Jisr affirmed a principle of harmony between philosophy/science/ knowledge and revelation, which principle he found in the writings of the great twelfth-century Muslim philosopher, Averroes (Guessoum, 310): well-established knowledge is always in harmony with the proper understanding of the Quran. Such matters are, he argued, both *epistemological* (what is well-established knowledge) and *hermeneutical* (how Scripture should be interpreted). On the hermeneutical side he defended *ta'wil*, metaphoric/ analogical interpretations of the Quran, over literal readings of the Quran (unless the literal meaning was apparent). *Ta'wil* allowed him to reconcile apparent inconsistencies between established science and Scripture (Elshakry, 2011). Advocating a theology in which the "Word of God" (the Quran) coincided with the "Works of God" (i.e., nature), *ta'wil* offered a hermeneutical stance that reinterpreted and allegorized verses that were incongruent with science, including Darwinism. Finally, Al-Jisr believed that Islam supported all truths that either acknowledged or didn't challenge the notion of God (Guessoum, 2011: 310). Since he believed the Quran neutral with respect to creation in a few days or creation over a vast period of time, he claimed that the Quranic teaching on omnipotence and creation were more than compatible with evolutionary theory.

Al-Jisr had one serious reservation about Darwinism. He, like many Muslims after, believed Darwin's theory incompatible with a Quranic view of the creation of humanity. He believed that God's creation of humans was clearly outlined in the Quran: Adam was created from dust before receiving the breath of God (3.59). Al-Jisr conceded, however, that if there was proof of humanity's primate origins, Muslims should adopt this view. A proof of prehuman ancestry, he argued, would in no way detract from faith in a creator God (Elshakry, 2011).

Jamal Al-din al-Afghani (1838–97), born in Iran, initially and vociferously rejected Darwinism because he believed its materialistic assumptions denied the existence of God. Al-Afghani, considered the father of the modern Islamic revival, was a theologian and activist who advocated a Pan-Islamic unity in the response to European imperialism. He traveled to India, Egypt, Constantinople, Paris, London, Moscow, and Munich preaching his gospel of Islamic political reform. His critiques of Darwin, based on (at best) glimmers of the *Origin*, were sharply criticized as caricatures. He would come to accept some form of the transmutation of species, claiming that it was taught already in the Quran and was God's way of creating living beings. He refused, however, accept the evolution of human beings from apes.

Al-Afghani's varied responses, particularly his original rejection of evolution, demonstrate the bearing of wider cultural, political, and identity issues on the compatibility of evolution and Islam. Al-Afghani's dealings with

Darwin's theories, for example, should be understood within a larger cultural struggle, a struggle to understand and overcome Western imperialism. To this end, al-Afghani hoped to persuade Muslims that Darwin's theory, and therefore Europe, were materialistic (atheistic).[19]

How, then, could the decidedly anti-imperialist al-Afghani come to accept even portions of Darwin's theory? Al-Afghani claimed that an eleventh-century poem that deals with animals generated from inorganic material demonstrates the roots of evolution in Arab thought. He went on to state the following, "If the doctrine of evolution is based on these premises, then the Arab scientists preceded Darwin." By connecting evolution to Arab sources and diminishing its ties to European thought, al-Afghani was able to defuse the cultural threat posed by Darwin. The claim to Arab originality would be repeated by Muslims attempting to alleviate concerns about the compatibility of Islam and evolution.

Despite his initial rejection of evolution, al-Afghani influenced the "Manar School of Thought," which sought a reconciliation of modern science and the Quran. The Manar School sought to reverse Muslim anti-rationalism by treating modern science as the criterion for knowledge of the physical world (rather than the Quran). Such thinkers were part of the vanguard intellectual response and resistance to the European encroachment and domination of Muslim lands. Although ideologically opposed to European imperialism, they saw modern science as the path to independence and political ascendancy for the Muslim world.

The Quran and Evolution

The importance of the Quran to the debate over Islam and evolution is difficult to overstate, given that it is considered the all-sufficient word of God and as such has been deemed authoritative on all matters of faith and life.[20] The Quran, unlike the Hebrew Bible and the New Testament, isn't a linear, chronological narrative; its treatment of creation is brief, episodic, and ambiguous. Moreover, the Quran's mentions of creation are often subservient to wider or deeper matters such as the omnipotence of God; the overall topic of such passages is the divine nature, not the precise mode of creation. Focusing on details such as the mode of creation would miss the point of such passages.

For example, the fortieth chapter of the Quran is titled, "The Forgiver," and God is referred to as "The Forgiver of the faults and the Acceptor of repentance." Several verses in this chapter speak of God's severe judgment of those who don't believe ("they are the inmates of the fire"). Yet the focus is on God's mercy to those who believe, to those who are saved from the punishments of hell. God's mercy, then, is displayed by contrast: the saved can better glimpse God's mercy by virtue of comprehending what God has saved them from—instead of fire, the righteous will enter into the eternal garden (40.8). God's mercy begins when he grants each person life and sends down his sustenance from above and extends into eternity where God grants sustenance without measure (40.40). The chapter elicits praise: "It is God who has given you the earth for a dwelling place and the heavens for a canopy. He shaped you, formed you well, and provided you with good things. Such is God your Lord, so glory be to Him, the Lord of the Worlds" (40.64).

One Surah cited in favor of God's special creation of human beings reads as follows: "It is He who created you from dust, then from a drop of fluid, then from a tiny, clinging form, then He brought you forth as infants, then He allowed you to reach maturity, then He let you grow old—though some of you die sooner—and reach your appointed term so that you may reflect" (40.67). The point of the chapter is not the *how* of God's creation, but the *fact* of God's creation (and that it is good, that humans are good, that life is good, and that eternal life is unfathomably good). Focusing on the details of God's creation of human (from dust) is to miss the point of the chapter. The point is that Allah the Creator grants life and brings death, and every-thing is dependent on him ("It is He who gives life and death, and when He ordains a thing, He says only 'Be' and it is." [40.68]). God, we learn in Chapter 40, has granted us everything we need for our physical and spiri-tual well-being. Life, sustenance, the night (for rest), the prophets, wisdom, are all gifts from God, gifts that God has given as signs of the One God. Upon recognition of those signs, the proper response is to fall on one's knees in gratitude and praise. Given the point of the chapter, the details of the creation of the human seem at the same time insignificant and poetic (i.e., nonliteral).[21]

Consider the ambiguity of a text often claimed in support of a speedy, non-evolutionary creation. In Surah 7.54 the Quran states, "Your Lord is God, who created the heavens and earth in six Days, then established Himself on the throne; He makes the night cover the day in swift pursuit; He created the sun, moon, and stars to be subservient to His command; all creation and command belong to Him. Exalted be God, Lord of all the worlds!" Here the Quran seems to restrict the creation of the world, as does the Hebrew narra-tive, to six days (*ayyam*). Yet, in the Quran, *ayyam* sometimes means "age," "epoch," or "extended period of time." For example: "He runs everything, from the heavens to the earth, and everything will ascend to Him in the end, on a Day that will measure a thousand years in your reckoning" (32.5) and "…a Day that will measure a thousand years in your reckoning" (70.4). In Surah 7.54, some translators prefer "long period of time" to "day" for *ayyam*. Of course, *ayyam* could mean, in this passage, a period of 24 hours. But if in Surah 7.54 *ayyam* means a vast period of time, as the vast majority of contemporary Muslim scholars believe, then Quranic support for a six-day creation withers away.

Muslims, by and large, have come to accept a very old earth, some even claim contemporary Big Bang Theory as a scientific miracle.[22] The sticking point, though, is not the age of the earth but human evolution. Human evo-lution is a source of contention given the special status accorded to humans in the Quran. All humans, it is claimed, descended from Adam, who was created from the clay, not from apes.

Muslims widely believe that the Quran unambiguously teaches that humanity began with Adam, who was created from (depending on the Surah) dust, clay, or water. Consider the following passages:

- "We created man from an essence of clay." (23.12)
- "Who gave everything its perfect form. He first created man from clay." (32.7)
- "So [Prophet], ask the disbelievers: is it harder to create them than other beings We have created? We created them from sticky clay." (37.11)
- "He created mankind out of dried clay, like pottery." (55.14)
- "We created man from an essence of clay, then We placed him as a drop of fluid in a safe place, then We made that drop into a clinging form, and We made that form into a lump of flesh, and We made that lump into bones, and We clothed those bones with flesh, and later We made him into other forms—glory be to God, the best of creators!" (23.12–14)

All subsequent human beings are, it is believed, descendants of Adam and Eve. Humanity's superiority to animals is due to God breathing his spirit into Adam (which spirit is then passed on to the children of Adam) and Adam's naming of everything. Being instilled with the spirit of God, humans are superior to animals in terms of our ability to freely know and obey God. Adam, then, did not come from a preexisting species (usually claimed to be apes). Rather, God created Adam directly from the clay and then breathed life and spirit into him.

And yet, given the multiplicity of materials from which the Quran claims humans were created—dust (30.26), water (25.54), clay (15.26), clinging form (clot of blood) (96.2), nothing (3.47; 19.67)—one might think that such passages weren't intended to teach how humans were created. Rather, they teach the humble origin of humanity and humanity's dependence upon Omnipotence. Consider the following passage:

> "And God created each animal out of [its own] fluid: some of them crawl on their bellies, some walk on two legs, and some on four. God creates whatever He will; God has power over everything." (24.45)

The mode of creation is poetic, one might think, but the fact of creation is not.

ISLAM AND EVOLUTION TODAY

Evolution's acceptance or rejection by Muslims is deeply tied to cultural struggles, political contexts, and a myriad of overlapping and conflicting identities. An internally leaked document from the French Ministère de l'Éducation Nationale cited the rejection of Darwinism as a symptom of disaffected Muslim youth in French society. In the last few years, news stories have emerged of Muslim medical students boycotting classes in which biological evolution is taught, or, as discussed, an Imam threatened with death over his belief in the compatibility between biological evolution and Islam. It is not without cause that Muslims have come to believe that evolution is just atheistic materialism in disguise.[23] It should come as no surprise, then, when Muslims find evolution difficult to believe. Yet, as with Christianity and Judaism, leading Muslim thinkers endorse the truth of evolution without loss of authentic belief; Islam and evolution, so they argue, are perfectly compatible. Let us consider three approaches to evolution and the creation of humanity among Islamic thinkers.

Islam, Anti-evolution, and Intelligent Design

Responding to tropes and longstanding caricatures of Islam as a backward religion and Muslims as primitive peoples, proponents of Islamic creationism, with ample financial backing, are concerted and vocal propagators of "scientific" creationism. In 2007, tens of thousands of high schools, colleges, institutes, teachers, researchers, and professors around the world received *The Atlas of Creation* free of charge courtesy of Harun Yahya, and the Bilim Arastirma Vakfi (BAV), or Foundation for Research, a Turkish Muslim creationist group founded by Yahya. The *Atlas*, an 800-page, 12-pound volume with glossy illustrations, argues against evolution (the transmutation of species from one form into another) and in favor of every species' special creation by God. Adnan Oktar, pen-name Harun Yahya, is a Turkish Muslim who was trained as an artist and who has set himself against materialism, communism, and atheism all of which, he argues, undermine moral values and true religion. Oktar's attack on these philosophies focuses on Darwinism, which he claims is held only for ideological, not scientific reasons (because of the intellectual support it affords atheism and immorality).

Entirely separate from his rejection of evolution, Oktar has been accused of anti-Semitism, denying the holocaust, fomenting antigovernment conspiracy theories, and being mentally ill. Some allege that he claims to be the promised Mahdi (the prophesied messiah of Islam who will rule before the Day of Judgment). In the mid-1980s he was imprisoned for conspiracy and hospitalized for mental illness. Oktar, on the other hand, claimed that he was a persecuted political prisoner. His worldwide influence is undeniable: he has been ranked in the top 50 of the 500 most influential Muslims in the world (the current top 50 includes King Abdullah of Saudi Arabia, Prime Minister Erdogan of Turkey, the Ayatollah Khameini of Iran, Muhammad Morsi of Egypt, Queen Rania of Jordan, and distinguished Cambridge University professor Timothy Winter).[24]

Harun Yahya's more than 250 books translated into 57 languages, with titles such as *The Evolution Deceit, The Disasters Darwinism Brought to Humanity*, and *Uncle Darwin, We Haven't Changed*, have been liberally distributed around the world. Although not all of his books deal exclusively with Darwinism and the theory of evolution, they often deal with evolution within the context of Western cultural influences, such as communism and atheism. It is deeply ironic, then, that Yahya's arguments are inspired by (almost copied from) the Christian creationist and Intelligent Design movements in the United States. As with the Christian creationist movement, Yahya's attempts to refute evolution are often couched in "science." For example, he offers "refutations" of evolution by citing gaps in the fossil record and claiming that it violates the second law of thermodynamics. In 2008 he offered to pay 10 trillion Turkish Lira to anyone who produces a single intermediate-form fossil demonstrating evolution.

Yahya has effectively wielded the internet as a vehicle for the dissemination of his message (and to block his opponents). His website is chock full of books and videos available to download for free. Yahya's populist rhetoric resonates with Muslims worldwide. He and his organization have yielded significant results. In Turkey, the BAV has helped create such a climate of fear that very few professors are willing to speak out against creationism and few university courses are offered in evolution. In 2007 it was reported that the United Arab Emirates would be removing evolution from the twelfth-grade curriculum; an article in the Gulf News cited the influence Yahya and his group.

Yahya's influence, which vastly exceeds any other defender of Islamic creationism, also vastly outstrips his scholarly credentials. His shoddy scholarship betrays his lack of training in either science or religion. Fellow Muslim T. O. Shanavas criticizes Yahya's pretension to being scientific:

> Following the modus operandi of the fundamentalist Christian organization Institute for Creation Research (ICR), Yahya uses pseudoscience to promote his interpretation of the Quran. The references he cites in his book, if read in their entirety, usually accept and defend evolution. But he routinely selects just one sentence from an article, a line that can be construed to support his arguments, and uses it as a scientific reference. Like the ICR, he distorts single new items from popular journals to "prove" his conclusion. He conveniently ignores the rest of the article or other articles in the same issue that support evolution. (Shanavas, 2010: 2)

BAV sent a copy of *The Atlas of Creation* to Richard Dawkins who found countless serious errors in the book and concluded: "I am at a loss to reconcile the expensive and glossy production values of this book with the 'breathtaking inanity' of the content. Is it really inanity, or is it just plain laziness—or perhaps cynical awareness of the ignorance and stupidity of the target audience—mostly Muslim creationists." In 2008, Oktar succeeded in getting Dawkins' website banned in Turkey.

Islam and Evolution

The worldwide Muslim population accepts and rejects evolution in numbers similar to the percentage of US citizens (who have been influenced by Christian young earth creationists and Intelligent Design theorists). That means that worldwide, the majority of Muslims reject evolution (and more reject the evolution of humans from preexisting species). A recent study seems to show more openness to evolution than previously thought. A recent report released by the Pew Forum, "The World's Muslims: Religion, Politics and Society," surveyed Muslims on whether or not they believed "humans and other things have evolved over time" or "always existed in present form." In 13 of the 22 countries surveyed, over half said that "humans and other things evolved over time." Of course, it's one thing to think that humans and other things have evolved over time (gotten smarter, say, or taller), another to think that humans evolved from a preexisting primate species. One wonders if the survey results would have been so pro-evolution if humanity's primate origins had been more prominently featured.[25]

The issue of Islam and evolution has been taken up by Muslim scholars around the world. Prominent Muslim scientists, including Imam Hasan, Bruno Guiderdoni, Nidhal Guessoum, and Rana Dajani, have passionately and persuasively argued in favor of evolution. The Deen Institute, a Muslim organization, recently organized a conference in which Muslim scientists came together with one creationist and discussed evolution and Islam. The conference, "Have Muslims Misunderstood Evolution?" set out to answer the question: Can Muslims appropriate evolution into an Islamic worldview? To answer this, scientists and theologians set out to dispel some of the negative associations that bear on discussions of evolution: atheism, materialism, and so on. Except for the lone creationist presenter, they concluded that there was room within the Islamic worldview for evolution.

Dajani, professor of biology at the Hashemite University in Jordan, is an expert in molecular biology, genomic studies, stem cells, and bioinformatics. She typically writes articles with impressive and forbidding titles like "Structure-function analysis of HsiF, a gp25-like component of the type VI secretion system, in *Pseudomonas aeruginosa*" and "Pleiotropic functions of TNF-[alpha] determine distinct IKK[beta]-dependent hepatocellular fates in response to LPS." She also works to improve the education of young, Middle Eastern women in the sciences. On the side, she argues that there is no contradiction between Islam and evolution. Dajani contends that there are very serious problems with the Muslim rejection of evolution:

> The fact that a sound scientific theory is so vehemently denied by Muslim scientists, let alone the layperson, on the basis of belief not logic is scary because it makes one wonder what else is being denied in the name of religion and played upon by people who want to control others through ignorance and emotion. This position alienates the world of Islam from thinkers and deprives the individual Muslim of the full use of his mind. In addition, it gives a terrible representation of Islam to non-Muslims, leading them to believe that Islam is a religion that denies freedom of thinking when that is the exact opposite of the truth. Islam calls for thinking, contemplating, and using logic to reach the truth: "Behold! In the creation of the heavens and the earth, and the alternation of night and day, there are indeed Signs for men of understanding" (Quran 3.190). In Islam, there is no limit to your questioning unless you question the existence of a God and that has nothing to do with evolution (Dajani, 2012: 347–48).

Dajani contends that Quranic rejections of evolution are based on misunderstandings. For example, the Arabic term for creation, *khalaq*, does not mean, as is widely believed by evolution's Islamic critics, "instantaneous creation." Indeed, for a timeless God, creation cannot be understood temporally. She notes the irony that while Quranic scholars have agreed that divine creation of the cosmos took billions of years, they are reluctant to concede that God's creation of living creatures likewise could have taken a very long time. God's *khalaq* of living creatures, as properly understood, could have occurred (as it did in God's creation of the cosmos) through a natural, evolutionary process over a very long period of time.

She also argues from the Quran that God created what was most fit or suited (and so the Quran is consistent with and even supportive of evolution). Consider

- He Who has made everything which He has created most good (*Ahsan*): He began the creation of man with (nothing more than) clay." (Quran 32.7)
- "We create man in the (*Ahsan*) finest state." (Quran 95.4)

According to these verses, God created all living creatures, including human beings, in the *Ahsan* way. *Ahsan*, she contends, means "most fit," not "the best" (which, in Arabic, is *Afdal*). She argues that in 32.7, "Allah states that he created all organisms to be the best fit and even man was created from mud, which is the origin of all creatures." In 95.4, "Allah states that man was created to be fit for his environment." Rightly understood, she argues, these passages offer Quranic support for evolutionary theory.

Dajani should not be seen as suggesting that the Quran predicted or even anticipated the synthetic theory of evolution. Hers is not a project in *Ijaz* or Islamic science. She is quite clear: the Quran is not a scientific textbook and it is a mistake to conceive of it as one. Dajani's views on the Quran and science are descendants of Averroes' views on Islam and knowledge: well-established science is always in harmony with the Quran properly understood. Science does not stand in need of proof by Quranic texts—it has its own, Quran-independent, modes of confirmation, ones that are rooted in our God-created brains and encouraged by God's clear commands to understand his creation. If a passage in the Quran were taken in such a way that it contradicted a scientific fact, then, she argues, we do not really understand that passage. We need to find a new way to interpret the text, one in which God's two books—the book of nature and the book of revelation—coincide. She concludes with sage advice for Muslim students who are grappling with the issue of Islam and evolution:

Islam is a spiritual guide to life. It teaches us how to live in harmony with ourselves, fellow humans, and the world. Islam asks us to use our intelligence to explore the world around us. Islam calls for using scientific methodology and logic in our approach to understanding the world. The Qur'an contains verses that describe worldly phenomenon. These verses are presented as evidence of the elegance and simplicity of creation. The Qur'an is not a book of scientific facts. If there happens to be an apparent contradiction between a verse in the Qur'an and a scientific fact, one is advised to either revise one's scientific conclusion (which is never absolute) or to revise the interpretation of the Qur'anic verse. It is humans who interpret verses, and we are limited by the scientific knowledge of our era. I believe, therefore, that our encounter with an ostensible conflict between Islam and science is an opportunity for harmony. (Dajani, 2012: 353)

A Third Way

Some thoughtful Muslim scholars object to the claim that science requires accepting the full package of the theory of evolution. According to these scholars, it is an open question/problem to determine which assertions of the theory of evolution are true (established with certainty) and which ones are not. While they concur with current scientific views on the age and evolution of the cosmos and they accept the evolutionary transformation of nearly every biological species, they reject the claim that human beings descended from a preexisting species. Humans, they believe, were created as a special act of divine creation, from the clay as it were.

Such Muslims affirm the principle of seeking the truth wherever it can be found (even in China). Truth, they enthusiastically aver, can be found both through the judicious use of human reason and the careful study of the Quran. Whatever reason presents as decidedly true must fit with the Quran properly understood. They believe that modern science has clearly made the case for an ancient cosmos and the transmutation of species. However, it has not yet made a compelling case that humans evolved from apes. The former should be understood in the light of the Quran, but until there is compelling evidence for the latter, they will follow Quranic teachings on the special creation of human beings.

These Muslim thinkers take early Muslim scholars as their examples. Although they showed great respect for the wisdom of others, particularly the wisdom of the Greeks, they did not accept willy-nilly whatever the Greeks (or anyone else) affirmed. These early scholars enthusiastically sought out and then examined every piece of *scientia* (wisdom) with a critical mind. Despite their great respect for the Greek philosophers and scientists, they did not ignore problems detected in the works of masters. They kept what was established as knowledge, understood it within the context of the Quran, and dropped what could not be rationally established. They developed the tradition of *shukuk* (doubts) in response to contradictions they found in Greek texts, initially ones in the astronomical works that defended Ptolemy's system. The findings of the *shukuk* tradition would, in turn, influence the astronomical revolution of Copernicus, Galileo, and Kepler.

Muslims today, they argue, need not accept every assertion of modern science. The history of science, with its host of widely accepted but eventually discarded theories (from Aristotelian physics to phrenology), confirms the suspicion that some assertions of contemporary science are not so well established and may even be untrue.[26] So while these thinkers concur with both Averroes and Dajani that well-established science is always in harmony with the Quran properly understood, they reject the claim of prehuman ancestors as well-established science. This group of thinkers should be understood as pro-science, pro-reason, and pro-Quran. Yet they reject the claim that human beings descended from primates. The best view, all things scientifically and Quranically considered, is the view that human beings are the special creation of God.

THE PROBLEM WITH FUNDAMENTALISTS

Islam is a religion of overwhelming diversity and flexibility. Brittle, fundamentalist Islam, with its accompanying literalism, encouraged a devaluing of science. As science advanced, Muslim countries were intellectually left behind. A recent essay in *The Economist* laments the relatively recent Muslim lack of commitment to science:

> In 2005 Harvard University produced more scientific papers than 17 Arabic-speaking countries combined. The world's 1.6 billion Muslims have produced only two Nobel laureates in chemistry and physics. Both moved to the West: the only living one, the chemist Ahmed Hassan Zewail, is at the California Institute of Technology. By contrast Jews, outnumbered 100 to one by Muslims, have won 79. The 57 countries in the Organisation of the Islamic Conference spend a puny 0.81% of GDP on research and development, about a third of the world average. America, which has the world's biggest science budget, spends 2.9%; Israel lavishes 4.4%.[27]

As Muslim-majority countries regain economic and political stability, Muslims are returning, slowly but surely, to their historic commitment to science. Muslim scholars are keenly aware that the way forward involves an enthusiastic affirmation of science. They want to be able to say more than, "We were great once" (where that once was nearly a millennium ago). So they concur with the wise counsel of al-Afghani: "Those who forbid science and knowledge in the belief that they are safeguarding the Islamic religion are really the enemies of that religion" (in Keddie, 1983: 107).

We find in among some Muslims the old warfare metaphor. As a result, some Muslims embrace science (at the expense of religion) and others embrace religion (at the expense of science). Is the peaceful coexistence of science and Islam possible?

Our discussion of Islam and evolution has raised the same origins questions that motivated this book. Is it possible to embrace science without loss of faith? Can one be a faithful believer in both science and religion? Is God the author of two books—nature and Scripture—and if so, how are they properly understood?

When the ground rules of this debate are set by imperialists and colonialists on the one hand and secularists and fundamentalists on the other, faithful inquiry is likely to suffer. Truth is a casualty when religion is placed in the service of unquestioned adherence, exploitation, or even violence. Without addressing the sociopolitical issues that surround this debate, little genuine dialogue is likely to occur.[28] Moreover, truth is a casualty when secularists and fundamentalists are united in their belief that evolution is atheism. Both the scientific and religious fundamentalist have exceeded the bounds of good science, moving well into the domains of philosophy and theology (with little or no justification for their assertions). Dawkins and his ilk are as dangerous to the development of science in Muslim majority countries as a fundamentalist Imam.

God and the Virtue of Humility

We have been examining issues of origins from within the context of the Abrahamic religions, religions that conjointly concur that there is but one God. Radical monotheism, at least in the Abrahamic tradition, asserts a sharp contrast between Creator and the created. What are the implications of monotheism and of the doctrine of creation for Abrahamic believers? Divine creation asserts the fact, not the mode, of creation. The science of creation is uncannily absent from ancient Biblical texts. But the Creator is not. Divine creation, in the Abrahamic traditions, is not and never has been primarily a scientific issue—theologically, it has always been a reminder, both stern and gentle, that we are not gods (that God alone is Creator).

This "we-are-not-gods" theology reminds us of our creatureliness. Rightly humbled, knowing our place, we understand that we, lacking a God's-eye view, cannot arrogate to ourselves God-like properties of omniscience and omnipotence. Because our God-created finitude assures us of our place in the cosmos, we should not fear our creatureliness. We are not apes for sure, but we are not gods either. We are limited in knowledge and power, located within space and time, conditioned by this and that set of social circumstances. In short, we are finite and contingent, seeking the infinite and non-contingent from our tiny little corner in space and time. The doctrine of creation, then, forbids intellectual and religious arrogance. We see through a glass darkly.

But we *do see* through that glass, albeit not without great effort and not always cleanly. Creation in the image of God gives Muslims–Christians–Jews reason to trust their cognitive faculties. Such trust, given that we are not gods, should preclude proclamations of god-like certitude on all manner of faith and science. Both the fundamentalist cleric who thinks he is suited to pronounce on science and the atheistic scientist who thinks he is suited to pronounce on God have equally exceeded their bounds. Self-assured pronouncements well outside of one's expertise are arrogant whether religiously or secularly motivated. Muslims–Christians–Jews have God-given reasons to discipline this instinctual pride, one which finds scientific, religious and moral expression. Then, in humility, they can and should use their God-given brains to seek and find knowledge wherever it is (and adjust their beliefs, religious or otherwise, accordingly).

The doctrine of creation, while battling pride and prejudice, likewise ennobles humanity. Each and every person is a divine creation; each and every person is created in the divine image. So each and every person is worthy of all of the respect that we owe God himself. We can't, in good faith, ignore, denigrate, or demean a fellow human being. We can only respect, as is their due, every icon of the divine. The fundamentalist religious believer can and should learn, without fear, from the expert in this or that science (who may or may not be an unbeliever but is, according to the monotheistic religions, created in the divine image regardless). The religious believer can, then, take what she has learned from the expert in the book of Nature and use that knowledge to seek a better, deeper understanding of their book of Scripture.

Notes

1 Science and/or Religion

1. This comment is ironic. Light did not appear until hundreds of millions of years after the Big Bang. The period before the first stars is known as "the dark ages."
2. I use the term "God" in this context as synonymous with "theism." God, to clarify, is not a theory; no concrete object (i.e., individual existent like the cup of coffee I'm drinking as I type or the book you are now reading) is a theory. A theory is a conjunction of statements, and statements (or propositions) are abstract objects (like numbers). God, if God should exist, is not an abstract object; God, according to most Western understandings, is a person. Theism, on the other hand, could constitute a theory (and, so, theories are abstract objects, like numbers); theism is a set of statements that affirms the existence of at least one god (various versions of theism will assert or deny various properties of god or the gods and various ways that god or the gods stand in relation to the world (as, say, Creator)).
3. This is not to deny that various forms of theism, for example those that assert that God created the world in six days about 10,000 years ago, make scientific assertions and so those forms of theism, those whose theism *is* a scientific hypothesis, are in competition with evolution.
4. This makes most religious believers into philosophers (big mistake). So let me, at the risk of offending philosophers, put it more colloquially: God is not a scientific hypothesis; God is a person.
5. There is a perfectly sensible usage of "theory" according to which theism *is,* like naturalism and pantheism, a theory: it may be an explanatory hypothesis which can be confirmed or disconfirmed by its fit with and ability to explain data in our experience. An important contemporary account of scientific confirmation is "Inference to the Best Explanation" (IBE). IBE emphasizes the way theories weave stories out of data, and the data need not be scientific or even empirical. Philosopher Richard Swinburne, for example, famously uses something like scientific confirmation to make a cumulative case for theism (Swinburne, 2004). Nonetheless, I think Swinburne would share my sentiment: theism is not a *scientific* hypothesis (though, for him, it is science-like and admits of similar methods of confirmation and disconfirmation). Since it's not a scientific theory, for Swinburne, theism, though a theory, couldn't compete with say, evolutionary theory or the universal law of gravitation. One might write a Swinburnean defense of theism given the challenges addressed in this book. I am considering the perspective of those for whom belief in God is neither a scientific nor a quasi-scientific hypothesis.

2 CONFLICT, SEPARATION, INTEGRATION

1. http://edge.org/conversation/progress-in-religion.
2. As we will see, it is notoriously difficult to divorce "scientific" and "religious" motivations in the work of pre-nineteenth-century thinkers. Newton and Kepler are prime examples of this (Barker and Goldstein, 2001).
3. General Scholium of the *Principia mathematica* (first published in the 2nd [1713] edition).
4. These issues are raised historically in Harrison (2006a).
5. The most famous dream "discovery" was Friedrich Kekulé's (1829–96), one of the greatest chemists of the nineteenth century. Kekule claimed to have discovered the structure of the benzene molecule in a dream. Kekule had testified at the trial of a maid accused of murdering her mistress by setting her on fire. He identified a distinctive ring hidden in the maid's rooms as the same ring that belonged to the dead woman. The ring was easily identifiable because it consisted of two snakes biting their own tails. Let's pick up the story, many years later, at a time when most scientists had despaired of discovering the structure of molecules. Kekule, however, remained hopeful that these chemical structures could be determined. One night, while working on this problem, he fell asleep in front of a warm fire. In his dream, the fire changed into whirling and dancing atoms; the atoms then rearranged themselves into the shape of a snake biting its own tail. When he woke up, he realized he had discovered the chemical structure of the benzene ring. It's likely that this story, though proffered by Kekule himself, is apocryphal. It merits a footnote because, though likely false, it is widely repeated. But being widely repeated does not make it true!
6. Physician Peter Dunn (2006) calls him one of the greatest scientists who have ever lived. Philosopher Patrick Byrne (1997) claims that Aristotle's science has many similarities with modern scientific thought. Some object: Aristotle, while surely a great philosopher, wasn't much of a scientist. Scott Atran (1998) holds that Aristotle's ideas were elaborations of folk biology rather than science proper. We don't need to settle the matter for the purposes of this book.
7. Some will disagree about the propriety of including Aristotle's theories; perhaps it is not fruitful to incorporate ancient ideas into a definition of what science is. Putting up some historical boundaries would certainly be useful for definitional purposes. But where does one start? Starting with the scientific revolution of the sixteenth and seventeenth centuries would certainly be too restrictive. The scientific revolution didn't create science ex nihilo. It embraced and rejected, at various times, ancient and medieval ideas (Hannam, 2009). Aristotle's biology predominated until the time of Darwin. Since, by the end of the chapter, not much will hang on our getting the definition of science precisely correct, we can acknowledge the controversy and move on.
8. For an argument that science as we know it is a product of the nineteenth century, see Harrison, Numbers, and Shank (2011). One might make a similar claim about religion as we know it.
9. This is a modern paraphrase of things said much more formally and in Latin.
10. Some claim that we cannot go beneath or behind the appearances to some unobservable reality (a hidden world of, say, atoms or the strong nuclear force). French physicist and philosopher, Pierre Duhem (1861–1916), argued that science should not hypothesize about or infer to unobservable bodies or hidden properties that underlie observations but should restrict itself to

generalizing the laws that describe the regularities among the appearances (see Duhem, 1954). The most famous contemporary defender of this view is Bas Van Fraassen (1980). A recent defense of this view, which has come to be called "constructive empiricism," is Dicken (2010).

11. This is not as far-fetched as one might think. John Conway and Simon Kochen, professors of mathematics at Princeton University, argue that electrons have some measure of free will (analogous to human free will) (Conway and Kochen, 2009).

12. Some thinkers, including some scientists, are skeptical about the human ability to probe the invisible realm of quantum phenomena. They are unwilling to commit themselves to the existence of anything that can't be seen, heard, touched, tasted, or smelled. The invisible entities that scientific theories postulate—atoms, gravity, and dark matter—are treated as useful placeholders in mathematical models (and we don't need to take those models as reality). The mathematical model must do two things—capture the data and make accurate predictions. But we should not commit ourselves to the invisible entities that the theory uses to make those predictions. Let us leave this perfectly valid option aside and press on.

13. For a philosophical defense of fertility, see W. Whewell, *The Philosophy of the Inductive Sciences Founded Upon Their History* (London: John W. Parker, 1840, Chapter 5, paragraph 11).

14. Laudan's (1981) pessimistic meta-induction cautions us not to blindly accept the results of science.

15. Some argue that what I assert is not true of the "mature" (usually post-scientific revolution) sciences. While the immature sciences might not be cumulative—more folk biology and folk physics than science proper—the mature sciences are. For example, Ian Hacking claims: "Future large-scale instability seems quite unlikely. We will witness radical developments at present unforeseen. But what we have may persist, be modified and built upon. The old idea that sciences are cumulative may reign once more" (1999). Hacking's claims, it must be noted, are predictions based on what *seems* likely, what *may* persist, and so on. His predictions may turn out right. They may not—predictions are hard, especially about the future. At this point, it is difficult to maintain that science is any simple accumulation of theories.

16. I am focusing on the most obvious examples of rupture and replacement in the sciences. I have selected those theoretical entities or properties that have not survived into the so-called mature sciences. About the mature sciences, it is difficult to imagine that any future science will reject, for example, the periodic table of the elements, the kinetic theory of gases, or the universal law of gravitation; any future science will, very likely, preserve the truth or approximate truth of these scientific ideas. Structural realism is the view that, despite theory change, there is an accumulation of the mathematical structures of scientific theories. True enough, but the scientific ideas that are preserved are at the level of observables (natural laws concerning the behavior of observables), not at the deepest level of theoretical explanation. Preserving natural laws is consistent with deep ruptures, usually at the level of unobservables, in successive theories. In the twentieth-century alone, we have witnessed significant differences in, for example, the nature of atoms (indivisible particles, very small but divisible particles, waves, and wave-particle). So I stand by my claim that science is not a *simple* accumulation of theories.

17. I don't intend any of this as a rejection of scientific realism—the idea that as science progresses it approximates the truth better and better. I only mean to reject our often very simplistic claims about what science is and how it works. Scientific results are always provisional and subject to improvement. But the skeptical conclusion that science is unreliable because it changes all the time is unwarranted, at least according to several scientific realists. For instance, some scientific realists argue that we should not compare the imma-ture stages of a scientific domain (e.g., early phlogiston-based chemistry) to later, mature stages. If a science has some form of maturity, for example, as assessed by the fact that it has a body of well-accepted theories which are not radically overturned but tweaked, its results may be less susceptible to the pessimistic meta-induction (Fahrbach, 2011; Lewis, 2001).

18. Simplicity is widely used in both scientific and nonscientific contexts (Lombrozo, 2007).

19. McMullin (2011) rejects this view.

20. This definition, if rigidly applied, would seem to preclude some of the so-called historical sciences—those sciences, like geology and evolutionary biology—where all of the big events happened in the remote past and where precise predictions (or retrodictions) are impossible. Some historical sciences, such as evolutionary biology, have almost no empirical consequences for precise observation the way models in physics do (Cleland, 2002; Jeffares, 2008). One might simply claim that such disciplines are not, after all, science, or one might claim that because evolution and geology are science, we have not yet adequately defined science.

21. A recent defense of atheistic religion can be found in Dworkin (2013).

22. There is no denying that Christianity has been at the epicenter of the science and religion debate in the West since the sixteenth century. Yet Cantor and Kenny have rightly complained that in "the science and religion debate," all too often the term "religion" is a synonym for "Christianity" (Cantor and Kenny, 2001). This has led to a neglect of scholarship on non-Christian reli-gions and their relationship to science. We will partially redress this concern in the final chapters where we consider the relationship of Judaism and Islam to science.

23. For ease of learning, I will just discuss these three. Some argue that there are four models: conflict, integration, independence, and dialogue (Barbour, 2002). Others argue that there are three or four models, but they are differ-ent from the ones discussed by Barbour (Haught, 1995). Ted Peters claims that there are eight (Peters, 1997). I propose, for purposes of this book, just sticking with the three.

24. While this mythic Galileo story is continually repeated as gospel truth, it is no longer accepted by reputable scholars (Hummel, 1986).

25. Historian Peter Bowler (2007) refutes the warfare metaphor as applied to Darwin and his reception.

3 THE FABRIC OF THE UNIVERSE

1. Sadly, there were no mothers of the new science. Women were systematically excluded from the educational opportunities necessary to fully participate in learned society.

2. Not everyone agrees; see, for example, Cartwright (1999).

3. Many early modern scientists also believed that creation depends on the ongoing providential care of its Creator for its continued existence. The philosopher Rene Descartes represents the general outlook of early modern science with respect to the role of God in creation; he writes: "[T]he Architect is the cause of the house, and the father of the son, as to his coming-to-be, but the work can continue to exist without the cause ... but God is the cause of created things, not only as to their coming-to-be but also as to their being" ("Reply to Gassendi," quoted in Hooykaas, 2000: 42).

4. Kepler was likewise impressed with the match between mind and world. In 1597, he wrote to his teacher, Mastlin: "Man will at last measure the power of his mind on the true scale, and will realize that God, who founded everything in the world according to the norm of quantity, also has endowed man with a mind that can comprehend these norms."

5. We should be careful to note that science has also carried in its wake dreadful things that detract from the quality of human life, such as weapons of mass destruction, pollution, and other life-destroying technologies.

6. Rather, for Boyle, it was a deep interpenetration of the two (Davis, 2007).

7. In a letter to Robert Hooke, February 5, 1676.

8. Stark (2003) claims that Christianity alone birthed modern science. He seems blithely unaware of the contributions of other religions (and of thinkers that don't fit his paradigm). See Efron (2009).

9. *Qi* is the life energy believed to be present in all things (from Chinese thought).

10. Yet it is notoriously difficult to divorce "scientific" and "religious" motivations in the work of pre-nineteenth-century thinkers. Next to Newton, Kepler is an example of this (Barker and Goldstein, 2001).

4 "THE GALILEO AFFAIR"

1. Developmental psychology supports the case for geocentrism. Cross-cultural literature on models of the Earth shows that these intuitions are deep seated, so it is unsurprising that many authors in Antiquity (be they Greek philosophers or Biblical authors) appealed to them (Vosniadou, Brewer, 1992; Samarapungavan, 2005).

2. Or indifferent (Gingerich, 2004).

3. "Canonical" Decree, Concerning the Canonical Scriptures, Fourth Session Council of Trent, celebrated on the eighth day of April, 1546. http://www.csun.edu/~hcfll004/trent4.html.

4. Bellarmine made this determination in his famous letter to Foscarini in 1615. In his view, biblical authority was assaulted by Copernicanism, which was not perhaps a matter of faith in and of itself, but was a matter of faith because the Bible said the sun moves and the earth does not.

5. For a defense of methodological naturalism, see the end of the preceding chapter.

6. Galileo may not present a fully naturalistic stance here. For example, in the absence of scientific certainty, the traditional interpretation of the Bible remains authoritative. He did think that we should *start* from observations and reason, not from the Bible, for understanding natural phenomena. And this is sufficient for the naturalistic stance.

7. Galileo is assuming the high standard of proof bequeathed by Aristotle. On the issue of proof, he was a child of Aristotle.

5   DARWIN, GOD, AND CREATION

1. Ussher's dating was widely accepted and his chronology was included in many editions of the Bible. It was not until the late 1970s that it was removed from the Gideon Society Bibles placed in nearly every US hotel room.
2. Paley himself was not unaware of these sorts of phenomena and attempted to deal with them through a theodicy, an explanation of why a wholly good, omnipotent God might allow evil.
3. Rejecting an argument for the existence of God is not tantamount to rejecting God's existence. One might reject one argument but believe that there are other arguments on which to base one's belief in God. Or one's belief in God might be based on one's religious experience, not on an argument at all (Clark, 1990). Finally, one might cease being a Christian theist but be a theist of another stripe altogether, a deist, for example (someone who believes in God but denies God's action in history after the creation).
4. http://www.darwinproject.ac.uk/death-of-anne-darwin.
5. Martin Gardner offers this explanation of why Darwin included reference to the Creator in subsequent editions: "Darwin himself, as a young biologist aboard H.M.S. Beagle, was so thoroughly orthodox that the ship's officers laughed at his propensity for quoting Scripture. Then 'disbelief crept over me at a very slow rate,' he recalled, 'but was at last complete. The rate was so slow that I felt no distress.' The phrase 'by the creator,' in the final sentence of the selection chosen here, did not appear in the first edition of *Origin of Species*. It was added to the second edition to conciliate angry clerics. Darwin later wrote, 'I have long since regretted that I truckled to public opinion and used the Pentateuchal term of creation, by which I really meant 'appeared' by some wholly unknown process" (1984).
6. There are religious alternatives, which I don't commend, diminishing the immensity of the suffering as does the young earth creationist or denying it altogether as does the Christian Science practitioner.

6   EVIDENCE AND EVOLUTION

1. Although ultimately vindicated, this was controversial for a while. Because of the controversy some creationists came to believe this was a hoax or fraud. See: http://www.millerandlevine.com/km/evol/Moths/moths.html
2. I am indebted, from this point on in the chapter, to the kind assistance of Stephen Matheson, my friend and former colleague.
3. Although we are all related, the tree of life is not the tree of progress. While it is certainly true that some highly complex organisms have arisen relatively recently, it is a mistake to conclude that the history of life was governed by a principled ascent toward complexity or perfection.
4. Technically, "adapt or do not leave offspring;" if this happens often enough, a species will die off.
5. This is, to say the least, extremely simplified. Evolution is not, for example, linear; it is tremendously branching. And, again, it is not progressive.

7   CHANCE AND CREATION

1. http://www.policymic.com/articles/80179/14-states-use-tax-dollars-to-teach-creationism-in-public-schools.

2. http://www.darwinproject.ac.uk/entry-2743.

3. Like Behe and so many others, Nagel has been vehemently criticized for his attempts to defend ID. University of Chicago's Brian Leiter referred to Nagel's defense of ID as an endorsement of a "misleading and embarrassing" enterprise. Leiter went on to denounce Nagel as a "formerly reputable" philosopher. As a further result of his defense, Nagel has been accused of knowing nothing of science, labeled an "idiot" who has done "irreparable harm."

4. ID theorists contend that theirs is no argument from ignorance because they have proven that something is irreducibly complex and so it cannot have been created through a natural process. Instead of ignorance of how some complexity might have arisen naturally, they believe that they have proven that it cannot have arisen naturally. I believe, along with their critics, that their often ingenius claims to having proven that something is irreducibly complex (and so cannot have arisen step-by-step through a natural process) are failures of imagination.

5. http://www.nbcnews.com/id/40373523/ns/technology_and_science -science/t/dinosaur-die-off-cleared-way-gigantic-mammals/#.UwEFbHl4b4V.

6. This seems to be the view of Bartholomew, 2008.

7. Comments at the 'Shifting Ground' conference in Bedford, New Hampshire, March 24, 2007.

8. I don't intend anything derogatory by any of the names. They are simply mnemonic devices.

8   The Evolution of God?

1. I can't resist a joke. What did the Zen Buddhist say to the hot dog vendor? "Make me one with everything."

2. Jack Hitt, "This is Your Brain on God" *Wired*. Vol. 7, no. 11 (November 1999).

3. A biblical name for God, the Beginning and the End, that draws from the first and last letters of the Greek alphabet implying that God is both the source and origin of reality and its ultimate purpose or goal.

4. "Is God in Our Genes?" *Time*. 1.64 (2004): 62–70.

5. Tom Stoppard, *Jumpers* (London, 1972).

6. I recommend that you stop reading now and go directly to the internet. You can experience these experiments in the various videos found at http://viscog .beckman.illinois.edu/djs_lab/demos.html.

7. Not everyone agrees. Some contend that all or nearly all rational beliefs must be based on evidence. For a critical discussion of this view, see Dougherty, 2011.

8. The best, single-volume introduction to this topic is Barrett, 2004.

9. I mean "belief in God," not "God." And I mean "belief in gods," not "belief in an omnipotent, omniscient creator of the universe." Although we are naturally disposed to beliefs in gods, the god-faculty is not so fine-tuned as to produce any single belief about God's nature.

10. Interestingly, contemporary science is not natural. See McAuley, 2011.

11. St Augustine, long before he became a saint or even a Christian, would attend religious services to pick up young women. So perhaps religious practices do conduce our reproductive advantage!

12. The technical term, coined by Gould and Lewontin (1979) for such traits is "spandrels."

13. They might not be irrelevant to everyone's judgments, although I suspect philosophers more highly value such criteria for ordinary beliefs than is necessary or even good.

14. Even equipped with a ToM, humans have not always done well in identifying persons. Consider the 1879 court case involving Standing Bear, a Native American who sued the US government to gain the legal status of a person (Dando-Collins, 2004). He was obliged to overcome the government's claim that Native Americans are neither persons nor citizens. In order to demonstrate his personhood, he had to establish the reality of his inner life. In his own defense, he argued through an interpreter, "My hand is not the color of yours, but if I pierce it, I shall feel pain." Judge Elmer Dundy, using ToM and plain good sense, found in favor of Standing Bear, ruling that "an Indian is a person"; for the first time Native Americans were granted the rights of a US citizen. It may be that we have an evolutionarily shaped cognitive faculty that leads us to distrust people who aren't kin or members of our community. The easiest way to make that judgment would be based on skin color. This distrust could distort information given to ToM and lead to wrong beliefs about persons.

9 EVOLUTION AND ETHICS

1. Although virtue ethicists might oppose rules ethics, they do not commend murder, say, or stealing. The virtuous person would never be disposed to take another's life or property.

2. This is the widely stated figure. The actual figure is closer to 96 percent.

3. Unlike kin selection and reciprocity, group selection is not generally accepted by biologists.

11 IN SEARCH OF THE SOUL

1. In an Address to the Pontifical Academy of Sciences on October 22, 1996.

2. There are countless views in between radical reductive materialism and radical separationist dualism. It is the purpose of this chapter to get a very general sense of the issues, not to canvass every possible position. We will restrict our discussion to reductive materialism, which we will call simply materialism, and dualism.

3. This would, of course, require a complete revision in our common sense understanding of our selves. Folk psychology is so prevalent in our self-understanding that philosopher Jerry Fodor has remarked that if this sort of common sense psychology were mistaken, it would be "the greatest intellectual catastrophe in the history of our species" (Fodor, 1987, p. xii).

4. Christian materialists tend not to be reductionists about the mind. Such a view, usually called "nonreductive physicalism," is most ably defended by Nancey Murphy (2005). I leave that subtlety aside for this discussion.

5. Christian materialists, those who deny mind–body dualism, include Lynne Rudder Baker (2005); Trenton Merricks (2007); Peter Van Inwagen (1995); and, as already noted, Nancey Murphy. It should be noted that Christian materialists are only materialists about human persons. They believe that a nonphysical God exists.

6. http://www.newstatesman.com/ideas/2012/02/consciousness-mind -brain.

7. Along these same lines, Thomas Nagel has argued that there is something that it is like to be a bat, which no human could understand on the basis of purely objective scientific data (Nagel, 1974). Similarly, John Foster argues that deaf persons possess knowledge regarding their condition that cannot be accessed via third-person objective inspection (Foster, 2001).

8. In order to reduce the number of theories the reader must keep in mind, I have considered only substance dualism and reductive materialism. As noted, a number of religious thinkers, among many others, are nonreductive materialists. The arguments I offer here against materialism being unable to account for mental properties or phenomena apply only to reductive materialism, not to nonreductive materialism. Nonreductive materialists claim that although humans are material objects, mental properties are not reducible to physical processes taking place in the brain. You can add reductive materialism to the list of viable options at the end of this chapter.

9. Descartes, *Meditations* §81, in *Philosophical Writings,* 2.56; cf. *Discourse on Method* §59, in *Philosophical Writings,* 1.141; Descartes, *Objections and Replies* §227, in *Philosophical Writings,* 2.160.

10. While Swinburne believes that normal soul functioning (possessing mental states) is possible only if there is a body, he holds that it is nonetheless logically possible that the soul can exist without the body. Swinburne says little of the functioning of the soul in this disembodied state. Swinburne makes the distinction between existing and functioning, but he does not believe that the disembodied soul part would be considered a "human person" in the sense in which Descartes would have maintained.

11. Descartes located the seat of the interaction in the pineal gland at the bottom of the brain.

12. http://www.telegraph.co.uk/science/8058541/Neuroscience-free-will-and -determinism-Im-just-a-machine.html.

13. http://select.nytimes.com/gst/abstract.html?res=F50910FE3E550C728D DDAA0894DF404482&fta=y&incamp=archive:article_related.

14. http://www.usatoday.com/news/opinion/forum/story/2012–01–01/free -will-science-religion/52317624/1. All of the Coyne quotations that follow are from this essay.

15. http://www.samharris.org/free-will.

16. http://www.usatoday.com/news/opinion/forum/story/2012–01–01/free -will-science-religion/52317624/1.

17. Coyne, "You Don't Have Free Will," *The Chronicle Review.*

18. http://www.telegraph.co.uk/science/8058541/Neuroscience-free-will-and -determinism-Im-just-a-machine.html.

19. http://www.nature.com/neuro/journal/v11/n5/abs/nn.2112.html 2008, p. 544.

20. These experiments have been widely criticized (Mele, 2009).

12 THIS MOST BEAUTIFUL SYSTEM

1. Isaac Newton. *Sir Isaac Newton's Mathematical Principles of Natural Philosophy and His System of the World.* Translated into English by Andrew Motte in 1729. http://hss.fullerton.edu/philosophy/GeneralScholium.htm <date accessed 23 December 2010>.

2. This important distinction helps us focus on where the real conflict often lies in the so-called battle between religion and science (Plantinga, 2011).

3. "Everything and Nothing: An Interview with Laurence Krauss," http://www.samharris.org/blog/item/everything-and-nothing/.
4. You can find similar claims and fallacies in Hawking and Mlodinow (2010). See John Horgan's scathing review (Horgan, 2010).
5. For a critique of Leslie's argument see Elliot Sober in Dembski and Ruse, 2008.
6. Nathan Schneider. "Is Theoretical Physics Becoming the Next Battleground in the Culture Wars?," http://seedmagazine.com/content/article/the_multiverse_problem/March 30, 2009 <date accessed 23 December 2010>.
7. "What I Wish My Pastor Knew about Multiverses," http://ministrytheorem.calvinseminary.edu/essays/wiwmpk/Cosmology.pdf.
8. None of this should suggest that theism should be treated as a *scientific* theory that makes predictions about our universe or multiverse. Theism is not a scientific theory. But it does lead us to expect a life-sustaining universe.

13   JUDAISM AND EVOLUTION

1. Bohr, while ethnically Jewish, was baptized a Christian. Like Kierkegaard, he was a Danish Lutheran. Unlike Kierkegaard, he later renounced his childhood faith.
2. "Rabbi" literally means "My Master" and refers to a teacher, a master, of Torah. Some early rabbis, those whose writings were collected in the Talmud, were considered sages and their teachings of great authority.
3. Babylonian Talmud, *Eruvin* 13b.
4. Bamidbar Rabbah 13.15.
5. It was widely believed, despite no textual support, that Abraham and his wise son, Solomon, passed on astronomy and mathematics to the Egyptians who then passed them on to the Greeks.
6. Maimonides' arguments here are not unlike those offered by Augustine and Galileo, as discussed in earlier chapters.
7. Other Orthodox Jewish attempts to reconcile contemporary science and Torah include Carmell and Domb (1988); Schroeder (1991).
8. "Ultra-Orthodox" is a term used by outsiders. Those within the group call themselves Haredi Jews. Haredi Jews oppose any secularization or cultural accommodation or assimilation of Judaism. They base their beliefs and practices entirely on Torah and Talmud.
9. See "Rationalist vs. Mystical Judaism," *Rationalist Judaism* (website), September 1, 2010, http://www.rationalistjudaism.com/2010/09/rationalist-vs-mystical-judaism.html.
10. One might see Slifkin's thought as an extension of the Haskala, the so-called Jewish Enlightenment, dating roughly 1770s–1880s. Haskala, which was opposed to mystical understanding of Judaism, comes from the Hebrew word *sekhel* which means "reason." It sought to rationalize and secularize Jewish beliefs and practices. Orthodox Jews opposed the Haskala from the outset because it downplayed Torah and Talmud studies in favor of a secular education and sought to develop a rationalized form of the Jewish faith that seemed little different from secular, Enlightenment values and beliefs.
11. Alexander Nussbaum, "Orthodox Jews and Science: An Empirical Study of their Attitudes toward Evolution, the Fossil Record, and Modern Geology," *Skeptic*, Vol. 12, no. 3.

12. I simply present his views. Interested readers are welcome to seek out criticisms of Spetner's premises and his calculations. Spetner, as one might imagine, has likewise responded to his critics.
13. See Lee Spetner, "Evolution, Randomness and Hashkafa," http://rbsp.info/rbs/RbS/CLONE/VGS/spetner_evol1.html.
14. Mishnah (Pirkei Avot/Ethics of our Fathers 5.17).

14 ISLAM AND EVOLUTION

1. Roy F. Baumeister et al., "Bad Is Stronger than Good," *Review of General Psychology* 5, no. 4 (2001), 323–70, http://www.carlsonmba.umn.edu/Assets/71516.pdf.
2. Jon Ponder, "Poll: 93% of Muslims Worldwide Condemn 9/11 Attacks—0% Approve of Attacks on Religious Grounds," *Pensito Review*, February 27, 2008, http://www.pensitoreview.com/2008/02/27/poll-majority-muslims-worldwide-condemn-9-11/.
3. The word "Allah" is also used by Arab Christians and in the Arabic version of the Bible.
4. Hadiths include Prophet Muhammad's sayings, actions, and approval of his companions' actions.
5. All passages of the Quran are from Abdel Haleem's recent translation (2005).
6. There are, it must be conceded, nonpeaceful verses as well.
7. You can read essays by five prominent Muslims defending religious liberty and tolerance in Clark (2012).
8. "The World's Muslims: Religion, Politics and Society: Execute Summary," Pew Research, Religion and Public Life Project, April 30, 2013, http://www.pewforum.org/2013/04/30/the-worlds-muslims-religion-politics-society-exec/.
9. "Muslim Americans: Middle Class and Mostly Mainstream," Pew Research, Center for the People and the Press, May 22, 2007, http://www.people-press.org/2007/05/22/muslim-americans-middle-class-and-mostly-mainstream/.
10. Recent data suggest nearly a half million civilian deaths due to the US invasion of Iraq. See A. Hagopian, A. D. Flaxman, T. K. Takaro, S. A. Esa Al Shatari, J. Rajaratnam et al. (2013), Mortality in Iraq Associated with the 2003–11 War and Occupation: Findings from a National Cluster Sample Survey by the University Collaborative Iraq Mortality Study.
11. See Living Under Drones website, http://www.livingunderdrones.org/.
12. "Signature Strike Investigation," Brave New Foundation, June 19, 2013, YouTube (website), http://www.youtube.com/watch?v=SsuhoVDm-Ag.
13. At the time China was widely believed, not without justification, to have all sorts of important and, of course, non-Islamic knowledge—paper, explosives, and literature. This is often alleged to be a Hadith (a quote from the Prophet) but is not.
14. He wrote *The Book of Addition and Subtraction According to the Hindu Calculation* to introduce the Indian decimal system to the Islamic World. Westerners got it centuries later.
15. The sermon can be viewed at "Usama Hasan Claims We Evolved from Apes," YouTube (website), January 25, 2011, http://www.youtube.com/watch?v=TgR-xfJbQcQ.

16. "Abu Zabair's Response to Usama Hasan," YouTube (website), January 26, 2011, http://www.youtube.com/watch?v=Cf1Rwfeuk7Y.

17. The causes were, among other things, mostly economic and political. Science, a geographical and historical rarity, thrives in times of economic affluence and political security. Many attribute the demise of science in the Islamic world to religious opposition to rational investigation (replaced with the study of revelation). Some allege that the work of al-Ghazali (1058–111), who asserted that mathematics is the work of the devil, was the death-knell of science in the Islamic world (Ofek, 2011). This view is rejected by George Saliba (2011).

18. Islam's Ahmadiyya Movement, with millions of followers in nearly 150 countries, has long endorsed evolution.

19. Afghani's original comments on Darwinism/evolution were part of a wider critique of another Muslim Reformer who embraced Darwinism more liberally than Al-Jisr. He was calling Darwinism "materialistic" to delegitimize this other scholar.

20. Contemporary science, it is claimed, establishes the miraculous nature of the Quran, which is widely believed to have prefigured, even precisely predicted, any number of scientific theories. This apologetic approach, called *Ijaz*, is based on "scientific miracles" in the text. The seventh-century prescientific text, it is alleged, affords insight into contemporary scientific theories from embryology to $E = mc^2$. If confirmed, such predictions would surely attest to the divine nature of the Quran (and, hence, the truth of Islam). This strategy was first developed in the late 1970s by French surgeon Maurice Bucaille in his hugely influential *The Bible, the Qur'an and Science* (Bucaille, 1976) and is widely employed by Haran Yahya, whom we will consider shortly. Websites proclaim the conversion of prominent Western scientists to Islam when apprised of the scientific miracles. Muslim scientists, Bruno Guiderdoni and Nidhal Guessoum, among other Muslim scholars, reject scientific miracles apologetics. I set aside discussion of those who commend a distinctly Muslim science, one concerned with, among other things, using the Quran to calculate the precise temperature of hell.

21. Only one knowledgeable in the discipline of Quranic exegesis would be able to make this assertion with the care and expertise it deserves.

22. There is a Quranic difficulty for Big-Bang cosmology. There are passages in the Quran that state that God made the earth first and then the heavens. For example in Quran 2.29 we read:

> It was He who created all that is on the earth for you,
> then turned to the sky and made the seven heavens; it is He who has knowledge of all things.

Two things are worth noting. First, the Surah doesn't state that God made the earth first—only that before turning heaven into the seven heavens (whatever that means), he made all that is *on* Earth. Second, taken literally, it would conflict with Surah 79.27–30, which states, if likewise taken literally, that God created the earth second:

> Which is harder to create: you people or the sky that He built,
> raising it high and perfecting it,
> giving darkness to its night and bringing out its morning brightness,
> and the earth, too, He spread out,

Some Muslim commentators have concluded that neither passage should be taken literally.

23. Biologist Richard Lewontin, for example, proclaimed that "materialism is absolute [and] we cannot allow a Divine Foot in the door" (from his review of Carl Sagan's *The Demon-Haunted World: Science as a Cradle in the Dark*, in the *New York Review of Books*, January 9, 1997). Richard Dawkins famously claimed that evolution made it possible to be an "intellectually fulfilled atheist."

24. While Oktar's influence is undeniable, he is not well respected by scholars either in Turkey or worldwide.

25. In a 2007 study, Riaz Hassan found about half as much support for evolution as did the Pew Study (Hassan, 2007). Moreover, the Pew Study left out Saudi Arabia and Iran.

26. Other once widely accepted but now rejected theories include phlogiston, caloric, the Ptolemaic system of the universe, spontaneous generation, alchemy, vitalism, the aether, vis viva, and the steady-state theory of the cosmos.

27. http://www.economist.com/news/international/21570677-after-centuries -stagnation-science-making-comeback-islamic-world-road.

28. Given some Western scientists' arrogant assertions about science and materialism/atheism, the fault does not lie entirely with fundamentalist clerics.

BIBLIOGRAPHY

Alper, Matthew (2000). *The God Part of the Brain*. New York: Rogue Press.

Alston, William (1967). "Religion." In *Encyclopedia of Philosophy*, edited by Paul Edwards. New York: Macmillan.

Anscombe, Elizabeth, and Geach, Peter, eds. (1954). *Descartes: Philosophical Writings*. Indianapolis, IN: Bobbs-Merrill Company.

Ashworth, William, Jr. (2003). "Christianity and the Mechanistic Universe." In *When Science and Christianity Meet*, edited by David Lindberg and Ronald Lumbers. Chicago, IL: University of Chicago Press.

Atkins, Peter (1995). "The Limitless Power of Science." In *Nature's Imagination: The Frontiers of Scientific Vision*, edited by John Cornwell, 123–125. Oxford: Oxford University Press.

––––– (1996). "Professor Says Science Rules Out Belief in God." *Electronic Telegraph*. September 11.

––––– (1998). "Awesome Versus Adipose: Who Really Works Hardest to Banish Ignorance?" *Free Inquiry* 18(2).

Atran, Scott (1998). "Folk Biology and the Anthropology of Science." *Behavioral & Brain Sciences* 21: 547–609.

––––– (2002). *In Gods We Trust: The Evolutionary Landscape of Religion*. New York: Oxford University Press.

Augustine (1982). *The Literal Meaning of Genesis*. Trans. J. H. Taylor. New York: Newman Press.

Bacon, Francis (1605). *The Advancement of Learning*. 1962, edited by G. W. Kitchin, London and New York: Dent.

––––– (1620). *Novum Organum*. Edited by Joseph Devey. New York, Collier, 1902.

Baker, Lynne Rudder (2005). "Death and the Afterlife." In *The Oxford Handbook of Philosophy of Mind*, edited by William J. Wainwright, 366–391. Oxford: Oxford University Press.

Barbour, Ian (1997). *Religion and Science: Historical and Contemporary Issues*. San Francisco: Harper Collins.

––––– (2002). "On Typologies for Relating Science and Religion." *Zygon* 37(2): 345–359.

Barker, Peter and Goldstein, Bernard (2001). "Theological Foundations of Kepler's Astronomy." *Osiris*, 16: 88–113.

Baron-Cohen, Simon, Tager-Flusberg, Helen, and Cohen, Donald J. (2000). *Understanding Other Minds: Perspectives from Developmental Cognitive Neuroscience*. New York: Oxford University Press.

Bartholomew, David (2008). *God, Chance, and Purpose: Can God Have It Both Ways?* Cambridge: Cambridge University Press.

Bateson, Melissa, Nettle, Daniel, and Roberts, Gilbert (2006). "Cues of Being Watched Enhance Cooperation in a Real-World Setting." *Biology Letters* 2(3): 412–414.

Behe, Michael (1998). *Darwin's Black Box: The Biochemical Challenge to Evolution*. New York: Free Press.

———(2001). "Molecular Machines: Experimental Support for the Design Inference." In *Intelligent Design Creationism and Its Critics: Philosophical, Theological and Scientific Perspectives*, edited by Roger T. Pennock, 241–256. Boston, MA: MIT Press.

Bering, Jesse and Parker, Becky D. (2006). "Children's Attributions of Intentions to an Invisible Agent." *Developmental Psychology* 42: 253–262.

Berlinski, David (2008). *The Devil's Delusion: Atheism and Its Scientific Pretensions*. New York: Crown Forum.

Bloom, Paul (2004). *Descartes' Baby: How the Science of Child Development Explains What Makes Us Human*. New York: Basic Books.

——— (2005). "Is God an Accident?" *Atlantic Monthly*. December 1.

Bowler, Peter (2007). *Monkey Trials & Gorilla Sermons*. Boston, MA: Harvard University Press.

Boyle, Robert (1663). "Usefulness of Natural Philosophy." *The Works of Robert Boyle, Vol. II*. Edited by Michael Hunter and Edward Davis. London: Pickering and Chatto.

——— (1690). *The Christian Virtuoso*. London.

——— (1996 [1686]). *A Free Enquiry into the Vulgarly Received Notion of Nature*. Edited by E. B. Davis and M. Hunter. Cambridge: Cambridge University Press.

Brooks, Arthur (2006). *Who Really Cares?* New York: Basic Books.

——— (2008). *Gross National Happiness: Why Happiness Matters for America—and How We Can Get More of It*. New York: Basic Books.

Browne, Thomas. (1974 [1643]). "Religio Medici." In *The Religion of Isaac Newton: The Freemantle Lectures*, edited by Frank Manuel. Oxford: Oxford University Press.

Bucaille, Maurice (1976). *The Bible, the Qur'an and Science*. Indianapolis, IN: American Trust Publications.

Byrne, Peter (1997). *Analysis and Science in Aristotle*. Albany, NY: SUNY Press.

Byrne, Peter (2008). "The Many Worlds of Hugh Everett." *Scientific American*. October 21.

Cahn, Stephen (1988). "The Challenge of Hume's Dialogue," *Newsletter on Teaching Philosophy* 88.

Cantor, Geoffrey and Kenny, Chris (2001). "Barbour's Fourfold Way: Problems with His Taxonomy of Science-Religion Relationships." *Zygon* 36: 765–781.

Carmell, Aryeh and Domb, Cyril (1988). *Challenge: Torah Views on Science and its Problems*. Spring Valley, New York: Feldheim Publishers.

Cartwright, Nancy (1999). *The Dappled World: A Study of the Boundaries of Science*. Cambridge: Cambridge University Press.

Chalmers, Alan F. (1999). *What Is This Thing Called Science?* Indianapolis, IN: Hackett Publishing Company.

Churchland, Paul (1988). *Matter and Consciousness*. Cambridge: The MIT Press.

Clark, Kelly James (1990). *Return to Reason*. Grand Rapids, MI: Eerdmans Publishing.

———, ed. (2012). *Abraham's Children: Liberty and Tolerance in an Age of Religious Conflict*. New Haven, CT: Yale University Press.

Cleland, Carol (2002). "Methodological and Epistemic Differences between Historical Science and Experimental Science." *Philosophy of Science* 69: 474–496.

Collins, Robin (2007). "The Multiverse Hypothesis: A Theistic Perspective." In *Universe or Multiverse?*, edited by Bernard Carr, 459–480. New York: Cambridge University Press.

Conway, John and Kochen, Simon (2009). "The Strong Free Will Theorem." *Notices of the AMS* 56(2).

Corcoran, Kevin, ed. (2001). *Soul, Body, and Survival: Essays on the Metaphysics of Persons*. Ithaca, NY: Cornell University.

Coulson, Charles (1953). "Christianity in an Age of Science." *25th Riddell Memorial Lecture Series*. Oxford: Oxford University Press.

Crabtree, Steve (1999). "New Poll Gauges Americans' General Knowledge Levels: Four-fifths Know Earth Revolves around Sun." http://www.gallup.com/poll /3742/new-poll-gauges-americans-general-knowledge-levels.aspx.

Crick, Francis (1994). *The Astonishing Hypothesis: The Scientific Search for the Soul*. New York: Charles Scribner's Sons.

Dajani, Rana (2012). "Evolution and Islam's Quantum Question." *Zygon* 47(2): 343–353.

Damasio, Antonio (1994). *Descartes' Error: Emotion, Reason and the Human Brain*. New York: Picador.

d'Aquili, Eugene and Newberg, Andrew (1993). "Religious and Mystical States: A Neuropsychological Model." *Zygon* 28: 177–200.

Dando-Collins, Stephen (2004). *Standing Bear Is a Person: The True Story of a Native American's Quest for Justice*. Cambridge, MA: Da Capo Press.

Darwin, Charles (1844). *Personal Communication with Leonard Homer*. http:// www.darwinproject.ac.uk/darwinletters/calendar/entry-771.html.

——— (1856). *Personal Communication with J. D. Hooker*. http://www.darwin project.ac.uk/letter/entry-1924.

——— (1859). *On the Origin of Species by Means of Natural Selection*. London: John Murray.

——— (1879). *Personal Communication with John Fordyce*. http://www.darwin project.ac.uk/letter/entry-12041

——— (1958). *The Autobiography of Charles Darwin*. London: Collins.

Davies, Paul (1995). *Are We Alone?* New York: Basic Books.

Davis, Edward (2007). "Robert Boyle's Religious Life, Attitude, and Vocation." *Science & Christian Belief* 19: 117–138.

Dawkins, Richard (1976). *The Selfish Gene*. Oxford: Oxford University Press.

——— (1986). *The Blind Watchmaker: Why the Evidence of Evolution Reveals a Universe Without Design*. New York: Norton and Company, Inc.

——— (1994). "Lecture from The Nullifidian." *The Nullifidian*: http://old.richard dawkins.net/articles/89.

——— (1995). *River Out of Eden*. New York: Basic Books.

——— (1996). *Climbing Mount Improbable*. London: Penguin Books.

——— (1999). "Is Science Killing the Soul?" *Edge* 8.

——— (2006). *The God Delusion*. New York: Bantam Books.

——— (2010). "The God Debate." Transcript: http://old.richarddawkins.net/articles /509756-live-14–30-bst-the-god-debate.

De Cruz, Helen and De Smedt, Johan (2010). "Science as Structured Imagination." *Journal of Creative Behavior* 44(1): 29–44.

Dembski, William and Ruse, Michael, eds. (2004). *Debating Design: From Darwin to DNA*. Cambridge: Cambridge University Press.

Dennett, Daniel (1991). *Consciousness Explained*. New York: Little, Brown and Co.

—— (1995). *Darwin's Dangerous Idea: Evolution and the Meanings of Life*. New York: Simon & Shuster.

—— (2003). *Freedom Evolves*. New York: Viking,

—— (2007). *Breaking the Spell: Religion as a Natural Phenomenon*. New York: Penguin Books.

Descartes, Rene (1993). *Meditations on First Philosophy*, edited by Donald Cress. Indianapolis, IN: Hackett Publishing Co.

de Waal, Frans (1996). *Good Natured*. Cambridge, MA: Harvard University Press.

Dewey, John (1998). *The Essential Dewey: Pragmatism, Education, Democracy*, edited by Larry Hickman and Thomas Alexander. Bloomington, IN: Indiana University Press.

Dicken, Paul (2010). *Constructive Empiricism: Epistemology and the Philosophy of Science*. New York: Palgrave Macmillan.

Dobzhansky, Theodosius (1973). "Nothing in Biology Makes Sense Except in the Light of Evolution." *American Biology Teacher* 35: 125–129.

Dougherty, Trent (2011). *Evidentialism and Its Discontents*. New York: Oxford University Press.

Drake, Stillman, ed. (1957). *Discoveries and Opinions of Galileo*. New York: Anchor-Doubleday.

Draper, John William (1898). *History of the Conflict between Religion and Science*. New York: D. Appleton and Company.

Duhem, Pierre (1954). *The Aim and Structure of Physical Theory*, edited by Phillip Wiener. Princeton: Princeton University Press.

Dunn, Peter (2006). *Arch Dis Child Fetal Neonatal Ed* 91(1): F75–F77.

Dworkin, Ronald (2013). *Religion without God*. Boston, MA: Harvard University Press.

Dyson, Freeman (1979). *Disturbing the Universe*. New York: Harper & Row.

—— (2000). "Progress in Religion." *The Edge* 68: www.edge.org/documents /archive/edge68.html.

Eddington, Arthur (2007). "Review of *Isaac Newton: 1642–1727.*" In *Alchemy Rediscovered and Restored*, edited by John William Navin Sullivan. New York: Cosimo.

Efron, Noah (2009). "[The Myth] That Christianity Gave Birth to Modern Science," In *Darwin Goes to Jail*, edited by Ronald L. Numbers. Boston, MA: Harvard University Press.

Einstein, Albert (1950). *Out of My Later Years*. New York: Philosophical Library.

Ellis, George (2011). "Does the Multiverse Really Exist?" *Scientific American*, August.

Elshakry, Marwa (2011). "Muslim Hermeneutics and Arabic Views of Evolution." *Zygon* 46(2): 330–344.

Eysenck, Michael and Keane, Mark T. (2010). *Cognitive Psychology: A Student's Handbook*, 6th Edition. Oxford: Psychology Press.

Fahrbach, Ludwig (2011). "How the Growth of Science Ends Theory Change." *Synthese* 180: 139–155.

Farrell, John (2005). *The Day without Yesterday*. New York: Thunder's Mouth Press.

Fodor, Jerry (1987). *Psychosemantics*. Cambridge, MA: Bradford Books/MIT Press.

Force, James (2000). "The Nature of Newton's 'Holy Alliance' between Science and Religion: From the Scientific Revolution to Newton (And Back Again)." In *Rethinking the Scientific Revolution*, edited by Margaret Osler. Cambridge: Cambridge University Press.

Forterre, Patrick and Philippe, Herve (1999). "Where Is the Root of the Universal Tree of Life?" *BioEssays* 21(10): 871–879.

Foster, John. "A Brief Defense of Cartesian Dualism." In Corcoran, *Soul, Body, and Survival*.

Freud, Sigmund (1975). *The Future of an Illusion*, Trans. Gregory C. Richter. New York: WW Norton & Co.

Futuyma, Douglas (1998). *Evolutionary Biology*, Third Edition. Sunderland, MA: Sinauer Associates.

Gardner, Martin (1984). *The Sacred Beetle and Other Great Essays in Science*. Amherst, NY: Prometheus Books.

——— (2001). "Multiverses and Blackberries." *The Skeptical Inquirer* 25(5).

Gaskin, John Charles Adam (1988). *Hume's Philosophy of Religion*, 2nd Edition, London: Macmillan.

Ghiselin, Michael T. (1974). *The Economy of Nature and the Evolution of Sex*. Berkeley, CA: University of California Press.

Gingerich, Owen (2004). *The Book Nobody Read: Chasing the Revolutions of Nicolaus Copernicus*. New York: Walker & Company.

Gould, Stephen Jay (1997). "Nonoverlapping Magisteria." *Natural History* 106: 16–22.

Gould, Stephen Jay and Lewontin, Richard (1979). "The Spandrels of San Marco and the Panglossian Paradigm: A Critique of the Adaptationist Programme." *Proceedings of the Royal Society of London*, Series B, 205(1161), 581–598.

Greco, John (2000). *Putting Skeptics in Their Place: The Nature of Skeptical Arguments and Their Role in Philosophical Inquiry*. Cambridge: Cambridge University Press.

Green, Joel, ed. (2005). *In Search of the Soul: Four Views of the Mind-Body Problem*. Downers Grove, IL: InterVarsity Press.

Greenstein. George (1988). *The Symbiotic Universe*. New York: William Morrow.

Guessoum, Nidhal (2011). *Islam's Quantum Question: Reconciling Muslim Tradition and Modern Science*. New York: I. B. Tauris.

Guthrie, Stewart (1995). *Faces in the Clouds: A New Theory of Religion*. New York: Oxford University Press.

Hacking, Ian (1999). *The Social Construction of What?* Boston, MA: Harvard University Press.

Haeckel, Ernst (1901). *The Riddle of the Universe at the Close of the Nineteenth Century*. New York: Harper and Brothers.

Haidt, Jonathan and Kesebir, Selin (2010). "Morality." in *Handbook of Social Psychology, 5th Edition*, edited by Susan Fiske and Daniel Gilbert. New York: Wiley.

Haley, Kevin and Fessler, Daniel (2005). "Nobody's Watching? Subtle Cues Affect Generosity in an Anonymous Economic Game." *Evolution and Human Behavior* 26: 245–256.

Hamer, Dean (2004). *The God Gene: How Faith Is Hardwired into Our Genes*. New York: Doubleday.

Hamilton, Virginia (1988). *In the Beginning: Creation Stories from Around the World*. New York: Harcourt, Inc.

Hannam, James (2009). *God's Philosophers: How the Medieval World Laid the Foundations of Modern Science*. London: Icon Books.

Harris, Sam (2006). "Science Must Destroy Religion." *Huffington Post*. January 2.

Harrison, Peter (2006a). ""Science" and "Religion": Constructing the Boundaries." *The Journal of Religion* 86: 81–106.

────── (2006b). "'The Book of Nature' and Early Modern Science." In *The Book of Nature in Early Modern and Modern History* (Groningen Studies in Cultural Change), edited by Klaas van Berkel and Arjo Vanderjagt (Editors). Leuven, Belgium: Peeters Publishers.

Harrison, Peter, Numbers, Ronald L., and Shank, Michael H. eds. (2011). *Wrestling with Nature: From Omens to Science* Chicago, IL: University of Chicago Press.

Hasker, William (2001). *The Emergent Self*. Ithaca, NY: Cornell University Press.

────── (2005). "On Behalf of Emergent Dualism," In Green, *In Search of the Soul*.

Hassan, Riaz (2007). "On Being Religious: Patterns of Religious Commitment in Muslim Societies." *The Muslim World* 97: 437–478.

Haught, John (1995). *Science and Religion: From Conflict to Conversation*. Mahwah, NJ: Paulist Press.

Hauser, Marc (2006). *Moral Minds: How Nature Designed Our Universal Sense of Right and Wrong*. New York: Ecco.

Hawking, Stephen and Mlodinow, Leonard. (2010). *The Grand Design*. New York: Bantam.

Highfield, Roger (2003). "Do Our Genes Reveal the Hand of God?" *The Telegraph*, March 20.

Hooykaas, Reijer (2000). *Religion and the Rise of Modern Science*. Vancouver: Regent College Publishing.

Horgan, John (2010). "Cosmic Clowning: Stephen Hawking's "New" Theory of Everything is the Same Old CRAP." *Scientific American*, September 13.

Hoyle, Fred (1981). "The Universe: Past and Present Reflections," *Engineering and Science*. November, 8–12.

────── (1983). *The Intelligent Universe*. New York: Holt, Rinehart & Winston.

Hummell, Charles (1986). *The Galileo Connection*. Downers Grove, IL: InterVarsity Press.

Hume, David (1957). *The Natural History of Religion*, edited by H. E. Root. Stanford, CA: Stanford University Press.

Huxley, Thomas Henry (1888). "The Struggle for Existence in Human Society." *Nineteenth Century*. February.

────── (1894). *Evolution and Ethics*. New York: D. Appleton and Co.

Iqbal, Muzzafar (2007). *Science and Islam*. Westport, CT: Greenwood Publishing Group.

────── (2009). "Darwin's Shadow: Context and reception in the Muslim World." *Islam & Science* 7(1).

Isaacson, Walter (2007). *Einstein: His Life and Universe*. New York: Simon & Schuster.

Jackson, Frank (1982). "Epiphenomenal Qualia." *The Philosophical Quarterly*, 127–136.

Jacquette, Dale (1994). *Philosophy of Mind*. New Jersey: Prentice Hall.

Jacob, Francois (1977). "Evolution and Tinkering." *Science* 196: 1161–1166.

Johnson, Dominic (2005). "God's Punishment and Public Goods: A Test of the Supernatural Punishment Hypothesis in 186 World Cultures." *Human Nature* 16: 410–446.

────── (Forthcoming). *Payback: God's Punishment and the Evolution of Cooperation*. New York: Oxford University Press.

Johnson, Dominic and Bering, Jesse (2006). "Hand of God, Mind of Man: Punishment and Cognition in the Evolution of Cooperation." *Evolutionary Psychology* 4: 219–233.

Joyce, Richard (2006). *The Evolution of Morality.* Cambridge, MA: MIT Press.

Kay, Joe (2007). "Science, Religion, and Society: Richard Dawkins' *The God Delusion.*" World Socialist Web Site. http://www.wsws.org/articles/2007/mar 2007/dawk-m15.shtml.

Keddie, Nikki (1983). *An Islamic Response to Imperialism: Political and Religious Writings of Sayyid Jamal ad-Din 'al-Afghani.'* Berkeley, CA: University of California Press.

Kim, Jaegwon (2001). "Lonely Souls: Causality and Substance Dualism." In Corcoran, *Soul, Body, and Survival.*

Kingsley, Charles (1871). "The Natural Theology of the Future." Lecture at Sion College.

Krauss, Laurence (2012). *A Universe from Nothing.* New York: Free Press.

Kuhn, Thomas (1977). "Objectivity, Value Judgment, and Theory Choice." In *The Essential Tension.* Chicago, IL: University of Chicago Press.

Larson, Edward (1997). *Summer for the Gods: the Scopes Trial and America's Continuing Debate Over Science and Religion.* New York: Basic Books.

Laudan, Larry (1981). "A Confutation of Convergent Realism." *Philosophy of Science* 48: 19–49.

Lemaitre, Georges (1950). *The Primeval Atom – An Essay on Cosmology.* New York: D. Van Nostrand Company, Inc.

Leslie, John (1989). *Universes.* London: Routledge.

Lewis, Peter (2001). "Why the Pessimistic Induction is a Fallacy." *Synthese* 129: 371–380.

Linde, Andrei (1994). "The Self-Reproducing Inflationary Universe." *Scientific American.* November.

Loder, James E. and Neidhardt, W. Jim (1996). "Barth, Bohr, and Dialectic." in *Religion and Science: History, Method, Dialogue,* edited by W. Mark Richardson and Wesley J. Wildman. New York: Routledge.

Lombrozo, Tanya (2007). "Simplicity and Probability in Causal Explanation." *Cognitive Psychology* 55: 232–257.

Lubbock, Constance (1933). *The Herschel Chronicle.* Cambridge: Cambridge University Press.

Maimonides, Moses (2006). *Guide for the Perplexed.* All references are to Friedlander's translation, Cosimo Ed.

Mackie, John Leslie (1977). *Ethics: Inventing Right and Wrong.* New York: Penguin.

Masserman, Jules H., Wechkin, Stanley, and Terris, William (1964). "'Altruistic' Behavior in Rhesus Monkeys." *The American Journal of Psychiatry* Vol 121. Dec. 584–585.

McAuley, Robert (2011). *Why Religion is Natural and Science is Not.* New York: Oxford University Press.

McGinn, Colin (2000). *The Mysterious Flame: Conscious Minds in a Material World.* New York: Oxford University Press.

McMullin, Ernan (2011). "Kepler: Moving the Earth." *HOPOS: The Journal of the International Society for the History of Philosophy of Science* 1(1): 3–22.

——— (2012). "Values in Science." *Zygon* 47(4): 686–709.

Mele, Alfred (2009). *Effective Intentions: The Power of Conscious Will.* New York: Oxford University Press.

Merricks, Trenton (2007). "Dualism, Physicalism, and the Incarnation." In *Persons: Human and Divine*, edited by Peter Van Inwagen and Dean Zimmerman, 281–300. Oxford: Oxford University Press.

Midgley, Mary (1978). *Beast and Man: The Roots of Human Nature*. Oxford: Routledge.

Miller, Kenneth (1999). *Finding Darwin's God*. New York: Cliff Street Books.

Monton, Bradley (2009). *Seeking God in Science: An Atheist Defends Intelligent Design*. Peterborough, Ontario: Broadview Press.

Murphy, Nancey. "Nonreductive Physicalism." In Green, *In Search of the Soul*.

Myers, David (1993). *The Pursuit of Happiness*. New York: William Morrow.

Nagel, Thomas (1974). "What Is It Like to Be a Bat?" *The Philosophical Review* 83(4): 435–450.

——— (2008). "Public Education and Intelligent Design."*Wiley InterScience Journal Philosophy and Public Affairs* 36(2).

——— (2012). *Mind and Cosmos: Why the Materialist Neo-Darwinian Conception of Nature Is Almost Certainly False*. New York: Oxford University Press.

Neher, Andre (1977). "Copernicus in the Hebraic Literature from the Sixteenth to the Eighteenth Century." *Journal of the History of Ideas* 38(2): 211–226.

Newberg, Andrew, d'Aquili, Emilio, and Rause, Vince (2001). *Why God Won't Go Away: Brain Science and the Biology of Belief*. New York: Ballantine Book.

Newport, Frank (2012). "In U.S. 46% Hold Creationist Views of Human Origins: Highly Religious Americans Most Likely to Believe in Creationism." *Gallup*. http://www.gallup.com/poll/155003/hold-creationist-view-human-origins.aspx.

Newton, Isaac (1687). *Philosophiae Naturalis Principia Mathematica*. London.

——— (1704). *Opticks, or a Treatise on the Reflections, Refractions, Inflections, and Colours of Light*. http://www.gutenberg.org/files/33504/33504-h/33504-h.htm.

——— (1713). "The General Scholium." In *Principia Mathematica*. http://www.isaac-newton.org/scholium.htm.

——— (1729). "The System of the World." *Philosophiae Naturalis Principia Mathematica*. Trans. Andrew Motte. http://archive.org/stream/newtonspmathema00newtrich/newtonspmathema00newtrich_djvu.txt.

——— (1974). "Yahida Manuscript." In *The Religion of Isaac Newton: The Freemantle Lectures*, edited by Frank Manuel. Cambridge: Cambridge University Press.

Ofek, Hillel (2011). "Why the Arabic World Turned Away from Science." *The New Atlantis* 30: 3–23.

Okasha, Samir (2002). *Philosophy of Science: A Very Short Introduction*. New York: Oxford University Press.

Origen (1966). *On First Principles: Being Koetschau's Text of the De Principiis Translated into English, Together with an Introduction and Notes*. Trans. G. W. Butterworth. New York: Harper & Row.

Orr, James (1897). *The Christian View of God and the World*. http://www.ccel.org/ccel/orr/view.html.

Paley, William (2006). *Natural Theology*. Oxford: Oxford University Press.

Parker, Katie Langloh (1905). *The Euahlayi Tribe: A Study of Aboriginal Life in Australia*. London: Archibald Constable and Company.

Pedersen, Olaf (1983). "Galileo and the Council of Trent: The Galileo Affair Revisited." *Journal for the History of Astronomy* 14: 1–29.

Penrose, Roger (1989). *The Emperor's New Mind*. New York: Penguin.

Peters, Ted (1997). "Theology and Natural Science." In *The Modern Theologians*, edited by David Ford. Oxford: Blackwell.

Philippe, Herve et al. (2009). "Phylogenomics Revives Traditional Views on Deep Animal Relationships." *Current Biology* 19: 706–712.

Pinker, Steven (1999). "Is Science Killing the Soul?" *Edge* 9.

Plantinga, Alvin (1993). *Warrant and Proper Function.* New York: Oxford University Press.

——— (2000). *Warranted Christian Belief.* New York: Oxford University Press.

——— (2011). *Where the Conflict Really Lies.* New York: Oxford University Press.

Plato, "Phaedo." In *Plato: Complete Works*, edited by John Cooper, 49–100. Indianapolis, IN: Hackett.

Polkinghorne, John (2009). *Theology in the Context of Science.* New Haven, CT: Yale University Press.

Polkinghorne, John and Beale, Nicholas (2009). *Questions of Truth.* Louisville, KY: Westminster John Knox.

Poole, Joyce (1997). *Coming of Age with Elephants: A Memoir.* New York: Hyperion.

Putnam, Robert (2000). *Bowling Alone.* New York: Simon & Shuster.

Rees, Martin (2001). *Our Cosmic Habitat.* Princeton: Princeton University Press, 2001.

——— (2003). "Numerical Coincidences and 'Tuning' in Cosmology." In *Fred Hoyle's Universe*, edited by Chandra Wickramasinghe, Geoffrey Burbidge, and Jayant Narlikar. Boston, MA: Kluwer.

Robinson, Richard (2005). "Jump-Starting a Cellular World: Investigating the Origin of Life, from Soup to Networks." *PLoS Biology* 3(11). doi:10.1371/journal.pbio.0030396.

Ross, Sydney (1962). "Scientist: The Story of a Word." *Annals of Science* 18(2): 65–85.

Ruse, Michael (1986). *Taking Darwin Seriously: A Naturalistic Approach to Philosophy.* New York: Blackwell.

Ruse, Michael and Wilson, Edward Osborne (1986). "Moral Philosophy as Applied Science." *Philosophy* 61(236): 173–192.

Ruse, Michael (1991). "The Significance of Evolution." In *A Companion to Ethics*, edited by Peter Singer. Cambridge: Blackwell.

Ryle, Gilbert (1949). *The Concept of Mind.* New York: Barnes and Noble.

Sagan, Carl (1980). *Cosmos.* New York: Ballantine.

Saliba, George (2011). *Islamic Science and Making of the European Renaissance.* Cambridge, MA: MIT Press.

Samarapungavan, Ala, Vosniadu, Stella and Brewer, William (1996). "Mental Models of the Earth, Sun, and Moon: Indian Children's Cosmologies." *Cognitive development* 11: 491–521.

Schierwater, B. et al. (2009). "Concatenated Analysis Sheds Light on Early Metazoan Evolution and Fuels a Modern "Urmetazoon" Hypothesis." *PLoS Biology* 7(1): e1000020.

Schroeder, Gerald (1991). *Genesis and the Big Bang.* New York: Bantam.

Shanavas, Tharackandathil (2010). *Islamic Theory of Evolution: The Missing Link between Darwin and the Origin of Species.* Tucson, AZ: Brainbow Press.

Shariff, Azim and Norenzayan, Ara (2007). "God is Watching You: Priming God Concepts Increases Prosocial Behavior in an Anonymous Economic Game." *Psychological Science* 18(9): 803–809.

Shubin, Neil (2009). *Your Inner Fish: A Journey into the 3.5-Billion-Year History of the Human Body.* New York: Vintage.

Silman, Shimon (2002). "Moshiah and Science," *The Voice of Moshiach*, 5763, November 8.

Simons, Daniel (2000). "Current Approaches to Change Blindness." *Visual Cognition* 7, 1–15.

Simons, Daniel and Levin, Daniel (1997). "Change Blindness." *Trends in Cognitive Science* 1, 261–267.

———— (1998). "Failure to Detect Changes to People in a Real-World Interaction." *Psychonomic Bulletin and Review* 5, 644–649.

Simpson, George (1967). *The Meaning of Evolution, Revised Edition*. New Haven, CT: Yale University Press.

Skinner, B. F. (1971). *Beyond Freedom and Dignity*. New York: Alfred Knopf.

Slifkin, Nathan (2006). *The Challenge of Creation: Judaism's Encounter with Science, Cosmology and Evolution*. Brooklyn, NY: Zoo Torah/Yashar Books.

Sosis, Richard (2000). "Religion and Intra-group Cooperation: Preliminary Results of a Comparative Analysis of Utopian Communities." *Cross-Cultural Research* 34: 70–87.

Sosis, Richard and Bressler, Eric (2003). "Cooperation and Commune Longevity: A Test of the Costly Signaling Theory of Religion." *Cross-Cultural Research* 37:211–239.

Sosis, Richard and Ruffle, Bradley (2003). "Religious Ritual and Cooperation: Testing for a Relationship on Israeli Religious and Secular Kibbutzim." *Current Anthropology* 44: 713–722.

Spetner, Lee (1988). *Not by Chance: Shattering the Modern Theory of Evolution*. New York: Judaica Press.

Sprat, Thomas (1722). *The History of the Royal Society of London, for the Improving of Natural Knowledge*. London: Samuel Chapman.

Sproul, Barbara C. (1979). *Primal Myths: Creation Myths Around the World*. New York: Harper Collins.

Sripada, Chandra (2008). "Nativism and Moral Psychology." In *Moral Psychology, Volume 1: The Evolution of Morality: Adaptations and Innateness*, edited by Walter Sinnott-Armstrong, Cambridge, MA: MIT Press.

Srivastava, Mansi, Simakov, Oleg, and Rokhsar, Daniel S. (2010). "The *Amphimedon queenslandica* Genome and the Evolution of Animal Complexity." *Nature* 466 (7307): 720–726.

Stark, Rodney (2003). *For the Glory of God: How Monotheism Led to Reformations, Science, Witch-Hunts and the End of Slavery*. Princeton, NJ: Princeton University Press.

Sternberg, Robert, and Sternberg, Karin (2012). *Cognitive Psychology*, 6th edition. Belmont, CA: Wadsworth.

Sturluson, Snorri (1987). *Edda*. Trans. Anthony Faulkes. London: J. M. Dent & Sons, Ltd.

Susskind, Leonard (2006). *The Cosmic Landscape*. New York: Little, Brown and Company.

Swinburne, Richard (1986). *The Evolution of the Soul*. Oxford: Clarendon Press.

Temple, William (1964). *Nature, Man and God*. London: Macmillan and Co.

Thagard, Paul (2010). *The Brain and the Meaning of Life*. Princeton, NJ: Princeton.

Thornhill, Randy and Palmer, Craig T. (2000). *A Natural History of Rape: Biological Bases of Sexual Coercion*. Cambride, MA: MIT Press.

Tipler, Frank (1994). *The Physics of Immortality*. New York: Anchor Books.

Trimble, Michael R. (2007). *The Soul in the Brain: The Cerebral Basis of Language, Art, and Belief.* Baltimore, MD: The Johns Hopkins University Press.

Trivers, Robert L. (1971). "The Evolution of Reciprocal Altruism." *The Quarterly Review of Biology* 46(1): 35–57.

Van Biema, David (2006). "God vs. Science." *Time Magazine.*

Van Fraassen, Bas (1980). *The Scientific Image.* New York: Oxford University Press.

Van Inwagen, Peter (1995). "Dualism and Materialism: Athens and Jerusalem." *Faith and Philosophy* 12(4): 475–488.

Vosniadou, Stella and Brewer, William (1992). "Mental Models of the Earth: A Study in Conceptual Change in Childhood." *Cognitive Psychology* 24: 535–585.

Vosniadou, Stella and Skopeliti, Irini. (2005). "Developmental Shifts in Children's Categorizations of the Earth." *Proceedings of the XXVII Annual Conference of the Cognitive Science Society,* Stresa, 2325–2330.

Watson, James (1968). *The Double Helix.* New York: Atheneum.

Weaver, Richard (1995). *Ethics of Rhetoric.* London: Routledge.

Weinberg, Steven (1994). *Dreams of a Final Theory: The Scientist's Search for the Ultimate Laws of Nature.* New York: Vintage.

——— (2000). "Free People from Superstition." *Freethought Today.* April.

——— (2008). "Without God." *The New York Review of Books.* November 20.

Whewell, William (1847). *History of the Inductive Sciences, from the Earliest to the Present Times.* London. 2nd ed.

White, Andrew Dickson (1908). *A History of the Warfare of Science with Theology in Christendom.* New York: D. Appleton and Company.

Wilson, Edward O. (1975). *Sociobiology: The New Synthesis.* Cambridge: Harvard University Press.

——— (1998a). *Consilience: The Unity of Knowledge.* New York: Alfred A. Knopf.

——— (1998b). "The Biological Basis of Morality," *The Atlantic Monthly,* April.

Wright, Robert (1994). *The Moral Animal.* New York: Vintage.

Yahya, Harun (2006). *The Atlas of Creation.* Istanbul, Turkey: Global Publishing.

INDEX

accommodationism, 52–4, 60, 70
Agency Detecting Device (ADD), 126–9, 133
Al-Afghani, Jamal Al-din, 231–3, 265
al-Haytham, Ibn (Alhazen), 229
al-Jisr, Hussein, 231–2, 256
al-Khwarizmi, Muhammad, 229
Allen, Bill, 26
Alston, William, 23, 259
altruism, 139, 141, 144–50, 150, 156–8, 160, 269
altruism dilemma, 144–5
Ambulocetus natans, 85–6
anatomy, comparative, 87, 89–90, 93, 95
anti-Semitism, 209, 212, 236
Aristotle, 5, 11, 13–14, 19–21, 46, 49, 55, 121, 141, 185, 246, 249, 260
atheism, 4, 7, 24, 31, 43, 67, 98–9, 119–20, 128, 165, 189, 236–7, 238, 242, 257
Atkins, Peter, 2, 4, 31, 259
Augustine, 7, 68–73, 95, 251, 254, 259
Averroes, 232, 239, 241

Bacon, Francis, 31–8, 40–1, 43–4, 46, 54, 259
Barbour, Ian, 27, 248, 259–60
Baron-Cohen, Simon, 124, 259
Baronius, Cardinal Caesar, 58
Barr, Stephen, 204
Barrett, Justin, 127, 251
Bellarmine, Cardinal Robert, 50–2, 249
Berg, Naftali, 219
Bering, Jesse, 161, 260, 265
Berlinski, David, 197, 204, 260
Big Bang theory, 1–4, 7, 8, 28, 64, 131, 188–9, 191–3, 208, 234, 245, 256
biogeography, 87–9
Bloom, Paul, 130, 167, 260, 262
Bohr, Niels, 207–8, 254, 265

Book of Nature, 7, 34, 37, 41–2, 49, 54, 58–60, 69, 79, 87, 95–6, 105, 239, 243, 264
Book of Scripture, 7, 34, 42, 44, 49, 54–6, 58, 60, 69, 79, 87, 95–6, 105, 243
Boyle, Robert, 21, 31–2, 37–44, 163, 249, 260–1
Brahe, Tycho, 20–1, 52, 212
Brooks, Arthur, 161–2, 260
Browne, Thomas, 35, 260

Cahn, Stephen, 119, 260
Carnegie, Andrew, 140–1, 149
catastrophism, 63, 82–3, 86
chance (random), 10, 102, 105–10, 112–14, 129, 192–4, 196–8, 200, 203, 220, 221, 259, 268
Churchland, Patricia, 169, 260
Clark, Kelly James, 125, 250, 255, 260
Cleaver, Gerald, 204
Cohen, Tobias, 209, 211–12
Collins, Robin, 192–3, 203, 261
colonialism, 228, 230–1, 242
common descent, 67, 80, 85–95, 215
compatibilism, 180–3
conflict (science and religion), 3, 8–10, 22, 24–5, 27–9, 31, 44, 49, 50, 52, 59–61, 64, 69, 73, 77, 98–9, 179, 208, 213, 218, 221, 235, 240, 248, 253, 256
consilience, 8, 86–7, 92, 96, 269
cooperation, 137–9, 143–4, 147–8, 151, 160, 163, 260, 265, 268
Copernicanism, 20, 21, 24, 25, 45, 46, 48, 49–52, 55, 59, 186, 212, 249
Copernicus, Nicholas, 21, 31, 37, 40, 42, 45–6, 48–50, 56, 163, 212, 214, 240, 263, 266
correspondence of mind and world, 35–6
Cotes, Roger, 40

Coyne, Jerry, 178–81, 253
creationism, young earth, 6, 25, 63, 76, 80, 113, 237, 250
Crick, Francis, 18, 32, 170, 261

Dajani, Rana, 238–41, 261
Damasio, Antonio, 174–5, 261
Darwin, Charles, 7, 9, 14, 19, 24, 25, 32, 61–77, 80–4, 86–91, 93, 98–103, 106, 145, 230–3, 246, 250, 261–2, 266–7
Darwinism, 7, 77, 138–9, 155, 230–2, 235–6, 256
Davies, Paul, 41–2, 199, 261
Dawkins, Richard, 5, 6, 9, 27, 31, 107, 117, 118–21, 130, 132–3, 135, 142, 144, 148, 153–6, 159–60, 170, 199, 237, 242, 257, 261, 265, 87, 90, 95, 256
Dawkinsian world, 153–6, 159
Dennett, Daniel, 117–21, 130, 133, 135, 159, 160, 166, 170–1, 262
Descartes, Rene, 46, 165–7, 169, 171, 174, 175, 249, 253, 259–62
Dewey, John, 121, 262
Dirac, Paul, 18
DNA, 17–18, 21, 32, 36, 43, 87, 90, 92–5, 170
Dobzhansky, Theodosius, 87, 262
Doctrine of Two Books, 34–5, 42, 44, 49, 52, 54, 56–60, 69, 87, 221, 239, 241
Draper, John William, 9, 24, 25, 262
dualism
    Cartesian, 165–6, 174–5, 263
    Christian, 168
    emergent, 176–8, 264
    mind-body, 165–9, 171–2, 174–8, 183, 252–3, 263–6, 269
    soft-dualism, 176–8

Eddington, Arthur, 3, 4, 13, 262
Einstein, Albert, 3, 4, 11–14, 19, 29, 32, 72–7, 79–96, 97–114, 207–9, 262, 264
Ellis, George, 203, 262
embryology, 87, 90–2, 95, 256
emergent dualism, 176–8, 264
empiricism, 121–5, 247, 262
Everett, Hugh, 201, 260

evil, natural, 74–6
evolution, 4–9, 26, 29, 61, 63–4, 66–8, 72–3, 77, 79–81, 83–95, 97–114, 117, 121–31, 133, 135–9, 143–56, 160, 182, 187, 190, 207, 214–15, 217–23, 228–42, 245, 248, 250–2, 254, 255–7, 259–65, 267–9
expectation principle, 187–8, 194, 199, 203, 205–6

Feynman, Richard, 207–8
fine-tuning, 8, 187, 189, 191, 192–4, 197–200, 202, 205–6
fitness, 80–1, 106, 148, 155–6
fossils, 67, 82–90, 93, 95, 98, 219, 237, 254
Foster, John, 174, 253, 263
free will, 74–5, 110, 111, 112, 116, 141, 149, 178–83, 247
free-rider problem, 160
Freud, Sigmund, 118–19, 263
Futuyma, Douglas, 106, 263

Gage, Phineas, 169
Galileo Galilei, 7, 24, 26, 31, 37–40, 42, 45–60, 70, 103, 163, 240, 248–9, 254, 262, 264, 266
Gans, David, 209, 211–13
Gardner, Martin, 203–4, 250, 263
Gell-Mann, Murray, 207
Genesis, 2, 4, 27, 61–4, 68–73, 77, 79, 82, 95, 116, 166, 168, 210, 214–18, 259, 267
genetics, 10, 87, 92–3, 95, 142
geocentrism, 46–8, 249
Ghiselin, Michael, 145, 263
God as scientific hypothesis, 5–6, 27
God helmet, 115, 117
God hypothesis, 5–6, 77, 132, 186, 202, 203, 204
god-faculty, 126, 128, 130–3, 135–6, 251–2
Golden Age of Islam, 228–9
Gould, Stephen Jay, 26–7, 85, 218, 251, 263
great chain of being, 205
Greco, John, 123, 125, 263
Greenstein, George, 189, 263
group selection, 144, 145, 147–51, 252
Guth, Alan, 194, 196, 263

Haeckel, Ernst, 137, 263
Haggard, Patrick, 178, 181
Haidt, Jonathan, 160, 263
Haldane, J. B. S., 145
Hamer, Dean, 116–17, 263
Hamilton, William, 145–6, 264
Harris, Sam, 31, 179, 181, 253–4
Hasan, Usama, 229–30
Hasker, William, 176–7, 264
Hauser, Marc, 134, 264
Hawking, Stephen, 9, 28, 32, 254, 264
heliocentrism, 47–8, 55–6, 59
Herschel, William, 186, 265
holism. *See* materialism, Christian
House of Wisdom, 228–9
Hoyle, Fred, 3, 4, 102, 189, 198,
    264, 267
Hume, David, 118–21, 260, 263, 264
Humility, 27, 52, 54–5, 57, 60, 242, 243
Huxley, T. H., 25, 138, 144, 200, 264
hypersensitive agency detecting device
    (HADD). *See* Agency Detecting
    Device
hypothetico-deductive method, 22

immediate beliefs, 6, 122, 125–8, 134
Intelligent Design (ID), 6, 99–100,
    102–4, 236–7
integration (science and religion), 10,
    24, 28–9, 39, 218, 221, 248
Islam, 223–8, 255–6

Jackson, Frank, 173, 264
Jacquette, Dale, 171, 174, 264
Johnson, Dominic, 160, 264–5
Joyce, Richard, 146, 154–5, 265, 267
Judaism, 210–11, 236, 254

Kepler, Johannes, 7, 21, 24, 42, 44,
    103, 212, 240, 246, 249, 259, 255
Kierkegaard, Søren, 208, 254
Kim, Jaegwon, 172, 265
kin selection, 145–7, 149, 150–1, 154,
    252
Kingsley, Charles, 77, 265
Krauss, Laurence, 194–6, 254, 265
Kuhn, Thomas, 17, 265

Laplace, Pierre, 103, 185–6
Lemaître, 1–4, 265

Leslie, John, 197, 254, 265
Letter to the Grand Duchess Christina,
    49, 52–60, 70
libertarianism, 181
Linde, Andrei, 201, 265
Loewi, Otto, 13
Lyell, Charles, 77, 82–4

Mackie, J. L., 154, 265
macroevolution, 80, 220
Maimonides, 210, 213–18, 254, 265
Marx, Karl, 118–19
materialism, materialistic, 165, 170–4,
    176–8, 232–3, 236, 238, 252–3,
    256–7, 266, 269
    Christian, 172–3
McGinn, Colin, 173, 176, 265
McMullin, Ernan, 17, 248, 265
Mele, Al, 182, 253, 266
microevolution, 80, 85, 220
Midgley, Mary, 142, 266
minds, other, 6, 124
Monton, Bradley, 103, 191, 266
moral faculty, 133–5
moral fiction, 154–6
morality, duty/rule, 139–41
morality, virtues, 141–2
multiverse, 194, 199–205, 254, 261–3

Napoleon, 185–6
natural philosophy, 14–15, 32, 35, 41,
    44, 209, 212–14, 253, 260
natural selection, 25, 61, 67, 80–2, 95,
    98–9, 101–3, 104, 106–7, 109, 129,
    138, 142, 144–8, 150, 154, 261
naturalism, metaphysical, 43, 164,
    186–7, 205–6, 245
naturalism, methodological, 42–3, 53,
    249
necessity, 198–9
Newberg, Andrew, 116, 261, 266
Newton, Isaac, 5, 7, 10, 13–14, 19, 24,
    31–2, 34, 39–44, 46, 59, 75, 103,
    185, 246, 249, 253, 260, 262–3,
    266
nothing, 194–6

Oppenheimer, Robert, 207
Origin of Species, 25, 61, 67, 77, 80,
    101, 231, 261, 267

Orr, James, 77, 266
Owen, Richard, 88–90

Paley, William, 64–7, 74, 103, 250, 266
Pauli, Wolfgang, 207
Penrose, Roger, 192–3, 266
Persinger, Michael, 115–17
Pinker, Stephen, 170, 267
Plantinga, Alvin, 125, 131, 253, 267
Plato, Platonic, 13, 90, 141, 153–4,
    166–8, 175, 177–8, 267
pseudogenes, 94
Ptolemaic system, 20, 21, 45, 48, 50,
    52, 55–6, 59, 185, 212, 214, 229,
    240, 257

Quine, Willard Van Orman, 5–6

random, 8, 17, 84, 105–10, 112–14,
    192, 198, 200, 203, 215, 220, 255
randomness. *See* chance
rationalism, Jewish, 216, 219
reciprocity, 147, 149, 150–1, 154, 252,
    269
Rees, Martin, 189, 192–4, 200, 202,
    267
Reformation, the, 46, 51
religion, definition of, 22–3
Rosen, Jeffrey, 178
Ruse, Michael, 146, 155–6, 254, 262,
    267
Russell, Bertrand, 124
Ryle, Gilbert, 166, 267

science, definition of, 11–22
scientia, 15, 42, 209, 240
separation (science and religion), 9–10,
    24, 26–9, 44, 218
Shanavas, T. O., 237, 267
Shubin, Neil, 89, 268
Silk, Joseph, 201
simplicity, 12, 18–21, 40, 41–1, 59,
    131–2, 203–4, 248, 265
Simpson, George Gaylord, 106, 268
Skinner, B. F., 28, 268
Slifkin, Natan, 215–19, 221, 254, 268
Sosis, Richard, 160, 268

soul, 8, 75, 112, 165–83
Spetner, Lee, 220–1, 255, 268
Sprat, Thomas, 37, 268
Sripada, Chandra, 135, 268
Stoppard, Tom, 119
Swinburne, Richard, 176–7, 245, 253,
    268

Talmud, 210–11, 213–22, 254
Teller, Edward, 207
Temple, William, 165, 268
Thagard, Paul, 116, 268
theism, 5–6, 74, 113, 119–20, 156–7,
    164, 177, 186–7, 189, 205–6, 245,
    254
theodicy, 74–6, 250
Theory of Mind (ToM), 123–4, 128,
    132–3, 252
Tiktaalikrosae, 85–6
Tipler, Frank, 205–6, 269
Torah, 210–21, 224, 254, 260
transitional organisms, 85–6, 219
tree of life, the, 80, 85, 250, 263
Trivers, Robert, 147, 269

uniformitarianism, 63, 82–3
uniformity of nature, 28, 124–5
unreliability argument, 132–3
Ussher, Bishop James, 61, 250

values in science, 16–21
von Neumann, John, 207

Watson, James, 18, 32, 43, 170, 269
Weinberg, Steven, 18, 42, 207–8, 269
Whewell, William, 86–7, 247, 269
White, Andrew Dickson, 9, 24–5, 269
Wilczek, Frank, 197
Wilson, E. O., 137, 145, 155, 170, 267,
    269
Wright, Robert, 155–6, 269

Yahya, Harun (Adnan Oktar), 236–7,
    256, 269

Zanchius, Hieronymus, 54
Zimmer, Carl, 116–17, 263

Printed in the United States of America